Strawberry Fields Once Again

Kazura Kinosaki

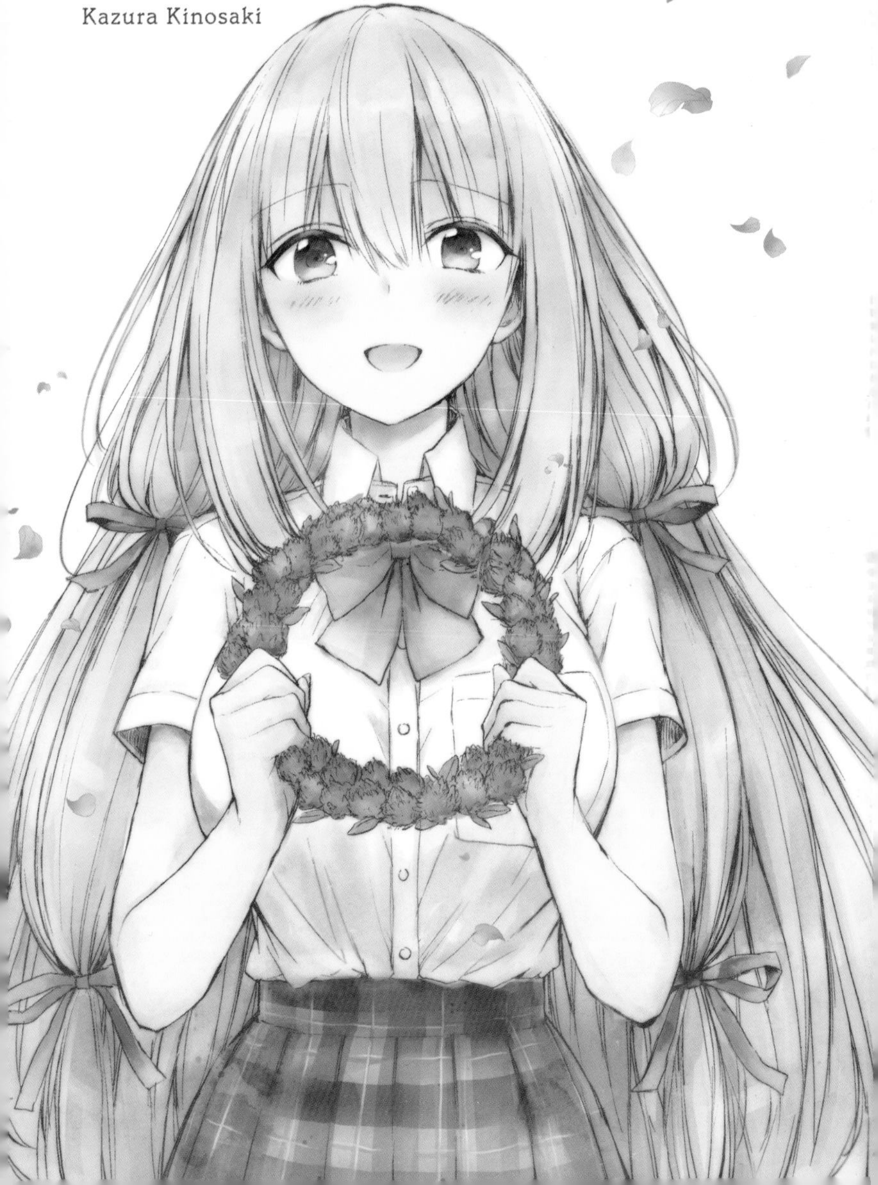

contents

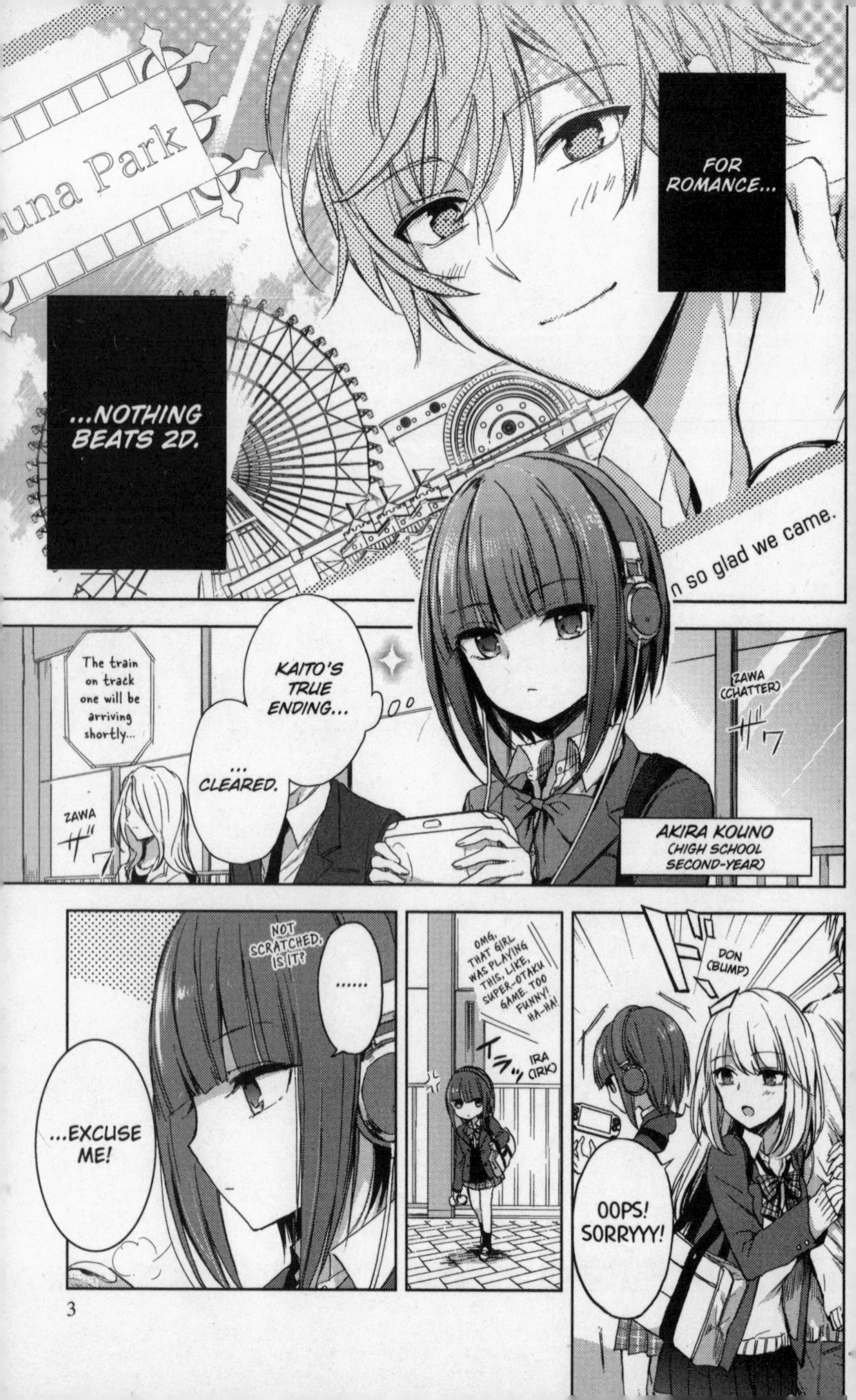

FOR ROMANCE...
...NOTHING BEATS 2D.
una Park
n so glad we came.
ZAWA (CHATTER)
KAITO'S TRUE ENDING...
... CLEARED.
AKIRA KOUNO (HIGH SCHOOL SECOND-YEAR)
The train on track one will be arriving shortly...
ZAWA
DON (BUMP)
OOPS! SORRYYY!
OMG, THAT GIRL WAS PLAYING THIS, LIKE, SUPER-OTAKU GAME. TOO FUNNY! HA-HA!
IRA (IRK)
NOT SCRATCHED, IS IT?
......
...EXCUSE ME!

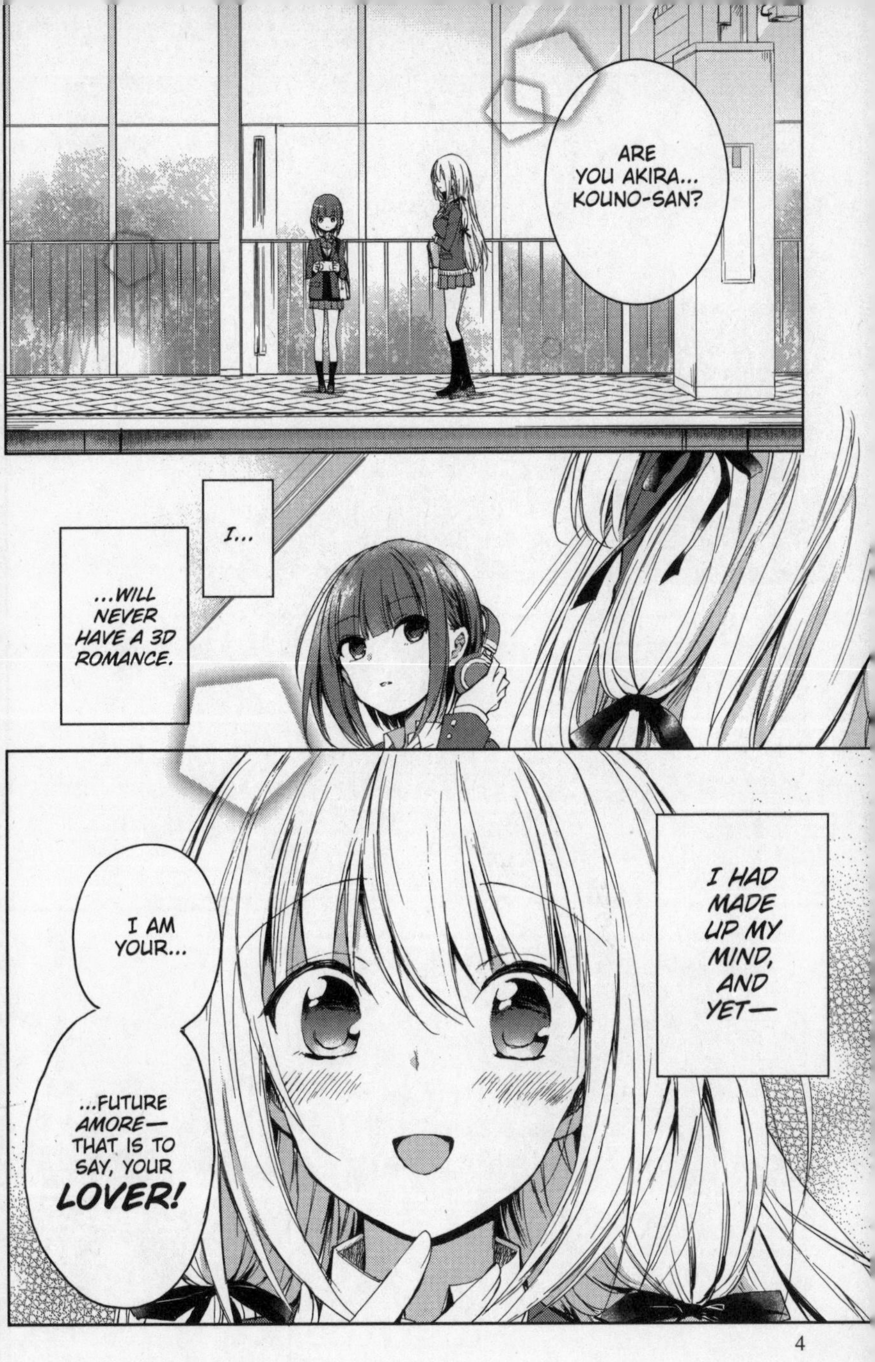
ARE YOU AKIRA... KOUNO-SAN?
I...
...WILL NEVER HAVE A 3D ROMANCE.
I HAD MADE UP MY MIND, AND YET—
I AM YOUR...
...FUTURE AMORE—THAT IS TO SAY, YOUR LOVER!

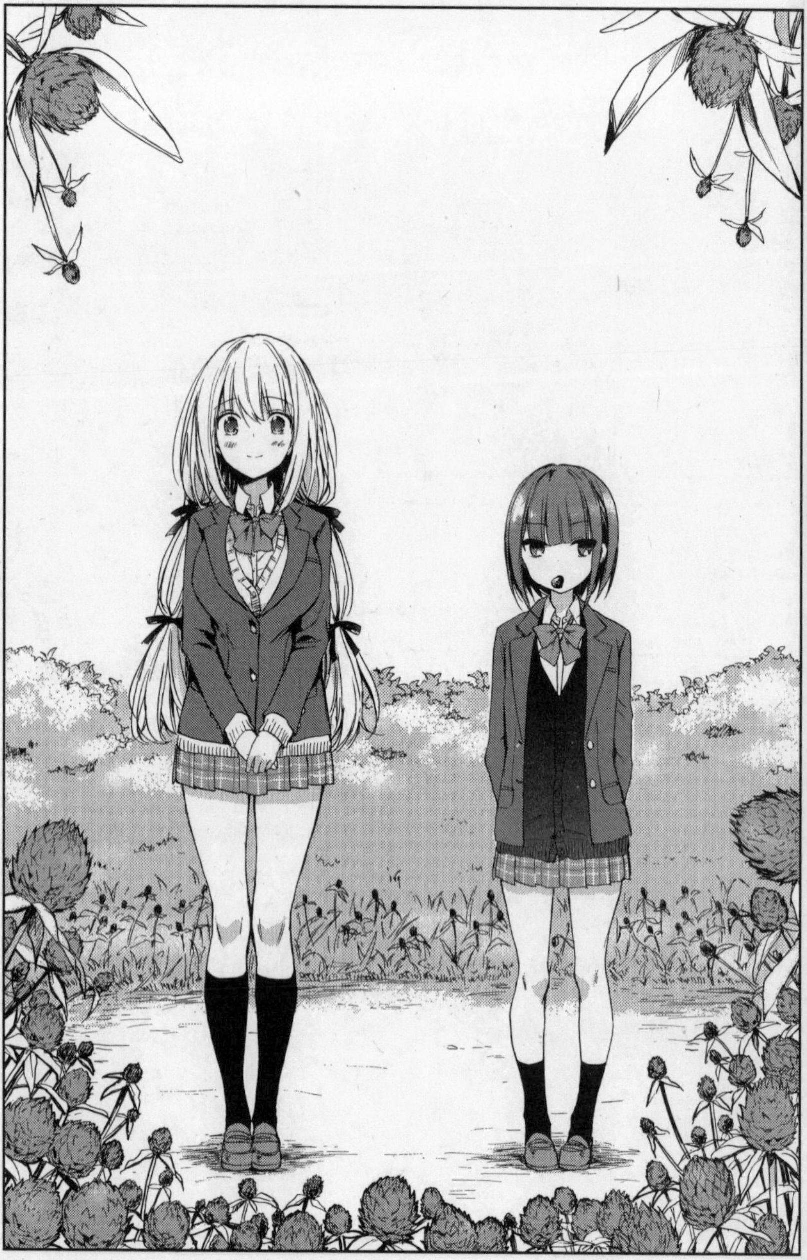

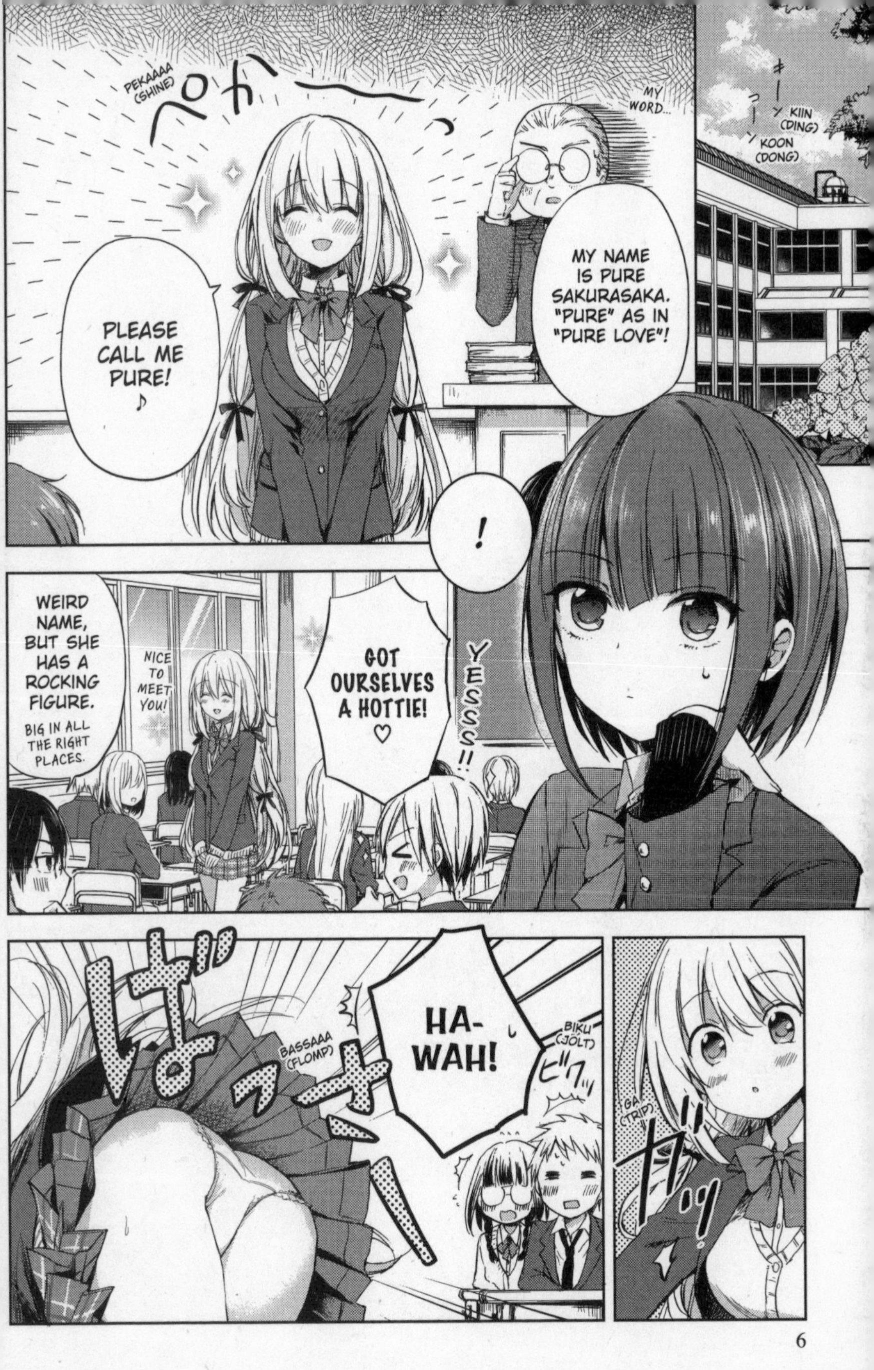
KIIN (DING)
KOON (DONG)
MY WORD...
MY NAME IS PURE SAKURASAKA. "PURE" AS IN "PURE LOVE"!
PEKAAAA (SHINE)
PLEASE CALL ME PURE! ♪
!
YESSS!!
GOT OURSELVES A HOTTIE! ♡
NICE TO MEET YOU!
WEIRD NAME, BUT SHE HAS A ROCKING FIGURE.
BIG IN ALL THE RIGHT PLACES.
GA (TRIP)
BIKU (JOLT)
HA-WAH!
BASSAAA (FLOMP)

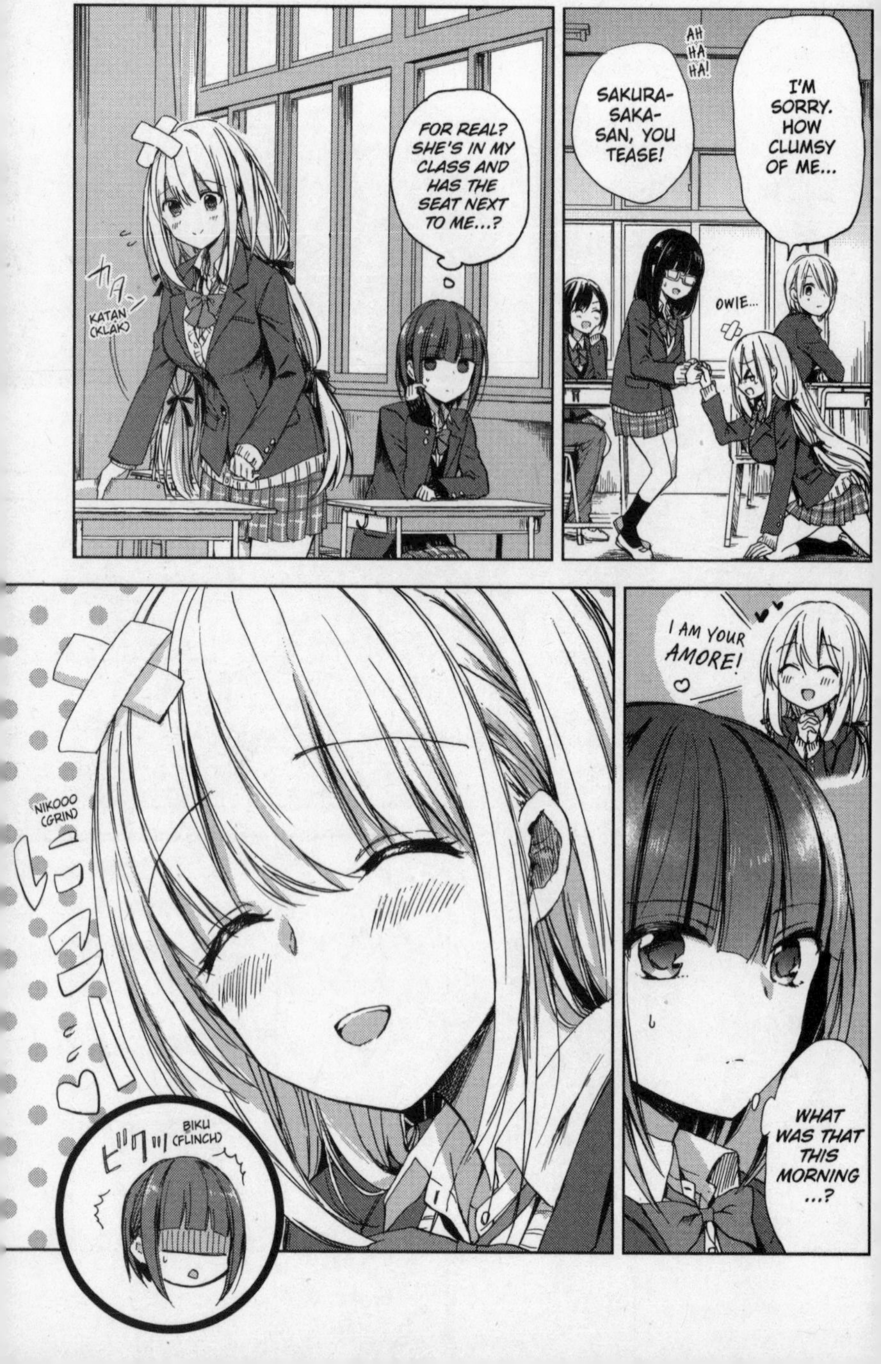
I'M SORRY. HOW CLUMSY OF ME...
AH HA HA!
SAKURA-SAKA-SAN, YOU TEASE!
OWIE...
FOR REAL? SHE'S IN MY CLASS AND HAS THE SEAT NEXT TO ME...?
KATAN (KLAK)
I AM YOUR AMORE!
WHAT WAS THAT THIS MORNING ...?
NIKOOO (GRIN)
BIKU (FLINCH)

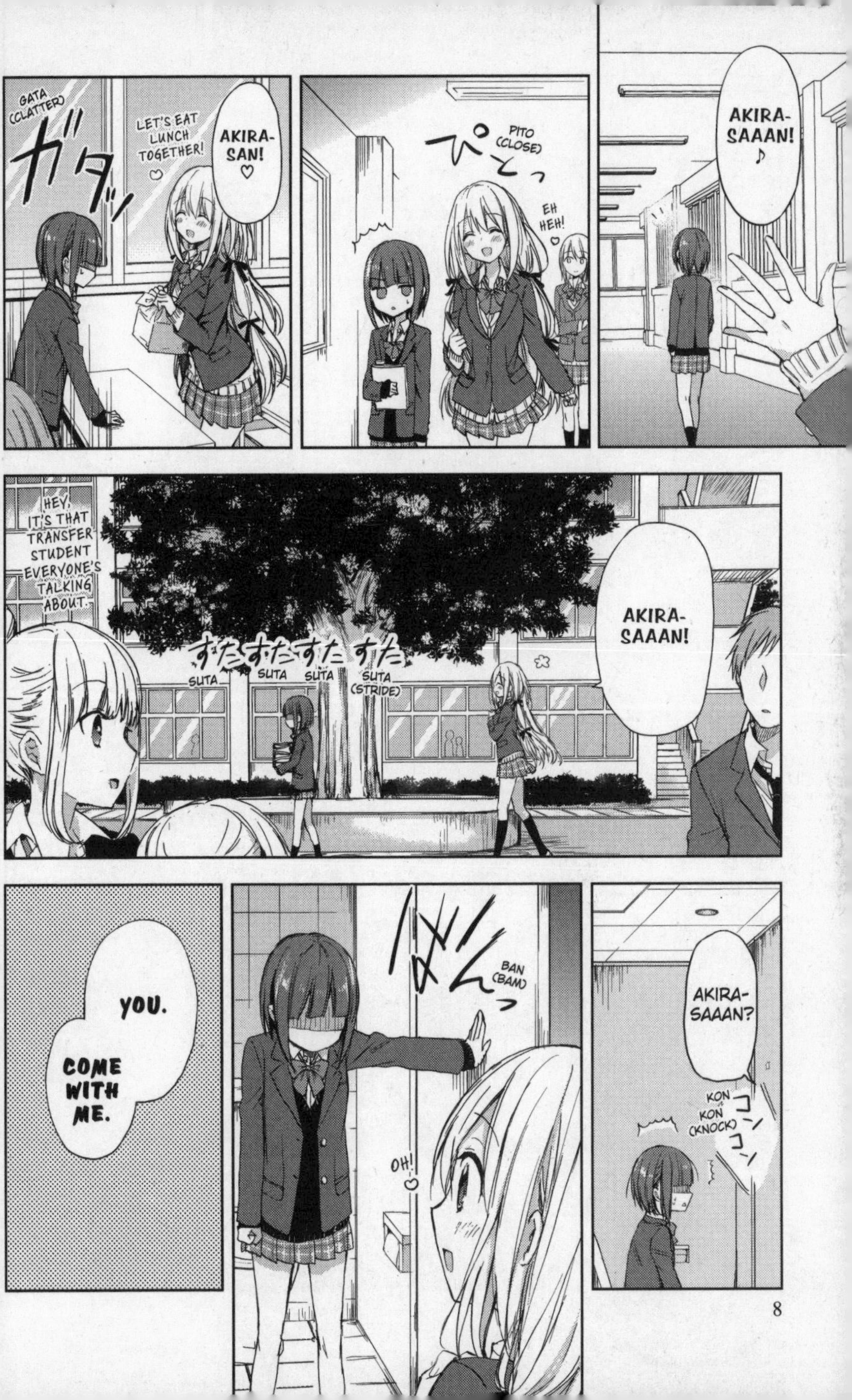
AKIRA-SAAAN! ♪
PITO (CLOSE)
EH HEH! ♡
AKIRA-SAN! ♡
LET'S EAT LUNCH TOGETHER! ♡
GATA (CLATTER)
AKIRA-SAAAN!
SUTA SUTA SUTA SUTA (STRIDE)
HEY, IT'S THAT TRANSFER STUDENT EVERYONE'S TALKING ABOUT.
AKIRA-SAAAN?
KON KON (KNOCK)
BAN (BAM)
OH! ♡
YOU.
COME WITH ME.

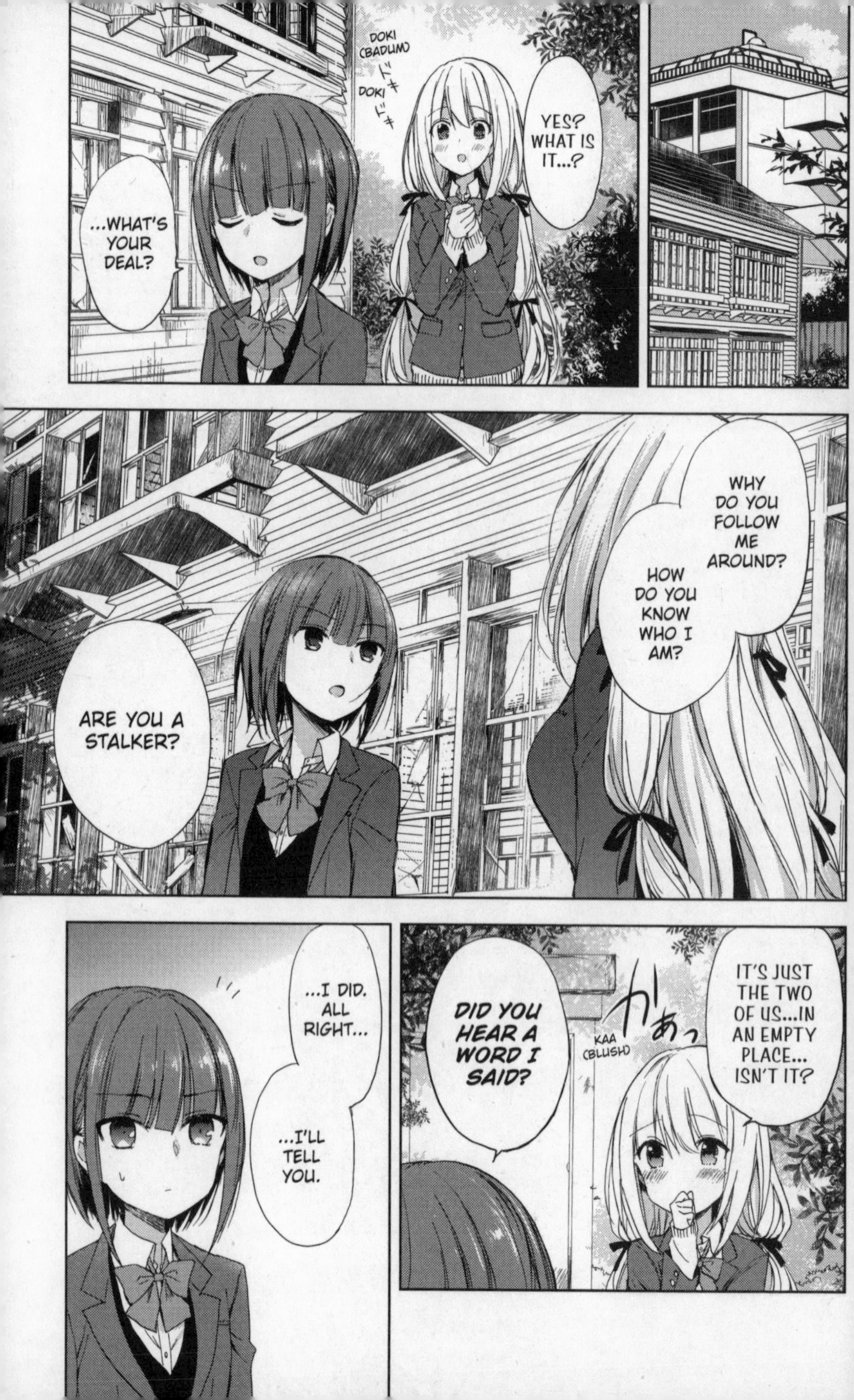
DOKI (BADUM)
DOKI
YES? WHAT IS IT...?
...WHAT'S YOUR DEAL?
WHY DO YOU FOLLOW ME AROUND?
HOW DO YOU KNOW WHO I AM?
ARE YOU A STALKER?
IT'S JUST THE TWO OF US...IN AN EMPTY PLACE... ISN'T IT?
KAA (BLUSH)
DID YOU HEAR A WORD I SAID?
...I DID. ALL RIGHT...
...I'LL TELL YOU.

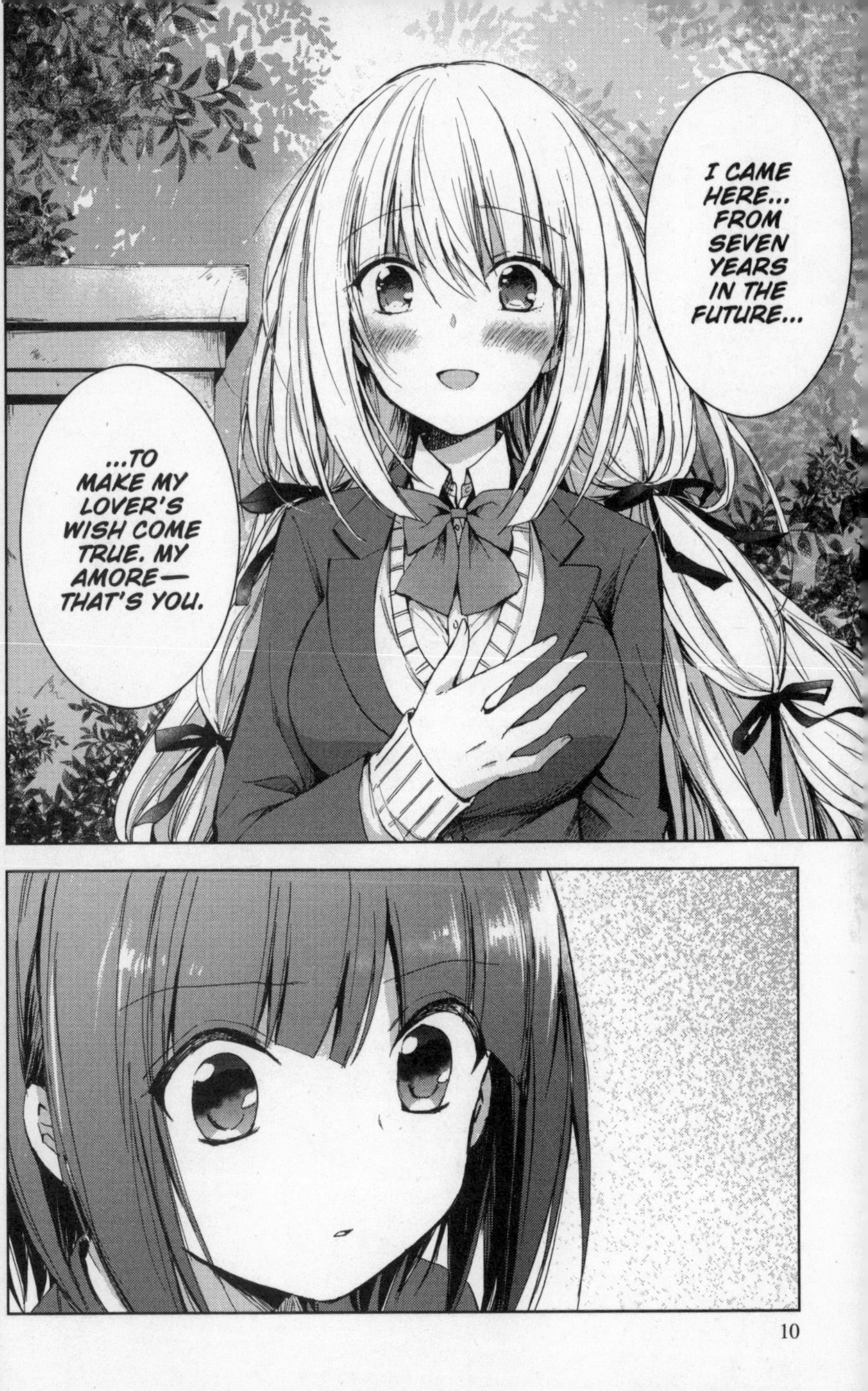
I CAME HERE... FROM SEVEN YEARS IN THE FUTURE...
...TO MAKE MY LOVER'S WISH COME TRUE. MY AMORE—THAT'S YOU.

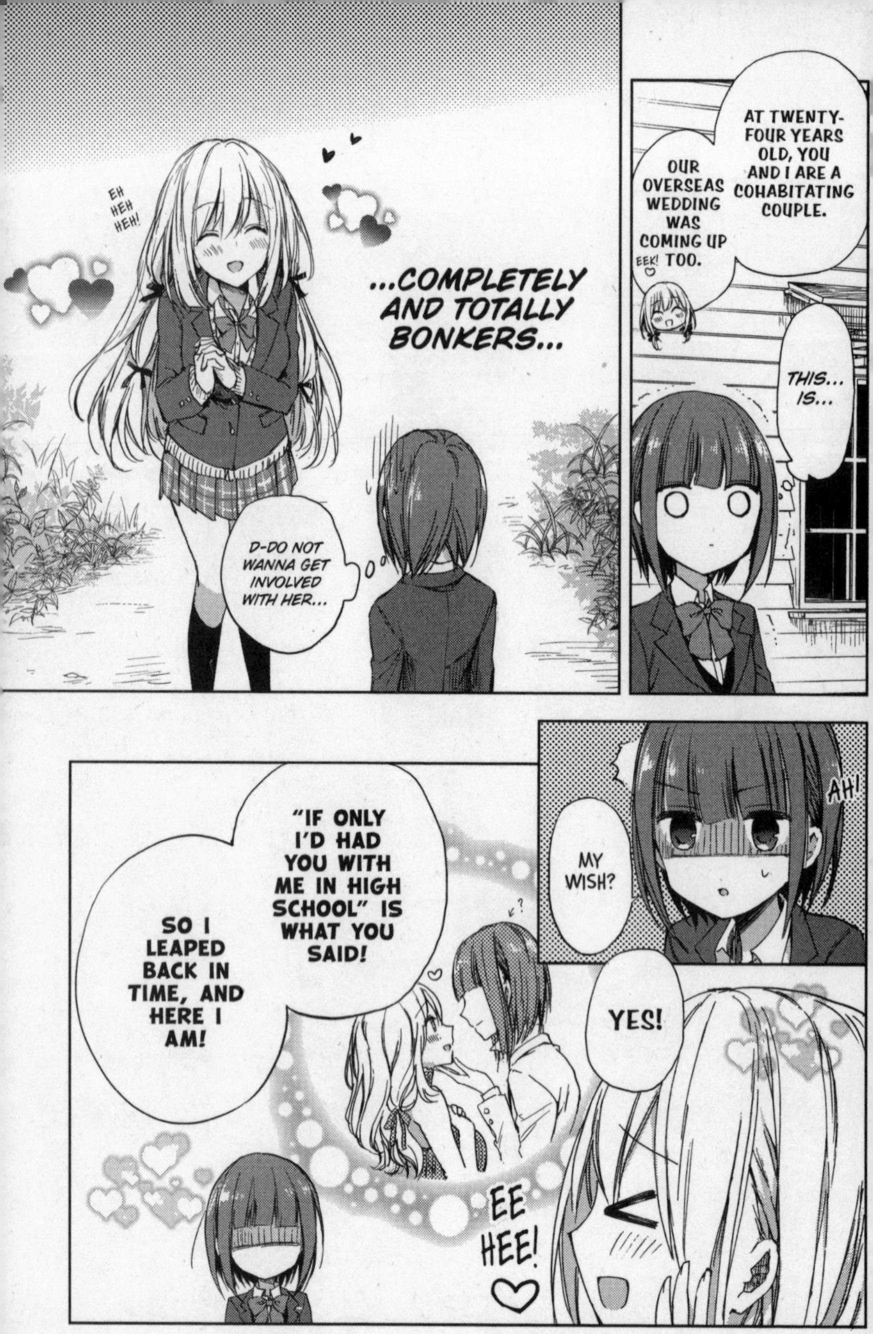
AT TWENTY-FOUR YEARS OLD, YOU AND I ARE A COHABITATING COUPLE.
OUR OVERSEAS WEDDING WAS COMING UP TOO.
EEK!
THIS... IS...
...COMPLETELY AND TOTALLY BONKERS...
EH HEH HEH!
D-DO NOT WANNA GET INVOLVED WITH HER...
AH!
MY WISH?
YES!
"IF ONLY I'D HAD YOU WITH ME IN HIGH SCHOOL" IS WHAT YOU SAID!
SO I LEAPED BACK IN TIME, AND HERE I AM!
EE HEE!

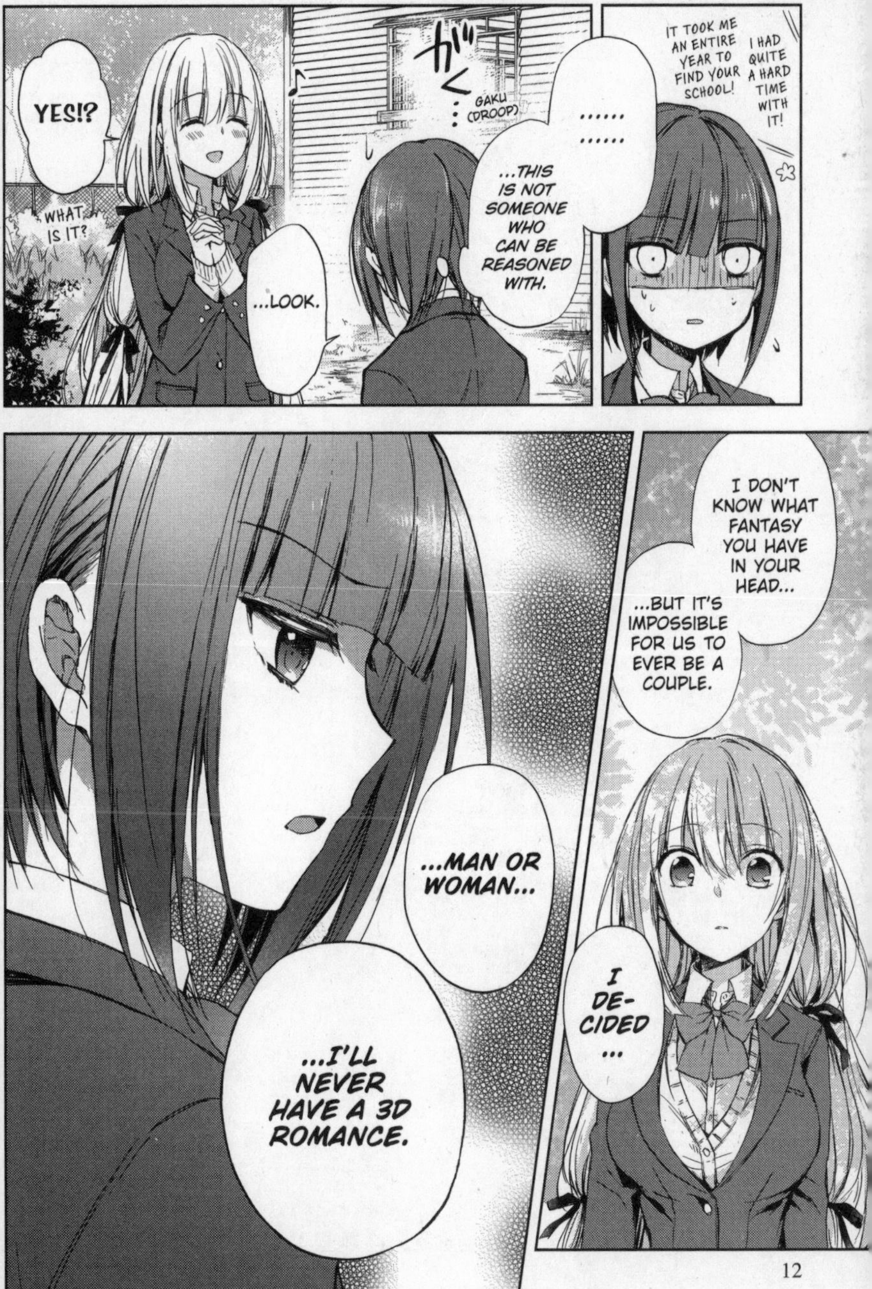
IT TOOK ME AN ENTIRE YEAR TO FIND YOUR SCHOOL!
I HAD QUITE A HARD TIME WITH IT!
GAKU (DROOP)
......
......
...THIS IS NOT SOMEONE WHO CAN BE REASONED WITH.
...LOOK.
YES!?
WHAT IS IT?
I DON'T KNOW WHAT FANTASY YOU HAVE IN YOUR HEAD...
...BUT IT'S IMPOSSIBLE FOR US TO EVER BE A COUPLE.
I DE-CIDED...
...MAN OR WOMAN...
...I'LL NEVER HAVE A 3D ROMANCE.

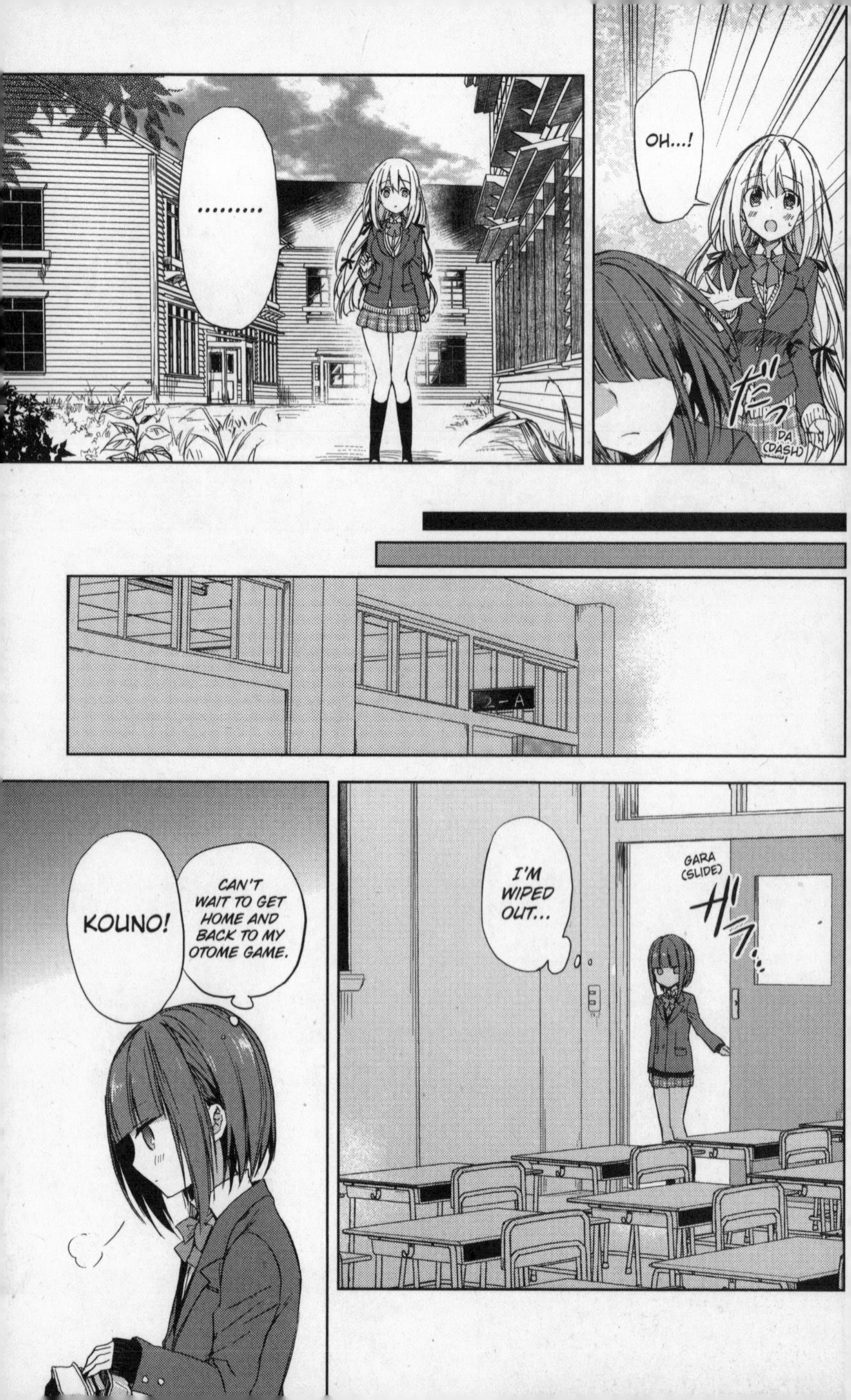
OH...!
DA (DASH)
....
2-A
GARA (SLIDE)
I'M WIPED OUT...
CAN'T WAIT TO GET HOME AND BACK TO MY OTOME GAME.
KOUNO!

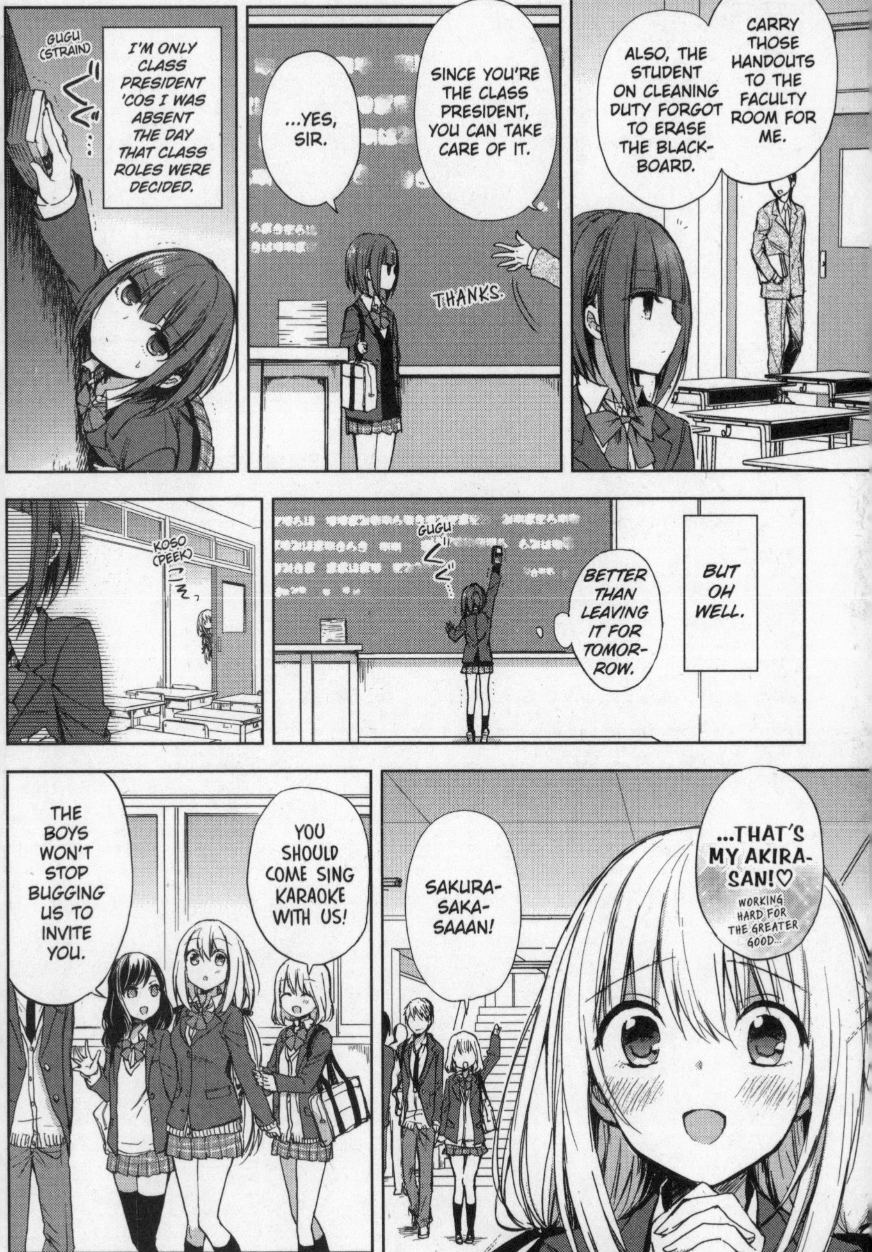
CARRY THOSE HANDOUTS TO THE FACULTY ROOM FOR ME.
ALSO, THE STUDENT ON CLEANING DUTY FORGOT TO ERASE THE BLACK-BOARD.
SINCE YOU'RE THE CLASS PRESIDENT, YOU CAN TAKE CARE OF IT.
...YES, SIR.
THANKS.
I'M ONLY CLASS PRESIDENT 'COS I WAS ABSENT THE DAY THAT CLASS ROLES WERE DECIDED.
GUGU (STRAIN)
BUT OH WELL.
BETTER THAN LEAVING IT FOR TOMOR-ROW.
GUGU
KOSO (PEEK)
...THAT'S MY AKIRA-SAN!♡
WORKING HARD FOR THE GREATER GOOD...
SAKURA-SAKA-SAAAN!
YOU SHOULD COME SING KARAOKE WITH US!
THE BOYS WON'T STOP BUGGING US TO INVITE YOU.

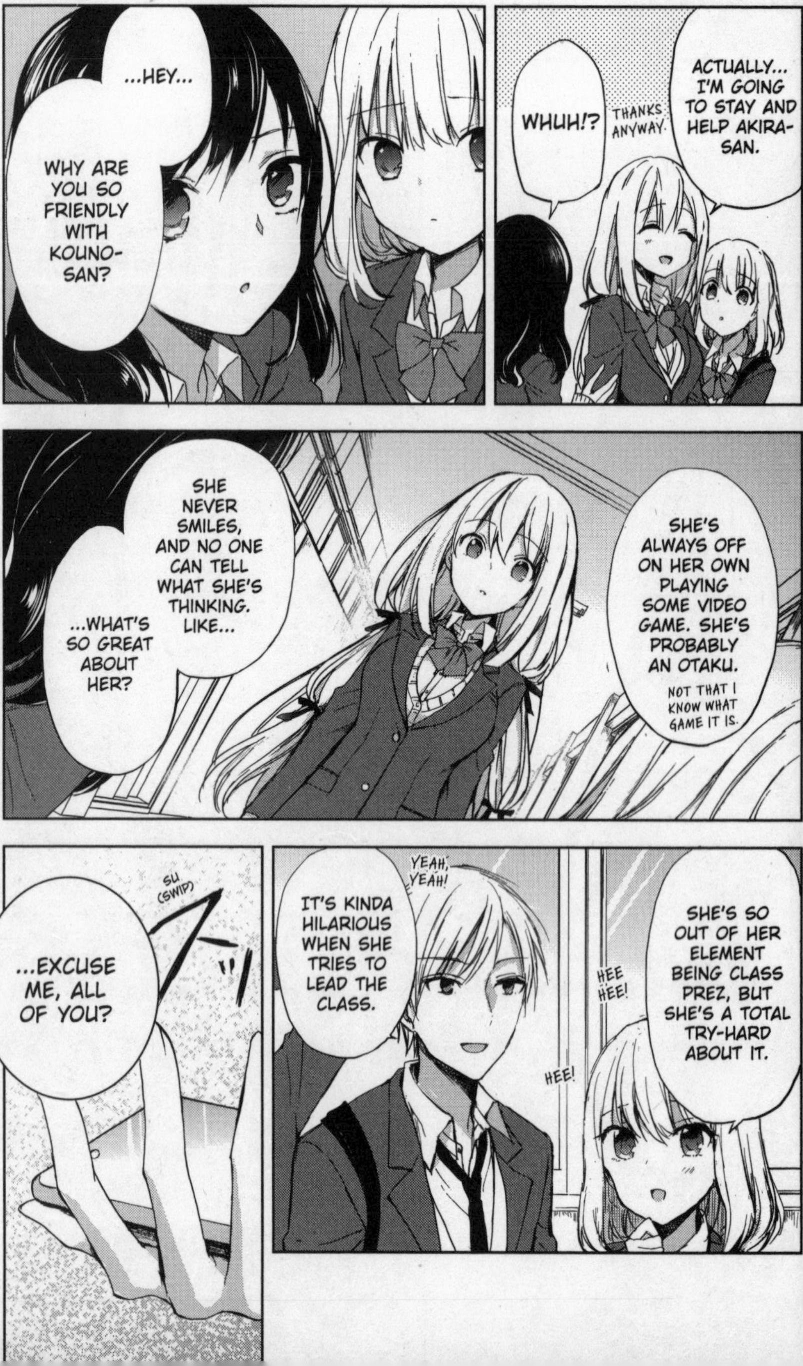
ACTUALLY... I'M GOING TO STAY AND HELP AKIRA-SAN.
THANKS ANYWAY.
WHUH!?
...HEY...
WHY ARE YOU SO FRIENDLY WITH KOUNO-SAN?
SHE'S ALWAYS OFF ON HER OWN PLAYING SOME VIDEO GAME. SHE'S PROBABLY AN OTAKU.
NOT THAT I KNOW WHAT GAME IT IS.
SHE NEVER SMILES, AND NO ONE CAN TELL WHAT SHE'S THINKING. LIKE...
...WHAT'S SO GREAT ABOUT HER?
SHE'S SO OUT OF HER ELEMENT BEING CLASS PREZ, BUT SHE'S A TOTAL TRY-HARD ABOUT IT.
HEE HEE!
HEE!
YEAH, YEAH!
IT'S KINDA HILARIOUS WHEN SHE TRIES TO LEAD THE CLASS.
SU (SWIP)
...EXCUSE ME, ALL OF YOU?

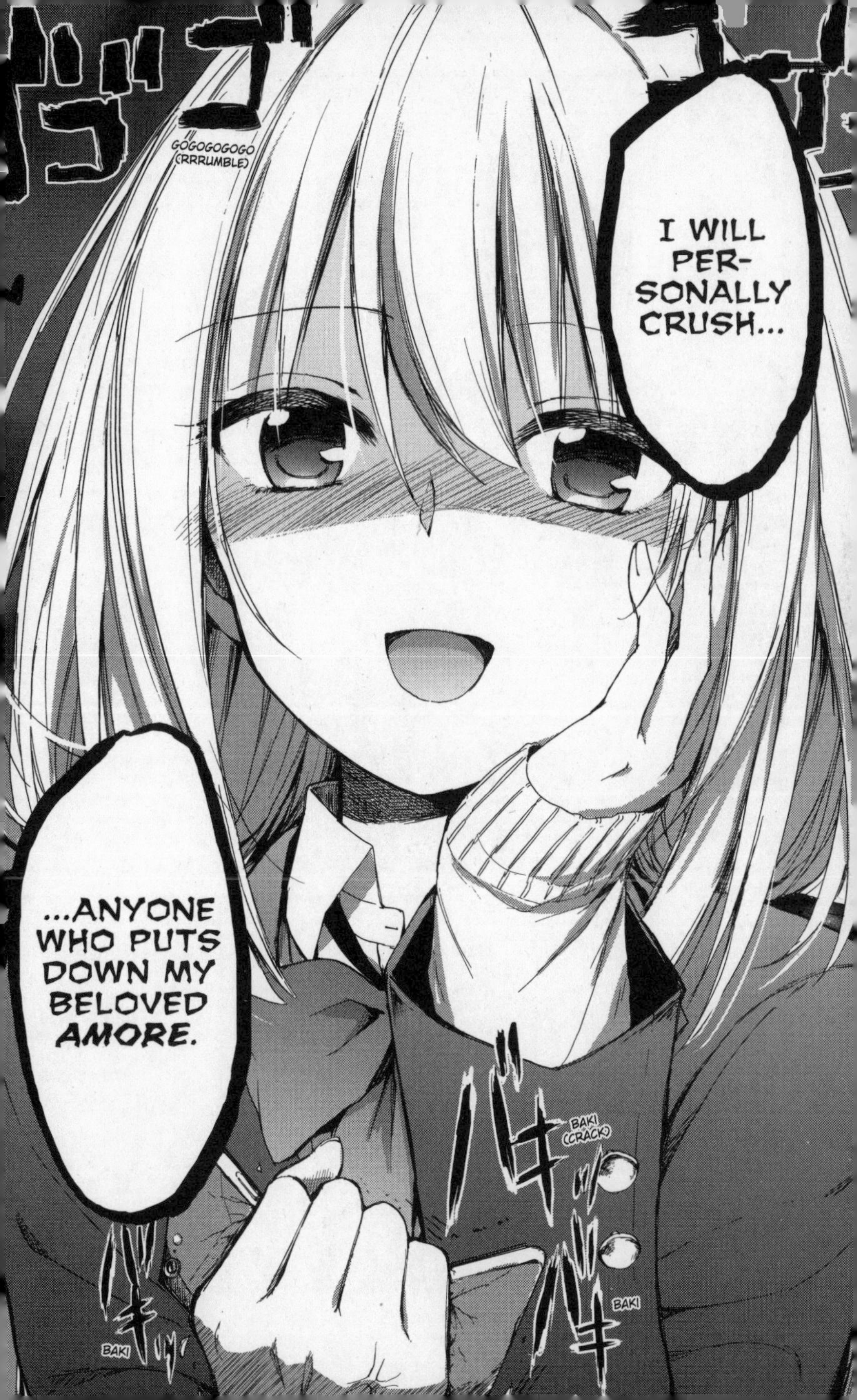
GOGOGOGOGO (RRRUMBLE)
I WILL PER-SONALLY CRUSH...
...ANYONE WHO PUTS DOWN MY BELOVED AMORE.
BAKI (CRACK)
BAKI
BAKI

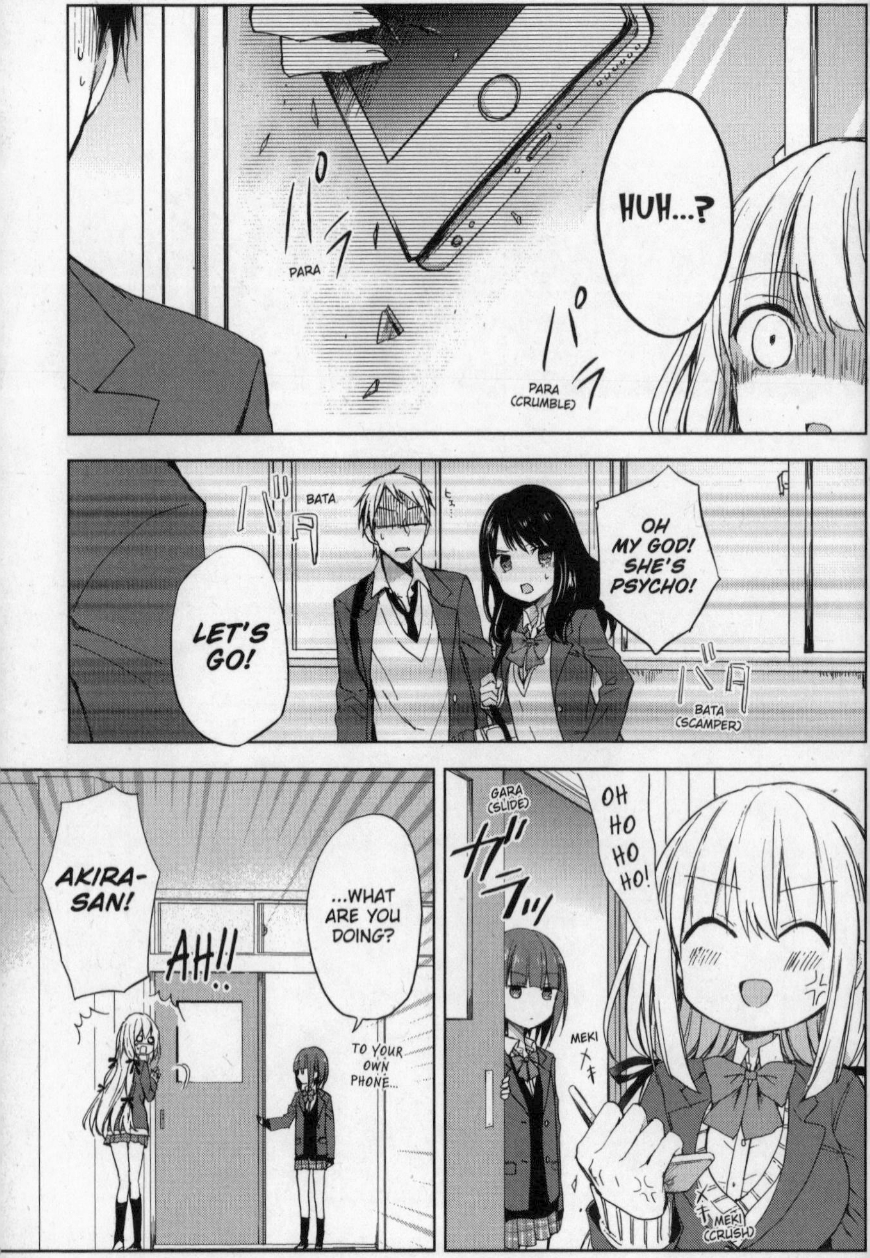
HUH...?
PARA
PARA (CRUMBLE)
OH MY GOD! SHE'S PSYCHO!
BATA
LET'S GO!
BATA (SCAMPER)
OH HO HO HO!
GARA (SLIDE)
MEKI
MEKI (CRUSH)
...WHAT ARE YOU DOING?
AKIRA-SAN!
AH!!
TO YOUR OWN PHONE...

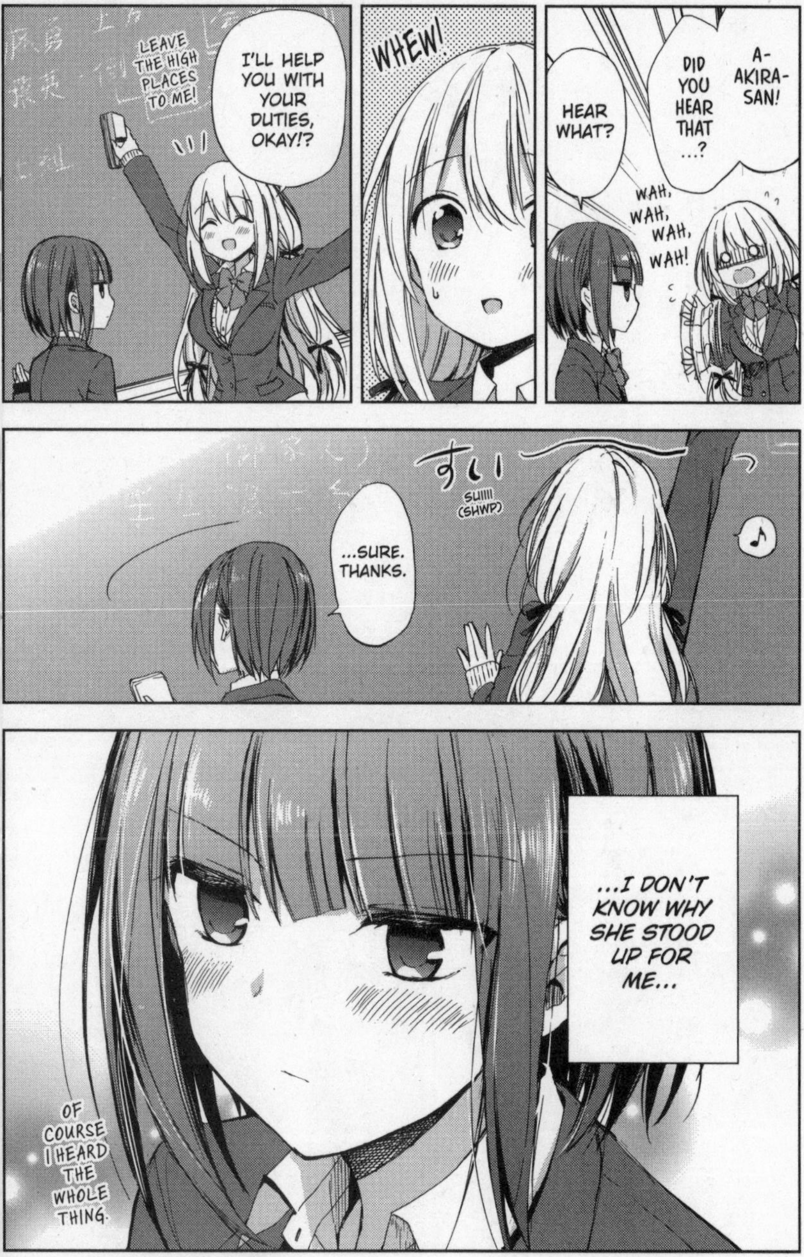
A-AKIRA-SAN!
DID YOU HEAR THAT ...?
HEAR WHAT?
WAH, WAH, WAH, WAH!
WHEW!
I'LL HELP YOU WITH YOUR DUTIES, OKAY!?
LEAVE THE HIGH PLACES TO ME!
すぃ
SUIIII (SHWP)
...SURE. THANKS.
...I DON'T KNOW WHY SHE STOOD UP FOR ME...
OF COURSE I HEARD THE WHOLE THING.

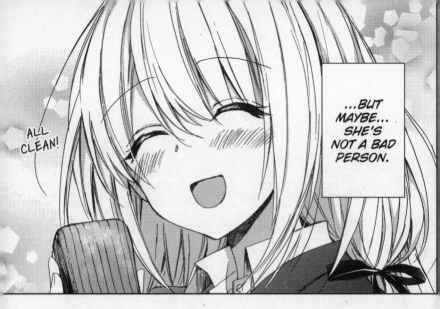

ALL CLEAN!

...BUT MAYBE... SHE'S NOT A BAD PERSON.

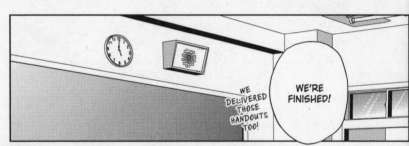

WE'RE FINISHED!

WE DELIVERED THOSE HANDOUTS TOO!

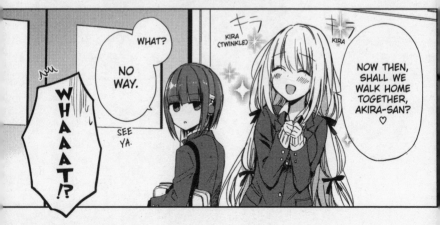

WHAT?

NO WAY.

SEE YA.

WHAAAT!?

KIRA (TWINKLE)

KIRA

NOW THEN, SHALL WE WALK HOME TOGETHER, AKIRA-SAN? ♡

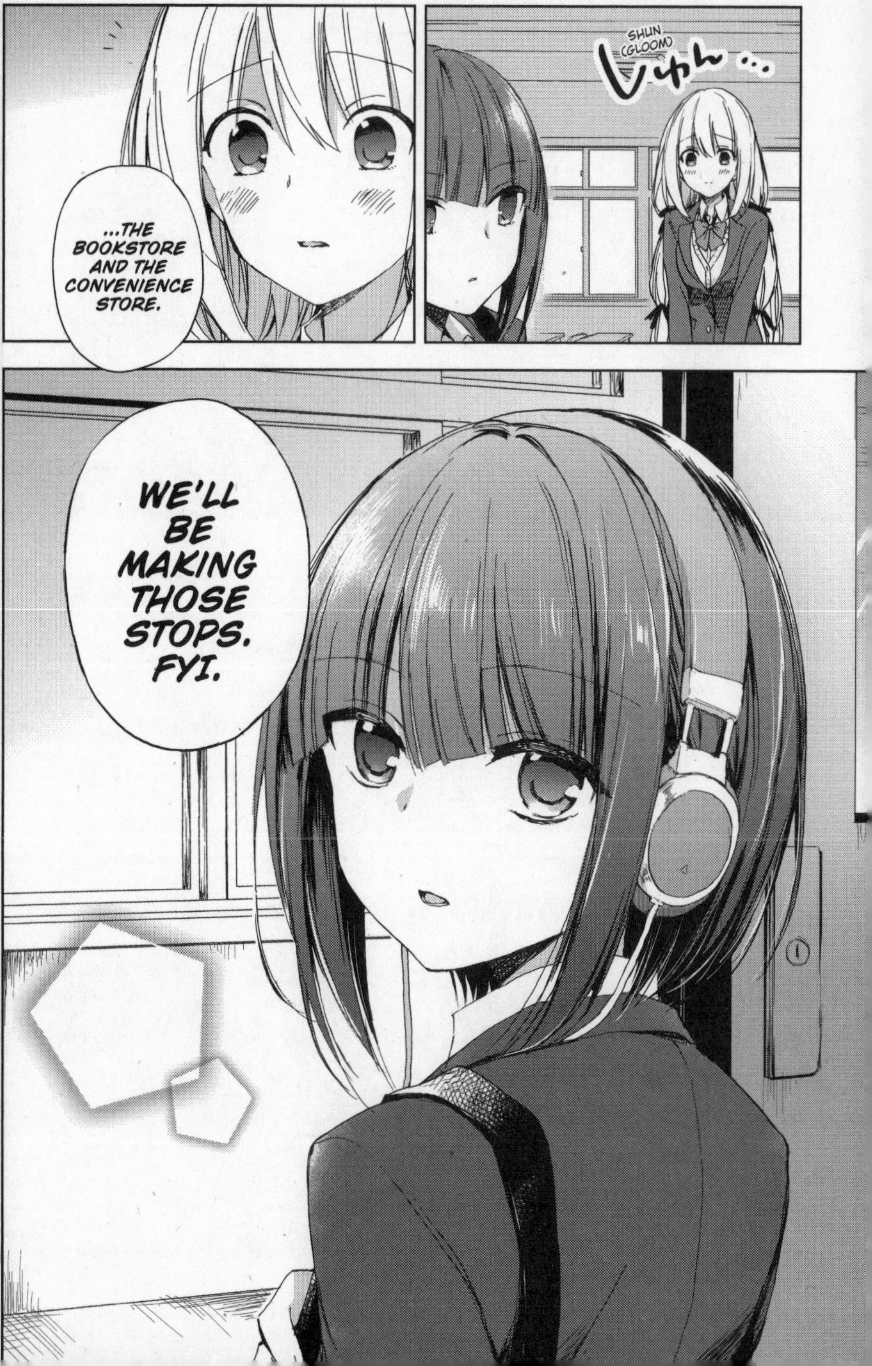
SHUN (GLOOM)
しゅん…
...THE BOOKSTORE AND THE CONVENIENCE STORE.
WE'LL BE MAKING THOSE STOPS. FYI.

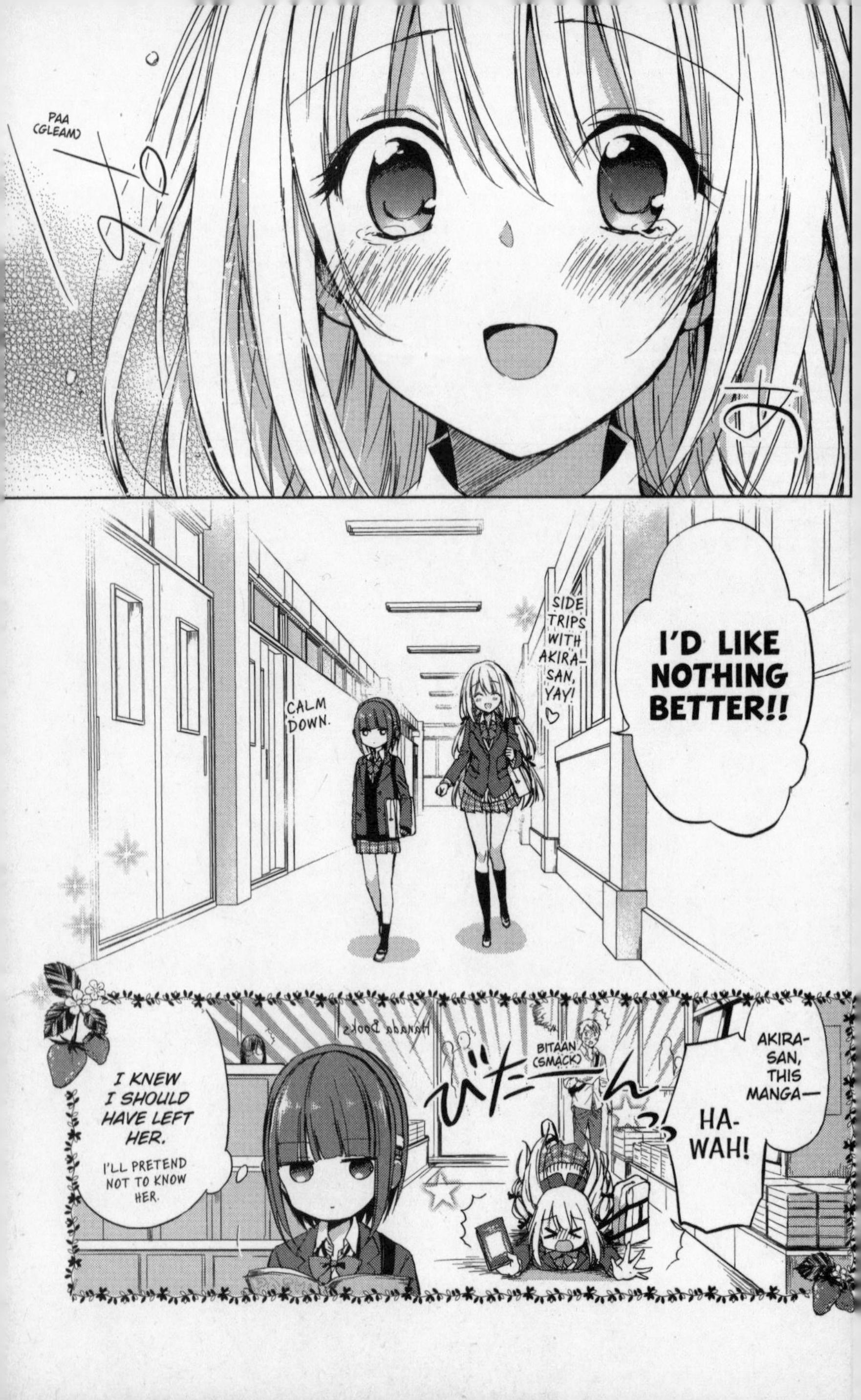
PAA (GLEAM)
I'D LIKE NOTHING BETTER!!
SIDE TRIPS WITH AKIRA-SAN, YAY! ♡
CALM DOWN.
AKIRA-SAN, THIS MANGA—
HA-WAH!
BITAAN (SMACK)
びたーん
I KNEW I SHOULD HAVE LEFT HER.
I'LL PRETEND NOT TO KNOW HER.

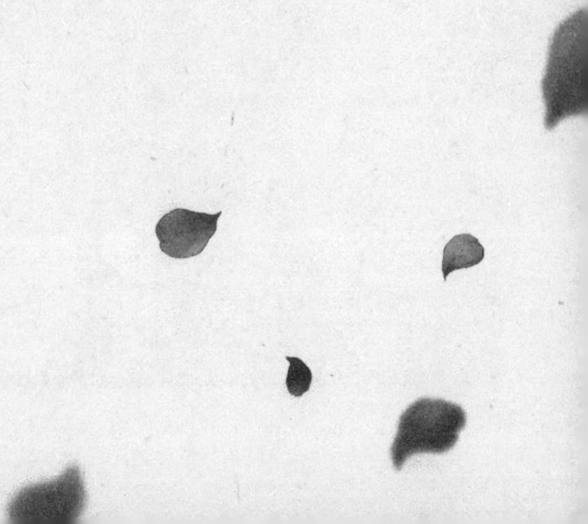

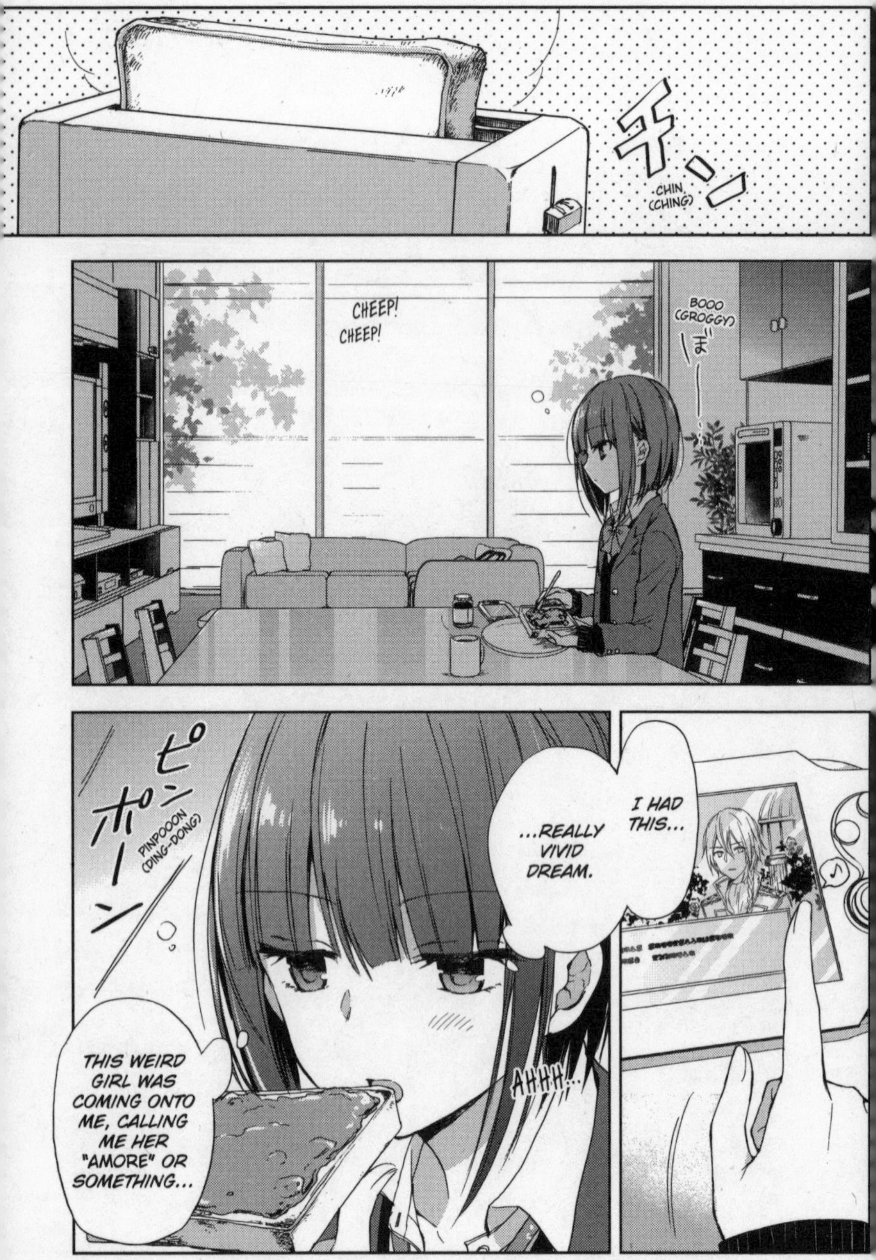
CHIN (CHING)
BOOO (GROGGY)
CHEEP! CHEEP!
I HAD THIS...
...REALLY VIVID DREAM.
PINPOOON (DING-DONG)
AHHH...
THIS WEIRD GIRL WAS COMING ONTO ME, CALLING ME HER "AMORE" OR SOMETHING...

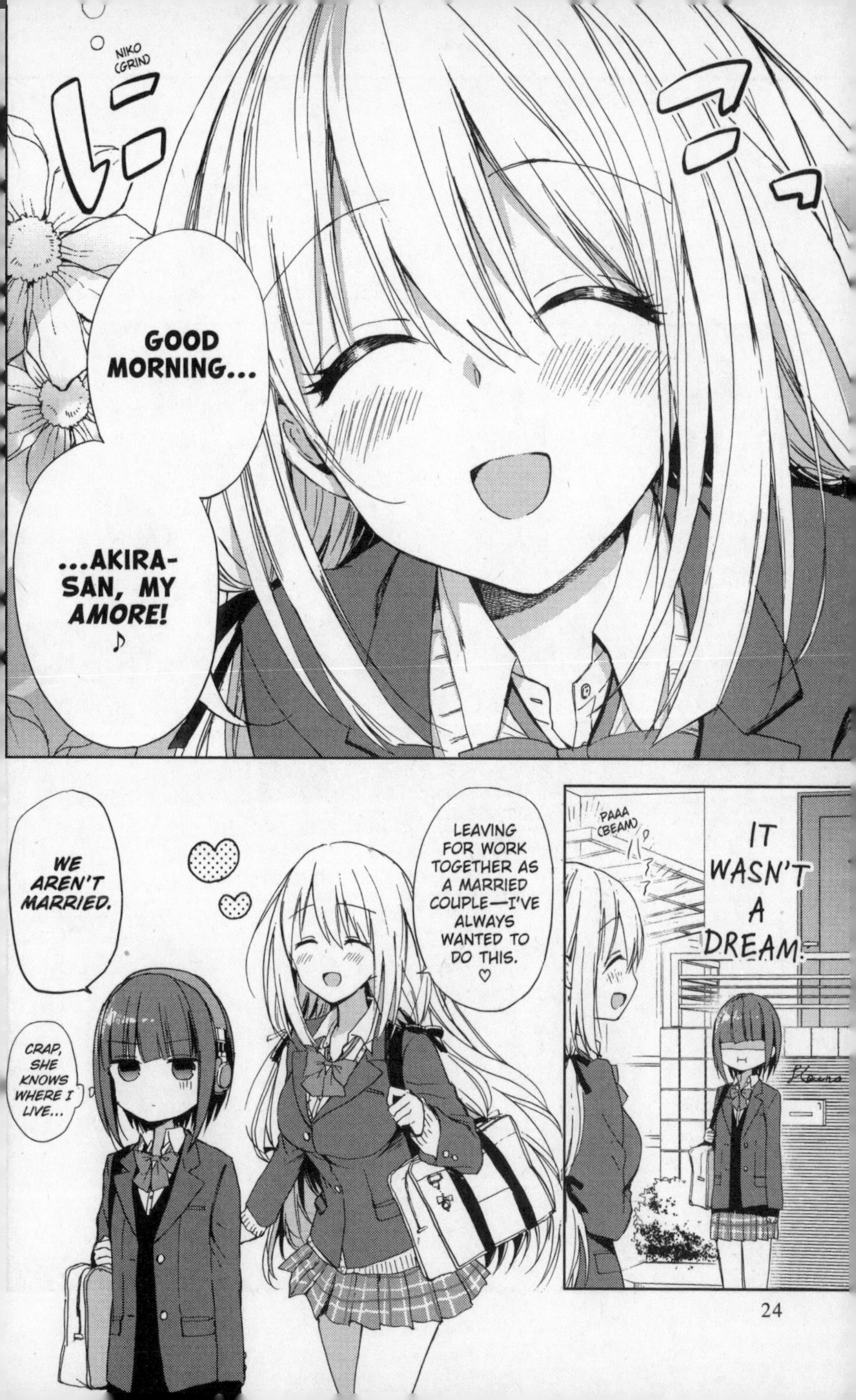
NIKO (GRIND
GOOD MORNING...
...AKIRA-SAN, MY AMORE! ♪
PAAA (BEAM)
IT WASN'T A DREAM.
LEAVING FOR WORK TOGETHER AS A MARRIED COUPLE—I'VE ALWAYS WANTED TO DO THIS. ♡
WE AREN'T MARRIED.
CRAP, SHE KNOWS WHERE I LIVE...

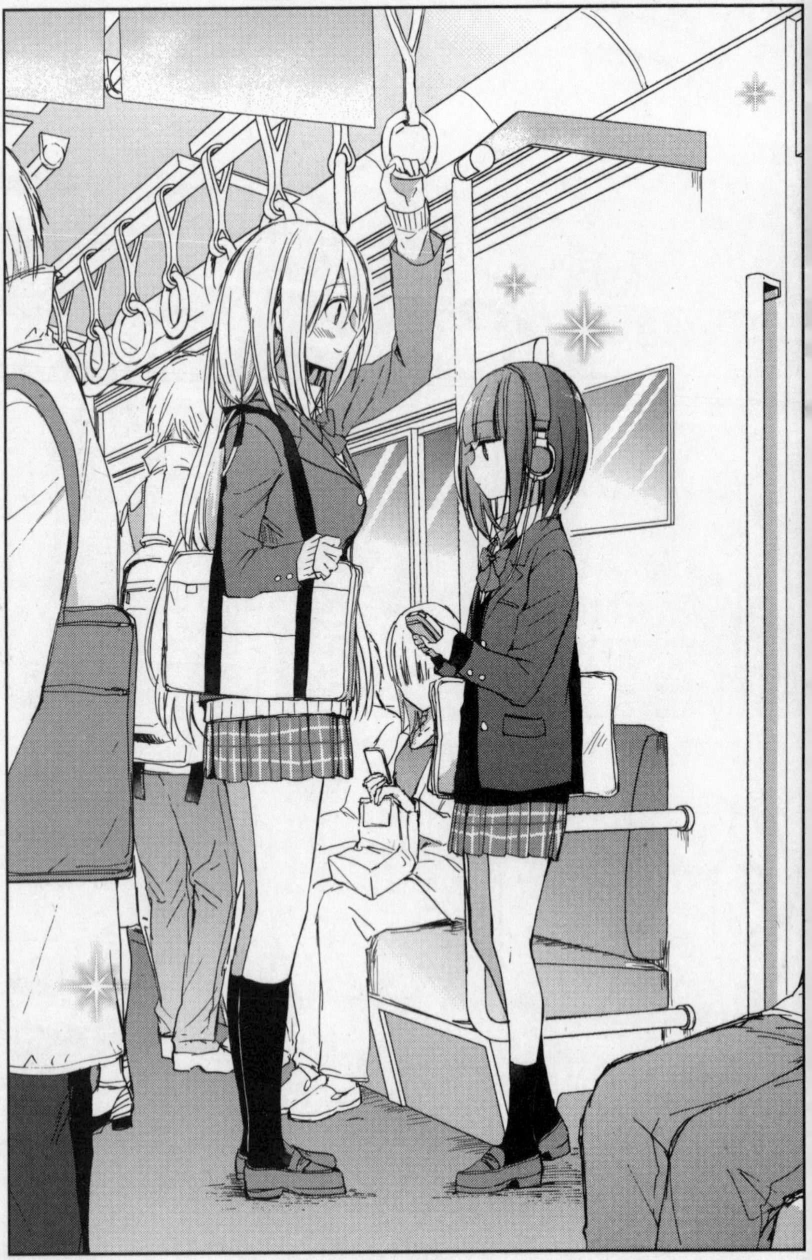

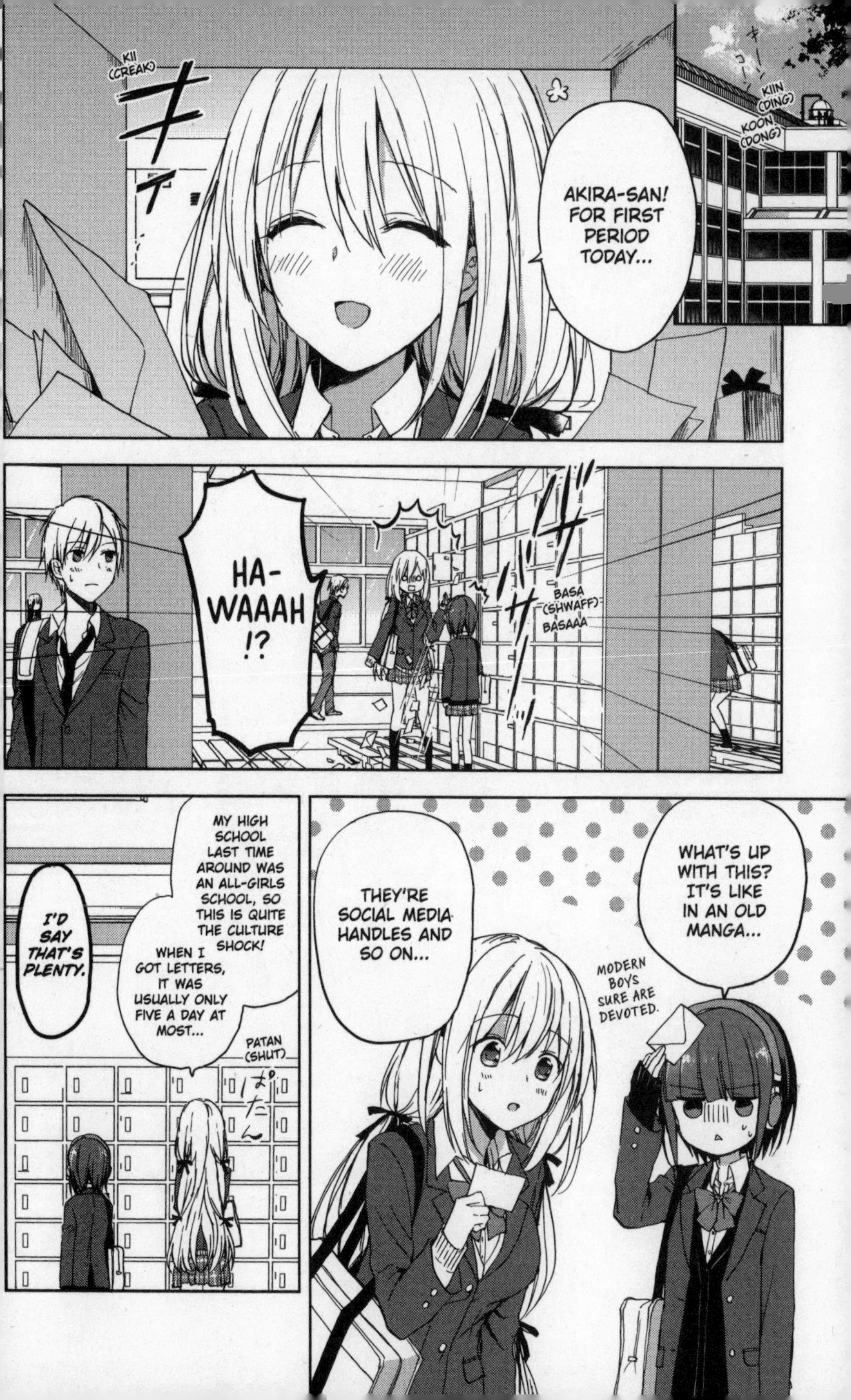
KIIN (DING)
KOON (DONG)
KII (CREAK)
AKIRA-SAN! FOR FIRST PERIOD TODAY...
BASA (SHWAFF) BASAAA
HA-WAAAH!?
WHAT'S UP WITH THIS? IT'S LIKE IN AN OLD MANGA...
MODERN BOYS SURE ARE DEVOTED.
THEY'RE SOCIAL MEDIA HANDLES AND SO ON...
MY HIGH SCHOOL LAST TIME AROUND WAS AN ALL-GIRLS SCHOOL, SO THIS IS QUITE THE CULTURE SHOCK!
WHEN I GOT LETTERS, IT WAS USUALLY ONLY FIVE A DAY AT MOST...
PATAN (SHUT)
I'D SAY THAT'S PLENTY.

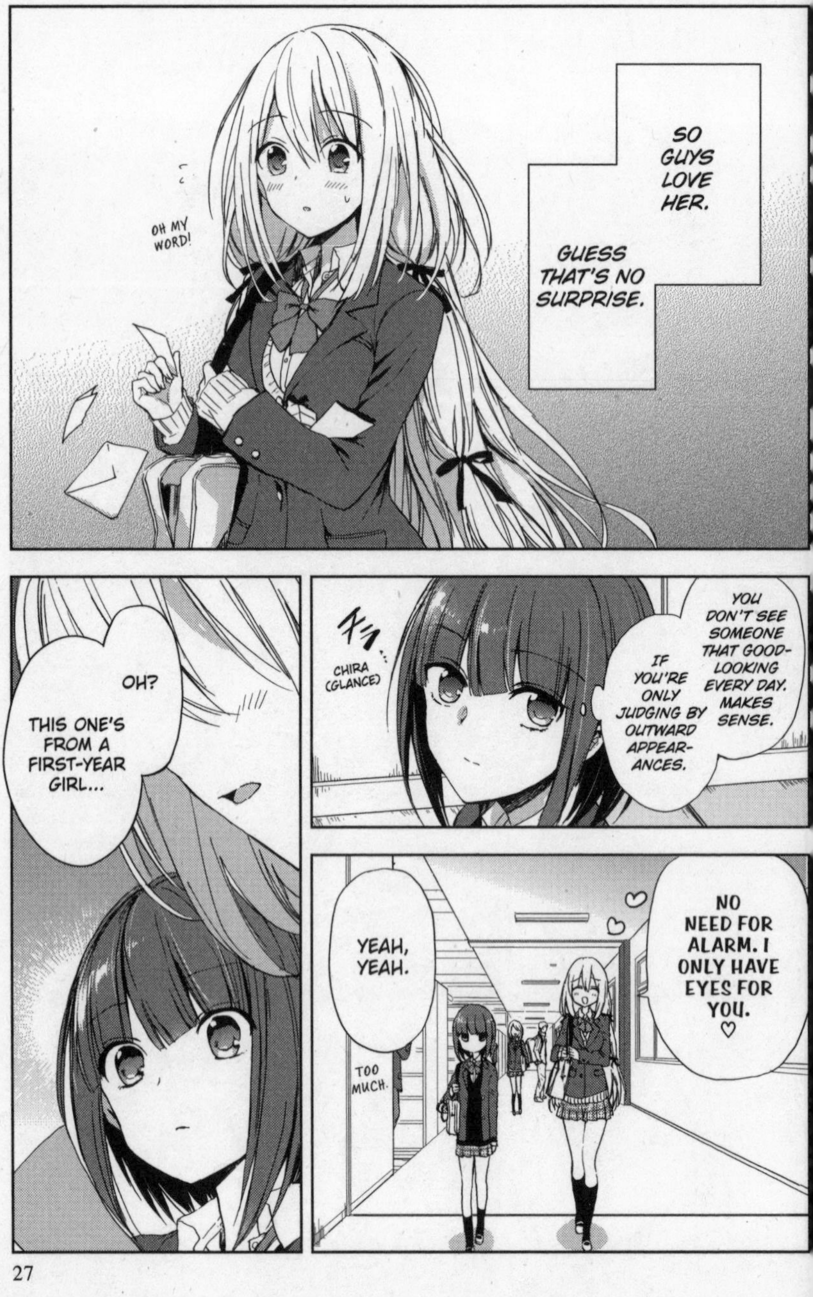
SO GUYS LOVE HER.
GUESS THAT'S NO SURPRISE.
OH MY WORD!
YOU DON'T SEE SOMEONE THAT GOOD-LOOKING EVERY DAY. MAKES SENSE.
IF YOU'RE ONLY JUDGING BY OUTWARD APPEARANCES.
チラ…
CHIRA (GLANCE)
NO NEED FOR ALARM. I ONLY HAVE EYES FOR YOU. ♡
YEAH, YEAH.
TOO MUCH.
OH?
THIS ONE'S FROM A FIRST-YEAR GIRL...

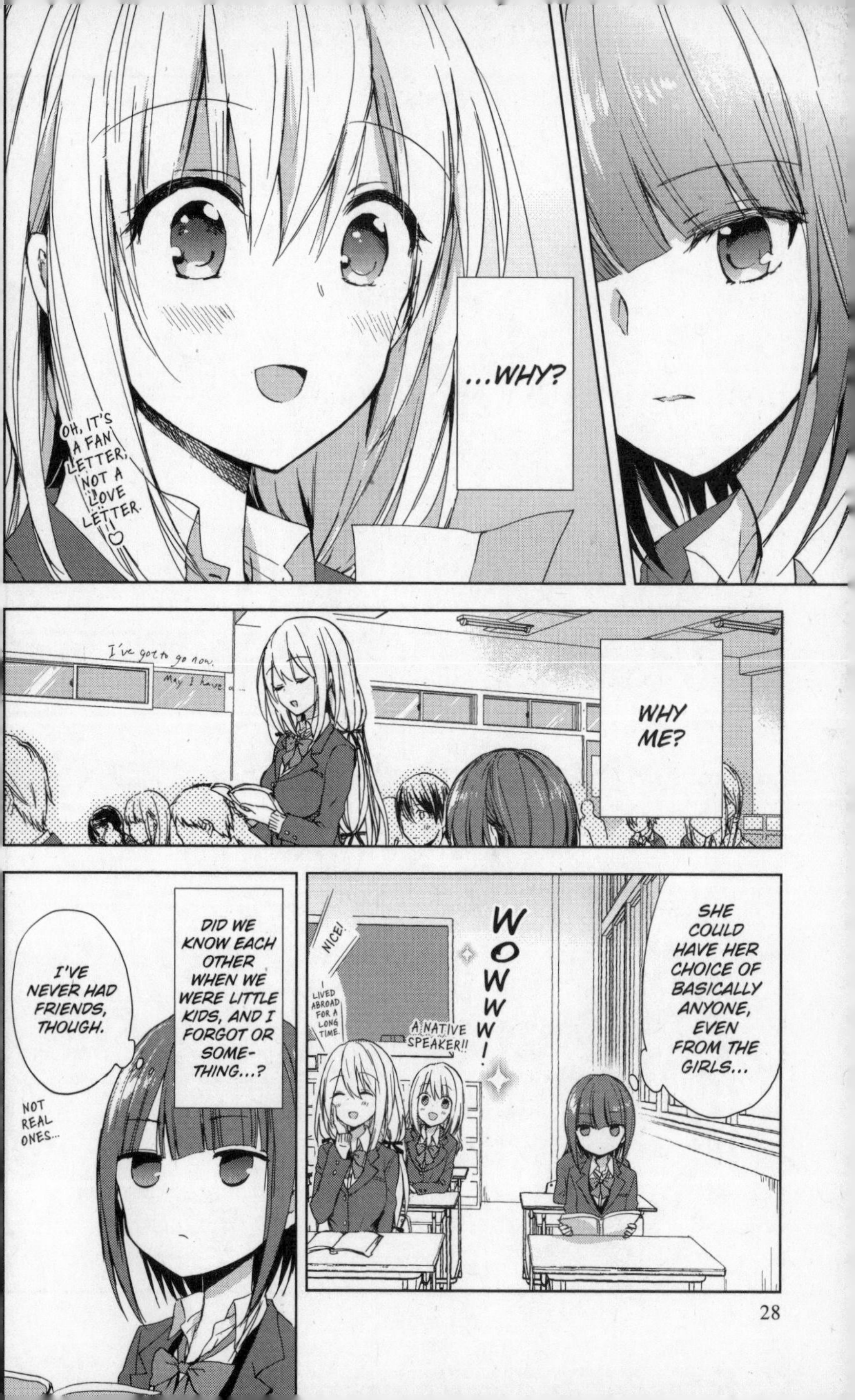
...WHY?
OH, IT'S A FAN LETTER, NOT A LOVE LETTER. ♡
WHY ME?
I've got to go now.
May I have a...
SHE COULD HAVE HER CHOICE OF BASICALLY ANYONE, EVEN FROM THE GIRLS...
WOWWWW!
NICE!
A NATIVE SPEAKER!!
I LIVED ABROAD FOR A LONG TIME.
DID WE KNOW EACH OTHER WHEN WE WERE LITTLE KIDS, AND I FORGOT OR SOME-THING...?
I'VE NEVER HAD FRIENDS, THOUGH.
NOT REAL ONES...

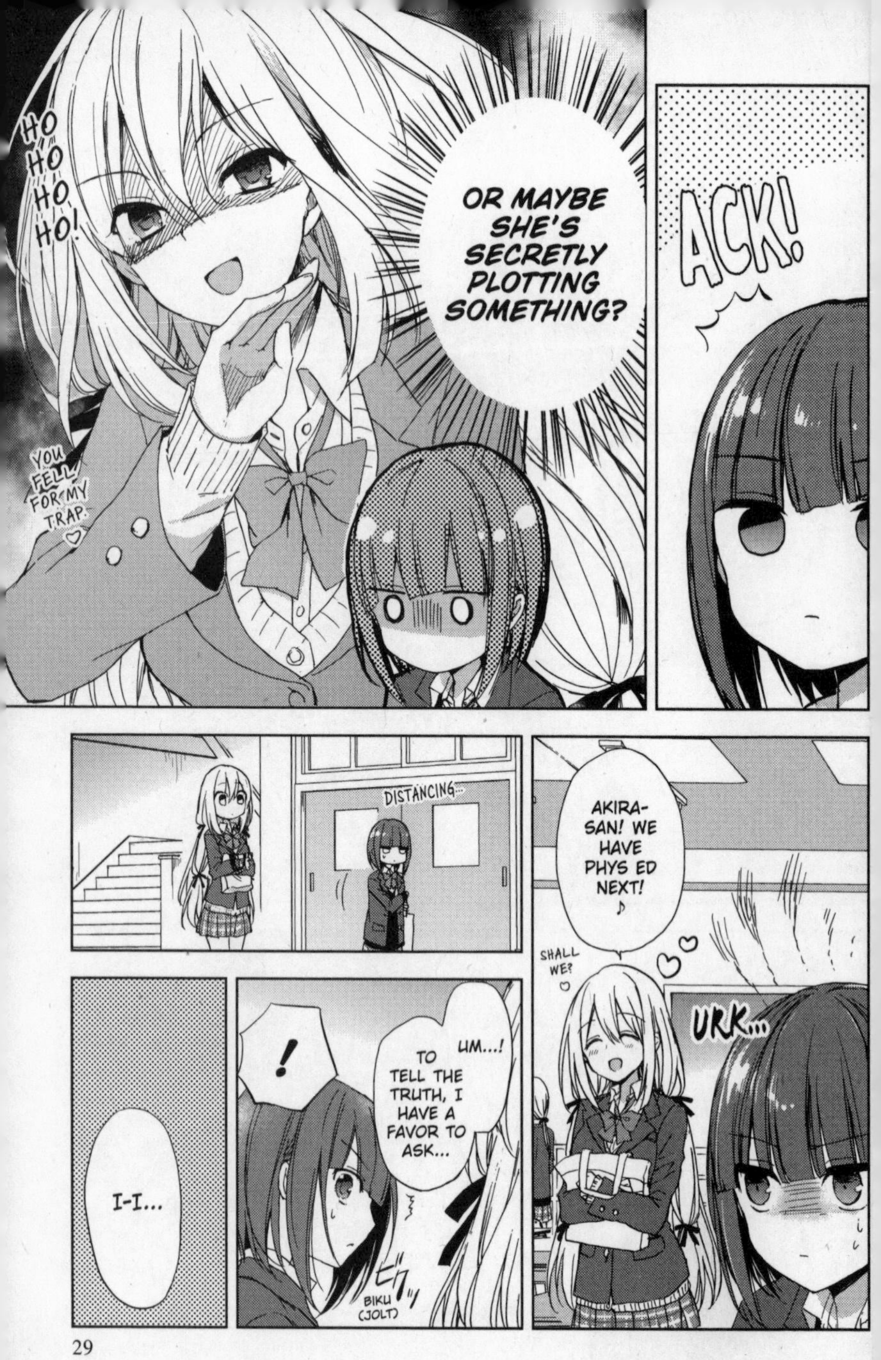
ACK!
OR MAYBE SHE'S SECRETLY PLOTTING SOMETHING?
HO HO HO HO HO HO!
YOU FELL FOR MY TRAP. ♡
AKIRA-SAN! WE HAVE PHYS ED NEXT! ♪
SHALL WE? ♡
URK...
DISTANCING...
UM...!
TO TELL THE TRUTH, I HAVE A FAVOR TO ASK...
!
BIKU (JOLT)
I-I...

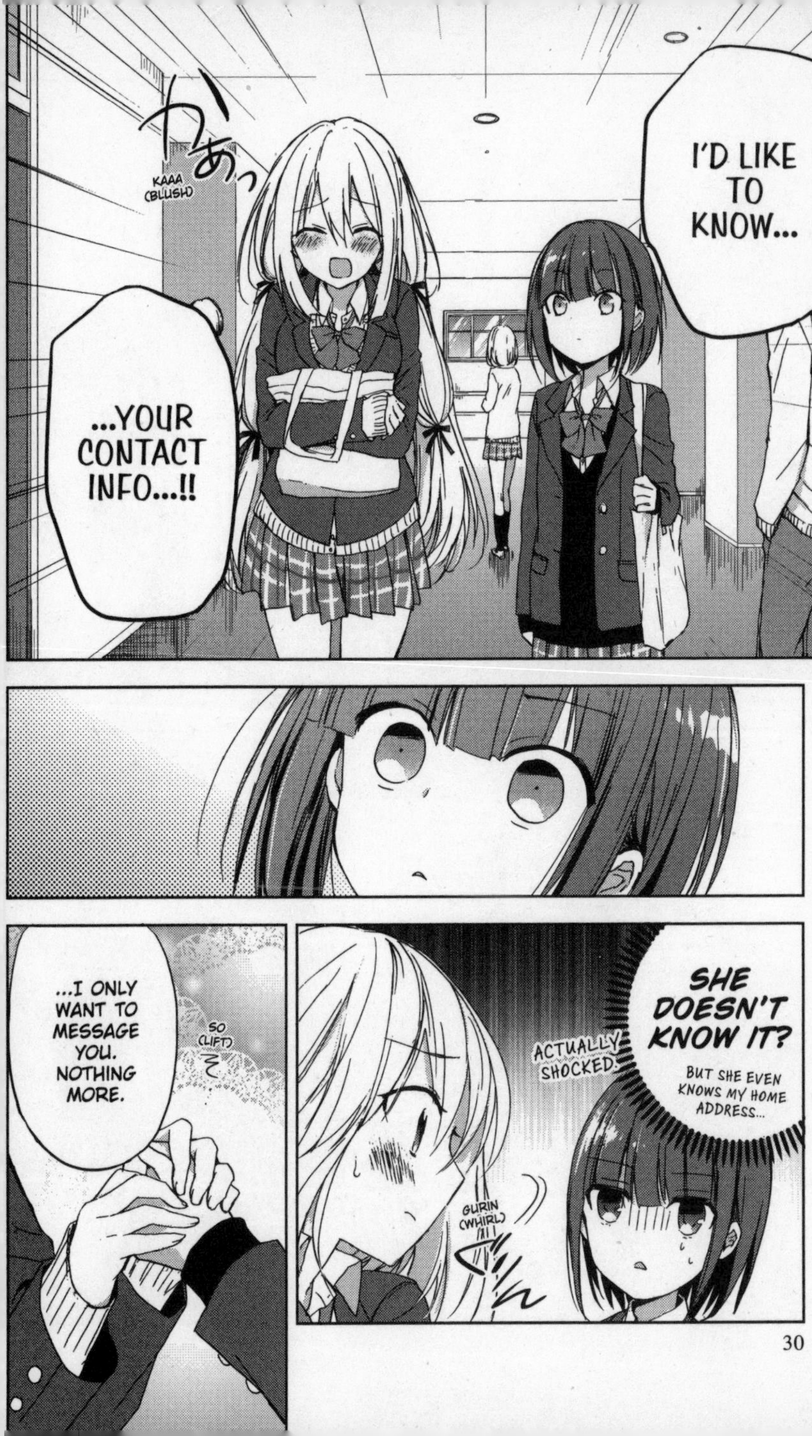

I'D LIKE TO KNOW...
かあっ
KAAA (BLUSH)
...YOUR CONTACT INFO...!!
SHE DOESN'T KNOW IT?
BUT SHE EVEN KNOWS MY HOME ADDRESS...
ACTUALLY SHOCKED.
GURIN (WHIRL)
...I ONLY WANT TO MESSAGE YOU. NOTHING MORE.
SO (LIFT)

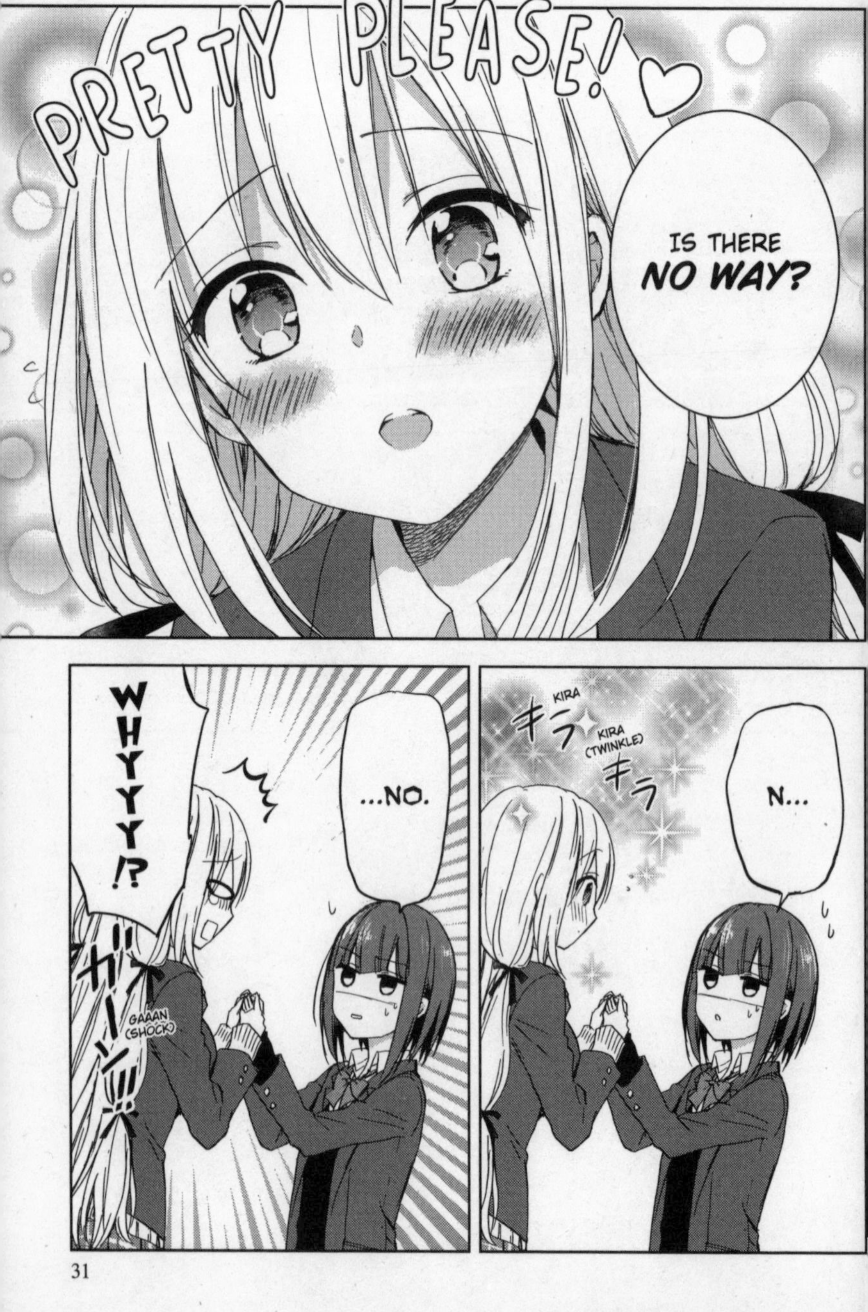
PRETTY PLEASE!
IS THERE NO WAY?
KIRA
KIRA (TWINKLE)
N...
...NO.
WHYYYY!?
GAAAN (SHOCK)

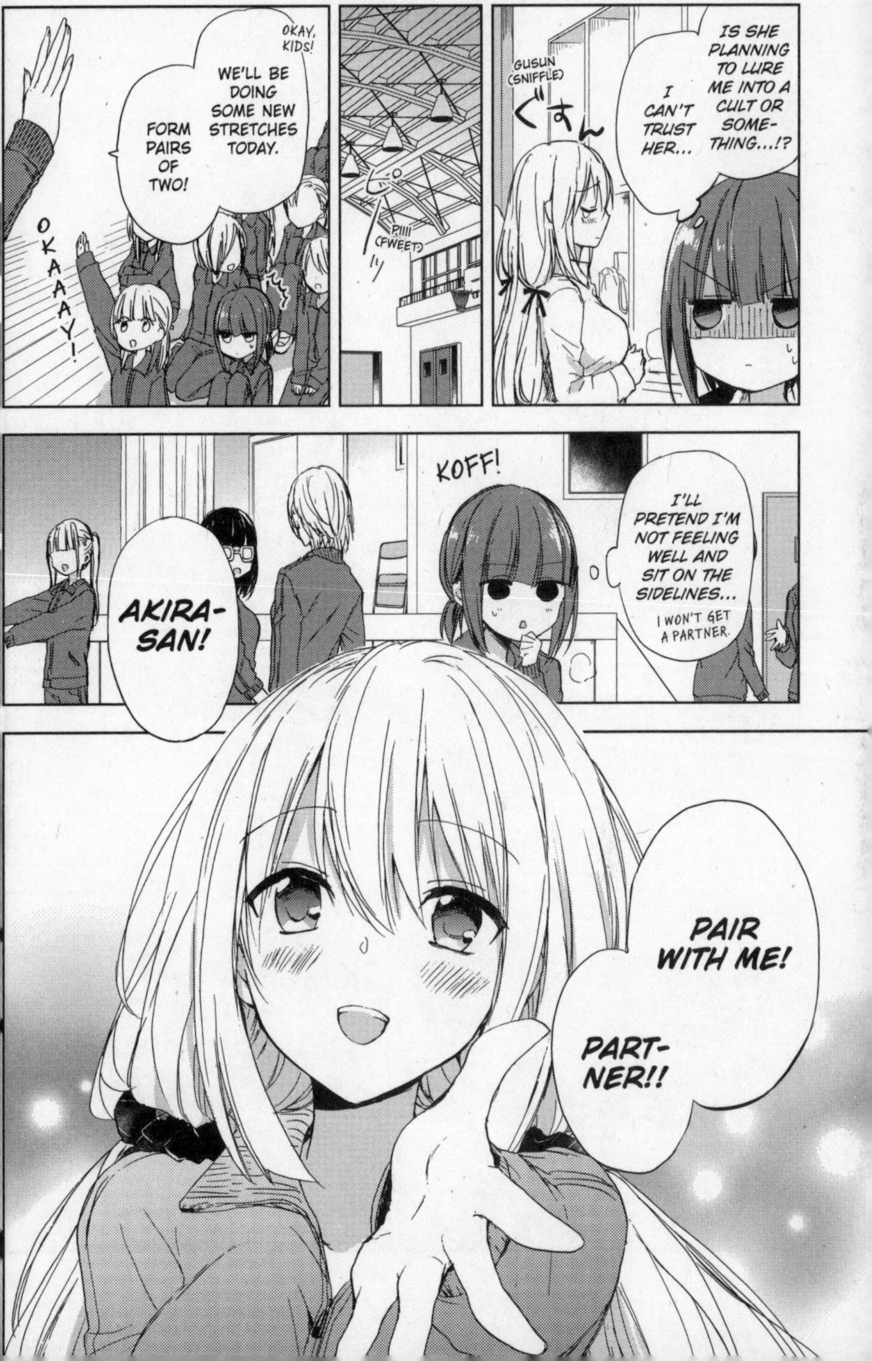
IS SHE PLANNING TO LURE ME INTO A CULT OR SOME-THING...!?
I CAN'T TRUST HER...
GUSUN (SNIFFLE)
ぐすん
P!!!! (FWEET)
OKAY, KIDS!
WE'LL BE DOING SOME NEW STRETCHES TODAY.
FORM PAIRS OF TWO!
OKAAAY!
KOFF!
I'LL PRETEND I'M NOT FEELING WELL AND SIT ON THE SIDELINES...
I WON'T GET A PARTNER.
AKIRA-SAN!
PAIR WITH ME!
PART-NER!!

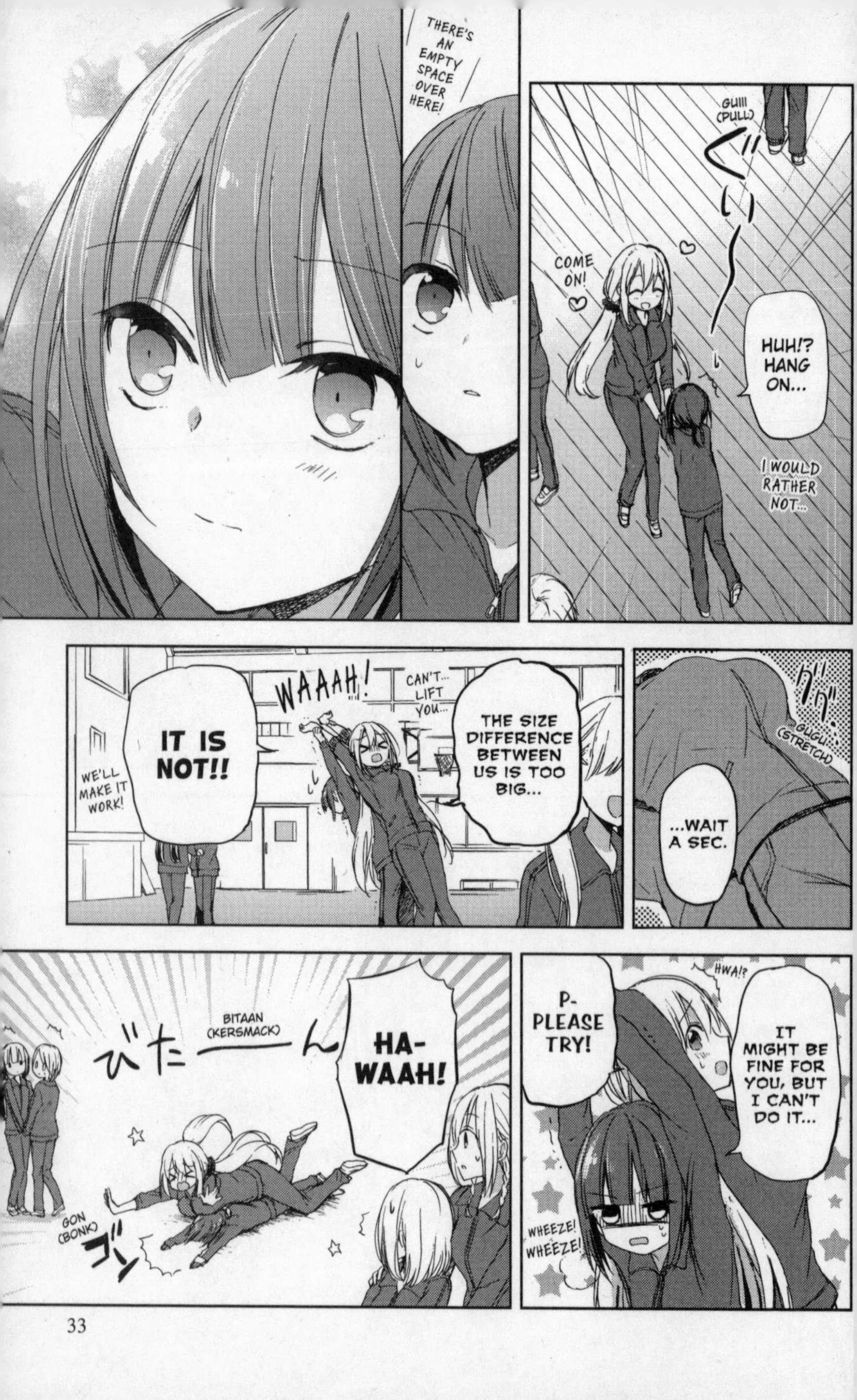
GUIII (PULL)
HUH!? HANG ON...
COME ON!
I WOULD RATHER NOT...
THERE'S AN EMPTY SPACE OVER HERE!
GUGU (STRETCH)
...WAIT A SEC.
THE SIZE DIFFERENCE BETWEEN US IS TOO BIG...
CAN'T... LIFT YOU...
WAAAH!
IT IS NOT!!
WE'LL MAKE IT WORK!
HWA!?
IT MIGHT BE FINE FOR YOU, BUT I CAN'T DO IT...
P-PLEASE TRY!
WHEEZE! WHEEZE!
HA-WAAH!
BITAAN (KERSMACK)
GON (BONK)

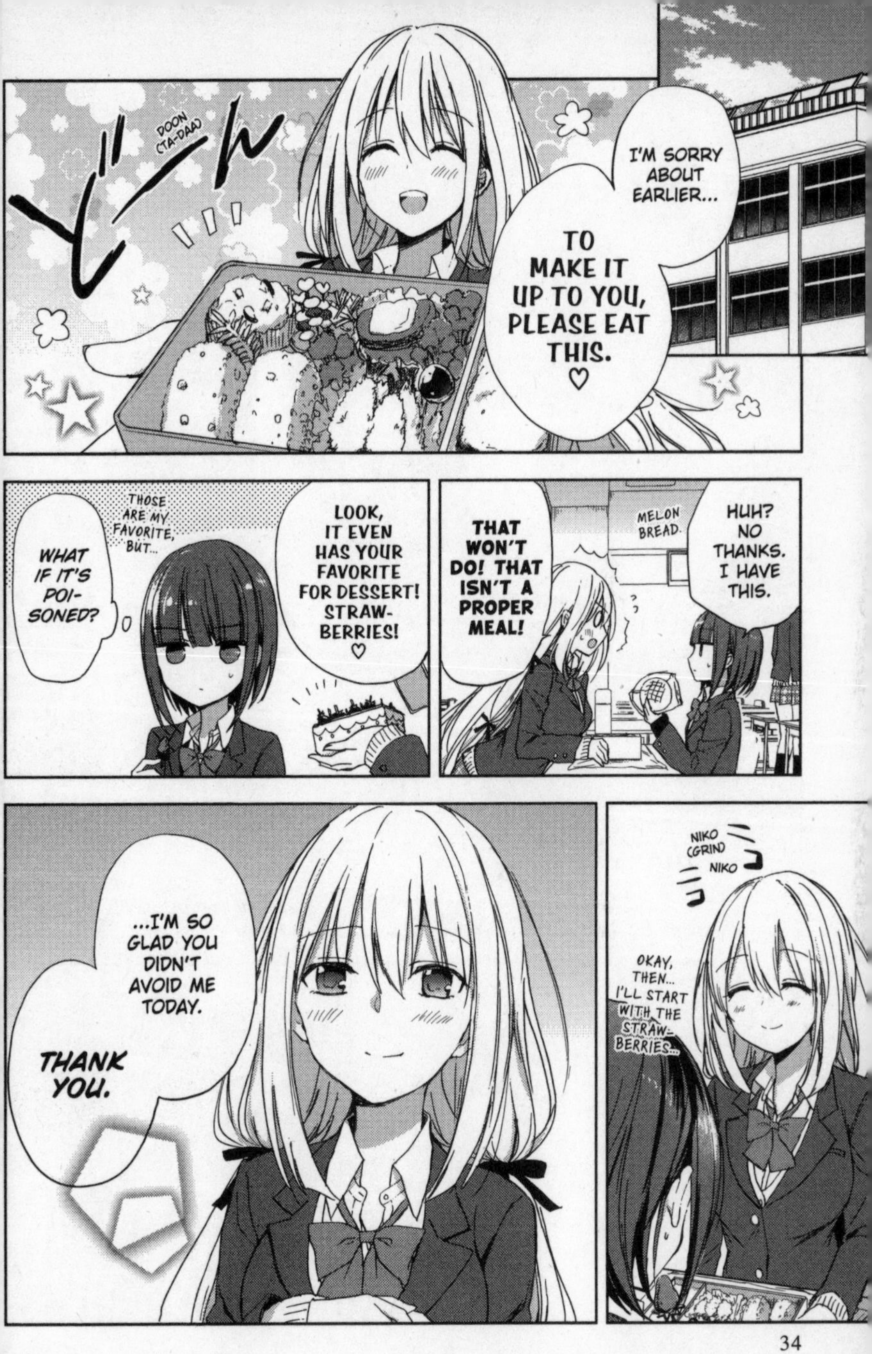
I'M SORRY ABOUT EARLIER...
TO MAKE IT UP TO YOU, PLEASE EAT THIS. ♡
DOON (TA-DAA)
HUH? NO THANKS. I HAVE THIS.
MELON BREAD.
THAT WON'T DO! THAT ISN'T A PROPER MEAL!
LOOK, IT EVEN HAS YOUR FAVORITE FOR DESSERT! STRAW-BERRIES! ♡
THOSE ARE MY FAVORITE, BUT...
WHAT IF IT'S POI-SONED?
NIKO (GRIN) NIKO
OKAY, THEN... I'LL START WITH THE STRAW-BERRIES...
...I'M SO GLAD YOU DIDN'T AVOID ME TODAY.
THANK YOU.

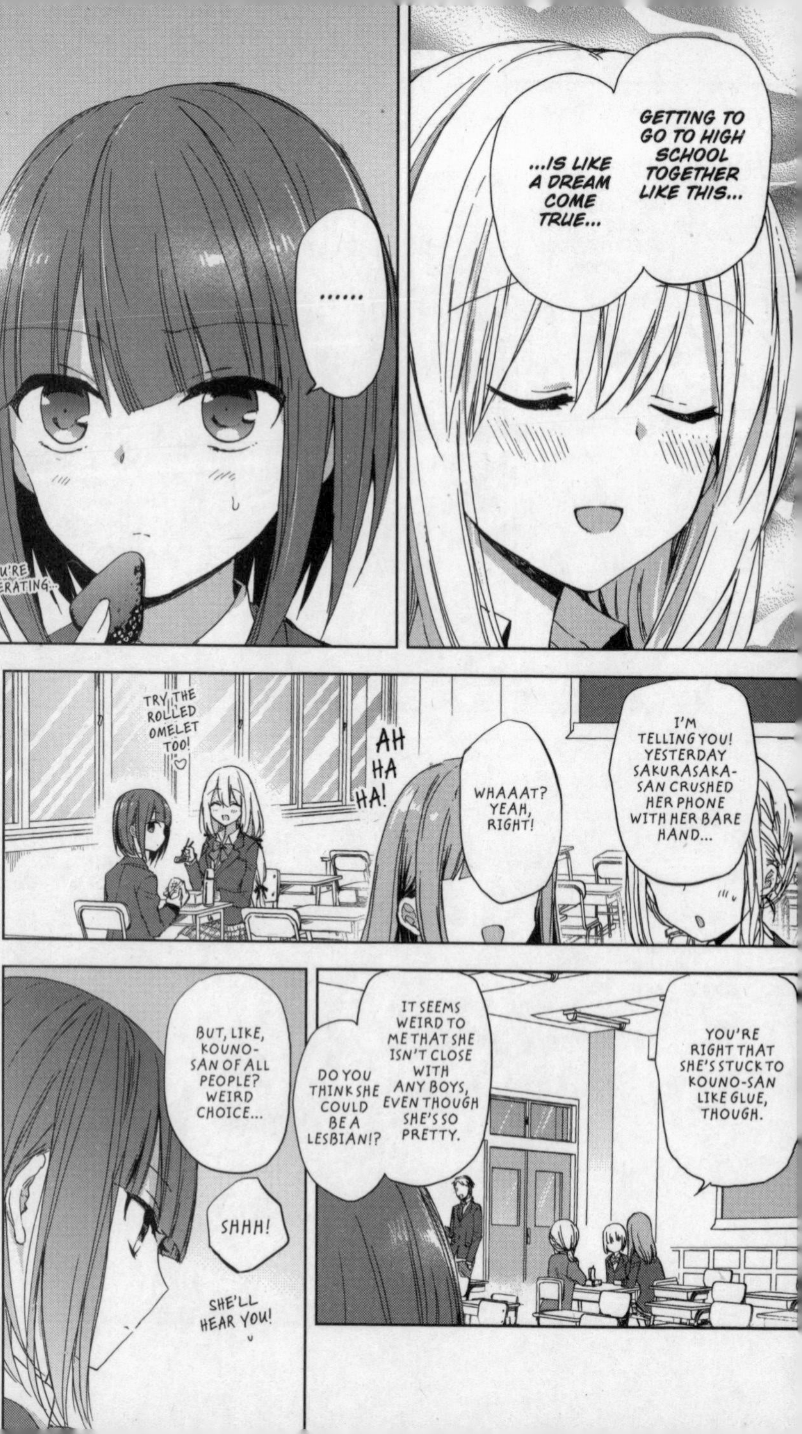
GETTING TO GO TO HIGH SCHOOL TOGETHER LIKE THIS...
...IS LIKE A DREAM COME TRUE...
......
YOU'RE EXAGGERATING...
I'M TELLING YOU! YESTERDAY SAKURASAKA-SAN CRUSHED HER PHONE WITH HER BARE HAND...
WHAAAT? YEAH, RIGHT!
AH HA HA!
TRY THE ROLLED OMELET TOO!
YOU'RE RIGHT THAT SHE'S STUCK TO KOUNO-SAN LIKE GLUE, THOUGH.
IT SEEMS WEIRD TO ME THAT SHE ISN'T CLOSE WITH ANY BOYS, EVEN THOUGH SHE'S SO PRETTY.
DO YOU THINK SHE COULD BE A LESBIAN!?
BUT, LIKE, KOUNO-SAN OF ALL PEOPLE? WEIRD CHOICE...
SHHH!
SHE'LL HEAR YOU!

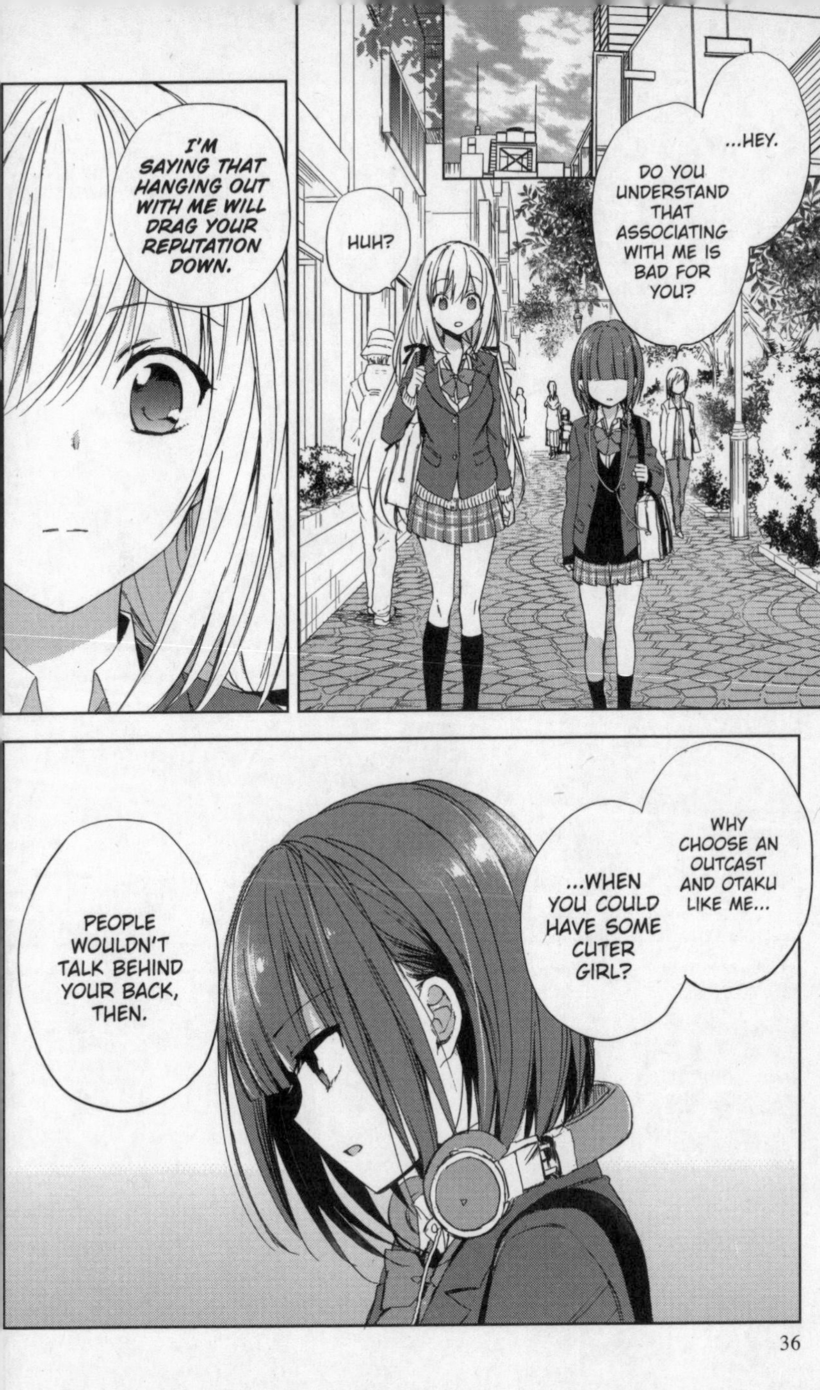
...HEY.
DO YOU UNDERSTAND THAT ASSOCIATING WITH ME IS BAD FOR YOU?
HUH?
I'M SAYING THAT HANGING OUT WITH ME WILL DRAG YOUR REPUTATION DOWN.
WHY CHOOSE AN OUTCAST AND OTAKU LIKE ME...
...WHEN YOU COULD HAVE SOME CUTER GIRL?
PEOPLE WOULDN'T TALK BEHIND YOUR BACK, THEN.

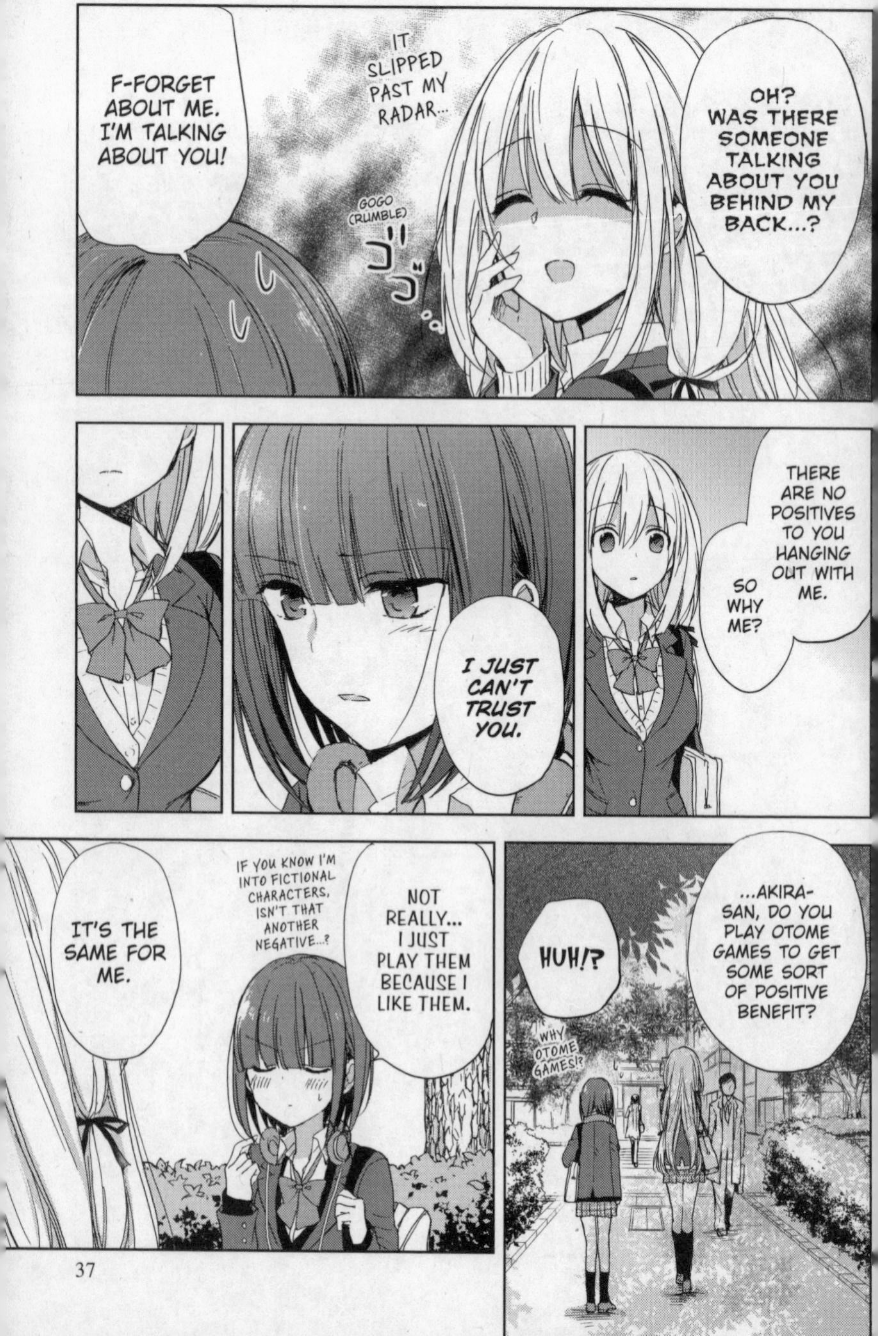
OH? WAS THERE SOMEONE TALKING ABOUT YOU BEHIND MY BACK...?
IT SLIPPED PAST MY RADAR...
F-FORGET ABOUT ME. I'M TALKING ABOUT YOU!
GOGO (RUMBLE)
THERE ARE NO POSITIVES TO YOU HANGING OUT WITH ME.
SO WHY ME?
I JUST CAN'T TRUST YOU.
...AKIRA-SAN, DO YOU PLAY OTOME GAMES TO GET SOME SORT OF POSITIVE BENEFIT?
HUH!?
WHY OTOME GAMES!?
NOT REALLY... I JUST PLAY THEM BECAUSE I LIKE THEM.
IF YOU KNOW I'M INTO FICTIONAL CHARACTERS, ISN'T THAT ANOTHER NEGATIVE...?
IT'S THE SAME FOR ME.

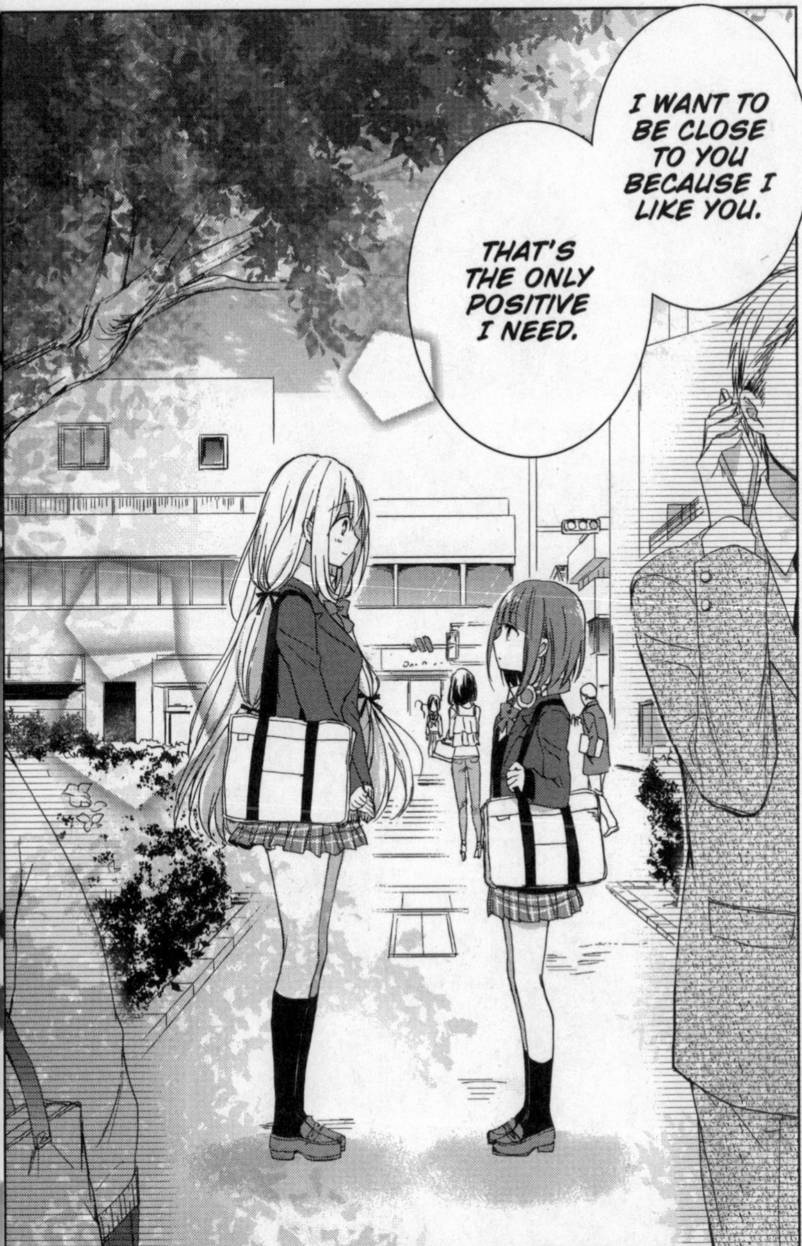
I WANT TO BE CLOSE TO YOU BECAUSE I LIKE YOU.
THAT'S THE ONLY POSITIVE I NEED.

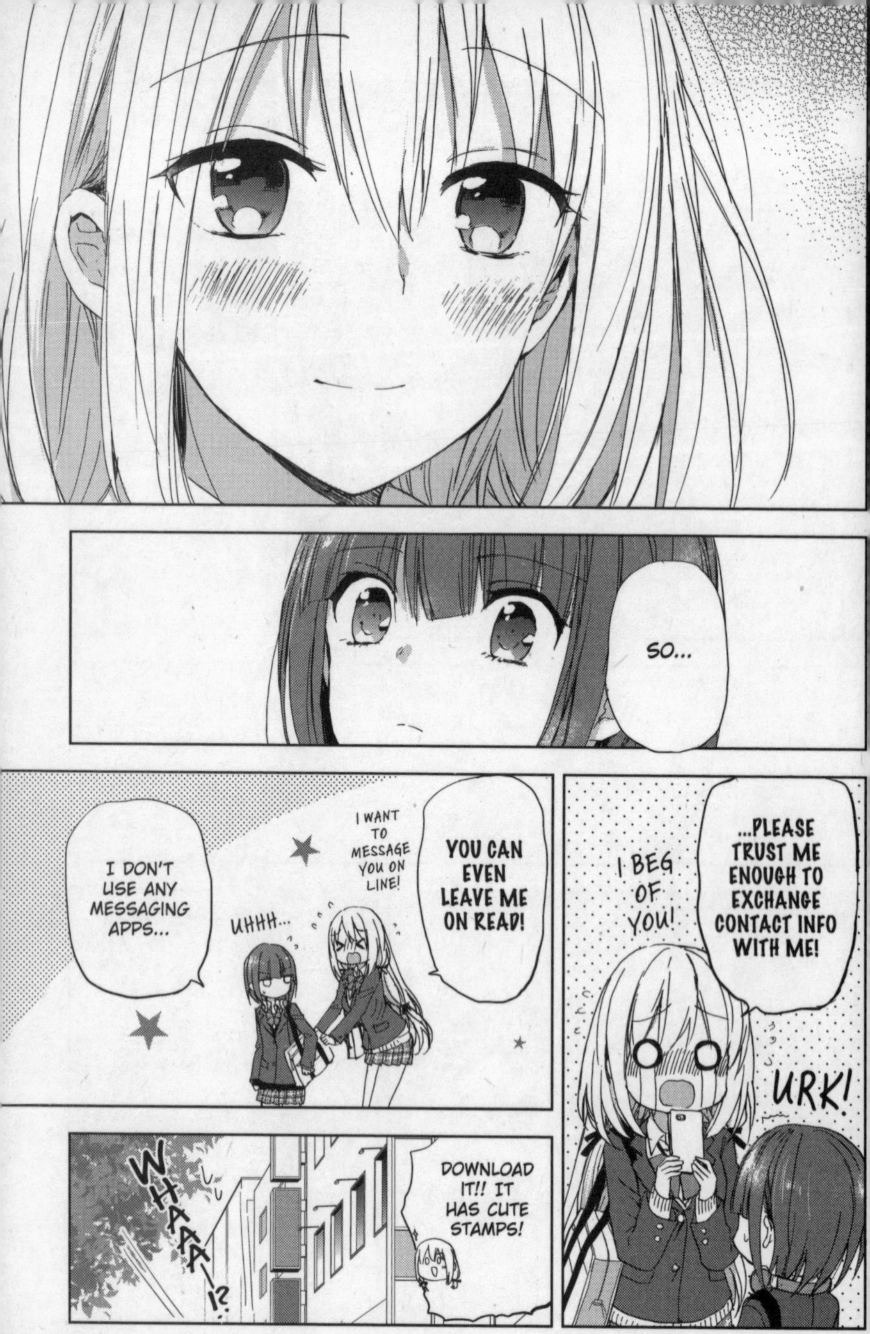
SO...
...PLEASE TRUST ME ENOUGH TO EXCHANGE CONTACT INFO WITH ME!
I BEG OF YOU!
URK!
YOU CAN EVEN LEAVE ME ON READ!
I WANT TO MESSAGE YOU ON LINE!
UHHH...
I DON'T USE ANY MESSAGING APPS...
DOWNLOAD IT!! IT HAS CUTE STAMPS!
WHAAA—!?

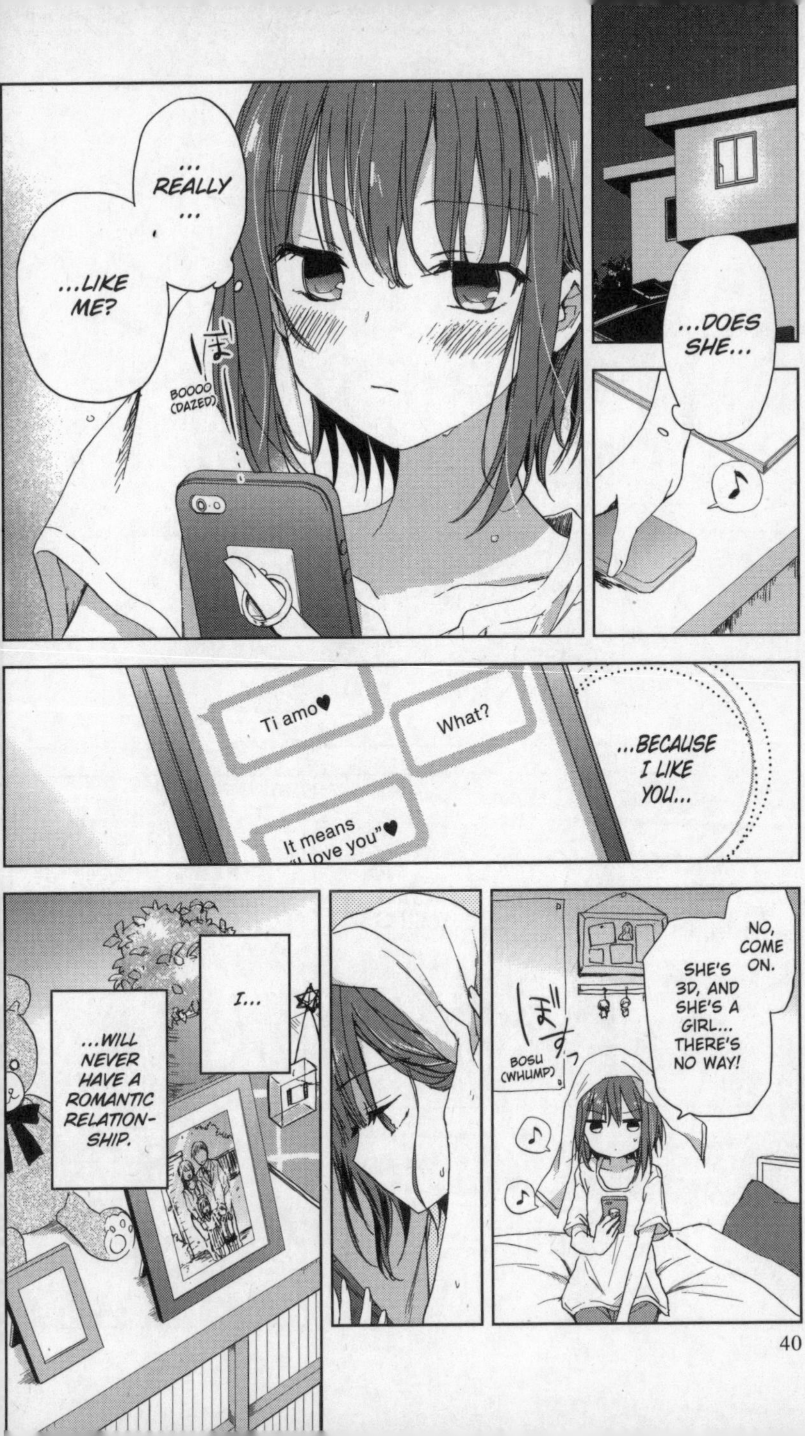
...DOES SHE...
... REALLY ...
...LIKE ME?
BOOOO (DAZED)
Ti amo♥
What?
It means "I love you"♥
...BECAUSE I LIKE YOU...
NO, COME ON.
SHE'S 3D, AND SHE'S A GIRL... THERE'S NO WAY!
BOSU (WHUMP)
I...
...WILL NEVER HAVE A ROMANTIC RELATION-SHIP.

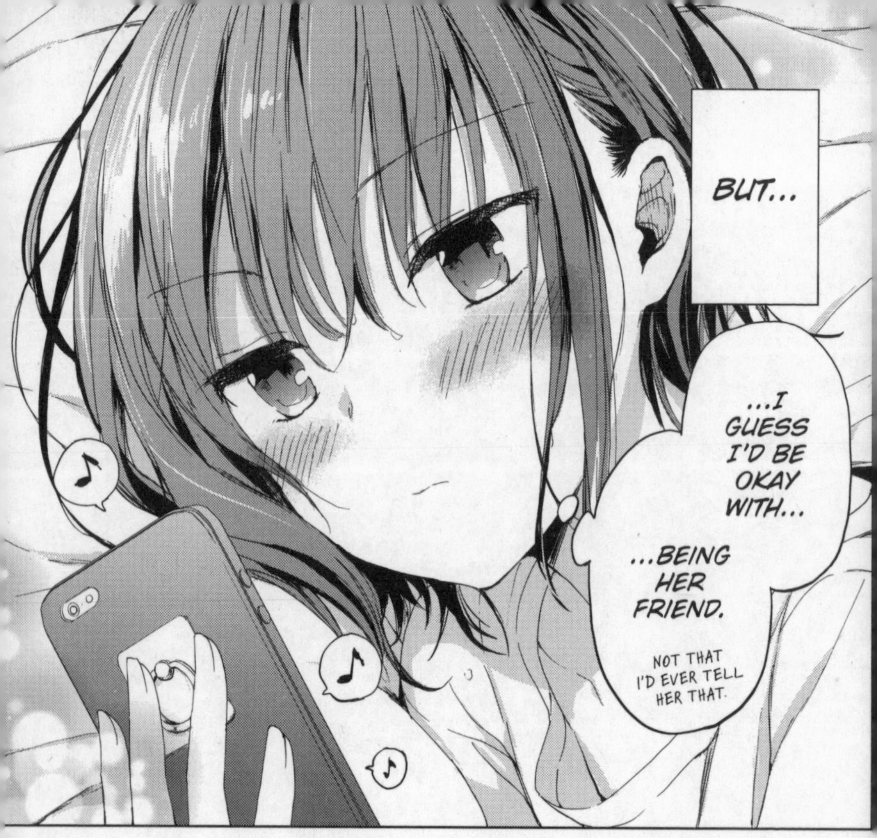
BUT...
...I GUESS I'D BE OKAY WITH...
...BEING HER FRIEND.
NOT THAT I'D EVER TELL HER THAT.

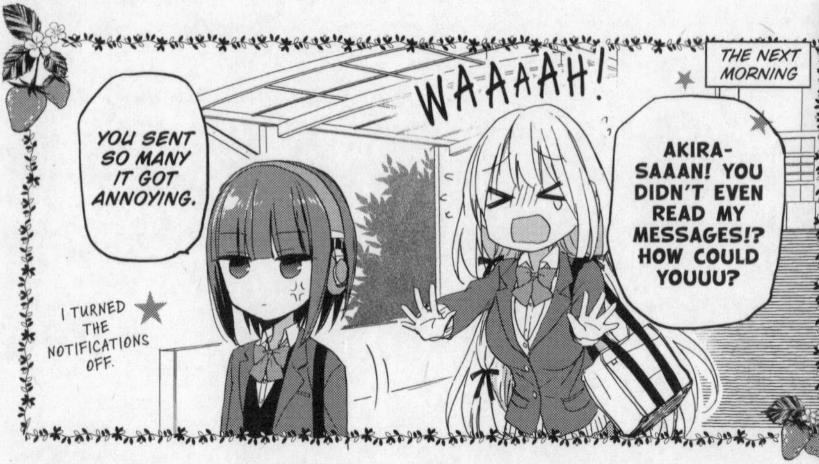
THE NEXT MORNING
WAAAAH!
AKIRA-SAAAN! YOU DIDN'T EVEN READ MY MESSAGES!? HOW COULD YOUUU?
YOU SENT SO MANY IT GOT ANNOYING.
I TURNED THE NOTIFICATIONS OFF.

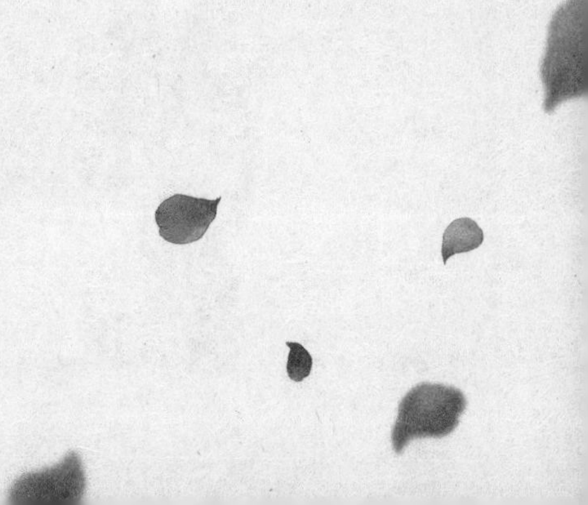

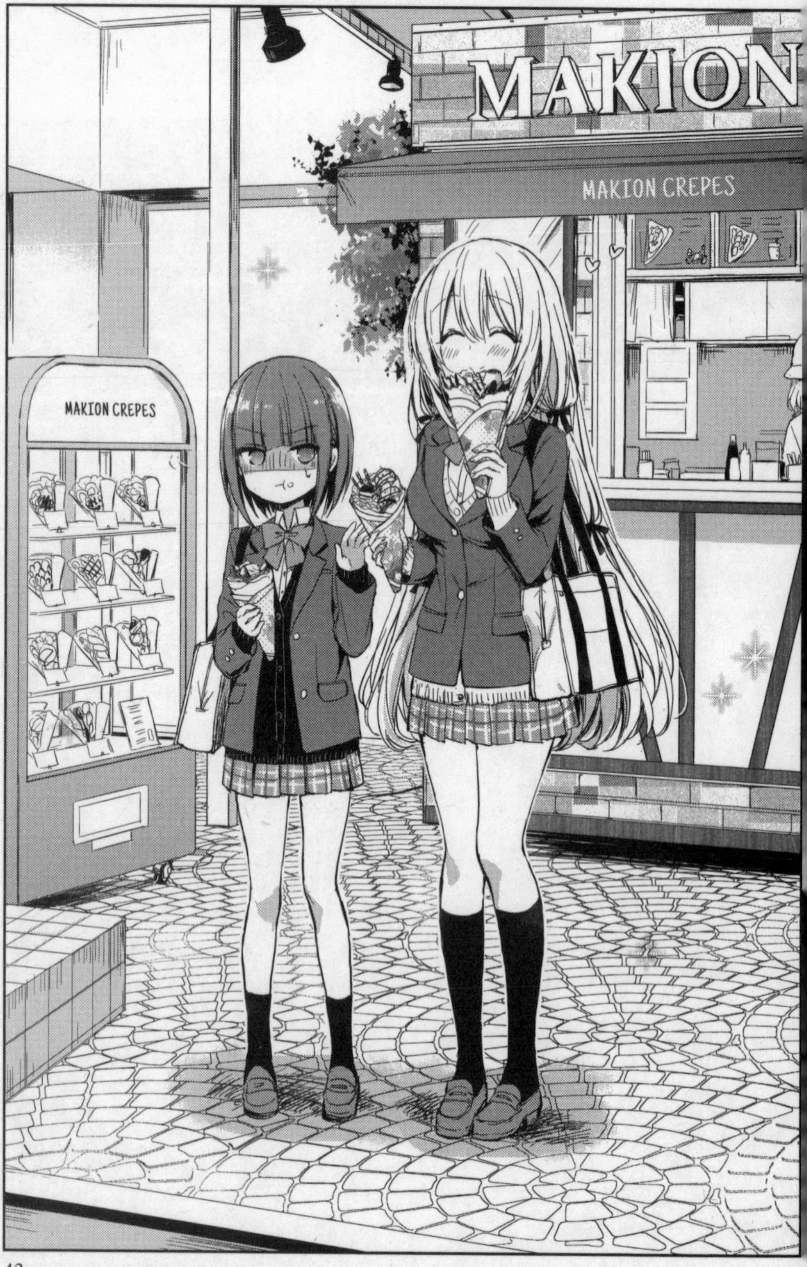
MAKION
MAKION CREPES
MAKION CREPES

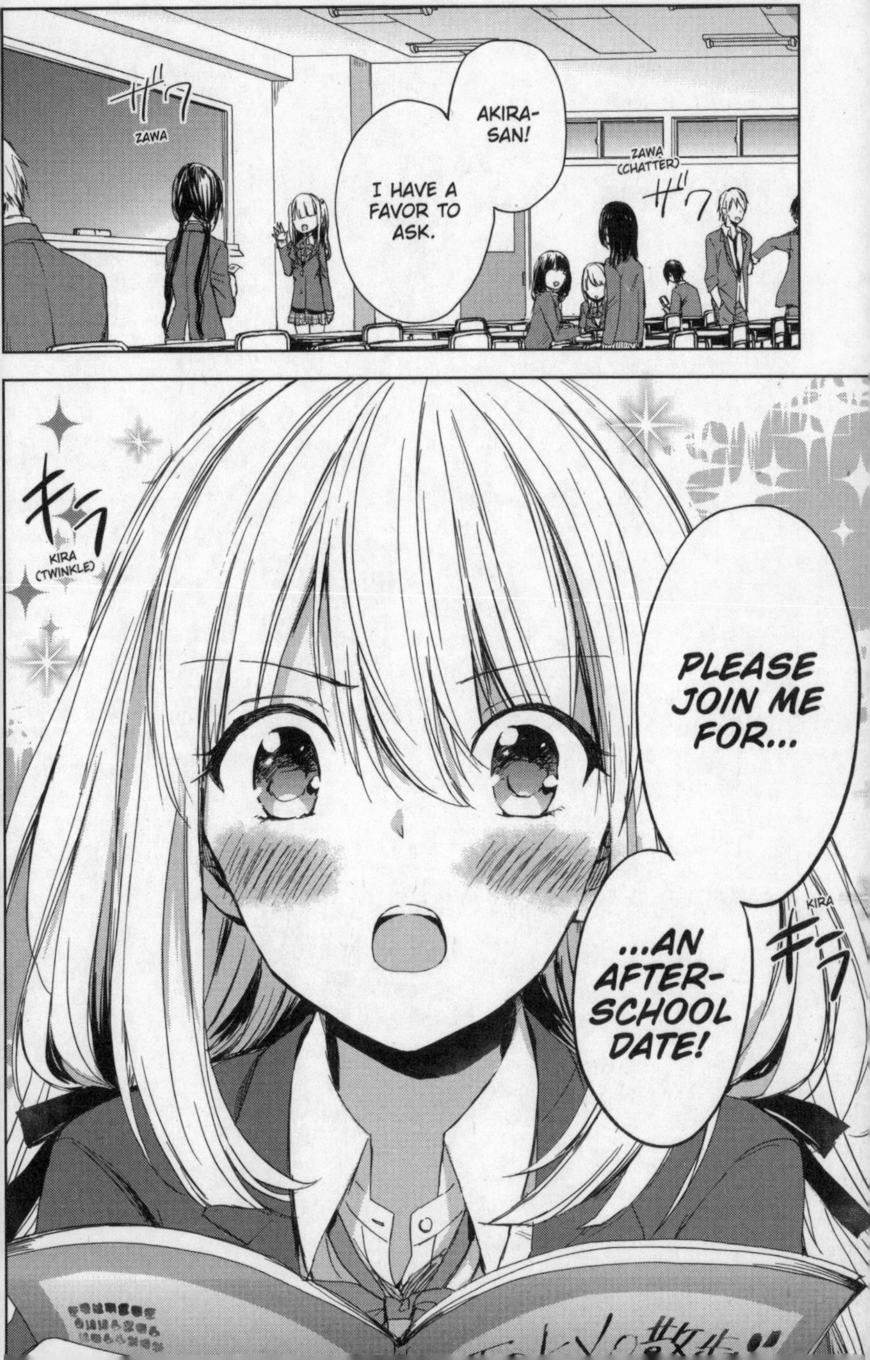
ZAWA (CHATTER)
AKIRA-SAN!
I HAVE A FAVOR TO ASK.
ZAWA
PLEASE JOIN ME FOR...
KIRA
...AN AFTER-SCHOOL DATE!
KIRA (TWINKLE)

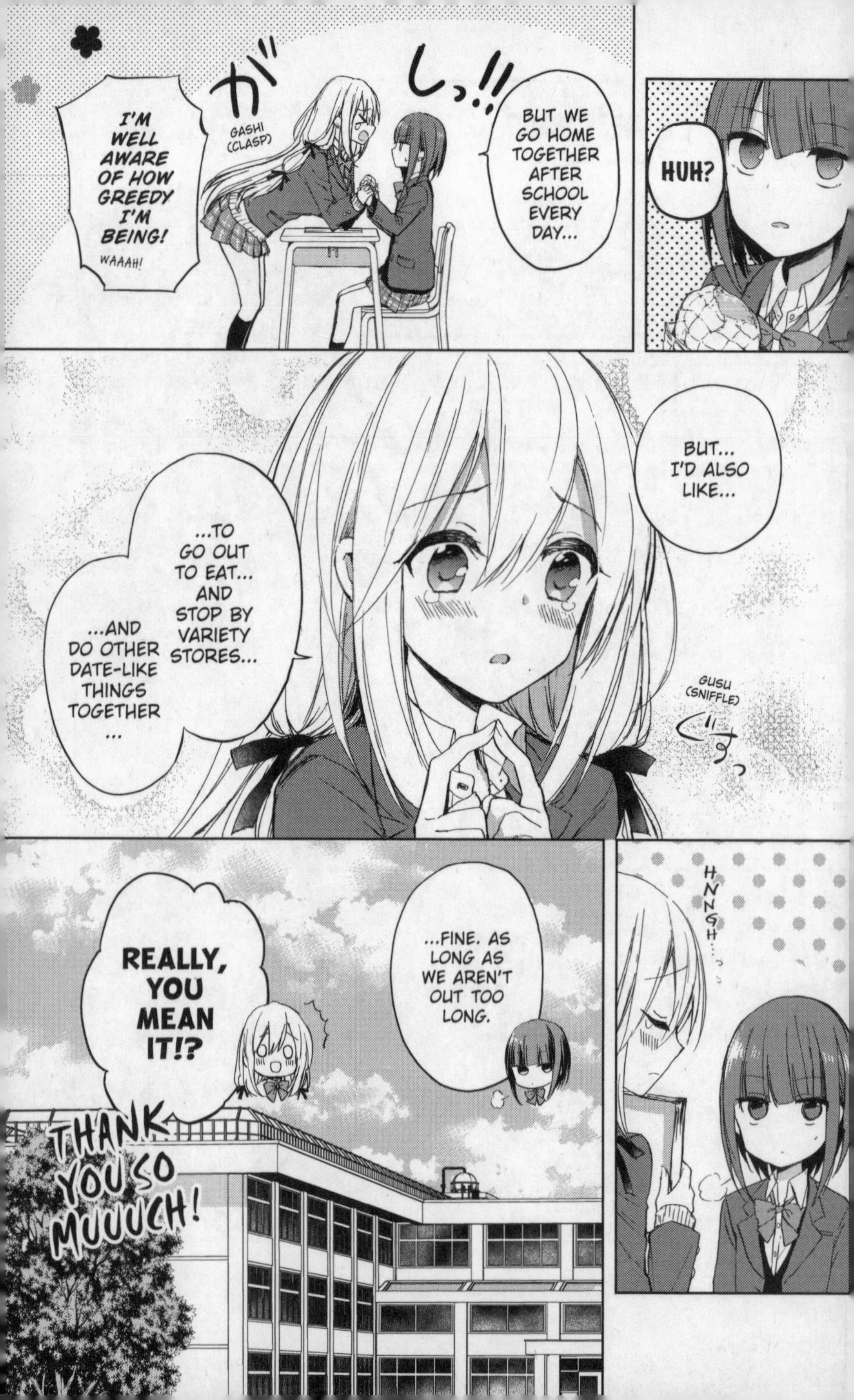

HUH?
がしっ!!
GASHI (CLASP)
BUT WE GO HOME TOGETHER AFTER SCHOOL EVERY DAY...
I'M WELL AWARE OF HOW GREEDY I'M BEING!
WAAAH!
BUT... I'D ALSO LIKE...
ぐすっ
GUSU (SNIFFLE)
...TO GO OUT TO EAT... AND STOP BY VARIETY STORES...
...AND DO OTHER DATE-LIKE THINGS TOGETHER...
HNNGH...
...FINE. AS LONG AS WE AREN'T OUT TOO LONG.
REALLY, YOU MEAN IT!?
THANK YOU SO MUUUCH!

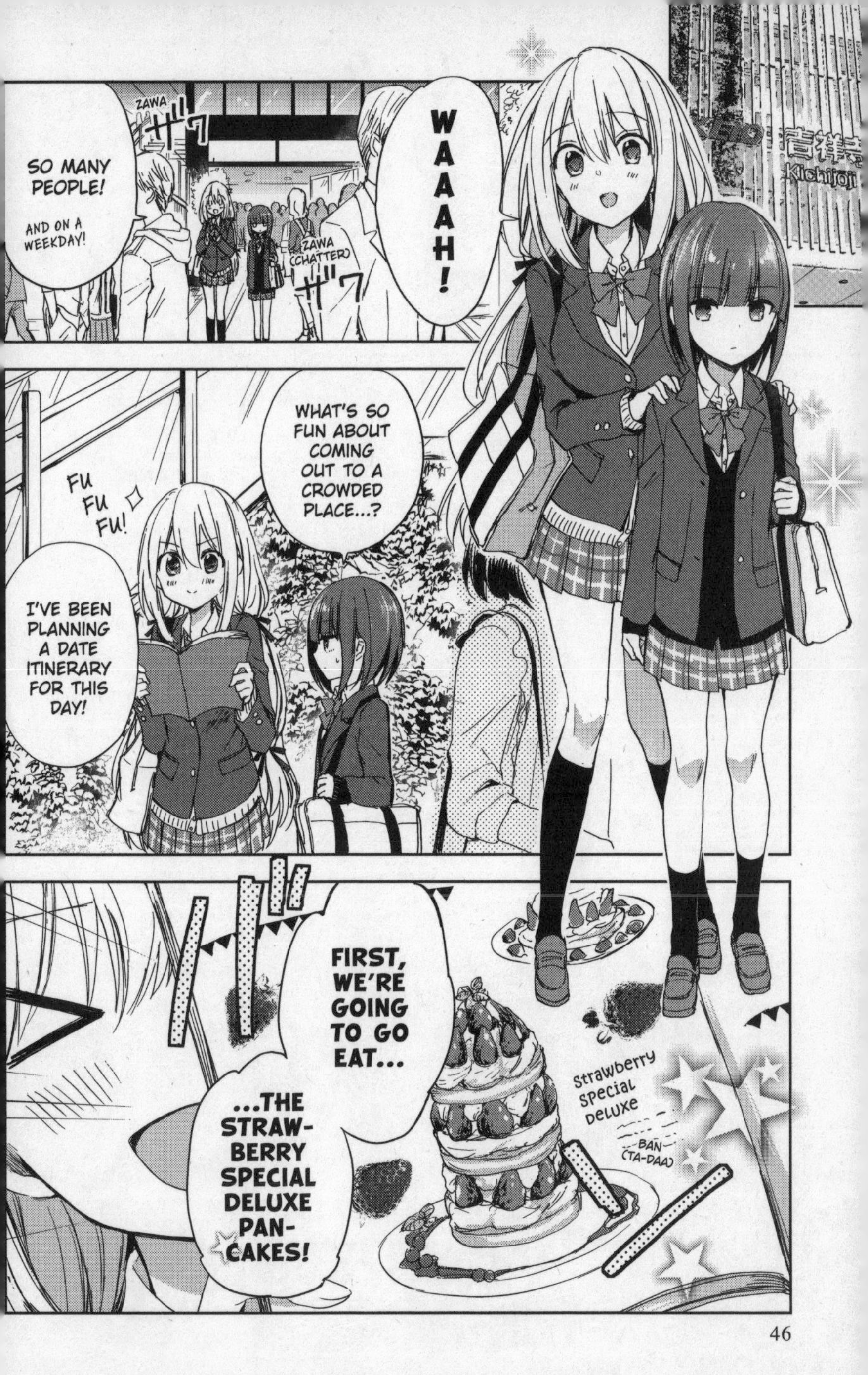

Kichijoji
WAAAH!
ZAWA (CHATTER)
ZAWA
SO MANY PEOPLE!
AND ON A WEEKDAY!
WHAT'S SO FUN ABOUT COMING OUT TO A CROWDED PLACE...?
FU FU FU!
I'VE BEEN PLANNING A DATE ITINERARY FOR THIS DAY!
FIRST, WE'RE GOING TO GO EAT...
...THE STRAWBERRY SPECIAL DELUXE PANCAKES!
Strawberry Special Deluxe
BAN (TA-DAA)

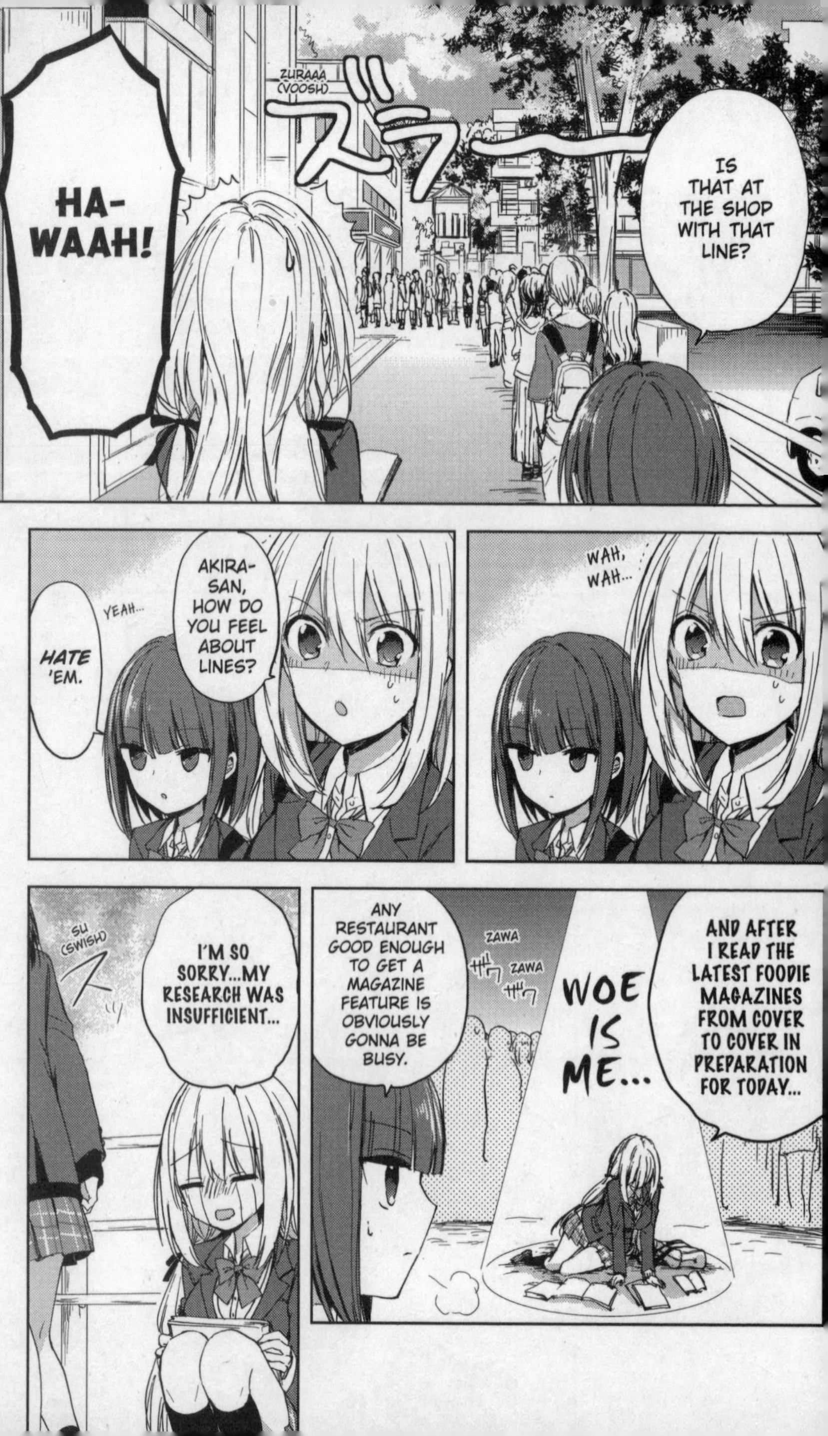
IS THAT AT THE SHOP WITH THAT LINE?
ZURAAA (VOOSH)
HA-WAAH!
WAH, WAH...
AKIRA-SAN, HOW DO YOU FEEL ABOUT LINES?
YEAH...
HATE 'EM.
AND AFTER I READ THE LATEST FOODIE MAGAZINES FROM COVER TO COVER IN PREPARATION FOR TODAY...
WOE IS ME...
ZAWA
ZAWA
ANY RESTAURANT GOOD ENOUGH TO GET A MAGAZINE FEATURE IS OBVIOUSLY GONNA BE BUSY.
I'M SO SORRY...MY RESEARCH WAS INSUFFICIENT...
SU (SWISH)

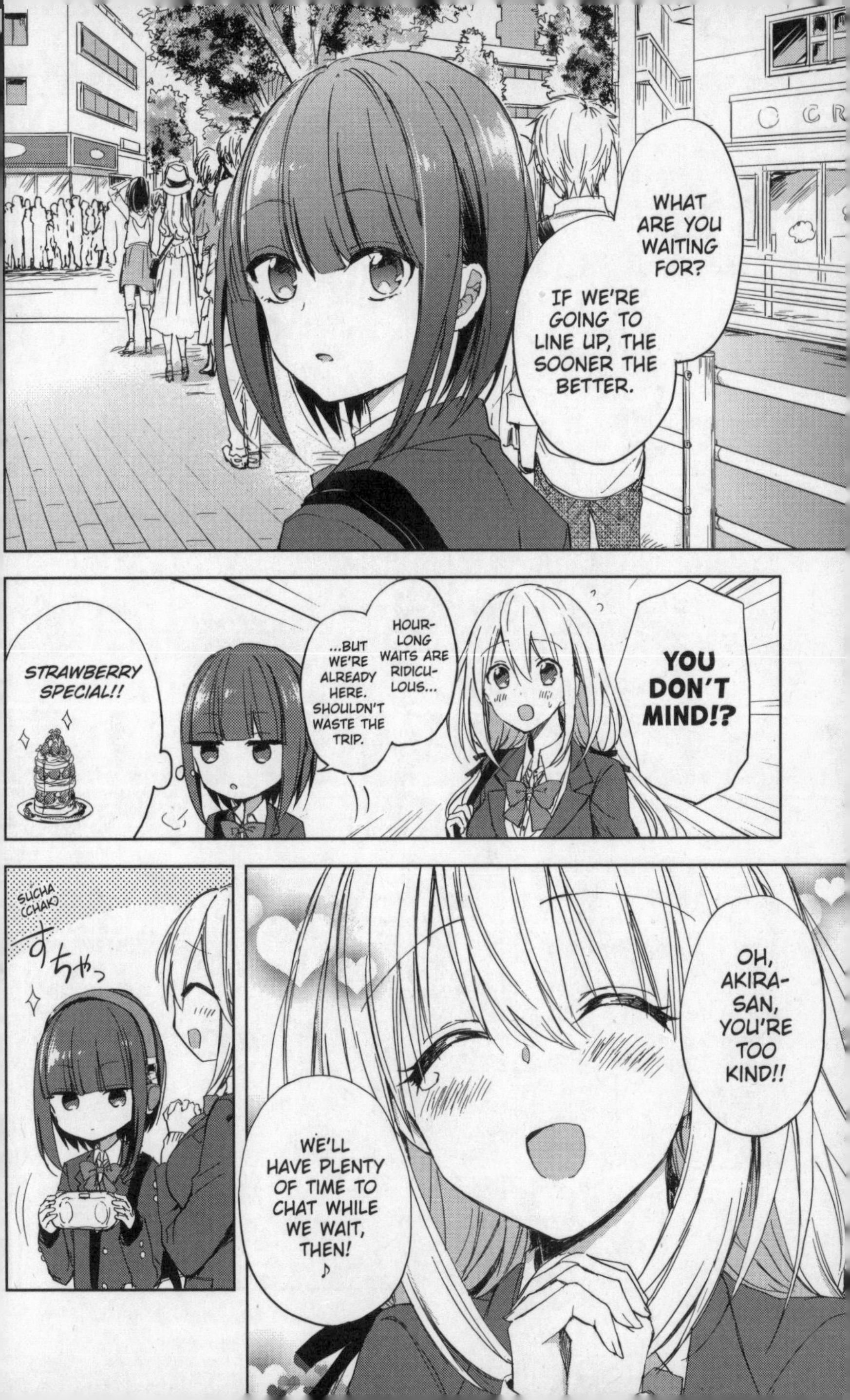
WHAT ARE YOU WAITING FOR?
IF WE'RE GOING TO LINE UP, THE SOONER THE BETTER.
YOU DON'T MIND!?
HOUR-LONG WAITS ARE RIDICULOUS...
...BUT WE'RE ALREADY HERE. SHOULDN'T WASTE THE TRIP.
STRAWBERRY SPECIAL!!
OH, AKIRA-SAN, YOU'RE TOO KIND!!
WE'LL HAVE PLENTY OF TIME TO CHAT WHILE WE WAIT, THEN! ♪
すちゃっ
SUCHA (CHAK)

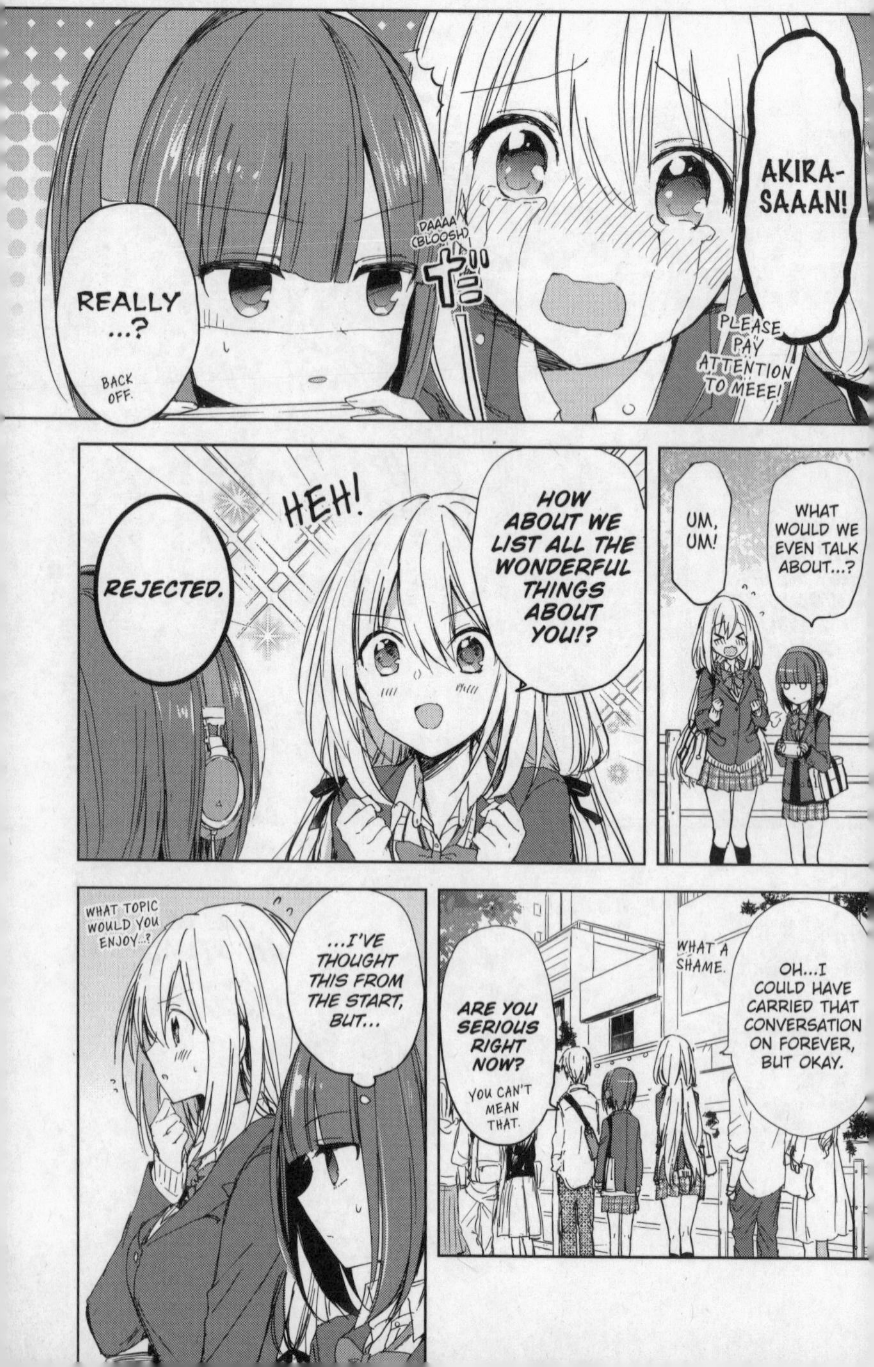
AKIRA-SAAAN!
PLEASE PAY ATTENTION TO MEEE!
DAAAA (BLOOSH)
REALLY ...?
BACK OFF.
WHAT WOULD WE EVEN TALK ABOUT...?
UM, UM!
HOW ABOUT WE LIST ALL THE WONDERFUL THINGS ABOUT YOU!?
HEH!
REJECTED.
OH...I COULD HAVE CARRIED THAT CONVERSATION ON FOREVER, BUT OKAY.
WHAT A SHAME.
ARE YOU SERIOUS RIGHT NOW?
YOU CAN'T MEAN THAT.
...I'VE THOUGHT THIS FROM THE START, BUT...
WHAT TOPIC WOULD YOU ENJOY...?

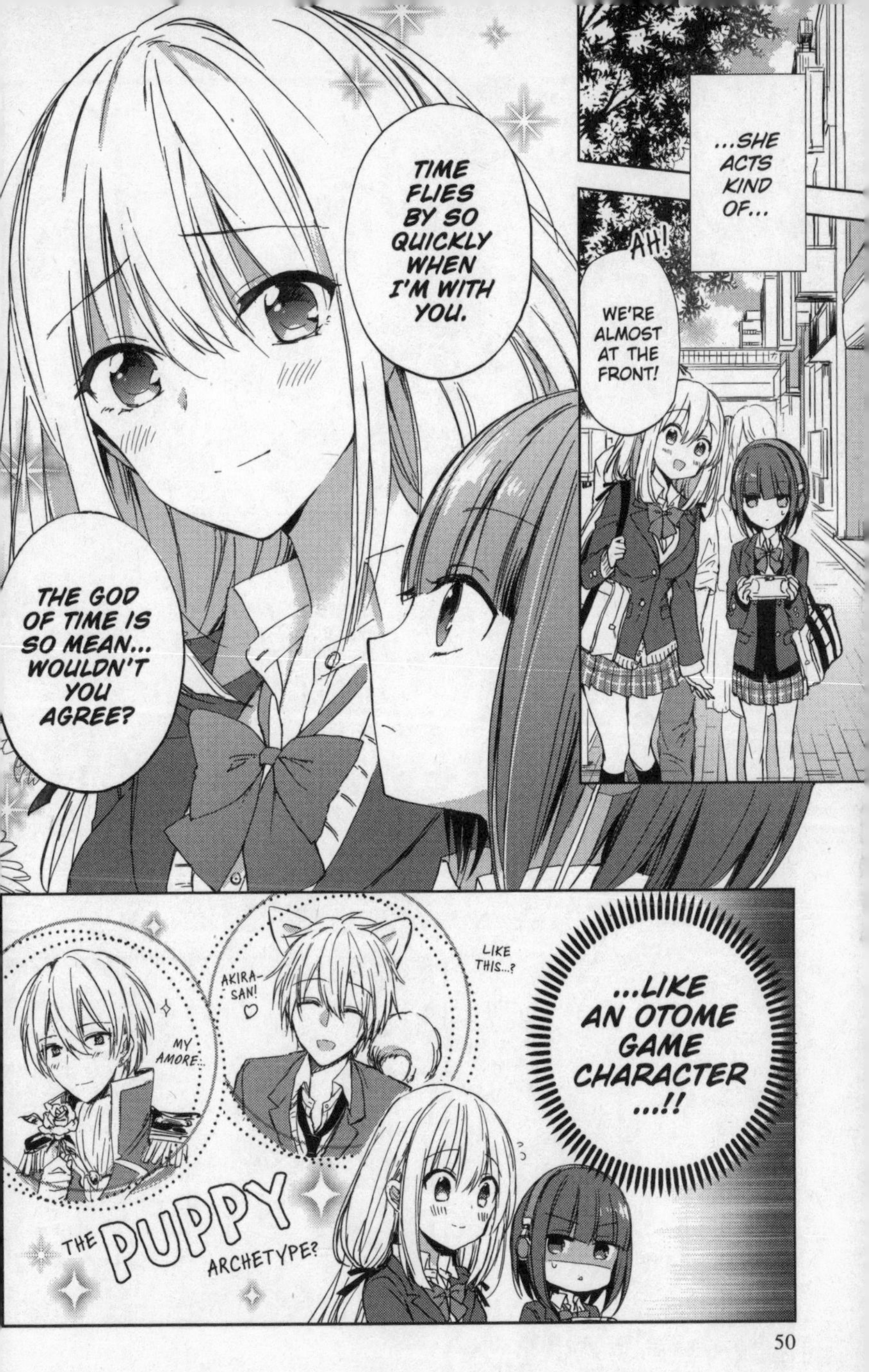
...SHE ACTS KIND OF...
AH!
WE'RE ALMOST AT THE FRONT!
TIME FLIES BY SO QUICKLY WHEN I'M WITH YOU.
THE GOD OF TIME IS SO MEAN... WOULDN'T YOU AGREE?
...LIKE AN OTOME GAME CHARACTER ...!!
LIKE THIS...?
AKIRA-SAN! ♡
MY AMORE...
THE PUPPY ARCHETYPE?

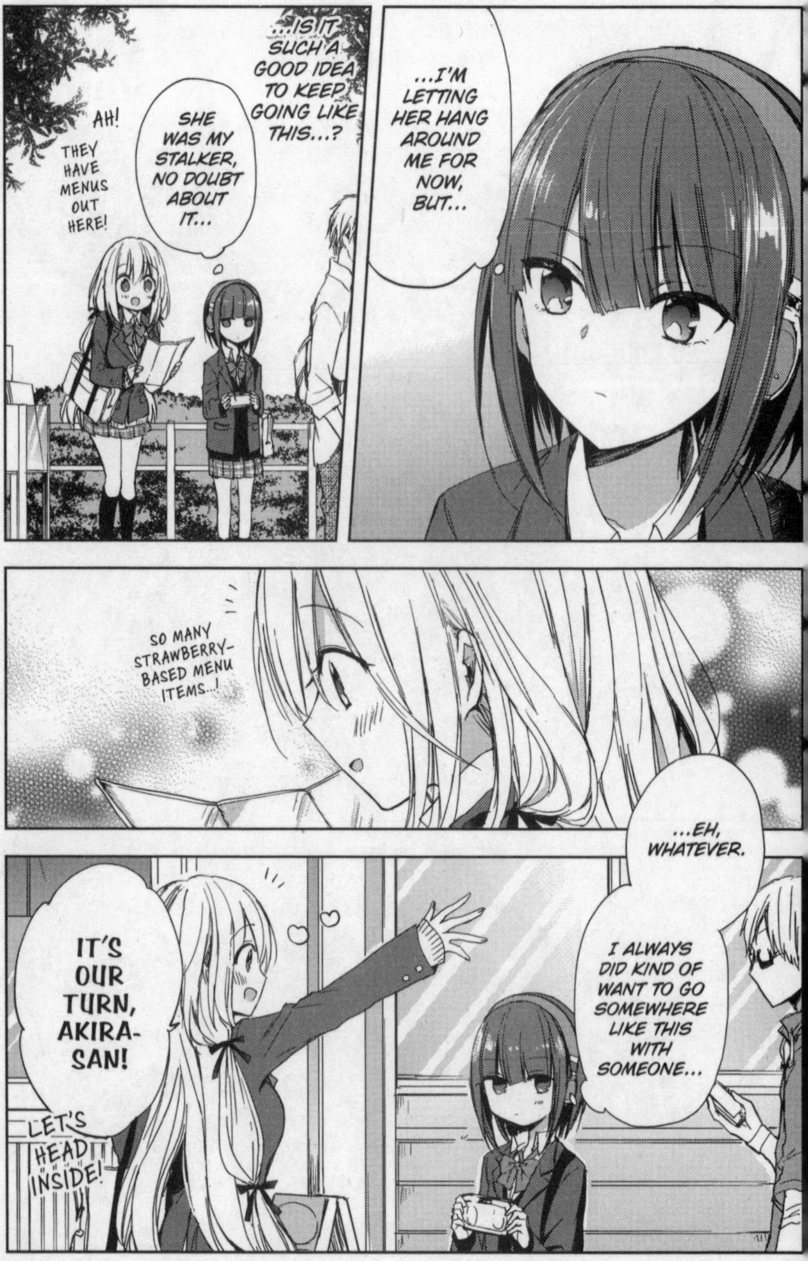
...I'M LETTING HER HANG AROUND ME FOR NOW, BUT...
...IS IT SUCH A GOOD IDEA TO KEEP GOING LIKE THIS...?
SHE WAS MY STALKER, NO DOUBT ABOUT IT...
AH! THEY HAVE MENUS OUT HERE!
SO MANY STRAWBERRY-BASED MENU ITEMS...!
...EH, WHATEVER.
I ALWAYS DID KIND OF WANT TO GO SOMEWHERE LIKE THIS WITH SOMEONE...
IT'S OUR TURN, AKIRA-SAN!
LET'S HEAD INSIDE!

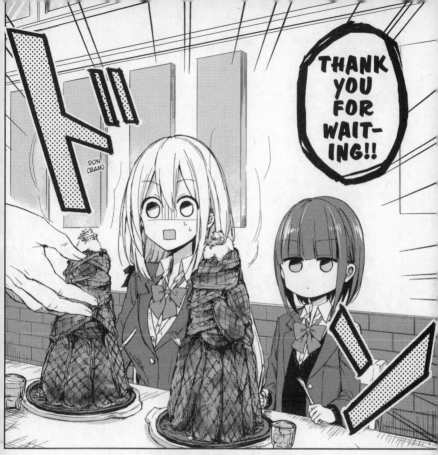

THANK YOU FOR WAIT-ING!!

DON (BAM)

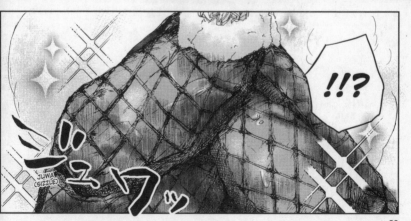

!!?

JUWA (SIZZLE)

52

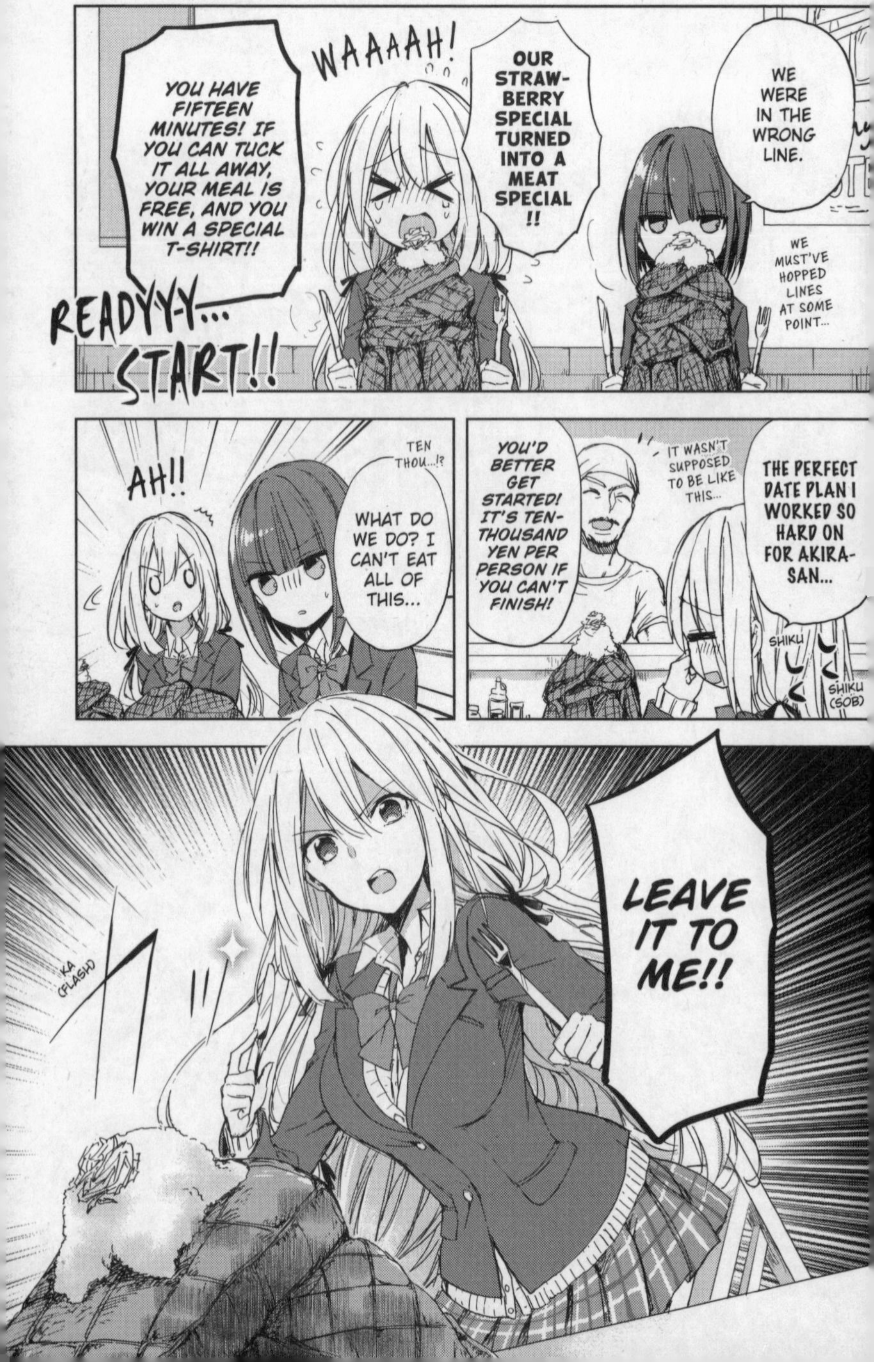
WE WERE IN THE WRONG LINE.
WE MUST'VE HOPPED LINES AT SOME POINT...
OUR STRAW-BERRY SPECIAL TURNED INTO A MEAT SPECIAL!!
WAAAAH!
YOU HAVE FIFTEEN MINUTES! IF YOU CAN TUCK IT ALL AWAY, YOUR MEAL IS FREE, AND YOU WIN A SPECIAL T-SHIRT!!
READYYY... START!!
THE PERFECT DATE PLAN I WORKED SO HARD ON FOR AKIRA-SAN...
SHIKU SHIKU (SOB)
IT WASN'T SUPPOSED TO BE LIKE THIS...
YOU'D BETTER GET STARTED! IT'S TEN-THOUSAND YEN PER PERSON IF YOU CAN'T FINISH!
TEN THOU...!?
WHAT DO WE DO? I CAN'T EAT ALL OF THIS...
AH!!
LEAVE IT TO ME!!
KA (FLASH)

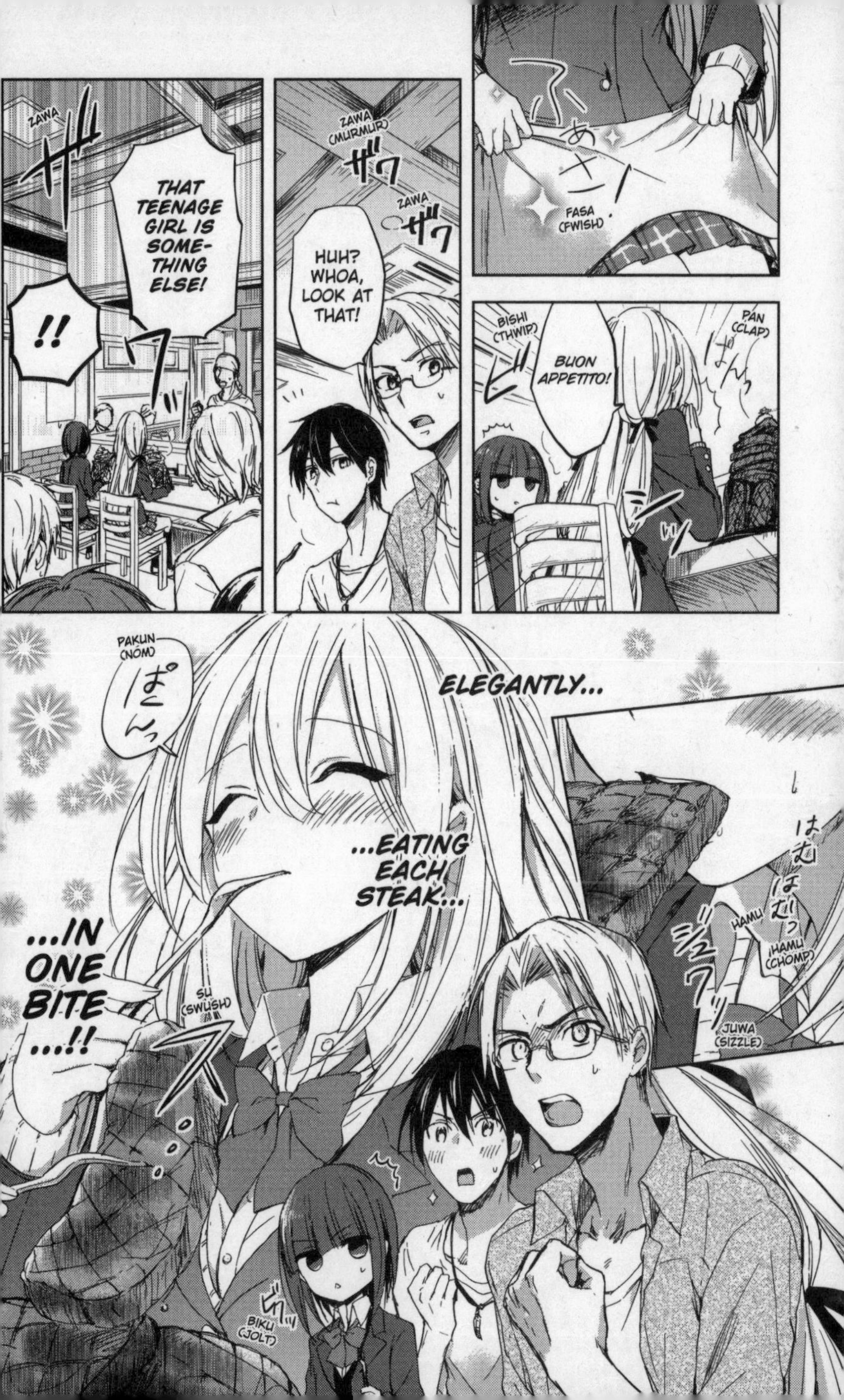
FASA (FWISH)
PAN (CLAP)
BISHI (THWIP)
BUON APPETITO!
ZAWA (MURMUR)
ZAWA
HUH? WHOA, LOOK AT THAT!
ZAWA
THAT TEENAGE GIRL IS SOME-THING ELSE!
!!
ELEGANTLY...
HAMU HAMU (CHOMP)
...EATING EACH STEAK...
JUWA (SIZZLE)
PAKUN (NOM)
SU (SWISH)
...IN ONE BITE ...!!
BIKU (JOLT)

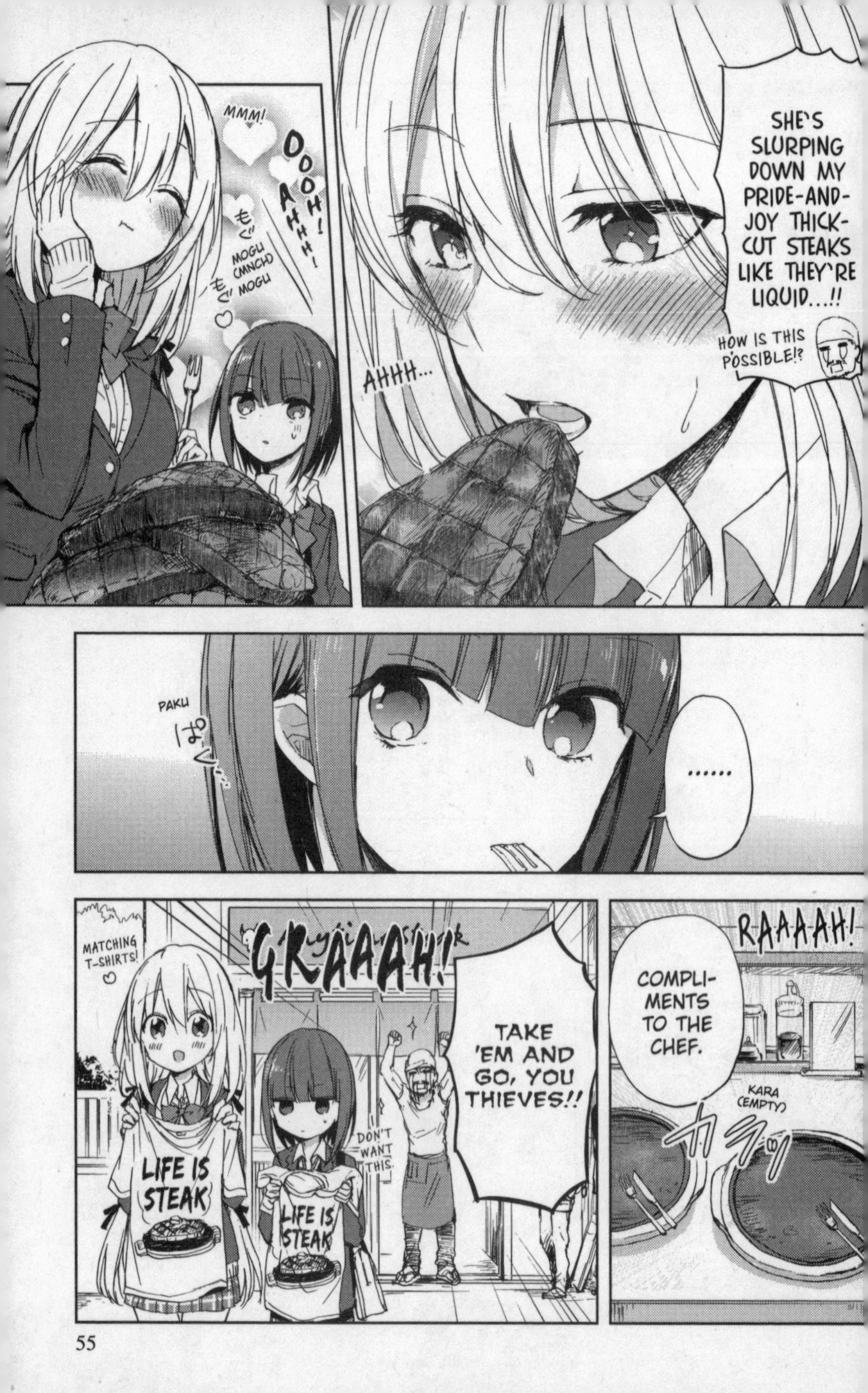
SHE'S SLURPING DOWN MY PRIDE-AND-JOY THICK-CUT STEAKS LIKE THEY'RE LIQUID...!!
HOW IS THIS POSSIBLE!?
AHHH...
MMM!
OOOH! AHHH!
もぐ もぐ
MOGU (MNCH) MOGU
PAKU
ぱく…
......
RAAAAH!
COMPLIMENTS TO THE CHEF.
KARA (EMPTY)
カラッ
GRAAAAH!
TAKE 'EM AND GO, YOU THIEVES!!
DON'T WANT THIS.
MATCHING T-SHIRTS!
LIFE IS STEAK
LIFE IS STEAK

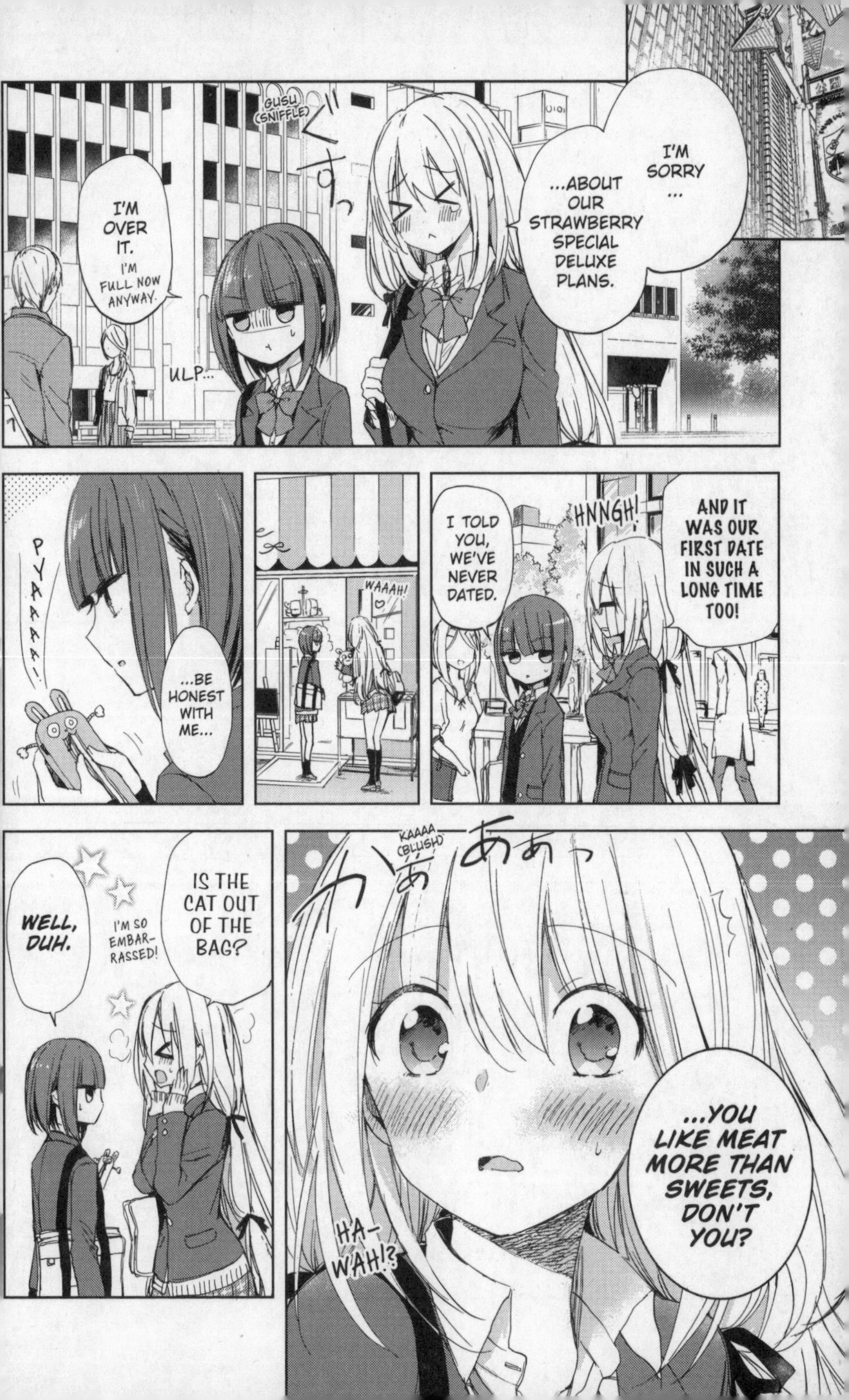
I'M SORRY ...
...ABOUT OUR STRAWBERRY SPECIAL DELUXE PLANS.
GUSU (SNIFFLE)
I'M OVER IT. I'M FULL NOW ANYWAY.
ULP...
AND IT WAS OUR FIRST DATE IN SUCH A LONG TIME TOO!
HNNGH!
I TOLD YOU, WE'VE NEVER DATED.
WAAAH!
...BE HONEST WITH ME...
PYAAAAA!
KAAAA (BLUSH)
...YOU LIKE MEAT MORE THAN SWEETS, DON'T YOU?
HA-WAH!?
IS THE CAT OUT OF THE BAG?
I'M SO EMBARRASSED!
WELL, DUH.

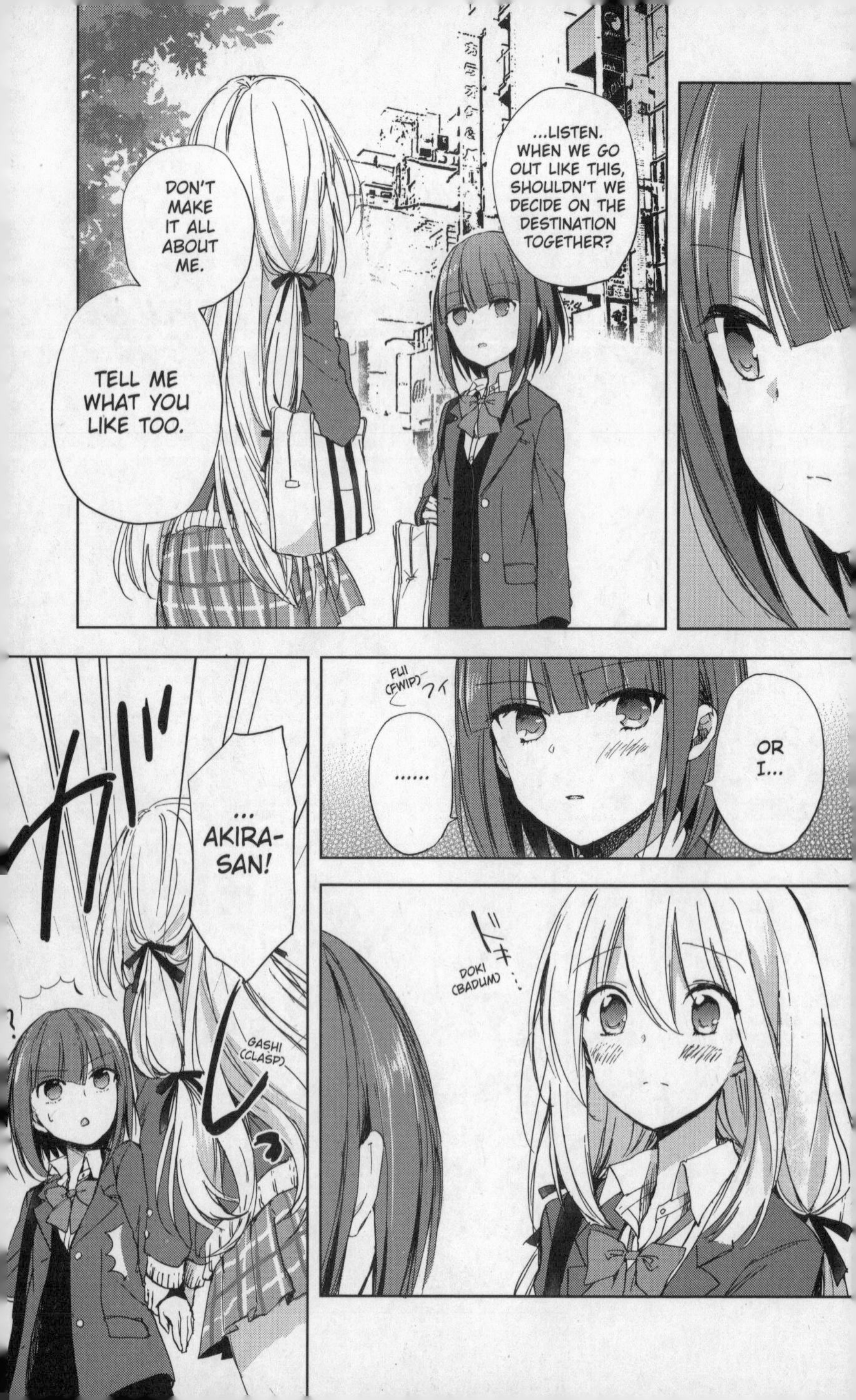
...LISTEN. WHEN WE GO OUT LIKE THIS, SHOULDN'T WE DECIDE ON THE DESTINATION TOGETHER?
DON'T MAKE IT ALL ABOUT ME.
TELL ME WHAT YOU LIKE TOO.
OR I...
FUI (FWIP)
フイ
......
DOKI (BADUM)
ドキ...
... AKIRA-SAN!
GASHI (CLASP)

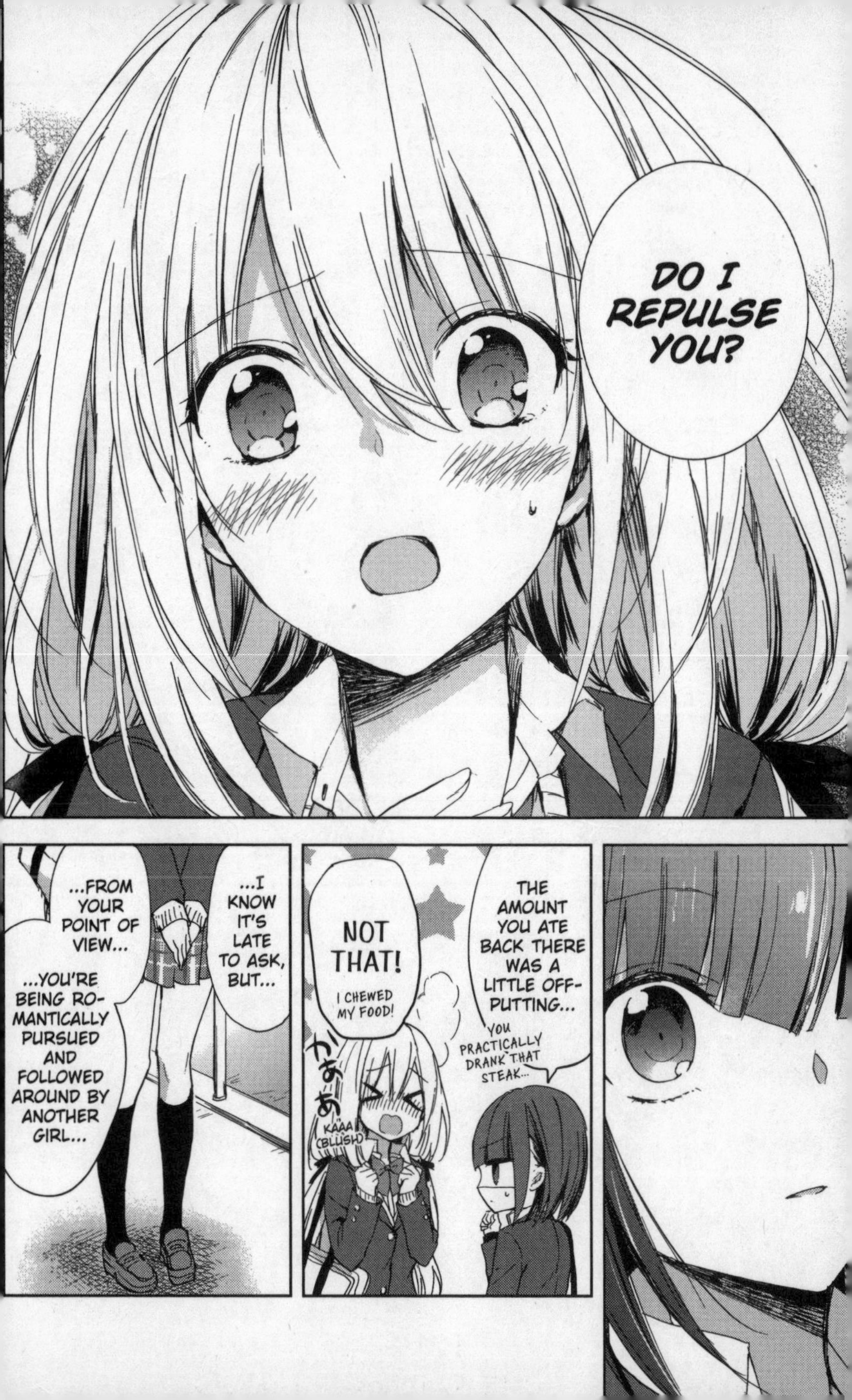
DO I REPULSE YOU?
THE AMOUNT YOU ATE BACK THERE WAS A LITTLE OFF-PUTTING...
YOU PRACTICALLY DRANK THAT STEAK...
NOT THAT!
I CHEWED MY FOOD!
かあぁ
KAAA (BLUSH)
...I KNOW IT'S LATE TO ASK, BUT...
...FROM YOUR POINT OF VIEW...
...YOU'RE BEING RO-MANTICALLY PURSUED AND FOLLOWED AROUND BY ANOTHER GIRL...

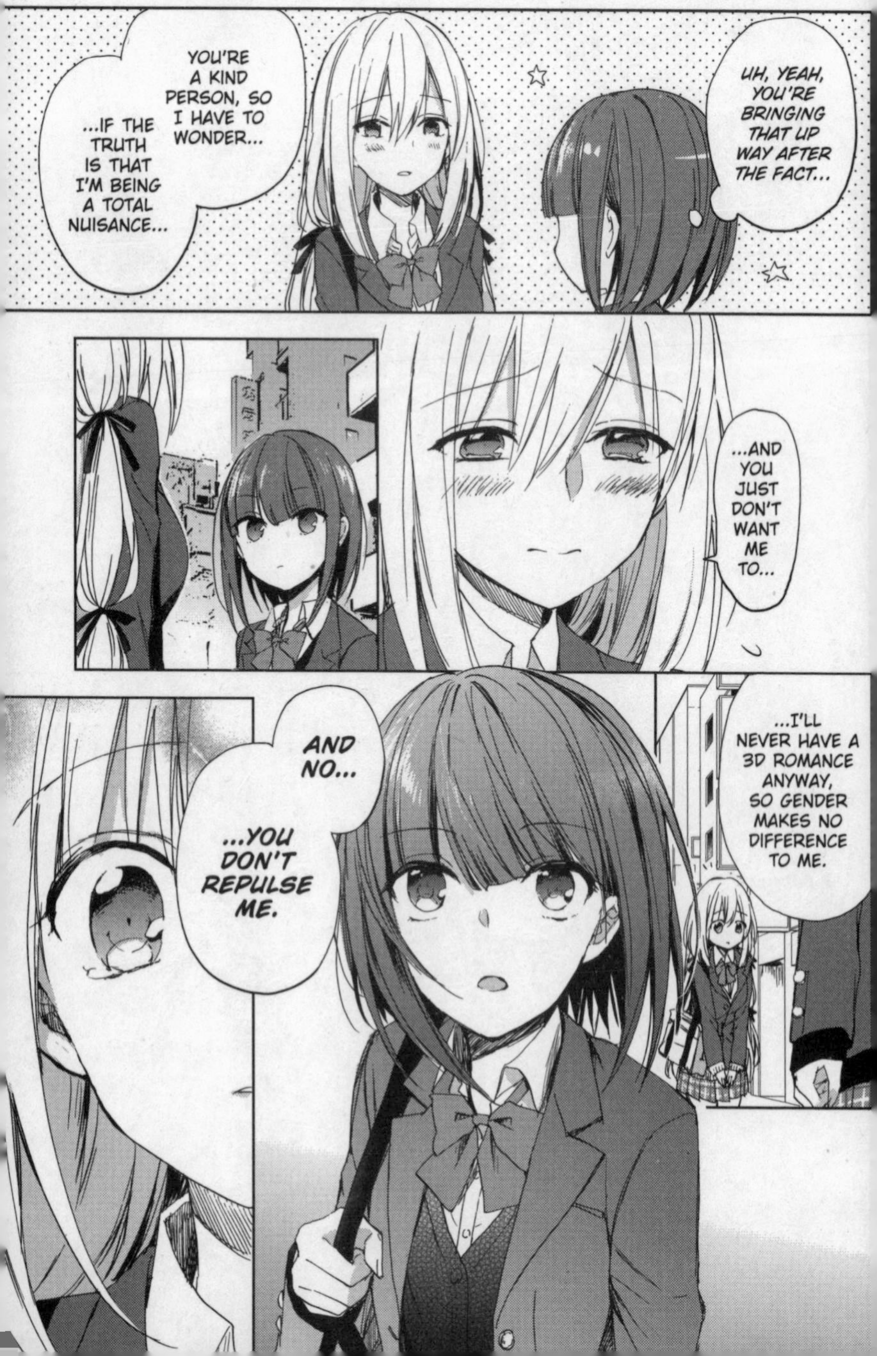
UH, YEAH, YOU'RE BRINGING THAT UP WAY AFTER THE FACT...
YOU'RE A KIND PERSON, SO I HAVE TO WONDER...
...IF THE TRUTH IS THAT I'M BEING A TOTAL NUISANCE...
...AND YOU JUST DON'T WANT ME TO...
...I'LL NEVER HAVE A 3D ROMANCE ANYWAY, SO GENDER MAKES NO DIFFERENCE TO ME.
AND NO...
...YOU DON'T REPULSE ME.

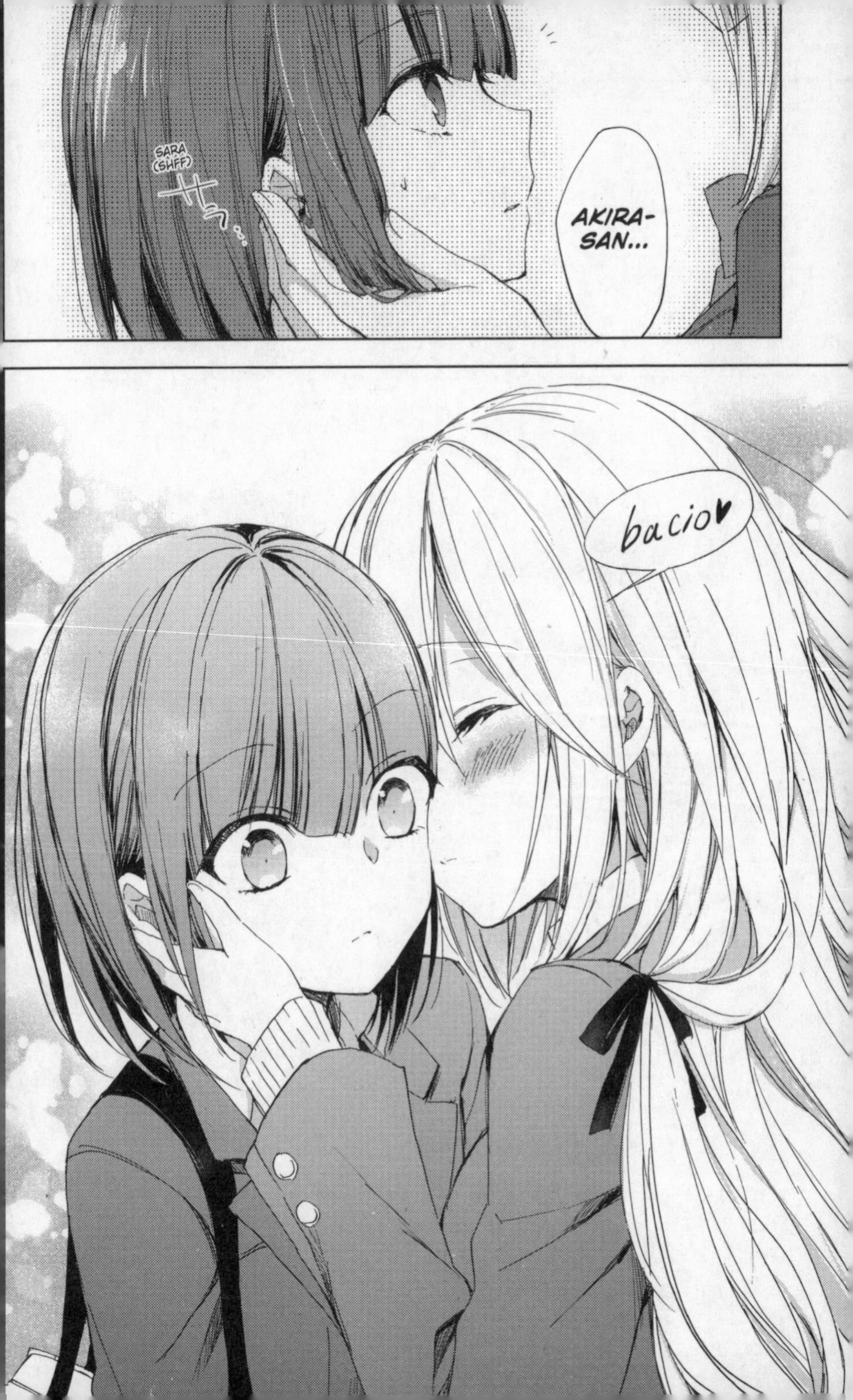
AKIRA-SAN...
SARA (SHFF)
bacio♥

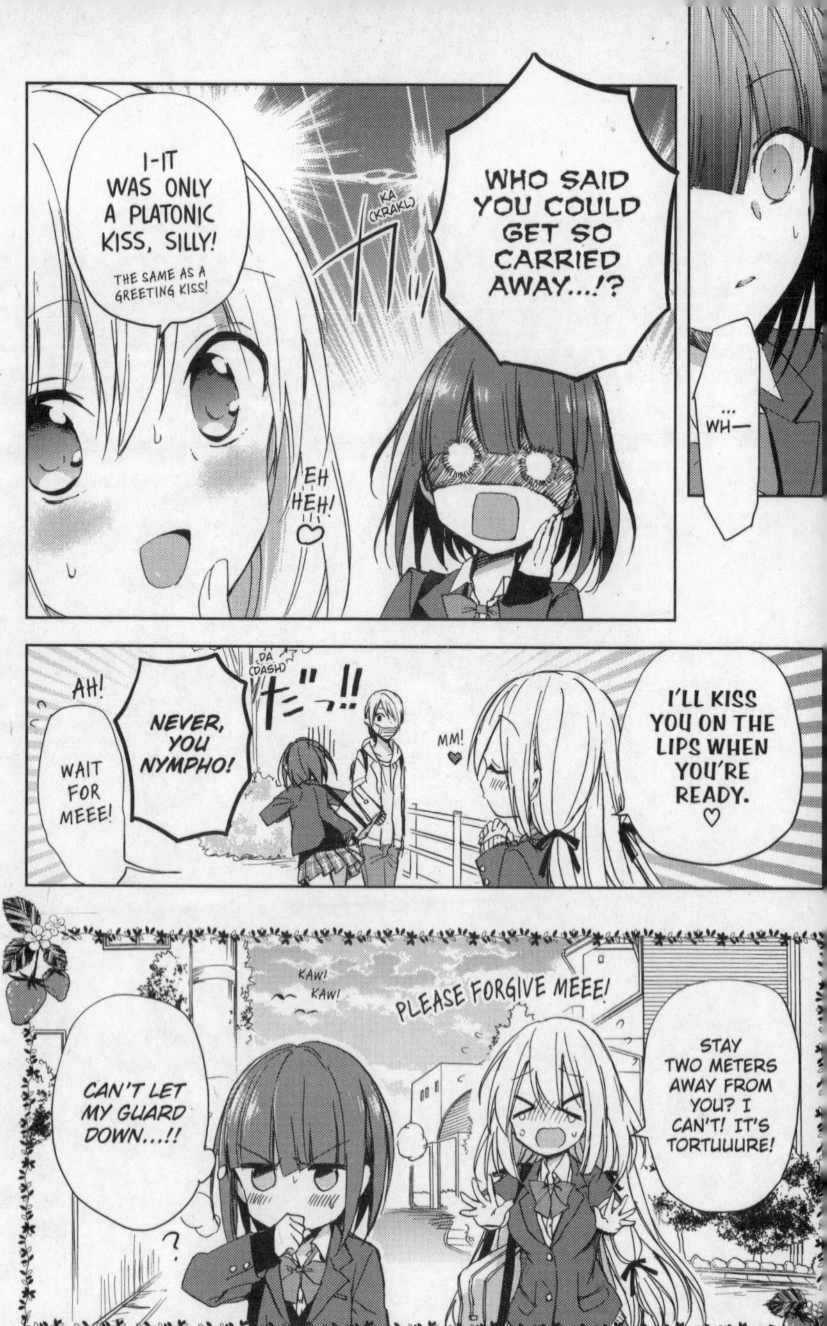
...WH—
WHO SAID YOU COULD GET SO CARRIED AWAY...!?
KA (KRAKL)
I-IT WAS ONLY A PLATONIC KISS, SILLY!
THE SAME AS A GREETING KISS!
EH HEH! ♡
I'LL KISS YOU ON THE LIPS WHEN YOU'RE READY. ♡
MM! ♥
DA (DASH)
NEVER, YOU NYMPHO!
AH!
WAIT FOR MEEE!
STAY TWO METERS AWAY FROM YOU? I CAN'T! IT'S TORTUUURE!
PLEASE FORGIVE MEEE!
KAW! KAW!
CAN'T LET MY GUARD DOWN...!!
?

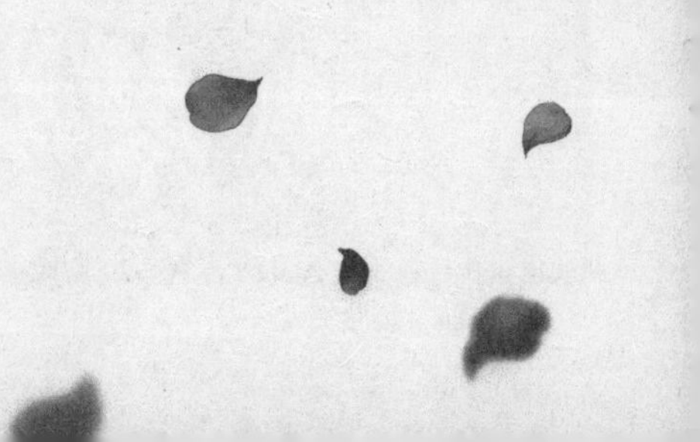

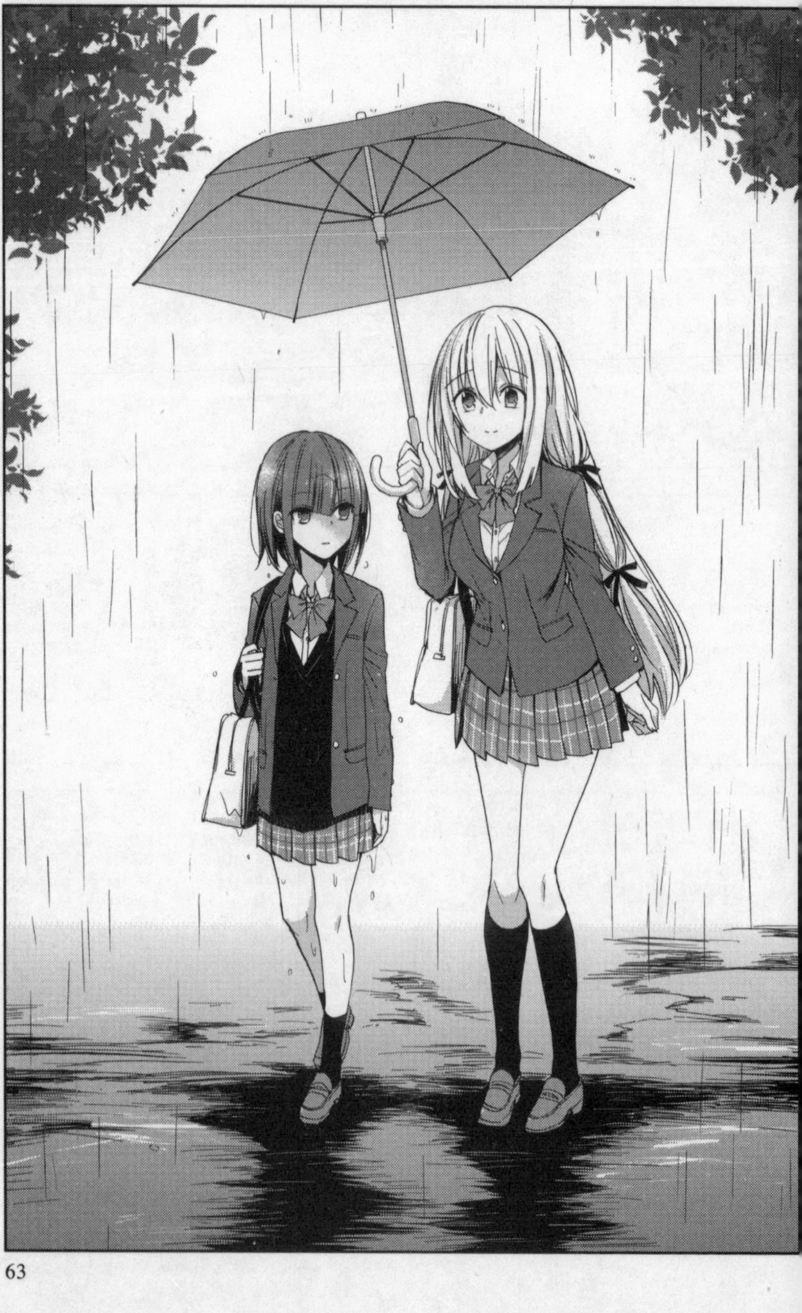

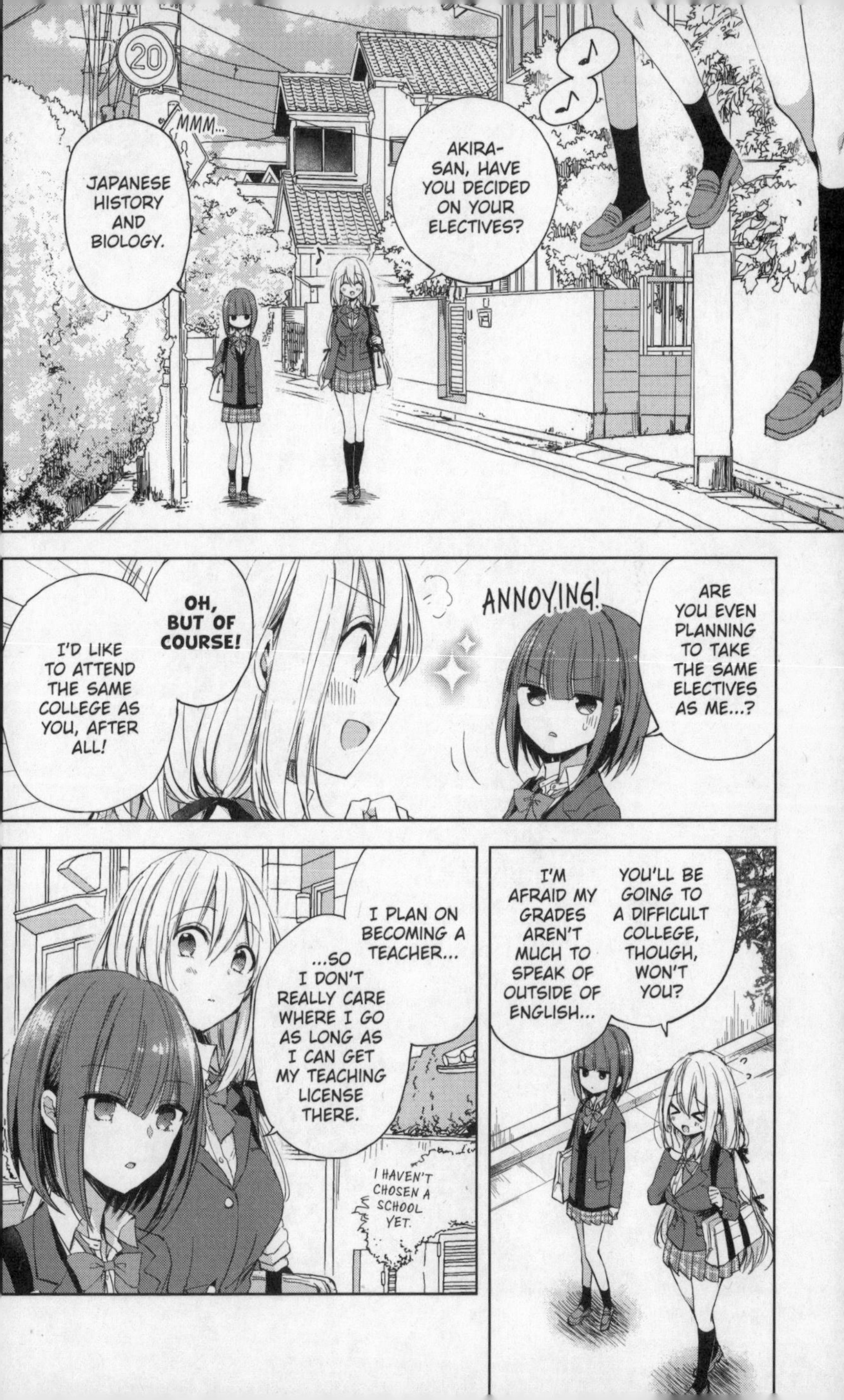

20
AKIRA-SAN, HAVE YOU DECIDED ON YOUR ELECTIVES?
MMM...
JAPANESE HISTORY AND BIOLOGY.
ARE YOU EVEN PLANNING TO TAKE THE SAME ELECTIVES AS ME...?
ANNOYING!
OH, BUT OF COURSE!
I'D LIKE TO ATTEND THE SAME COLLEGE AS YOU, AFTER ALL!
YOU'LL BE GOING TO A DIFFICULT COLLEGE, THOUGH, WON'T YOU?
I'M AFRAID MY GRADES AREN'T MUCH TO SPEAK OF OUTSIDE OF ENGLISH...
I PLAN ON BECOMING A TEACHER...
...SO I DON'T REALLY CARE WHERE I GO AS LONG AS I CAN GET MY TEACHING LICENSE THERE.
I HAVEN'T CHOSEN A SCHOOL YET.

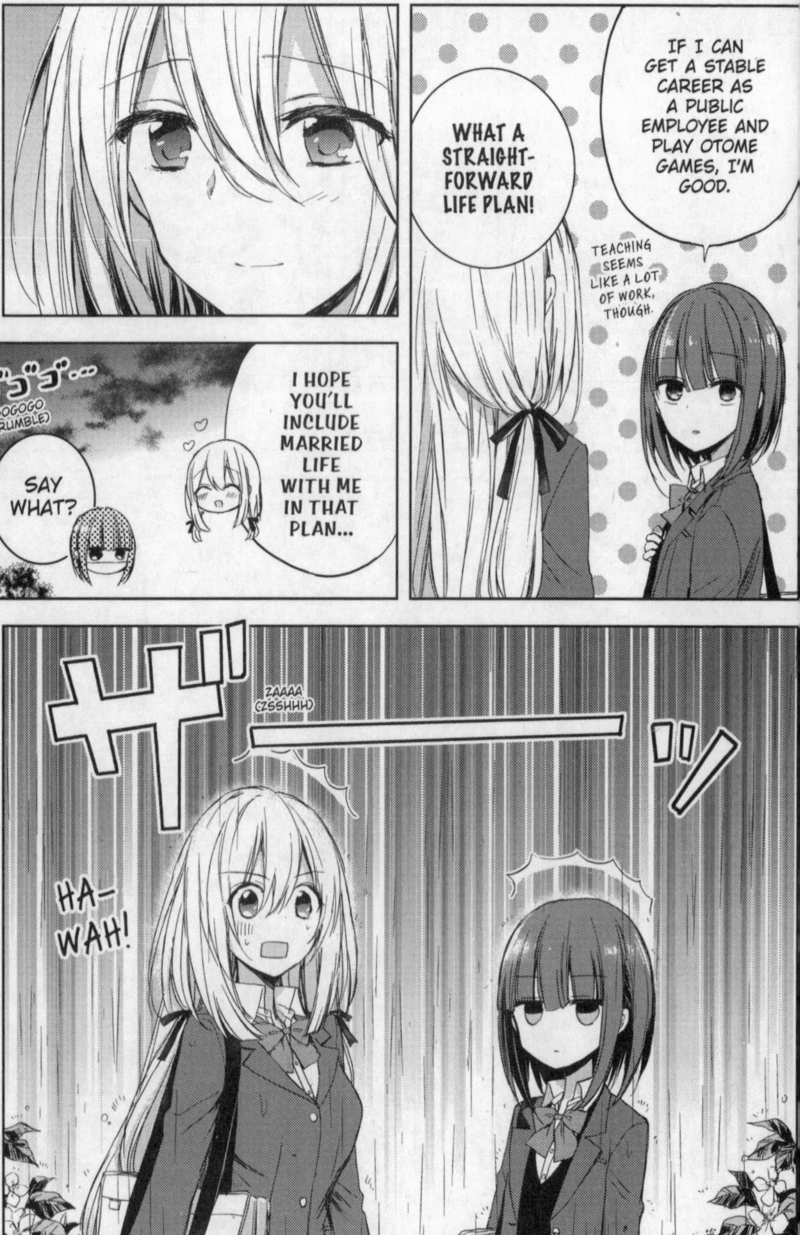
IF I CAN GET A STABLE CAREER AS A PUBLIC EMPLOYEE AND PLAY OTOME GAMES, I'M GOOD.
TEACHING SEEMS LIKE A LOT OF WORK, THOUGH.
WHAT A STRAIGHT-FORWARD LIFE PLAN!
I HOPE YOU'LL INCLUDE MARRIED LIFE WITH ME IN THAT PLAN...
ゴゴゴ...
GOGOGO (RUMBLE)
SAY WHAT?
ザーーッ
ZAAAA (ZSSHHH)
HA-WAH!

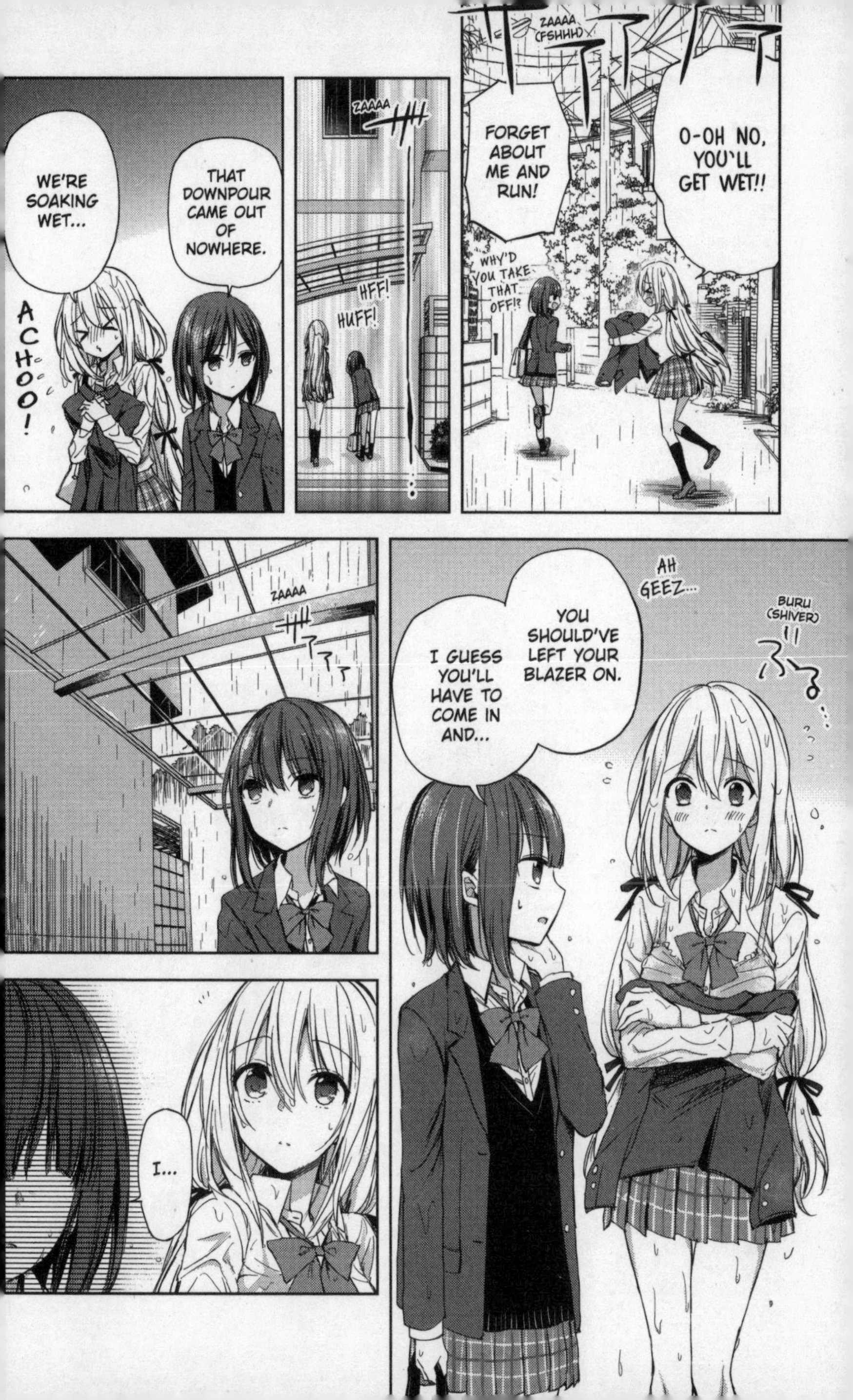
ZAAAA (FSHHH)
O-OH NO, YOU'LL GET WET!!
FORGET ABOUT ME AND RUN!
WHY'D YOU TAKE THAT OFF!?
ZAAAA
HFF!
HUFF!
THAT DOWNPOUR CAME OUT OF NOWHERE.
WE'RE SOAKING WET...
ACHOO!
AH GEEZ...
BURU (SHIVER)
YOU SHOULD'VE LEFT YOUR BLAZER ON.
I GUESS YOU'LL HAVE TO COME IN AND...
ZAAAA
I...

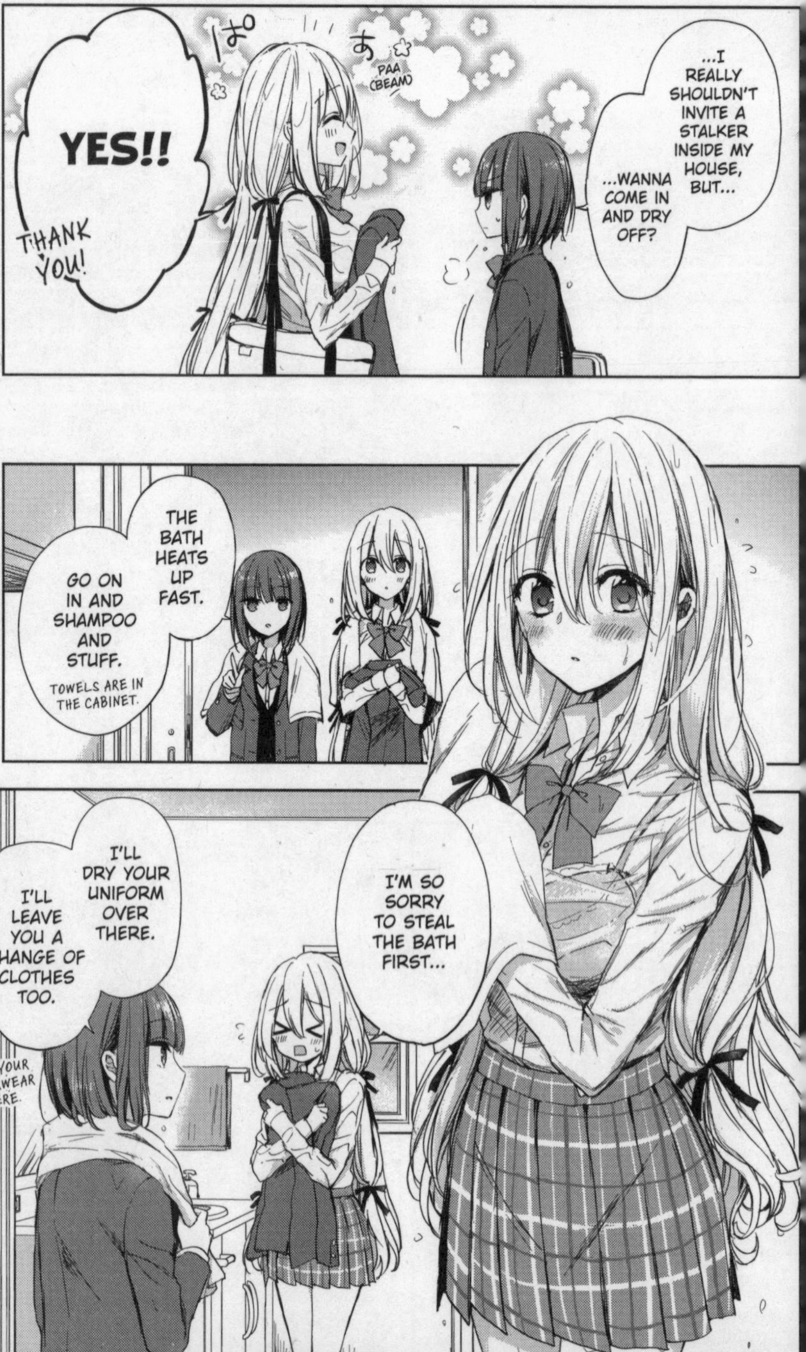
...I REALLY SHOULDN'T INVITE A STALKER INSIDE MY HOUSE, BUT...
...WANNA COME IN AND DRY OFF?
ぱあ
PAA (BEAM)
YES!!
THANK YOU!
THE BATH HEATS UP FAST.
GO ON IN AND SHAMPOO AND STUFF.
TOWELS ARE IN THE CABINET.
I'M SO SORRY TO STEAL THE BATH FIRST...
I'LL DRY YOUR UNIFORM OVER THERE.
I'LL LEAVE YOU A CHANGE OF CLOTHES TOO.
HANG YOUR UNDERWEAR THERE.

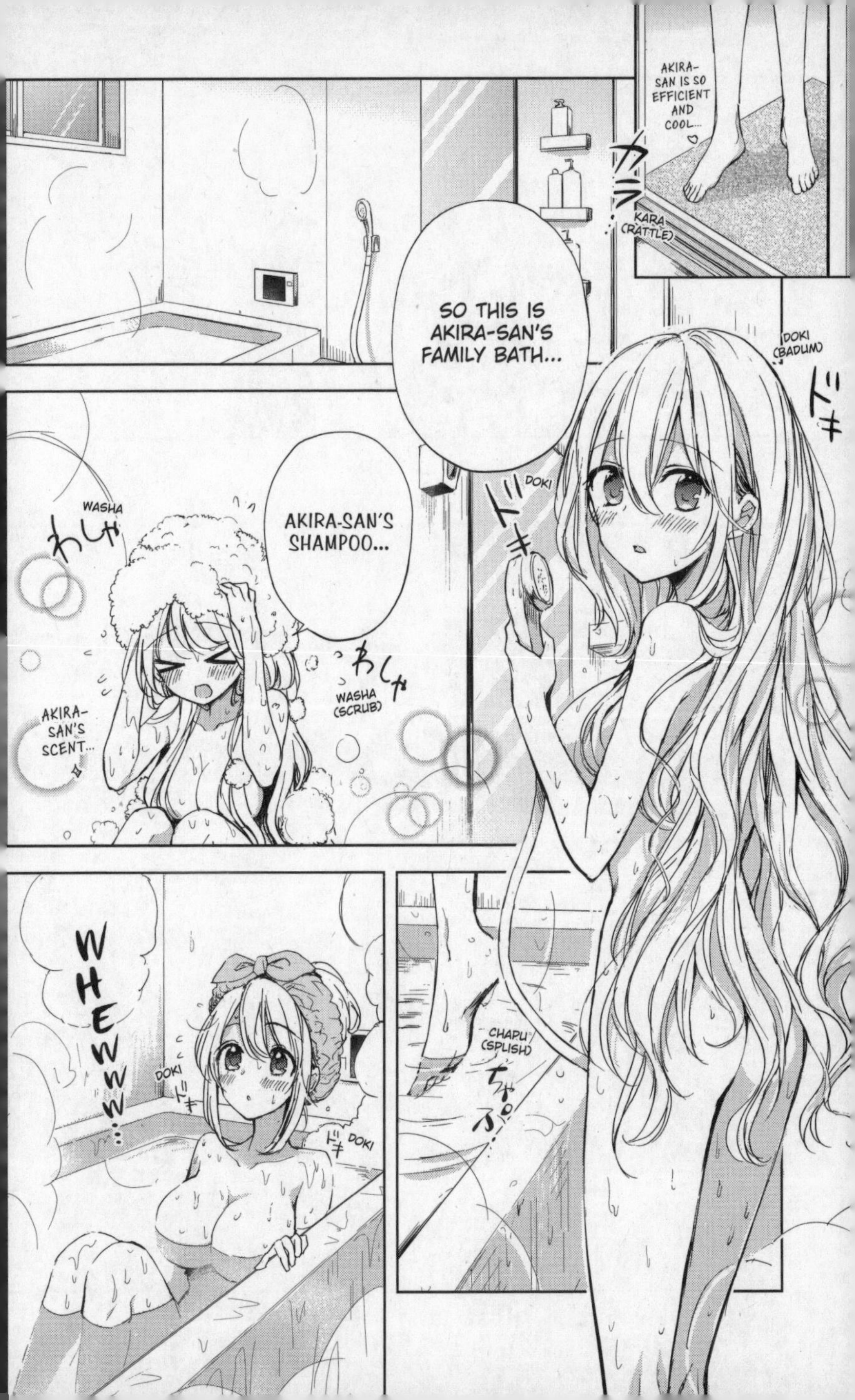

AKIRA-SAN IS SO EFFICIENT AND COOL...
KARA (RATTLE)
SO THIS IS AKIRA-SAN'S FAMILY BATH...
DOKI (BADUM)
DOKI
AKIRA-SAN'S SHAMPOO...
WASHA
WASHA (SCRUB)
AKIRA-SAN'S SCENT...
CHAPU (SPLISH)
WHEWWW...
DOKI
DOKI

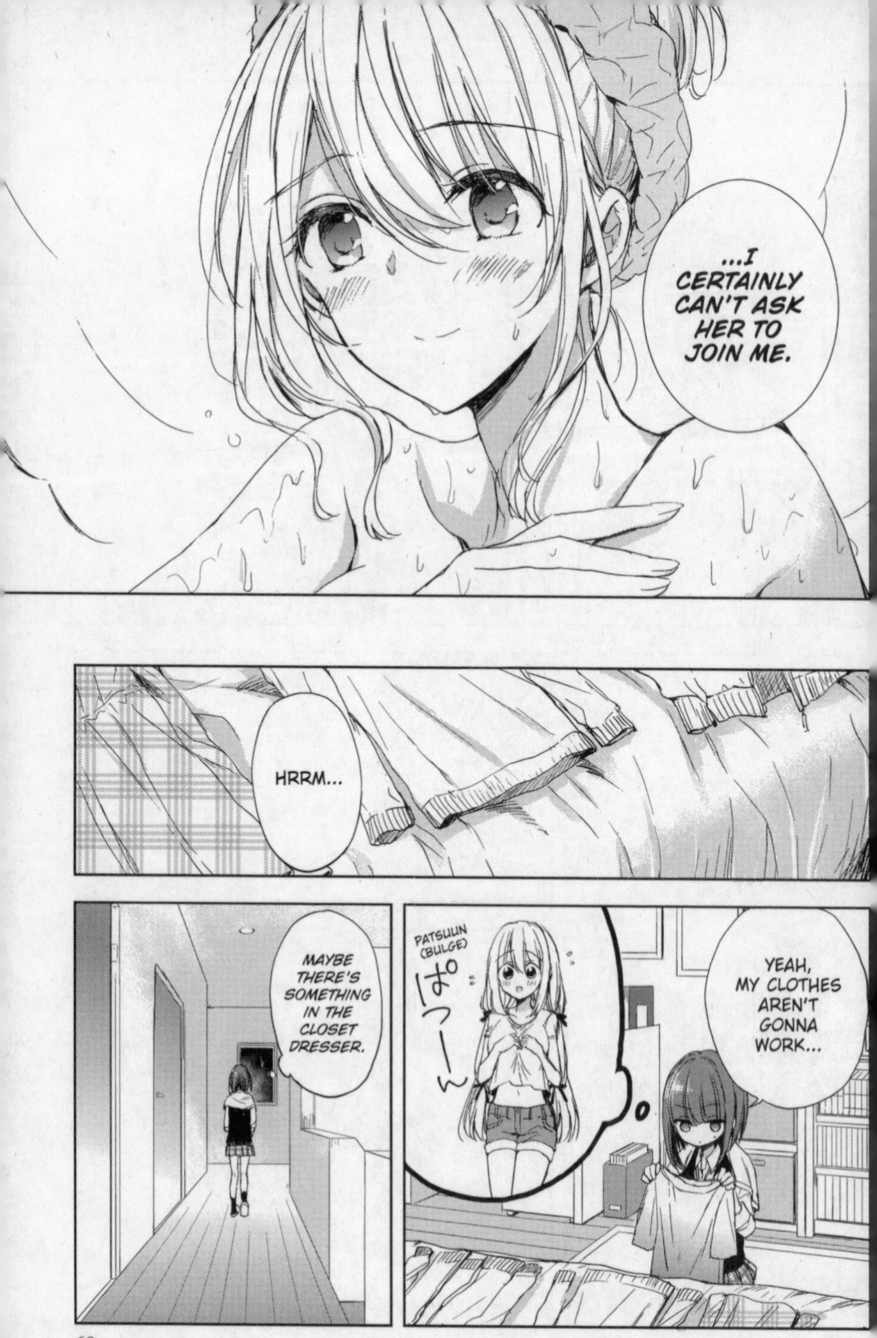
...I CERTAINLY CAN'T ASK HER TO JOIN ME.
HRRM...
YEAH, MY CLOTHES AREN'T GONNA WORK...
PATSUUN (BULGE)
ぱつーん
MAYBE THERE'S SOMETHING IN THE CLOSET DRESSER.

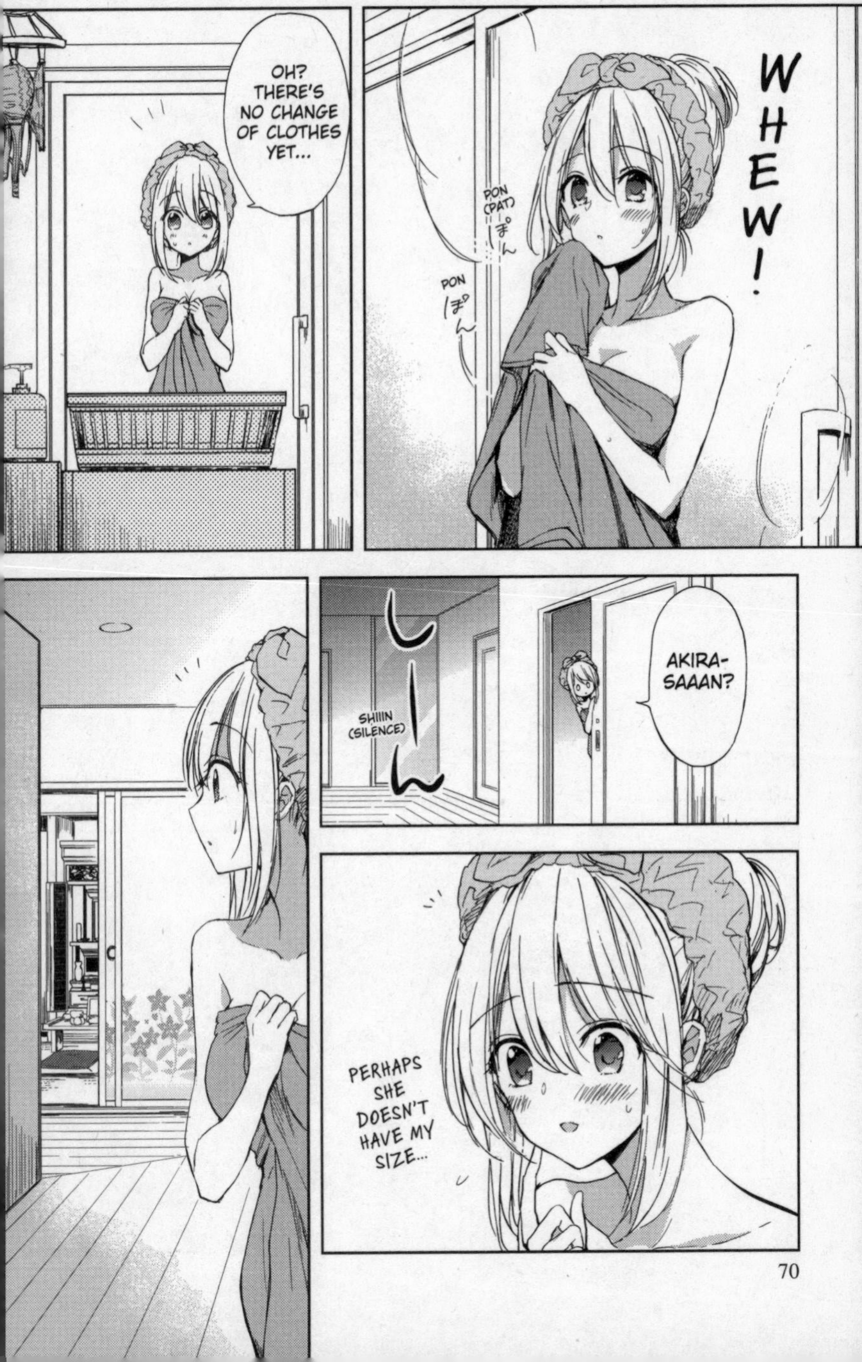
WHEW!
PON (PAT) ぽん
PON ぽん
OH? THERE'S NO CHANGE OF CLOTHES YET...
AKIRA-SAAAN?
しーん
SHIIN (SILENCE)
PERHAPS SHE DOESN'T HAVE MY SIZE...

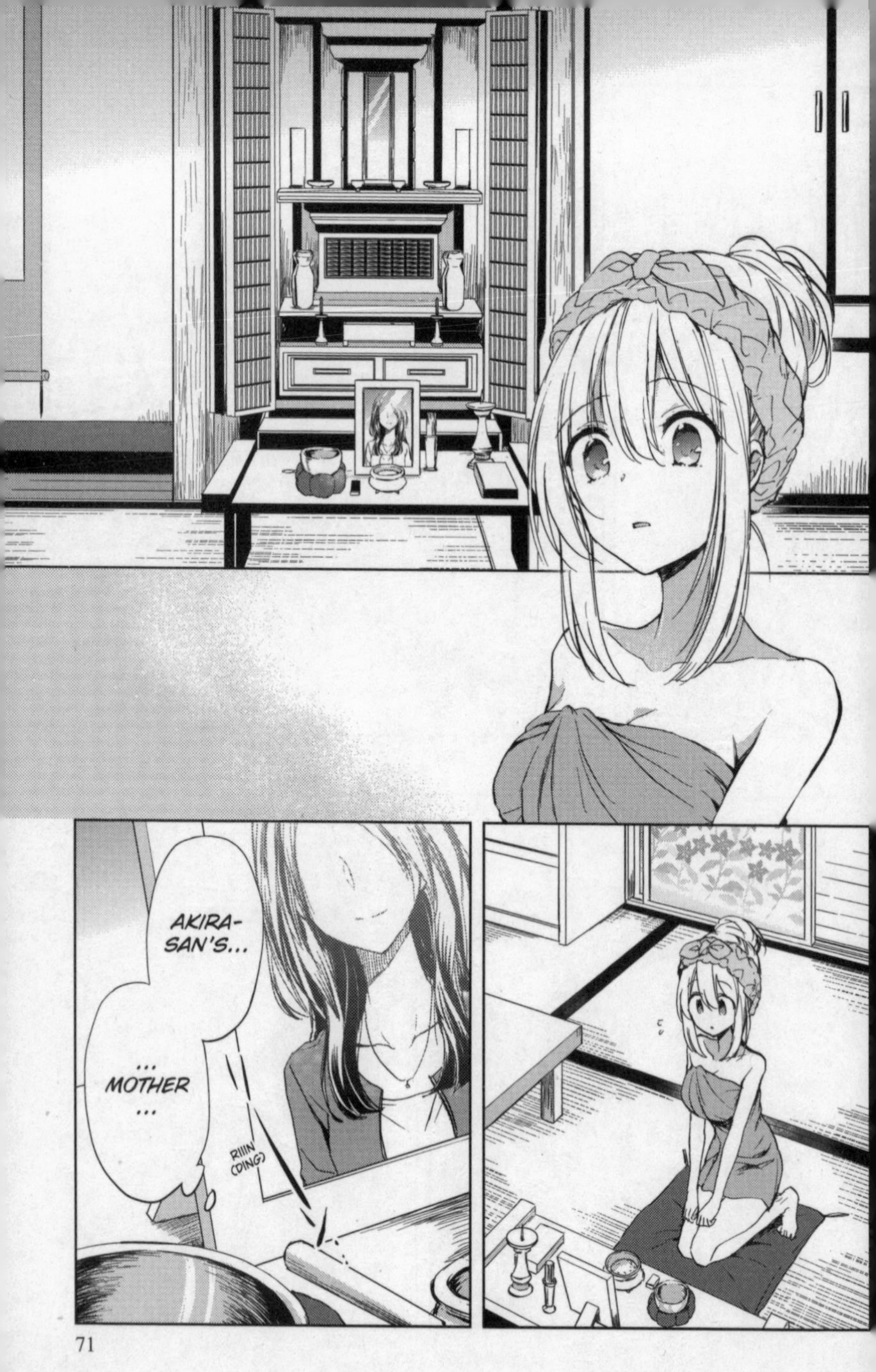
AKIRA-SAN'S...
...MOTHER...
RIIIN (DING)

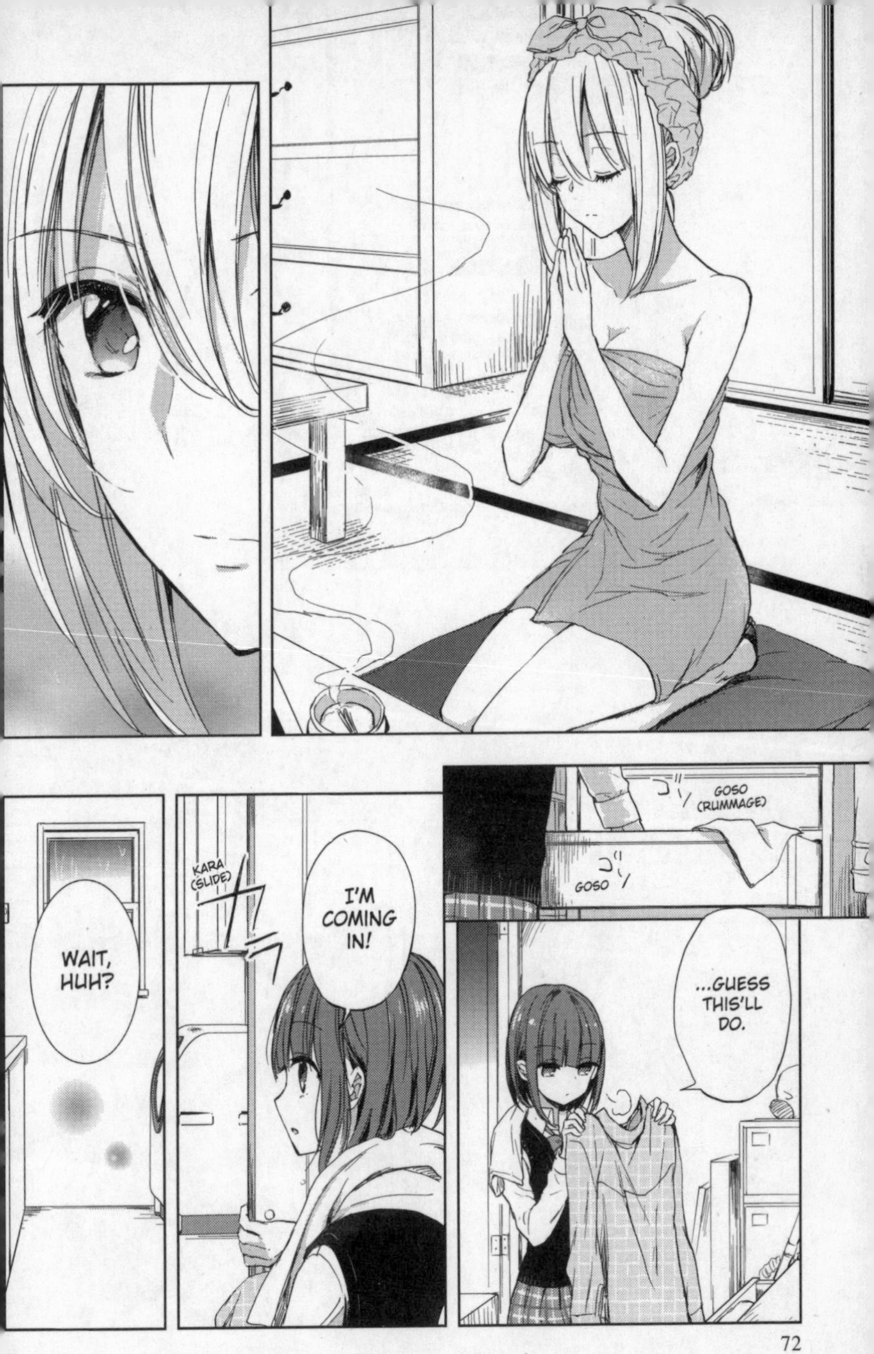
ゴソ
GOSO (RUMMAGE)
ゴソ
GOSO
...GUESS THIS'LL DO.
I'M COMING IN!
KARA (SLIDE)
WAIT, HUH?

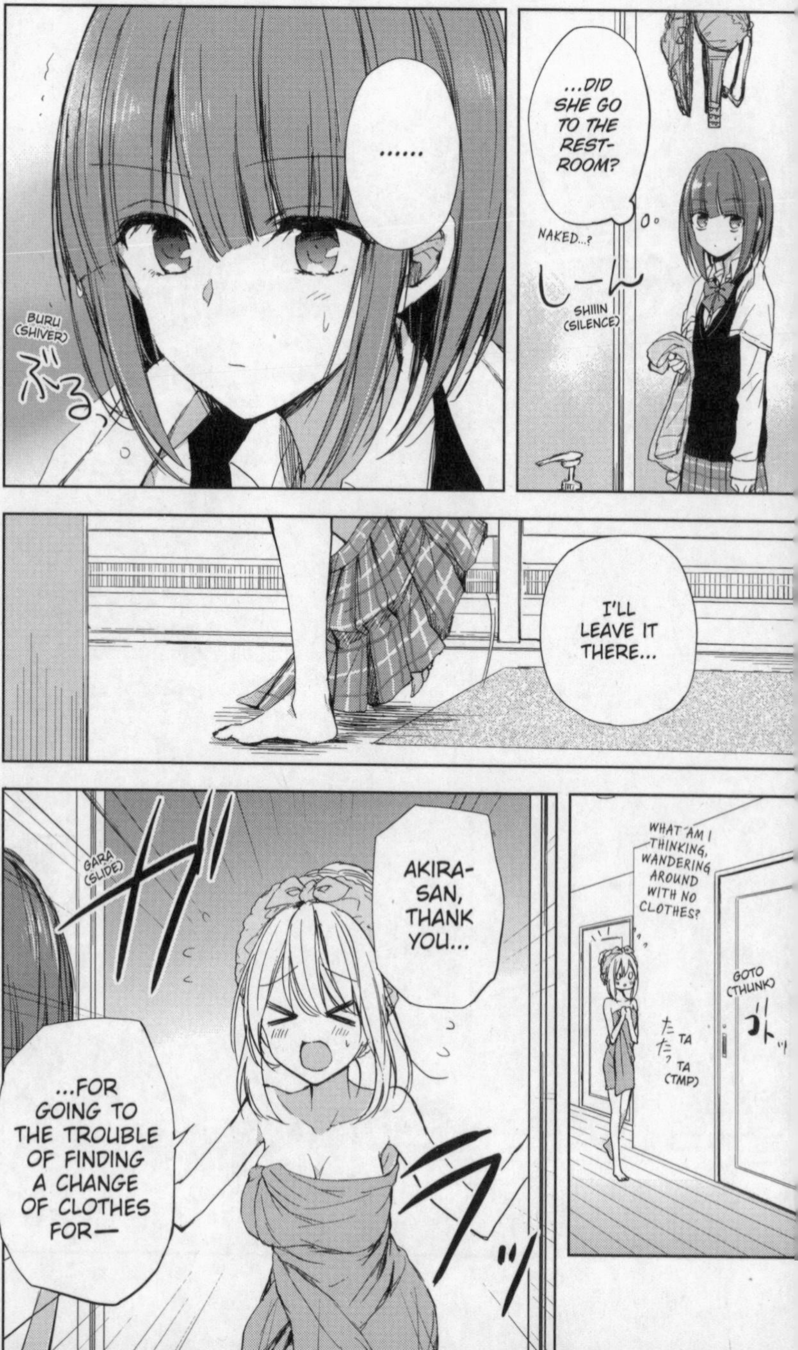
...DID SHE GO TO THE REST-ROOM?
NAKED...?
しーん
SHIIIN (SILENCE)
......
BURU (SHIVER)
ぶるっ
I'LL LEAVE IT THERE...
WHAT AM I THINKING, WANDERING AROUND WITH NO CLOTHES?
GOTO (THUNK)
ゴトッ
たたっ
TA TA (TMP)
GARA (SLIDE)
AKIRA-SAN, THANK YOU...
...FOR GOING TO THE TROUBLE OF FINDING A CHANGE OF CLOTHES FOR—

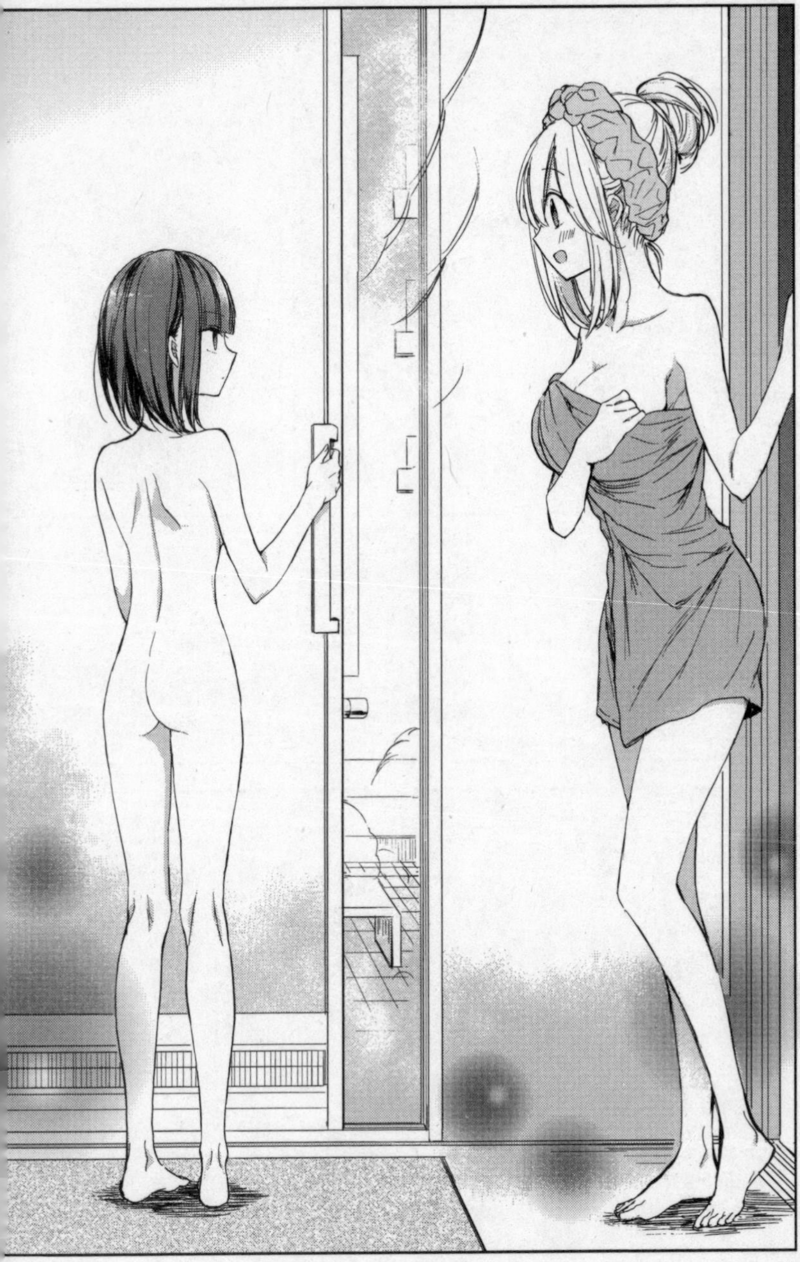

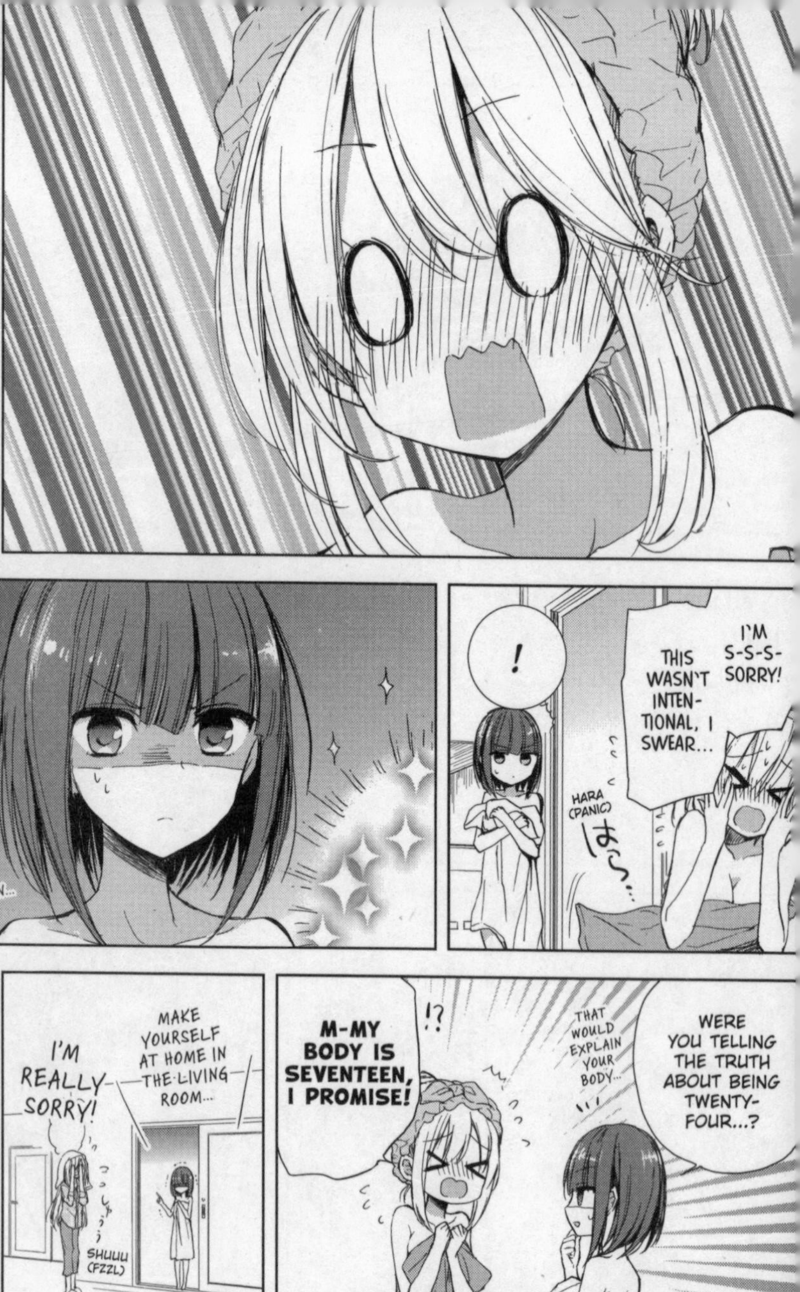
!
I'M S-S-S-SORRY!
THIS WASN'T INTENTIONAL, I SWEAR...
HARA (PANIC)
HNN...
WERE YOU TELLING THE TRUTH ABOUT BEING TWENTY-FOUR...?
THAT WOULD EXPLAIN YOUR BODY...
!?
M-MY BODY IS SEVENTEEN, I PROMISE!
MAKE YOURSELF AT HOME IN THE LIVING ROOM...
I'M REALLY SORRY!
SHUUU (FZZL)

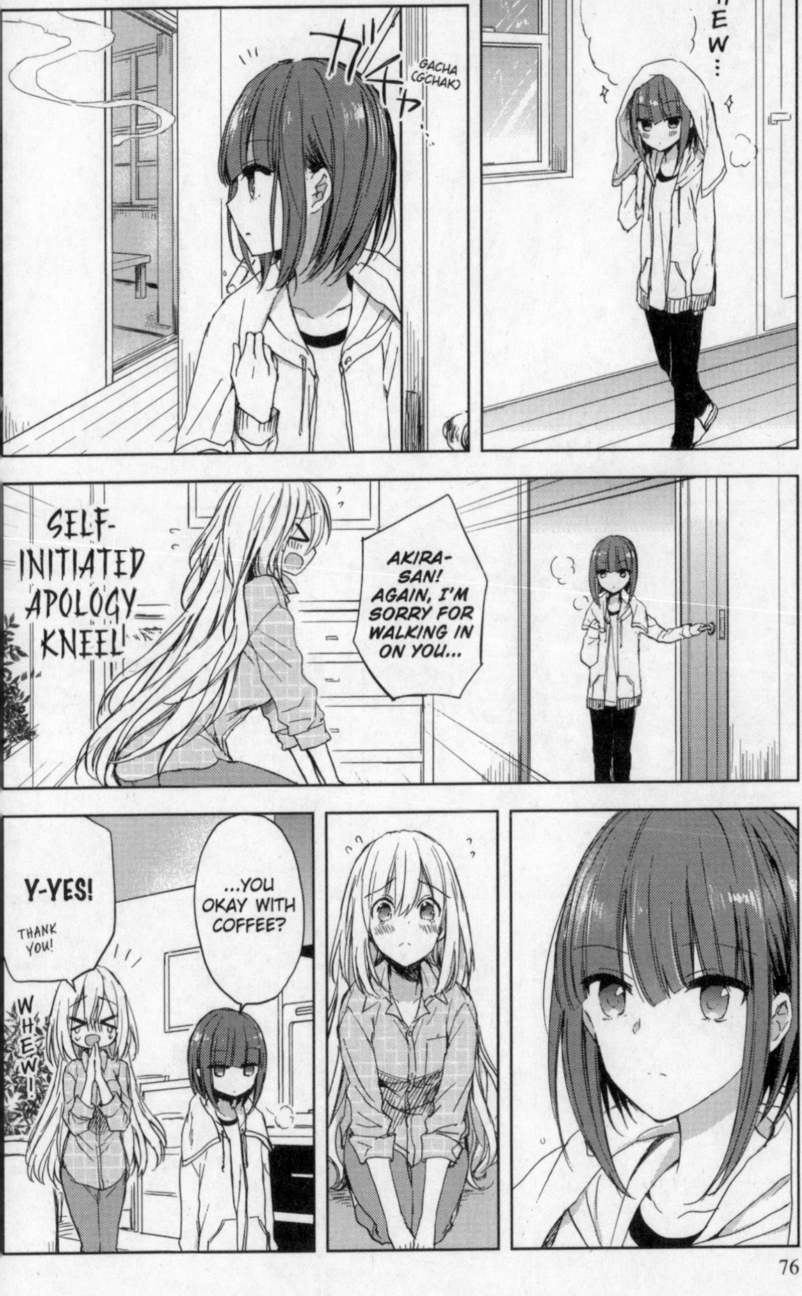
WHEW...
ガチャ
GACHA (G'CHAK)
AKIRA-SAN! AGAIN, I'M SORRY FOR WALKING IN ON YOU...
SELF-INITIATED APOLOGY KNEEL
...YOU OKAY WITH COFFEE?
Y-YES!
THANK YOU!
WHEW!

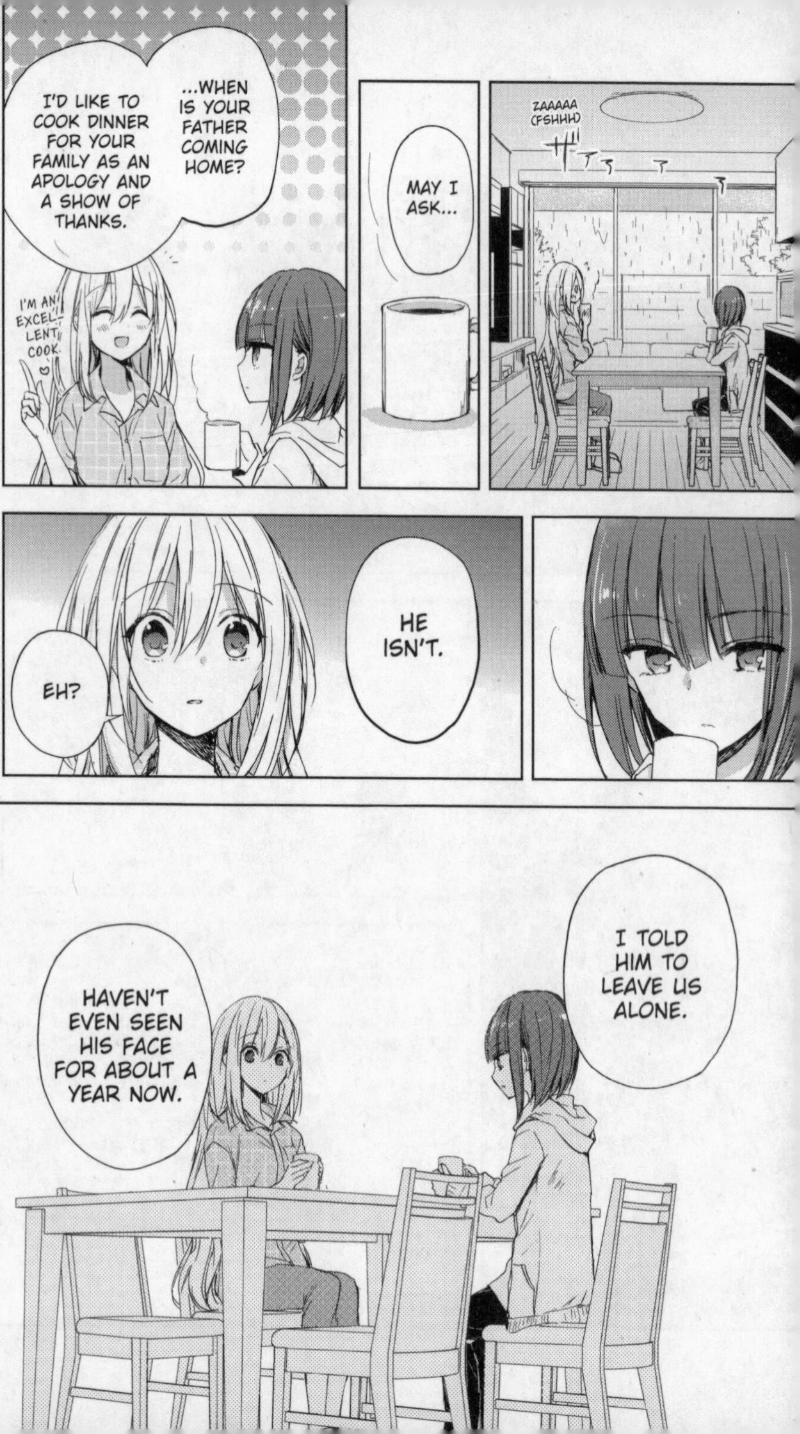
ZAAAAA (FSHHH)
MAY I ASK...
...WHEN IS YOUR FATHER COMING HOME?
I'D LIKE TO COOK DINNER FOR YOUR FAMILY AS AN APOLOGY AND A SHOW OF THANKS.
I'M AN EXCEL-LENT COOK.
HE ISN'T.
EH?
I TOLD HIM TO LEAVE US ALONE.
HAVEN'T EVEN SEEN HIS FACE FOR ABOUT A YEAR NOW.

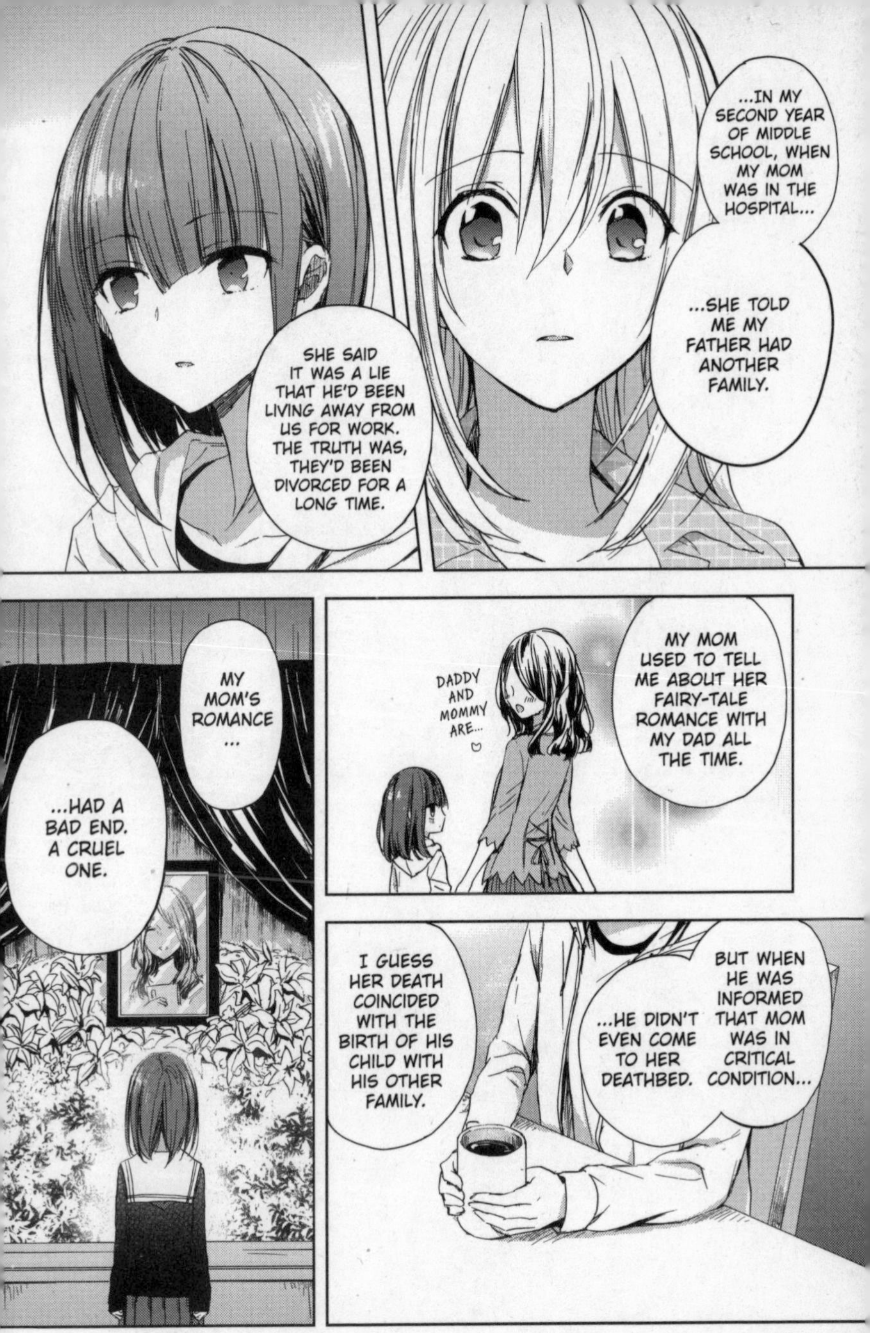
...IN MY SECOND YEAR OF MIDDLE SCHOOL, WHEN MY MOM WAS IN THE HOSPITAL...
...SHE TOLD ME MY FATHER HAD ANOTHER FAMILY.
SHE SAID IT WAS A LIE THAT HE'D BEEN LIVING AWAY FROM US FOR WORK. THE TRUTH WAS, THEY'D BEEN DIVORCED FOR A LONG TIME.
MY MOM USED TO TELL ME ABOUT HER FAIRY-TALE ROMANCE WITH MY DAD ALL THE TIME.
DADDY AND MOMMY ARE... ♡
BUT WHEN HE WAS INFORMED THAT MOM WAS IN CRITICAL CONDITION...
...HE DIDN'T EVEN COME TO HER DEATHBED.
I GUESS HER DEATH COINCIDED WITH THE BIRTH OF HIS CHILD WITH HIS OTHER FAMILY.
MY MOM'S ROMANCE...
...HAD A BAD END. A CRUEL ONE.

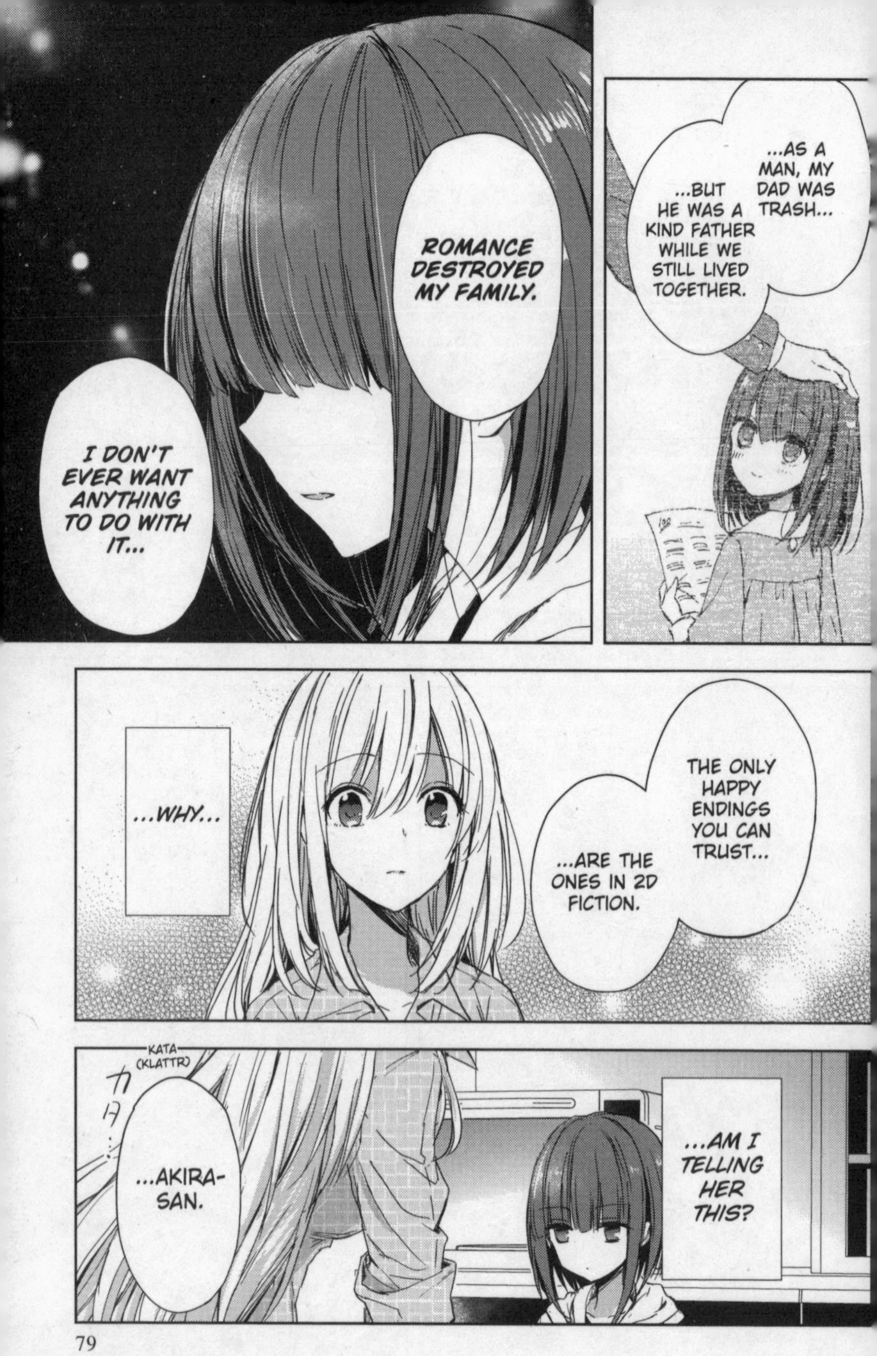
...AS A MAN, MY DAD WAS TRASH...
...BUT HE WAS A KIND FATHER WHILE WE STILL LIVED TOGETHER.
ROMANCE DESTROYED MY FAMILY.
I DON'T EVER WANT ANYTHING TO DO WITH IT...
THE ONLY HAPPY ENDINGS YOU CAN TRUST...
...ARE THE ONES IN 2D FICTION.
...WHY...
...AM I TELLING HER THIS?
カタ...
KATA (KLATTR)
...AKIRA-SAN.

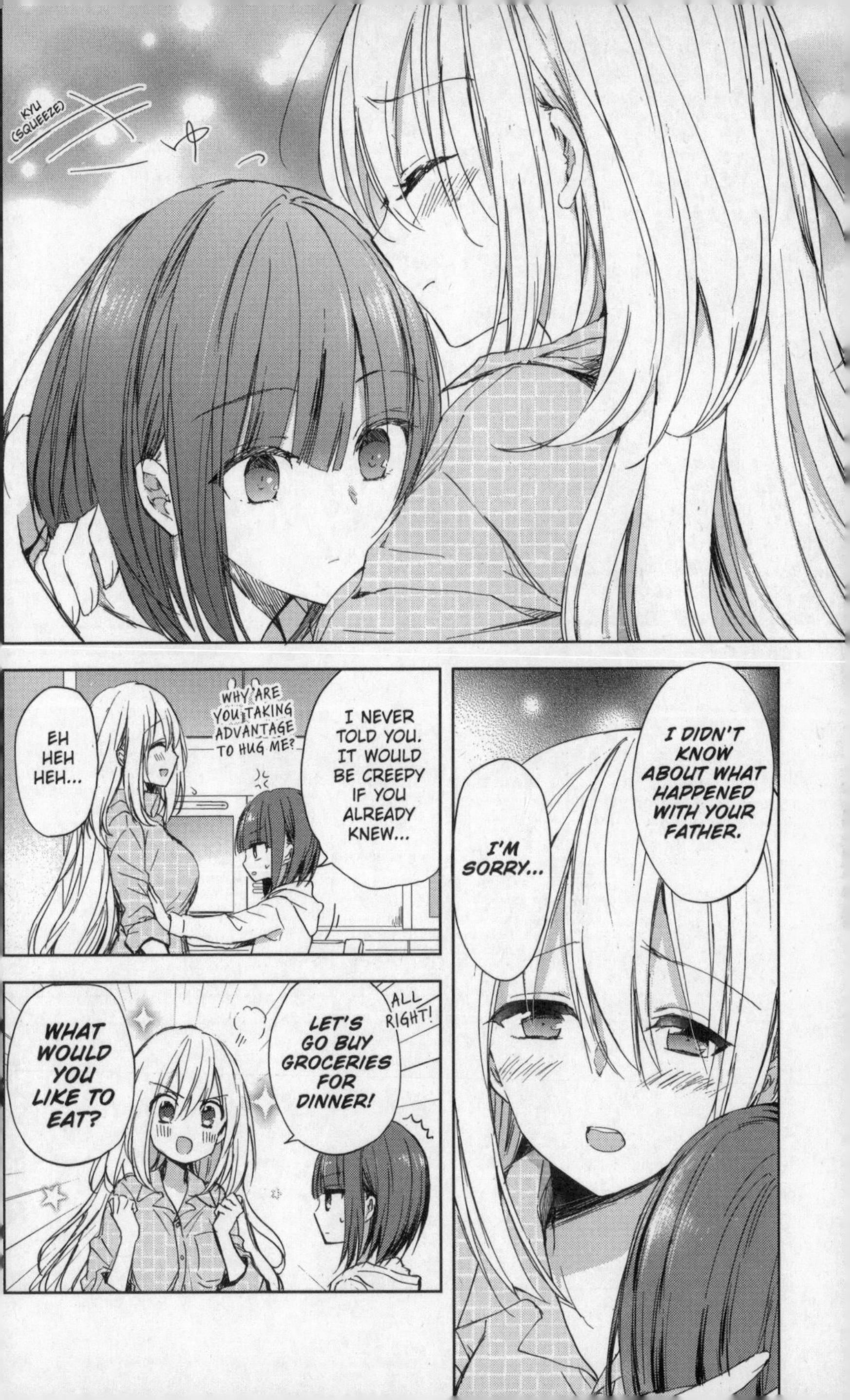
KYU (SQUEEZE)
I DIDN'T KNOW ABOUT WHAT HAPPENED WITH YOUR FATHER.
I'M SORRY...
I NEVER TOLD YOU. IT WOULD BE CREEPY IF YOU ALREADY KNEW...
WHY ARE YOU TAKING ADVANTAGE TO HUG ME?
EH HEH HEH...
ALL RIGHT!
LET'S GO BUY GROCERIES FOR DINNER!
WHAT WOULD YOU LIKE TO EAT?

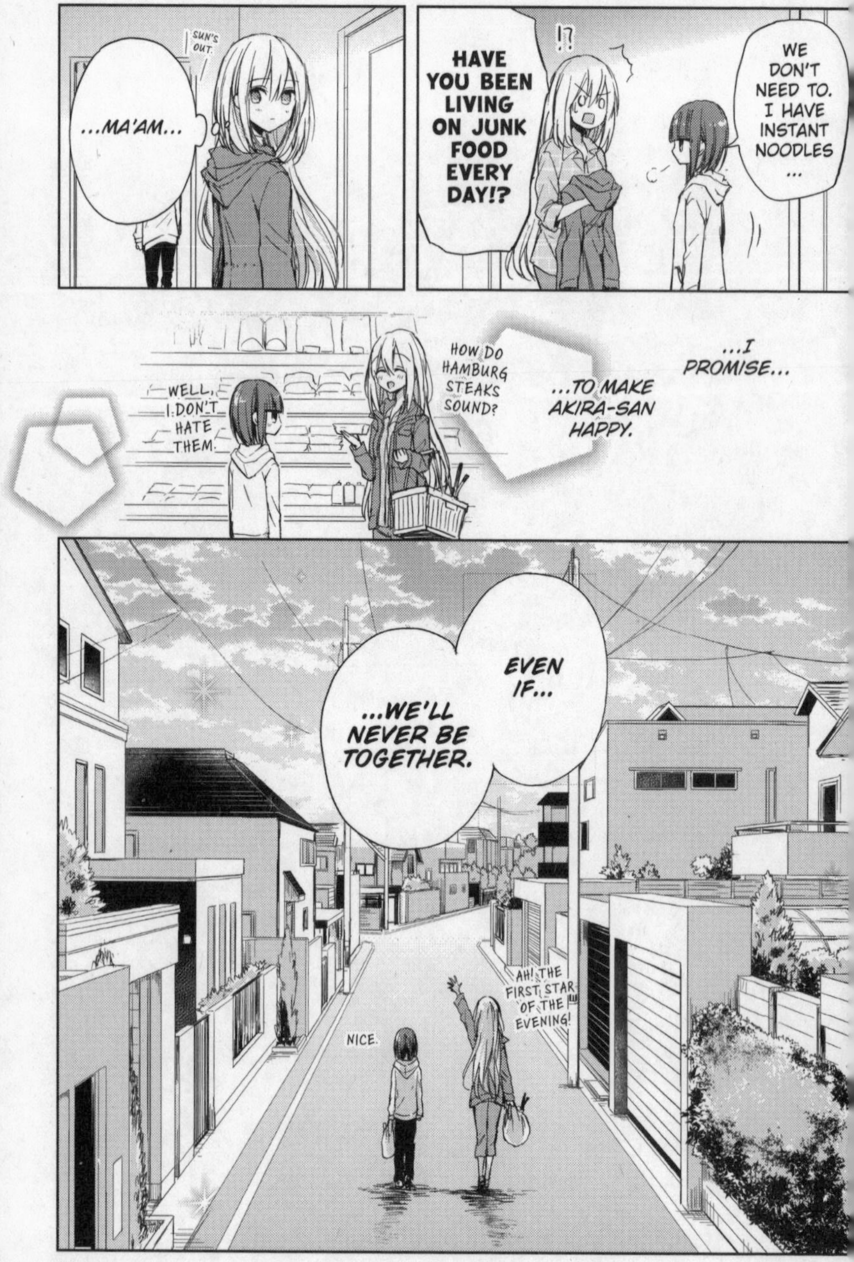
WE DON'T NEED TO. I HAVE INSTANT NOODLES ...
!?
HAVE YOU BEEN LIVING ON JUNK FOOD EVERY DAY!?
SUN'S OUT.
...MA'AM...
...I PROMISE...
...TO MAKE AKIRA-SAN HAPPY.
HOW DO HAMBURG STEAKS SOUND?
WELL, I DON'T HATE THEM.
EVEN IF...
...WE'LL NEVER BE TOGETHER.
AH! THE FIRST STAR OF THE EVENING!
NICE.

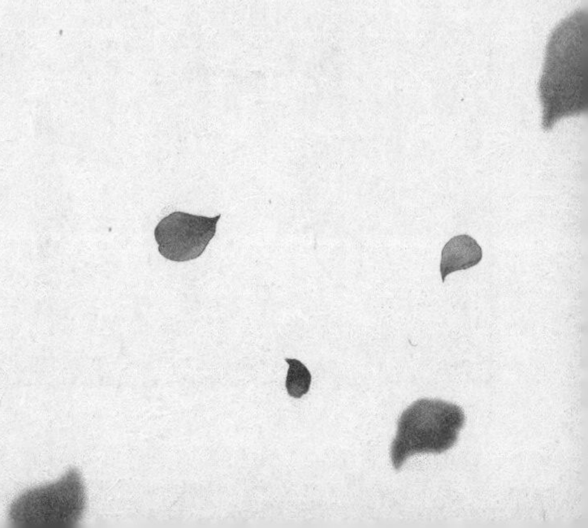

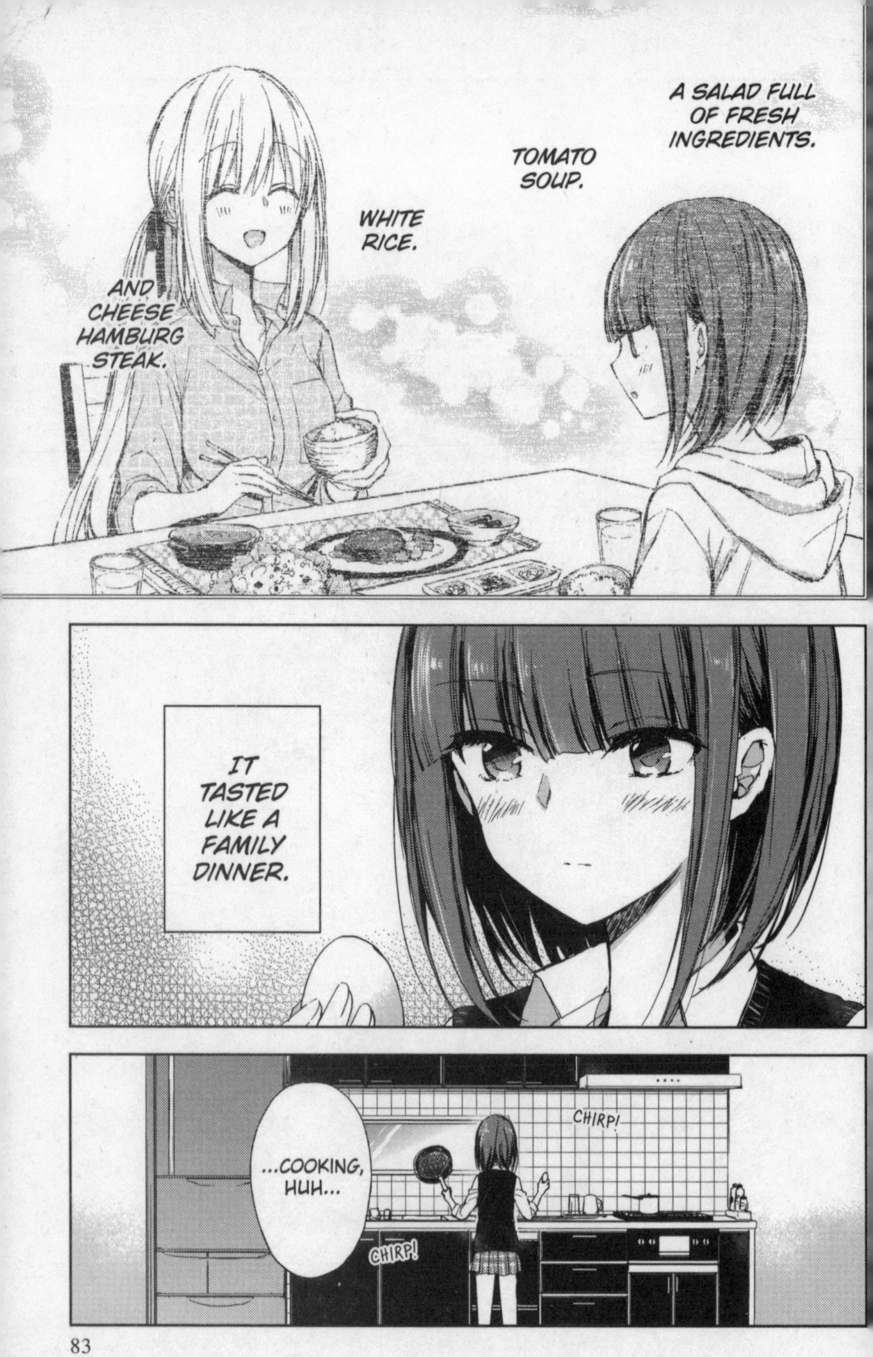
A SALAD FULL OF FRESH INGREDIENTS.
TOMATO SOUP.
WHITE RICE.
AND CHEESE HAMBURG STEAK.
IT TASTED LIKE A FAMILY DINNER.
CHIRP!
...COOKING, HUH...
CHIRP!

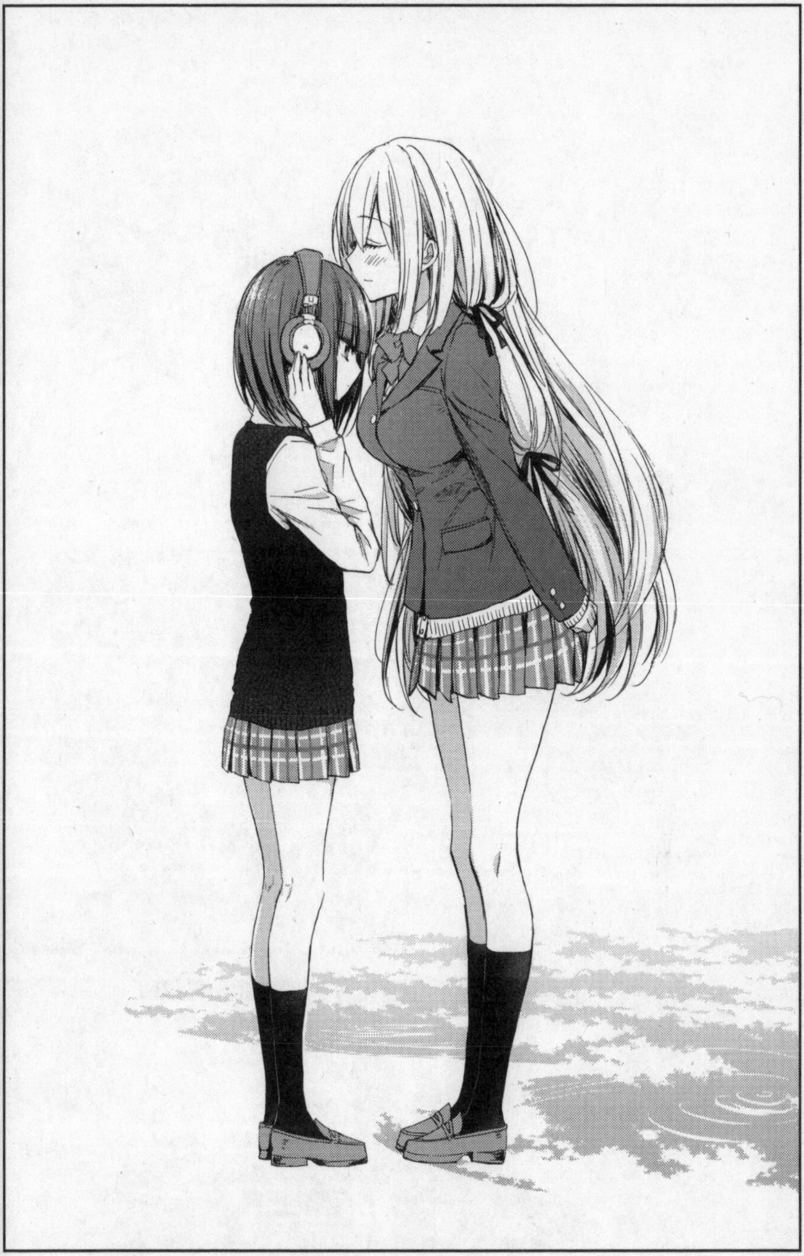

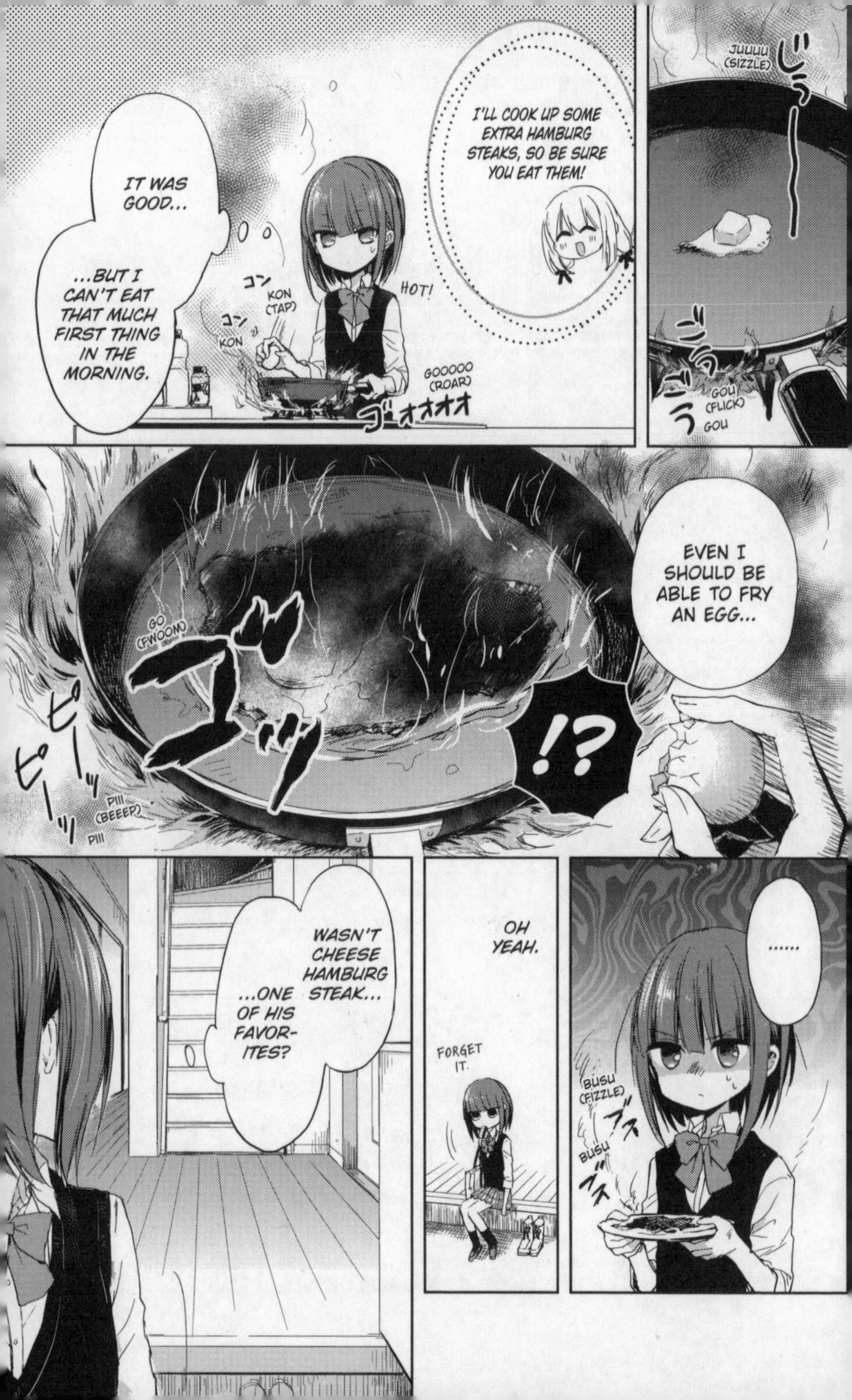
JUUUU (SIZZLE)
GOU (FLICK)
GOU
I'LL COOK UP SOME EXTRA HAMBURG STEAKS, SO BE SURE YOU EAT THEM!
IT WAS GOOD...
...BUT I CAN'T EAT THAT MUCH FIRST THING IN THE MORNING.
KON (TAP)
KON
HOT!
GOOOOO (ROAR)
EVEN I SHOULD BE ABLE TO FRY AN EGG...
!?
GO (FWOOM)
PIII (BEEEP)
PIII
......
BUSU (FIZZLE)
BUSU
OH YEAH.
FORGET IT.
WASN'T CHEESE HAMBURG STEAK...
...ONE OF HIS FAVOR-ITES?

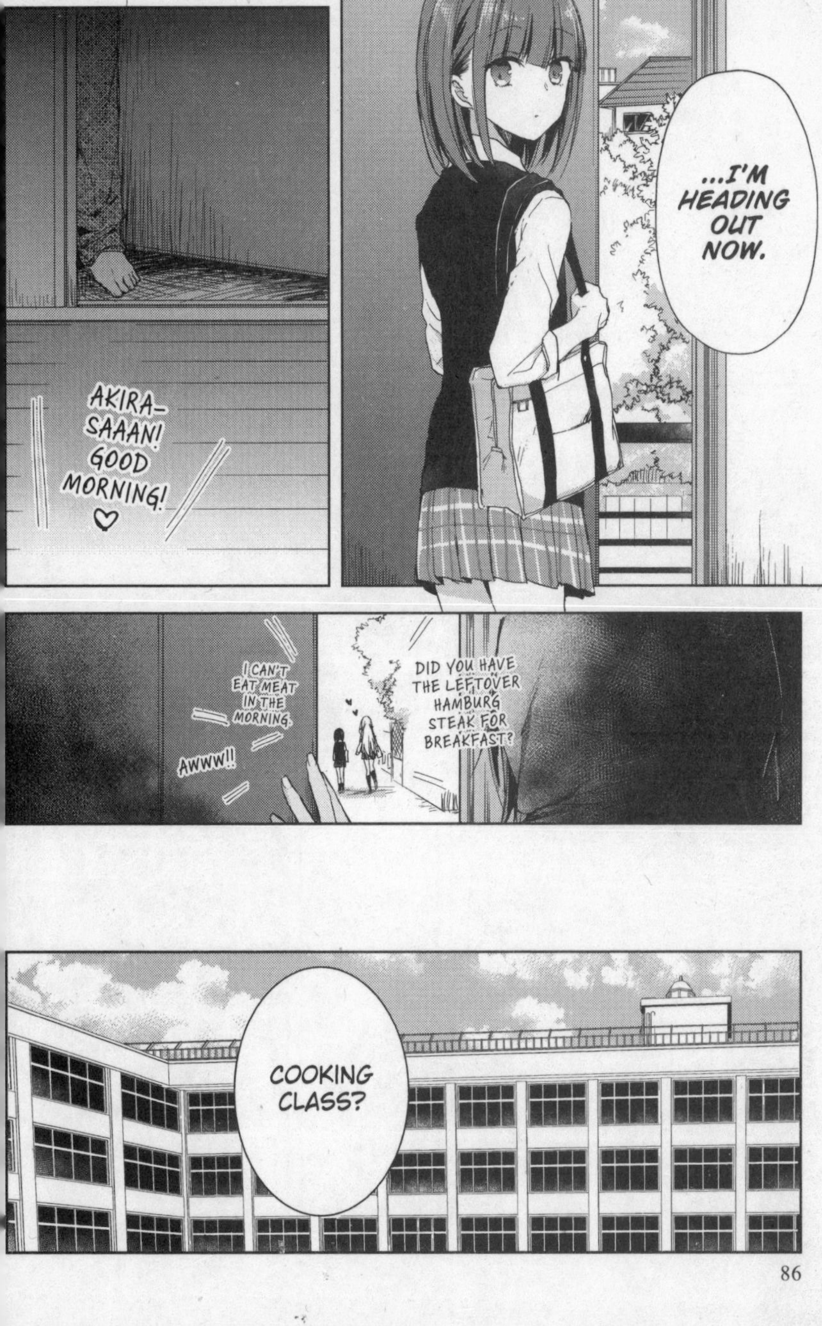
...I'M HEADING OUT NOW.
AKIRA-SAAAN! GOOD MORNING! ♡
DID YOU HAVE THE LEFTOVER HAMBURG STEAK FOR BREAKFAST?
I CAN'T EAT MEAT IN THE MORNING.
AWWW!!
COOKING CLASS?

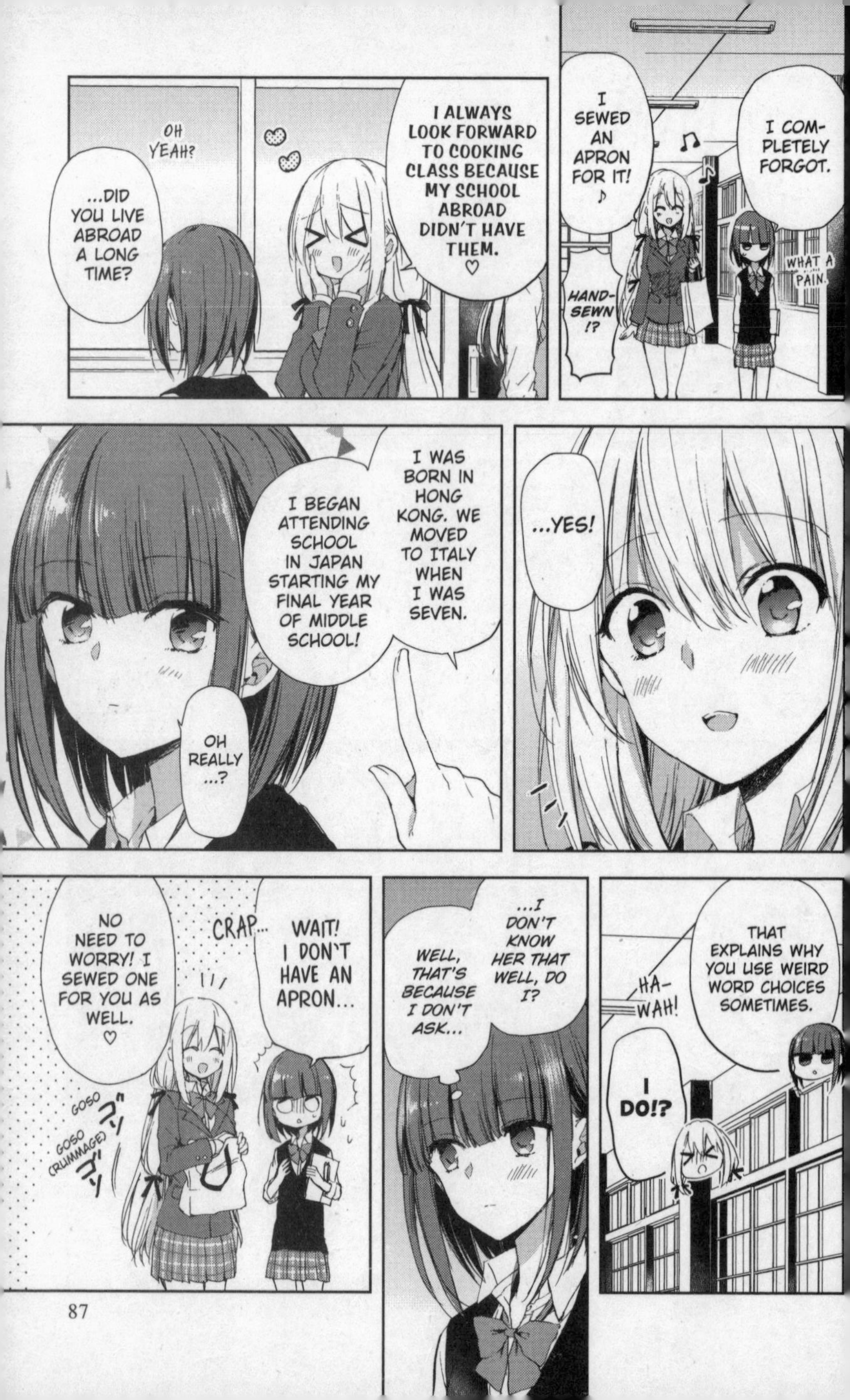
I COM-PLETELY FORGOT.
I SEWED AN APRON FOR IT! ♪
WHAT A PAIN.
HAND-SEWN!?
I ALWAYS LOOK FORWARD TO COOKING CLASS BECAUSE MY SCHOOL ABROAD DIDN'T HAVE THEM. ♡
OH YEAH?
...DID YOU LIVE ABROAD A LONG TIME?
...YES!
I WAS BORN IN HONG KONG. WE MOVED TO ITALY WHEN I WAS SEVEN.
I BEGAN ATTENDING SCHOOL IN JAPAN STARTING MY FINAL YEAR OF MIDDLE SCHOOL!
OH REALLY...?
THAT EXPLAINS WHY YOU USE WEIRD WORD CHOICES SOMETIMES.
HA-WAH!
I DO!?
...I DON'T KNOW HER THAT WELL, DO I?
WELL, THAT'S BECAUSE I DON'T ASK...
WAIT! I DON'T HAVE AN APRON...
CRAP...
NO NEED TO WORRY! I SEWED ONE FOR YOU AS WELL. ♡
GOSO GOSO (RUMMAGE)

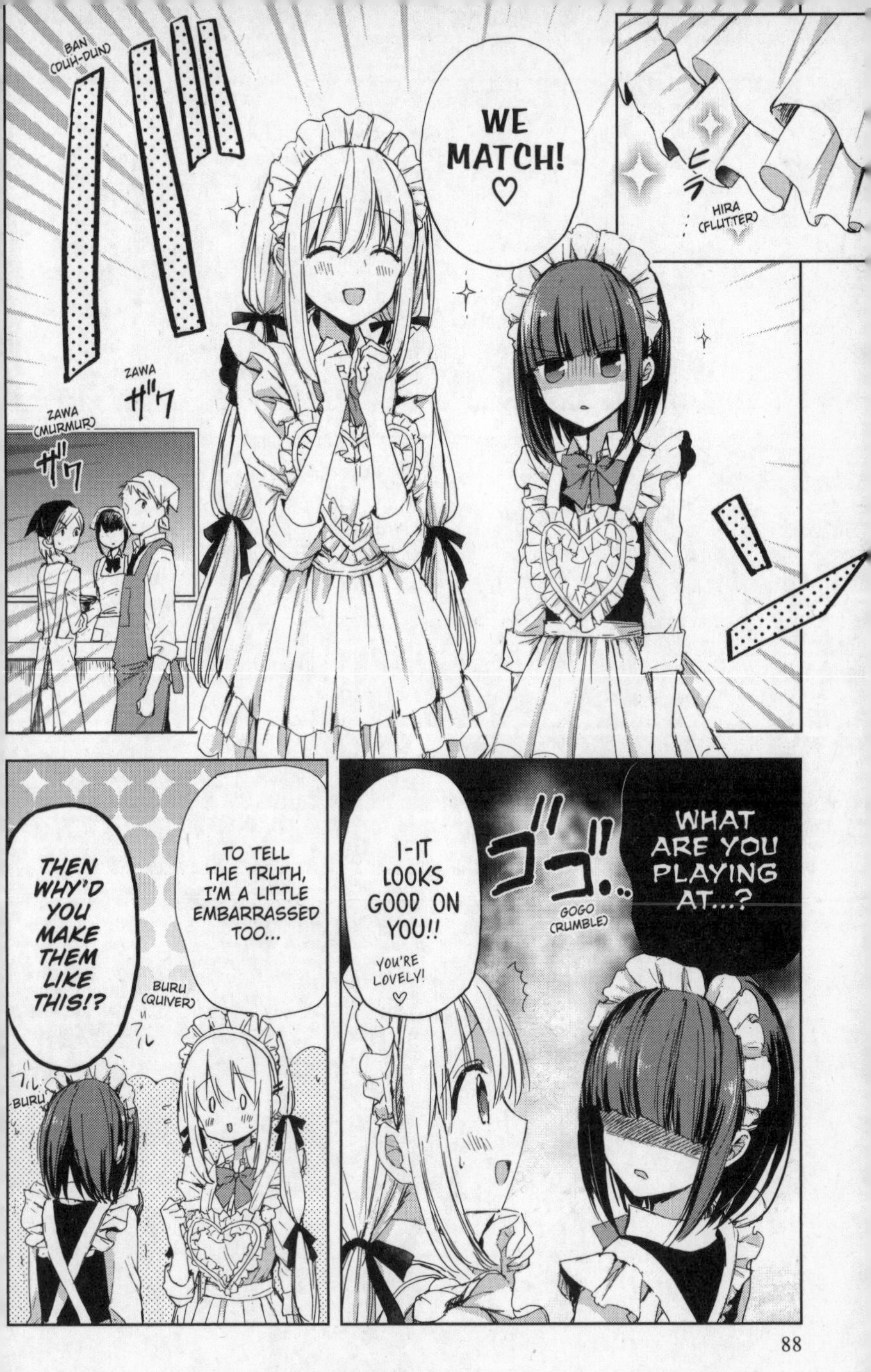
ヒラ
HIRA (FLUTTER)
BAN (DUH-DUN)
WE MATCH! ♡
ザワ
ZAWA (MURMUR)
ザワ
ZAWA
WHAT ARE YOU PLAYING AT...?
ゴゴ...
GOGO (RUMBLE)
I-IT LOOKS GOOD ON YOU!!
YOU'RE LOVELY! ♡
TO TELL THE TRUTH, I'M A LITTLE EMBARRASSED TOO...
ブル
BURU (QUIVER)
ブル
BURU
THEN WHY'D YOU MAKE THEM LIKE THIS!?

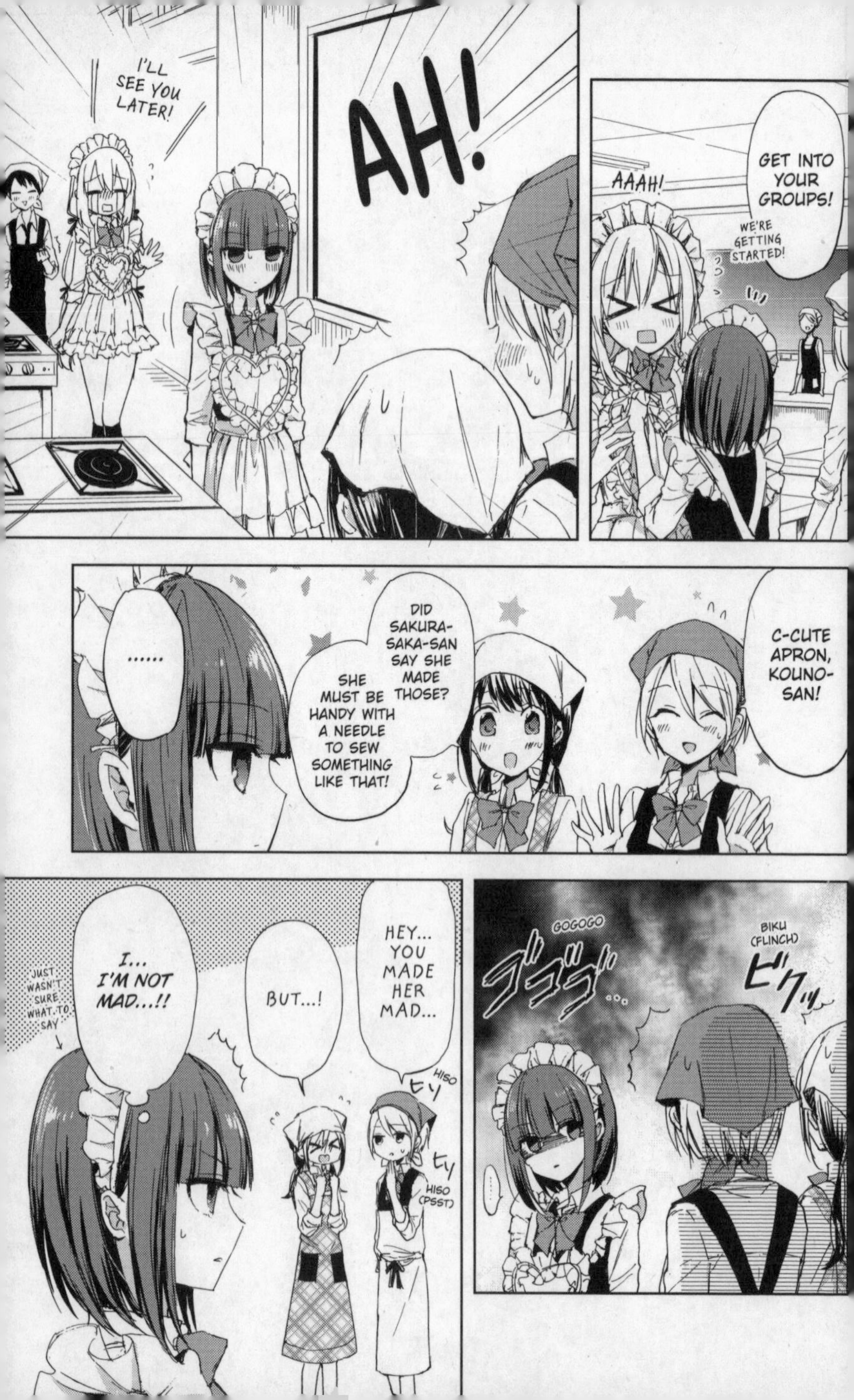
GET INTO YOUR GROUPS!
WE'RE GETTING STARTED!
AAAH!
AH!
I'LL SEE YOU LATER!
C-CUTE APRON, KOUNO-SAN!
DID SAKURA-SAKA-SAN SAY SHE MADE THOSE?
SHE MUST BE HANDY WITH A NEEDLE TO SEW SOMETHING LIKE THAT!
......
BIKU (FLINCH)
GOGOGO
HEY... YOU MADE HER MAD...
HISO
HISO (PSST)
BUT...!
I... I'M NOT MAD...!!
JUST WASN'T SURE WHAT TO SAY

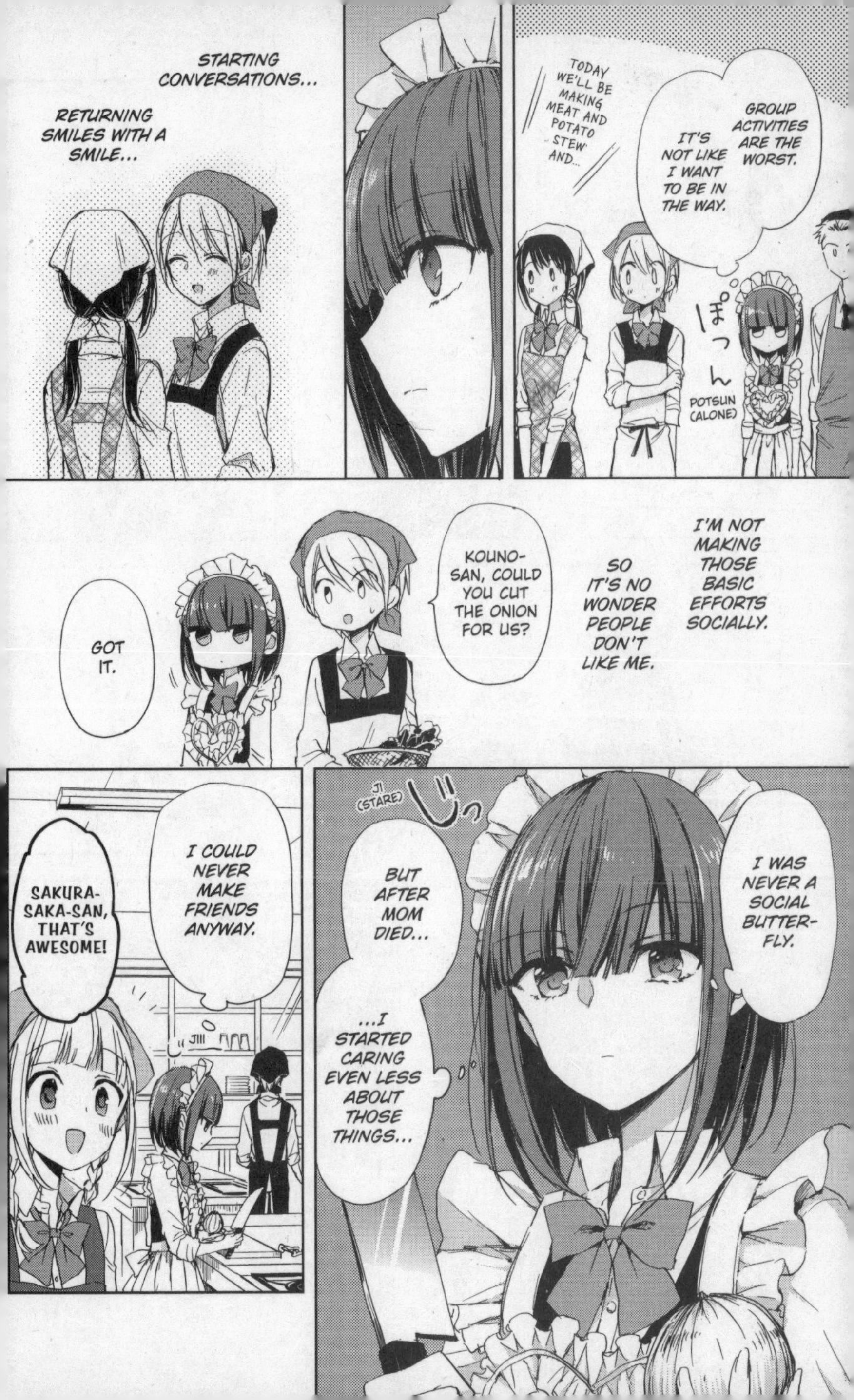
GROUP ACTIVITIES ARE THE WORST.
IT'S NOT LIKE I WANT TO BE IN THE WAY.
TODAY WE'LL BE MAKING MEAT AND POTATO STEW AND...
ぽつん
POTSUN (ALONE)
STARTING CONVERSATIONS...
RETURNING SMILES WITH A SMILE...
I'M NOT MAKING THOSE BASIC EFFORTS SOCIALLY.
SO IT'S NO WONDER PEOPLE DON'T LIKE ME.
KOUNO-SAN, COULD YOU CUT THE ONION FOR US?
GOT IT.
I WAS NEVER A SOCIAL BUTTERFLY.
じっ
JI (STARE)
BUT AFTER MOM DIED...
...I STARTED CARING EVEN LESS ABOUT THOSE THINGS...
I COULD NEVER MAKE FRIENDS ANYWAY.
SAKURA-SAKA-SAN, THAT'S AWESOME!
JIII

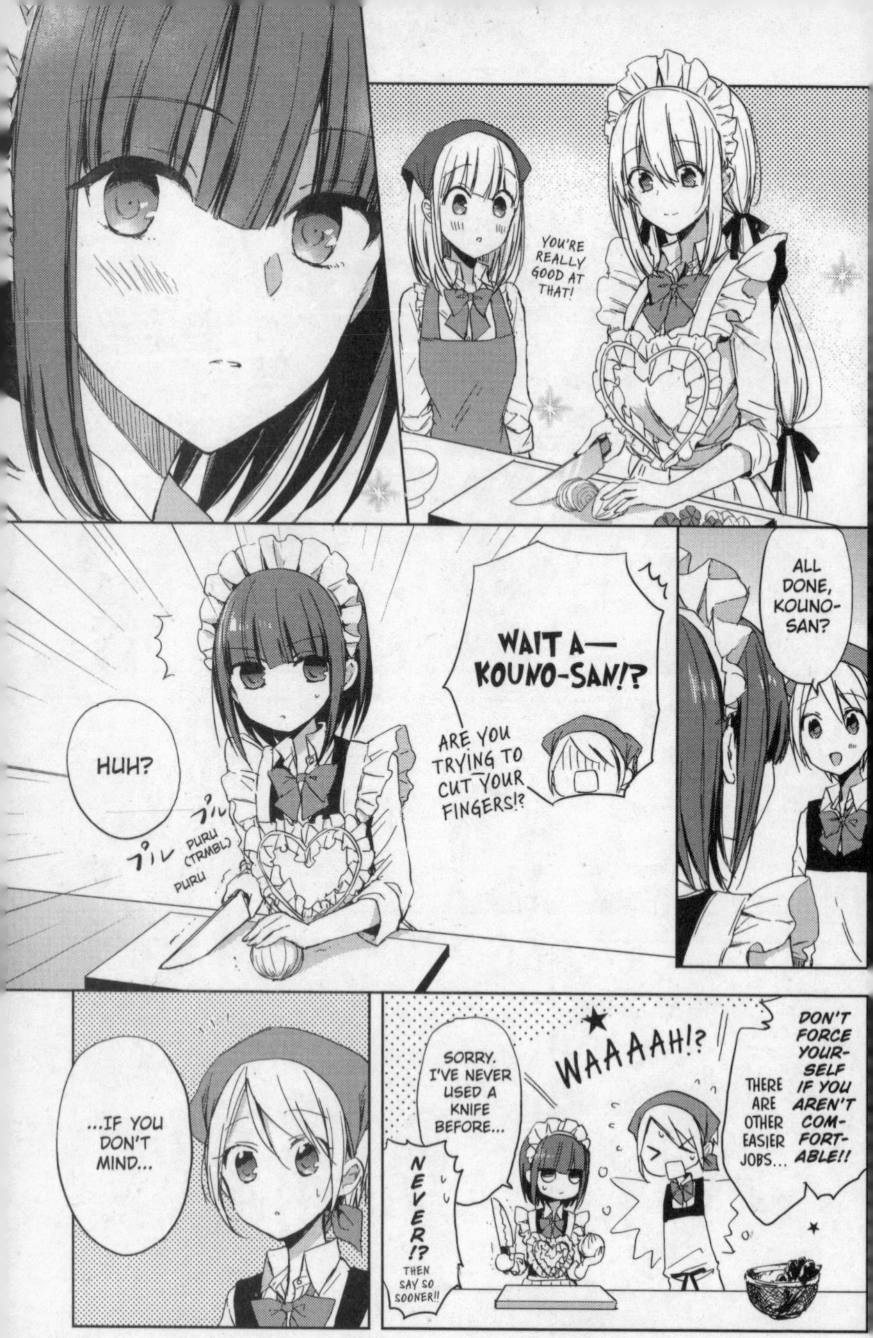
YOU'RE REALLY GOOD AT THAT!
ALL DONE, KOUNO-SAN?
WAIT A— KOUNO-SAN!?
ARE YOU TRYING TO CUT YOUR FINGERS!?
HUH?
プル PURU (TRMBL)
プル PURU
DON'T FORCE YOURSELF IF YOU AREN'T COMFORTABLE!!
THERE ARE OTHER EASIER JOBS...
WAAAAH!?
SORRY. I'VE NEVER USED A KNIFE BEFORE...
NEVER!? THEN SAY SO SOONER!!
...IF YOU DON'T MIND...

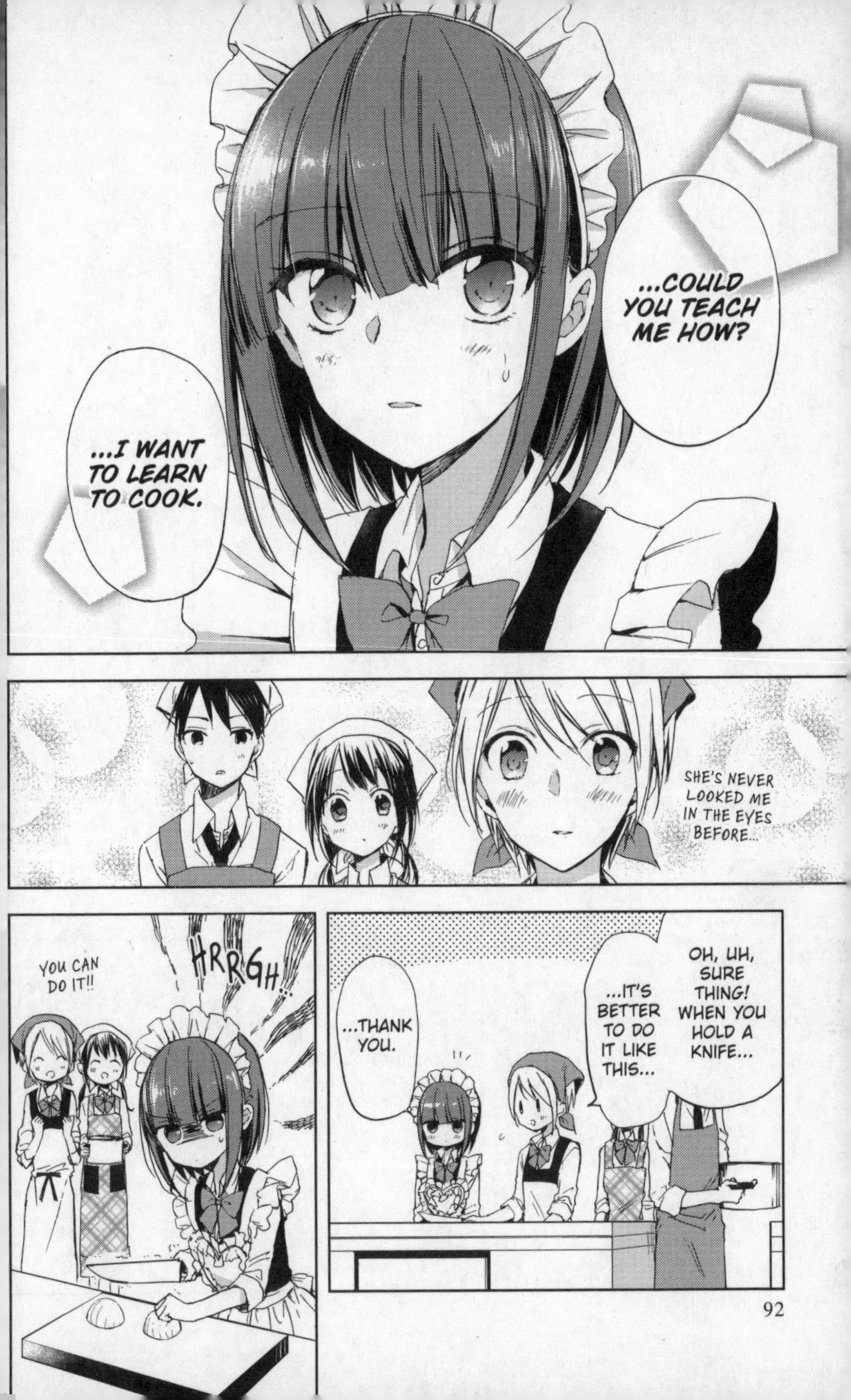
...COULD YOU TEACH ME HOW?
...I WANT TO LEARN TO COOK.
SHE'S NEVER LOOKED ME IN THE EYES BEFORE...
OH, UH, SURE THING! WHEN YOU HOLD A KNIFE...
...IT'S BETTER TO DO IT LIKE THIS...
...THANK YOU.
HRRGH!!
YOU CAN DO IT!!

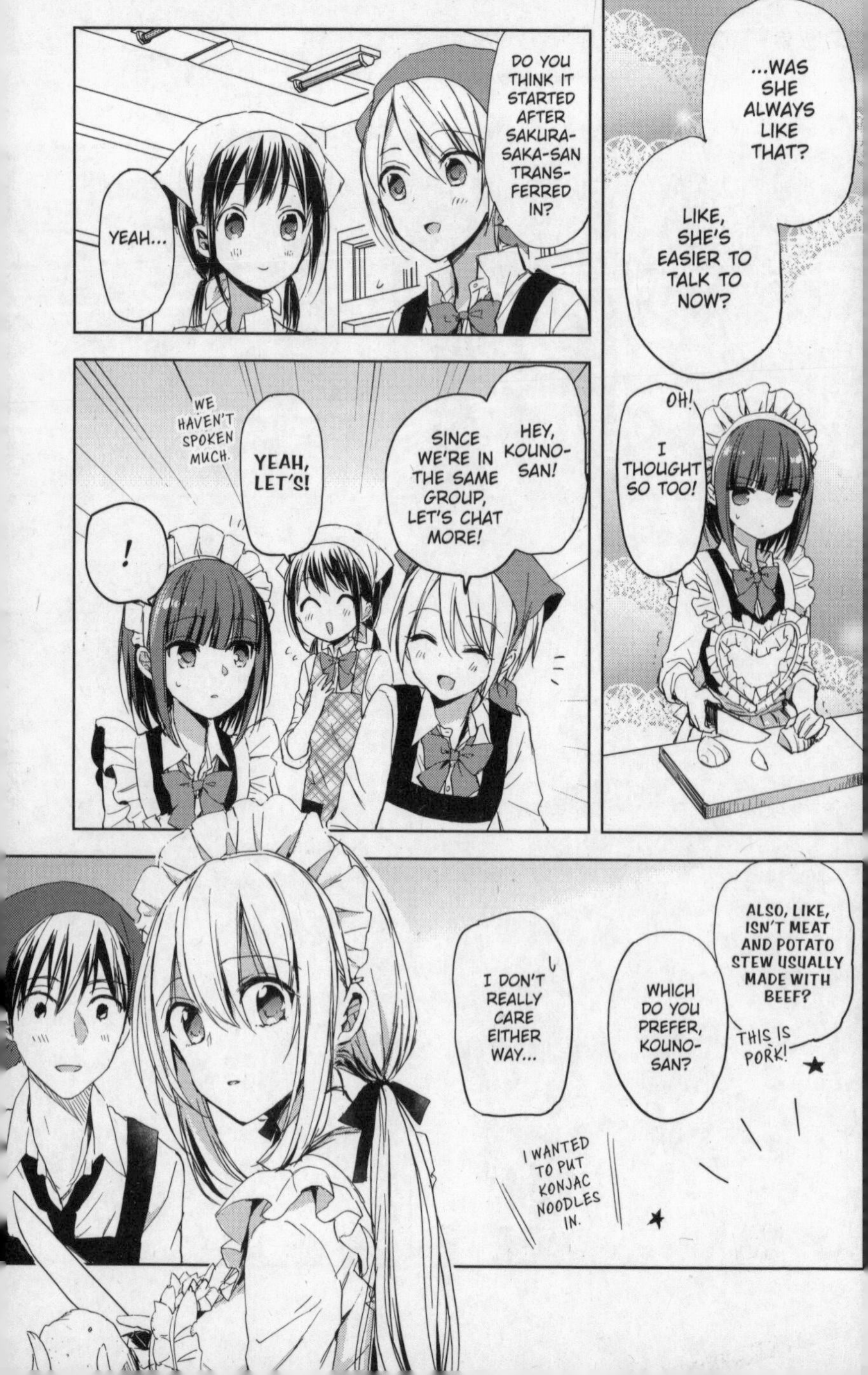

...WAS SHE ALWAYS LIKE THAT?
LIKE, SHE'S EASIER TO TALK TO NOW?
OH!
I THOUGHT SO TOO!
DO YOU THINK IT STARTED AFTER SAKURA-SAKA-SAN TRANS-FERRED IN?
YEAH...
HEY, KOUNO-SAN!
SINCE WE'RE IN THE SAME GROUP, LET'S CHAT MORE!
YEAH, LET'S!
WE HAVEN'T SPOKEN MUCH.
!
ALSO, LIKE, ISN'T MEAT AND POTATO STEW USUALLY MADE WITH BEEF?
THIS IS PORK!
WHICH DO YOU PREFER, KOUNO-SAN?
I DON'T REALLY CARE EITHER WAY...
I WANTED TO PUT KONJAC NOODLES IN.

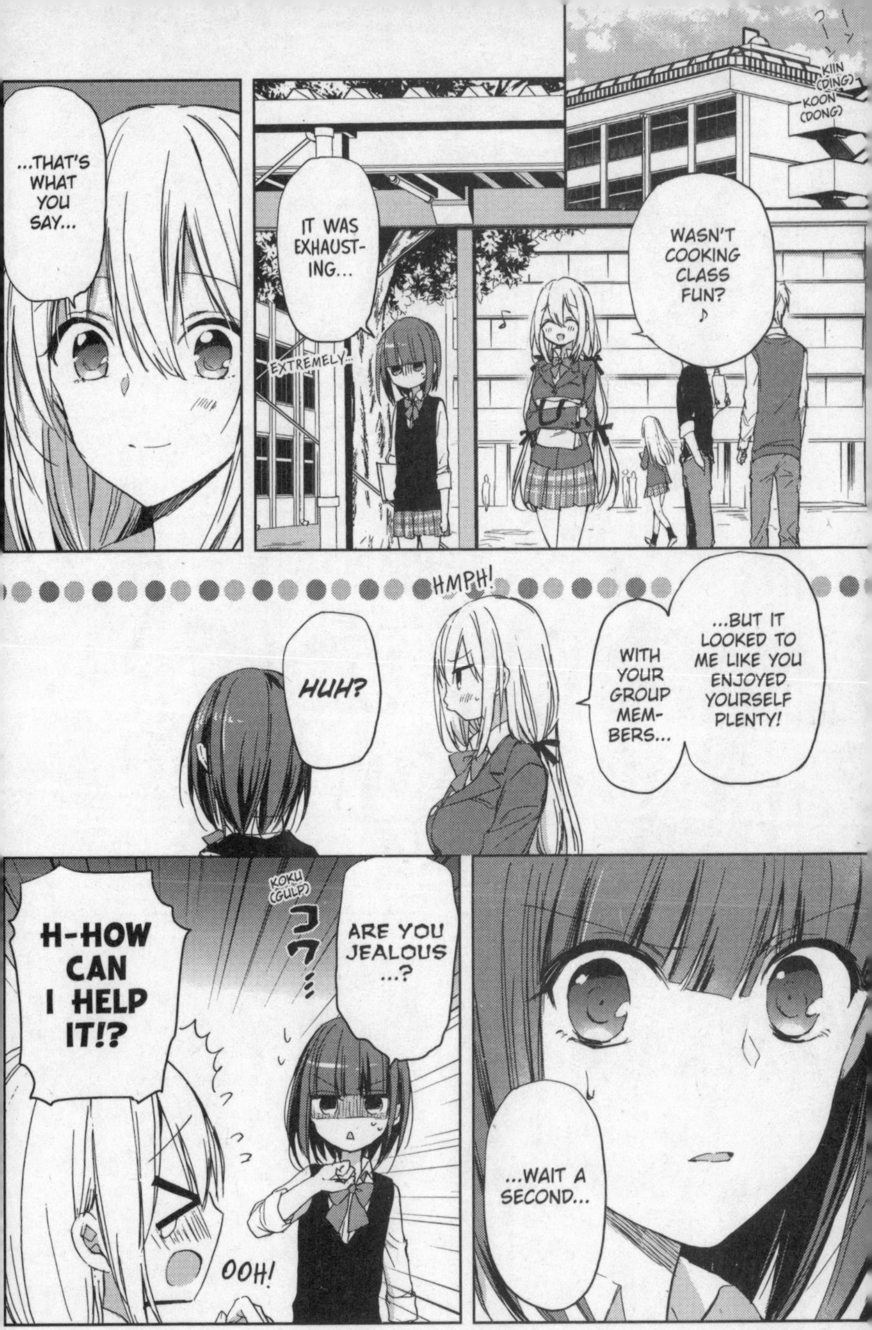
KIIN (DING)
KOON (DONG)
WASN'T COOKING CLASS FUN? ♪
IT WAS EXHAUSTING...
EXTREMELY...
...THAT'S WHAT YOU SAY...
HMPH!
...BUT IT LOOKED TO ME LIKE YOU ENJOYED YOURSELF PLENTY!
WITH YOUR GROUP MEMBERS...
HUH?
...WAIT A SECOND...
ARE YOU JEALOUS ...?
KOKU (GULP)
H-HOW CAN I HELP IT!?
OOH!

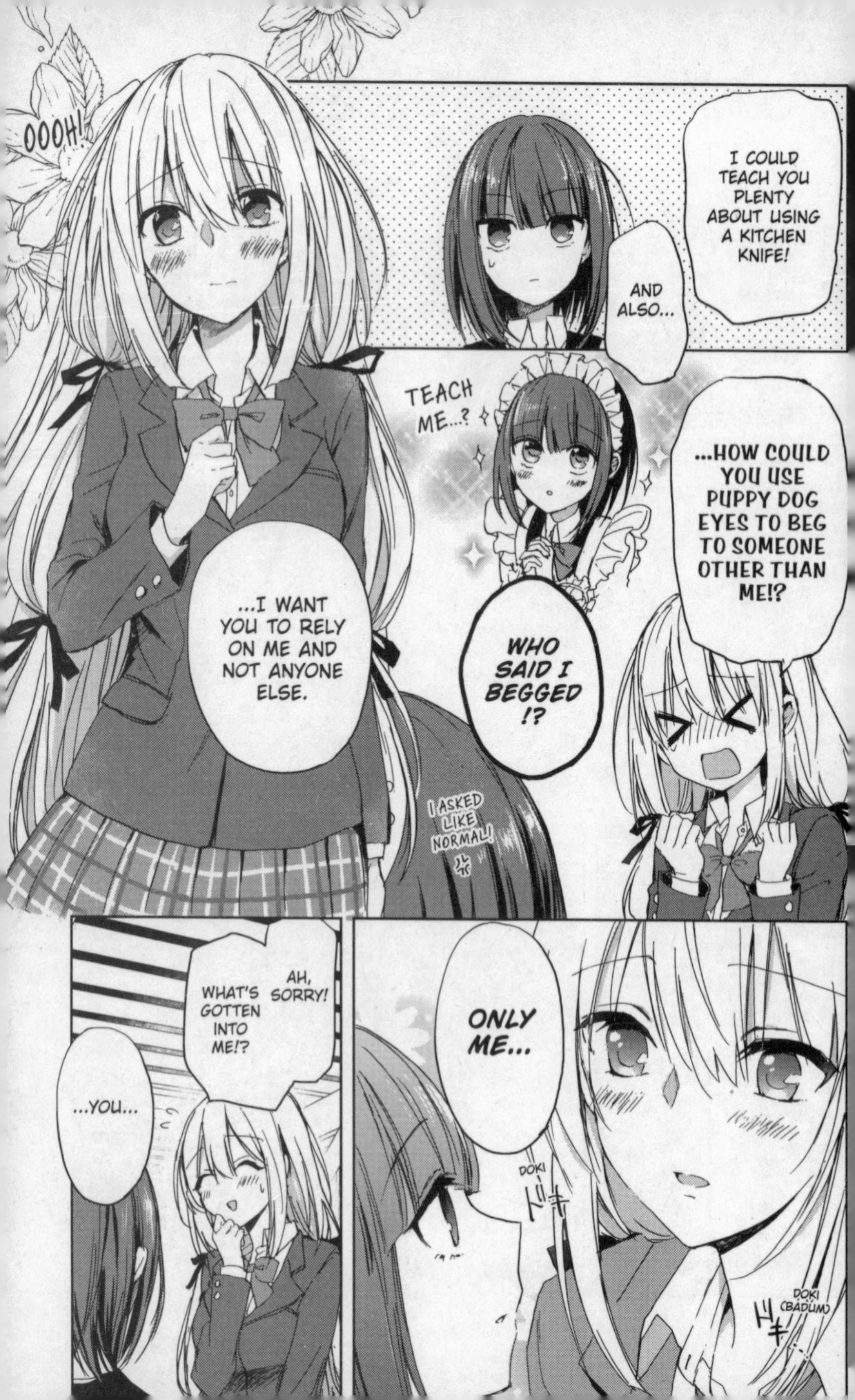
I COULD TEACH YOU PLENTY ABOUT USING A KITCHEN KNIFE!
AND ALSO...
TEACH ME...?
...HOW COULD YOU USE PUPPY DOG EYES TO BEG TO SOMEONE OTHER THAN ME!?
WHO SAID I BEGGED!?
I ASKED LIKE NORMAL!
OOOH!
...I WANT YOU TO RELY ON ME AND NOT ANYONE ELSE.
ONLY ME...
DOKI
ドキ
DOKI (BADUM)
ドキ...
AH, SORRY! WHAT'S GOTTEN INTO ME!?
...YOU...

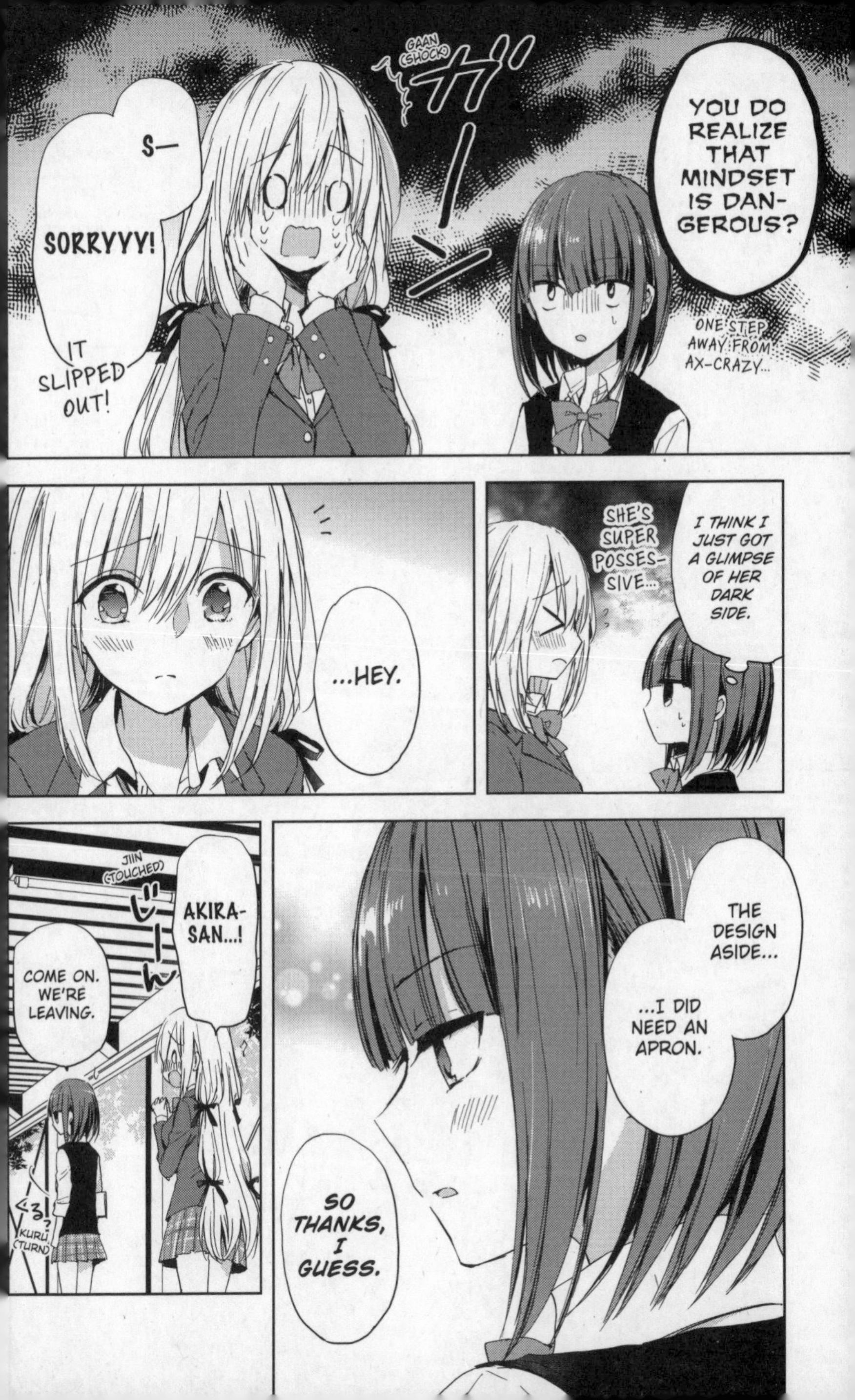
YOU DO REALIZE THAT MINDSET IS DANGEROUS?
GAAN (SHOCK)
ONE STEP AWAY FROM AX-CRAZY...
S— SORRYYY!
IT SLIPPED OUT!
I THINK I JUST GOT A GLIMPSE OF HER DARK SIDE.
SHE'S SUPER POSSESSIVE...
...HEY.
THE DESIGN ASIDE...
...I DID NEED AN APRON.
SO THANKS, I GUESS.
AKIRA-SAN...!
JIIN (TOUCHED)
COME ON. WE'RE LEAVING.
KURU (TURN)

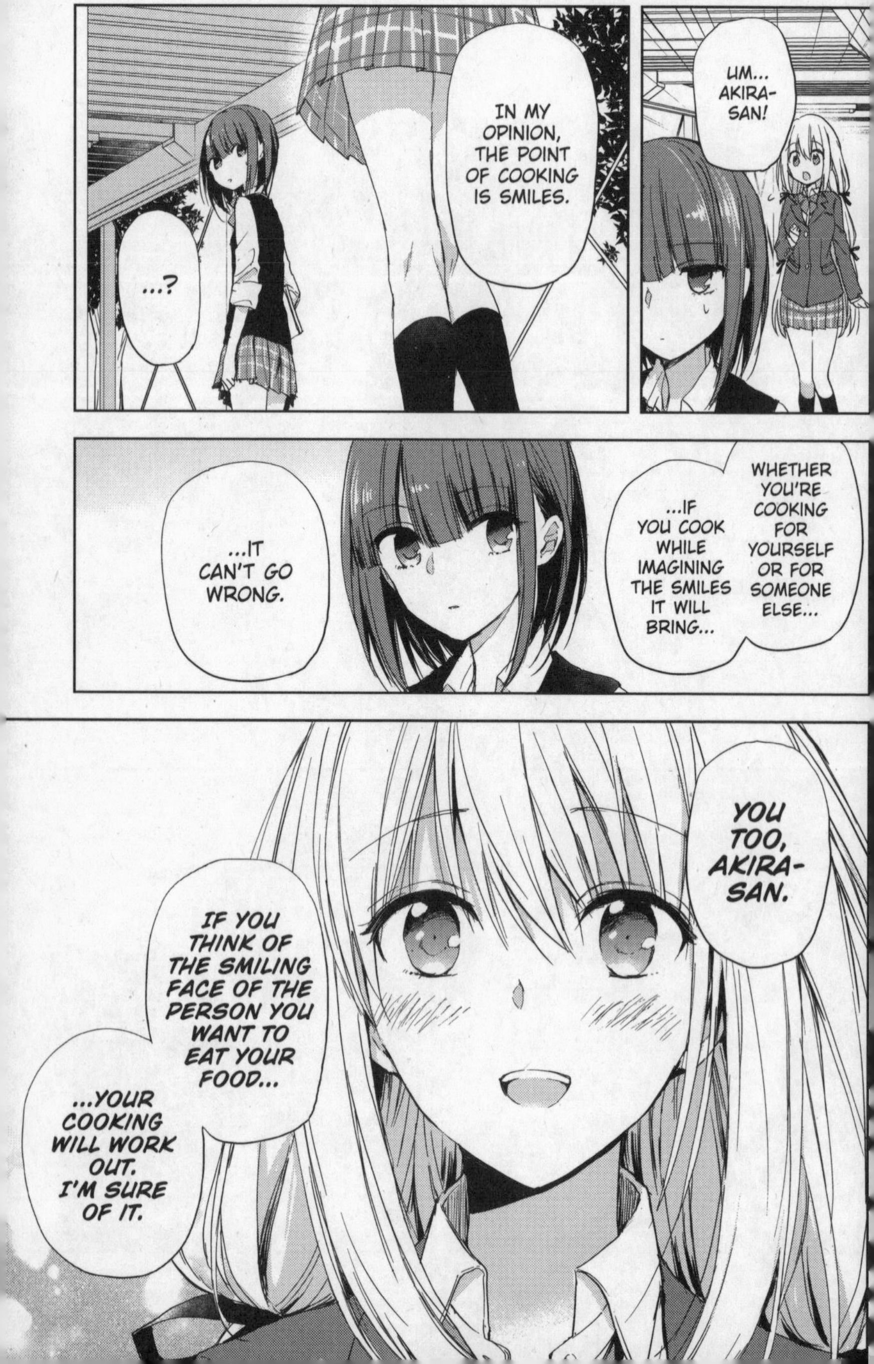
UM... AKIRA-SAN!
IN MY OPINION, THE POINT OF COOKING IS SMILES.
...?
WHETHER YOU'RE COOKING FOR YOURSELF OR FOR SOMEONE ELSE...
...IF YOU COOK WHILE IMAGINING THE SMILES IT WILL BRING...
...IT CAN'T GO WRONG.
YOU TOO, AKIRA-SAN.
IF YOU THINK OF THE SMILING FACE OF THE PERSON YOU WANT TO EAT YOUR FOOD...
...YOUR COOKING WILL WORK OUT. I'M SURE OF IT.

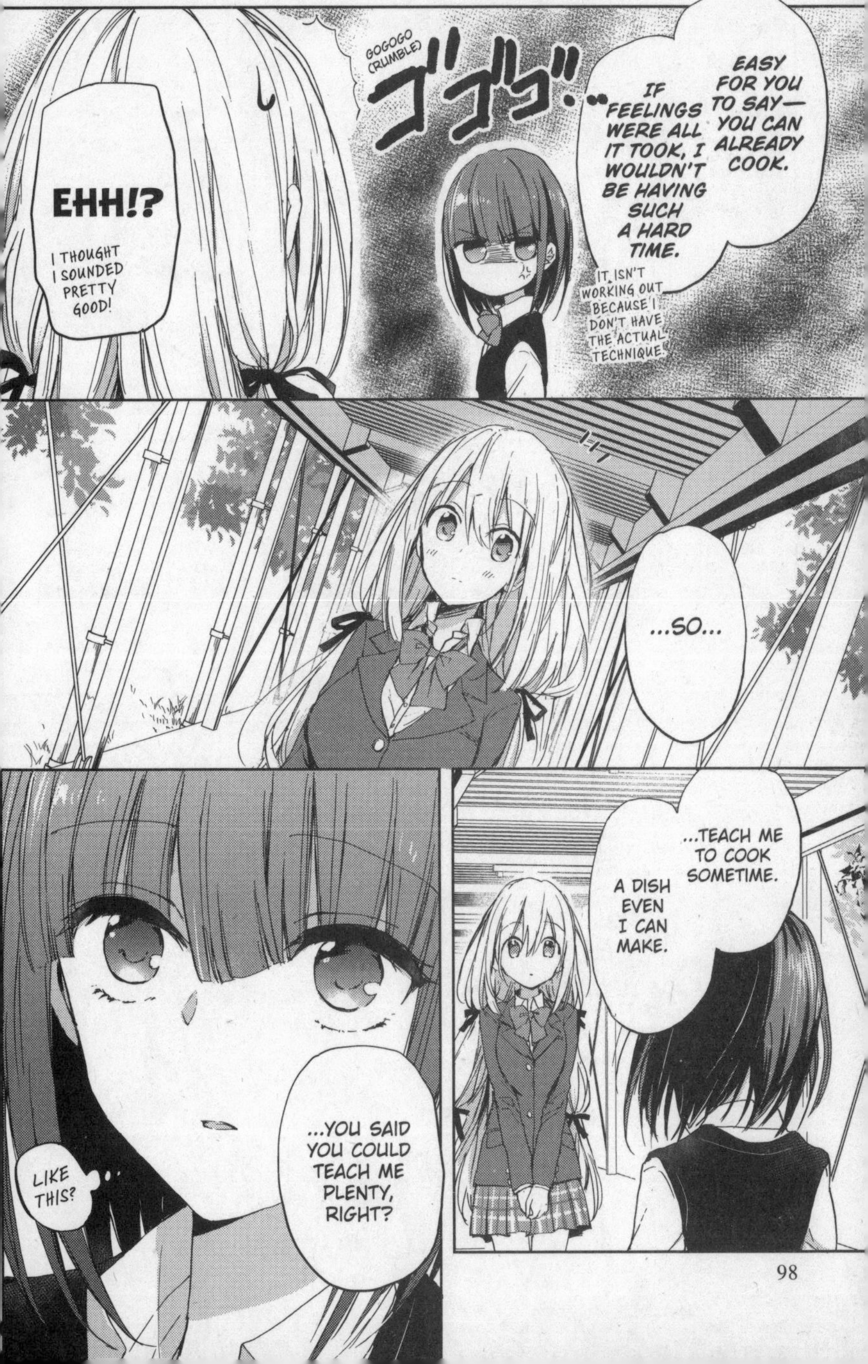
EASY FOR YOU TO SAY— YOU CAN ALREADY COOK.
IF FEELINGS WERE ALL IT TOOK, I WOULDN'T BE HAVING SUCH A HARD TIME.
GOGOGO (RUMBLE)
IT ISN'T WORKING OUT BECAUSE I DON'T HAVE THE ACTUAL TECHNIQUE.
EHH!?
I THOUGHT I SOUNDED PRETTY GOOD!
...SO...
...TEACH ME TO COOK SOMETIME.
A DISH EVEN I CAN MAKE.
...YOU SAID YOU COULD TEACH ME PLENTY, RIGHT?
LIKE THIS?

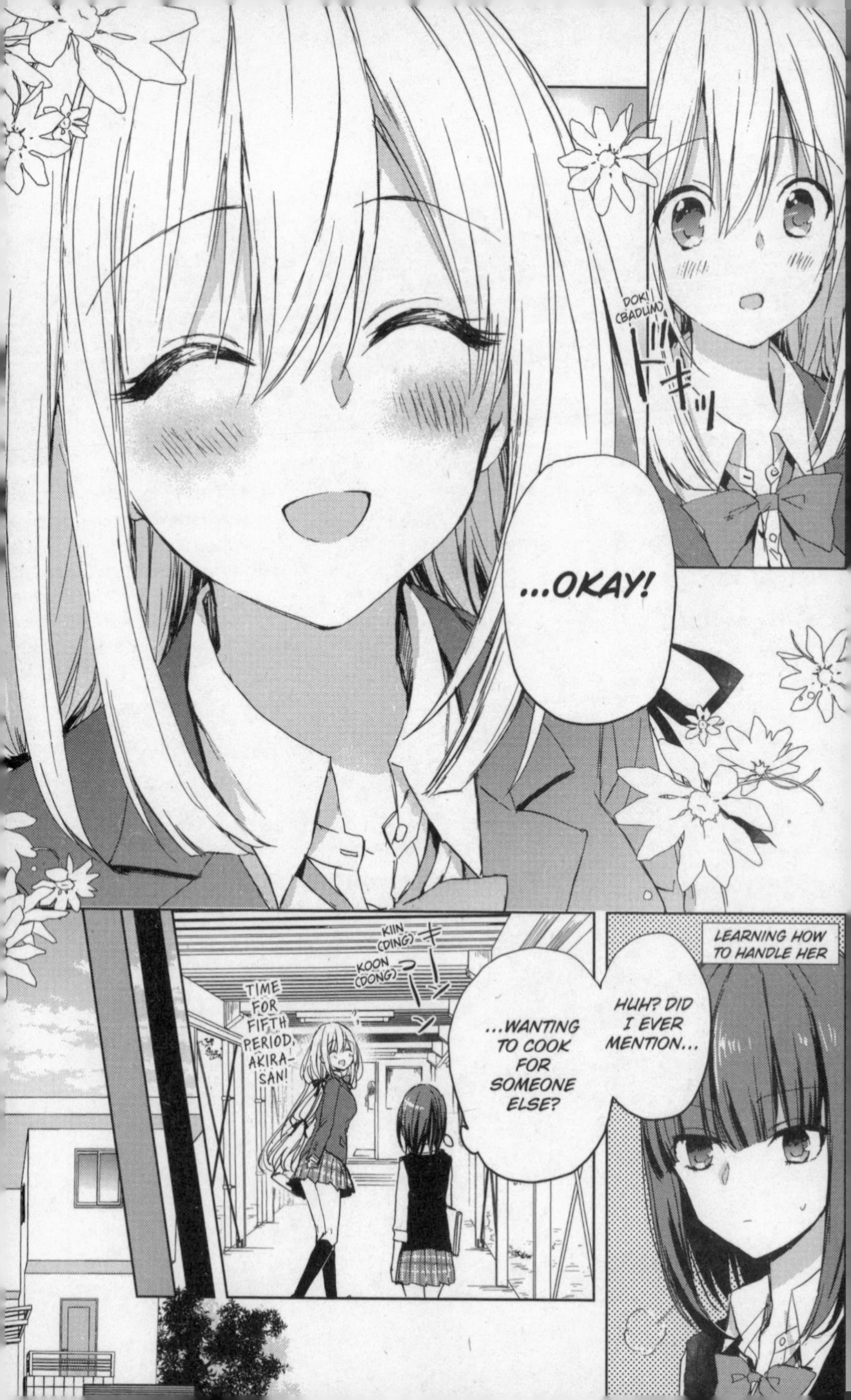
DOKI (BADUMP)
...OKAY!
LEARNING HOW TO HANDLE HER
HUH? DID I EVER MENTION...
...WANTING TO COOK FOR SOMEONE ELSE?
KIIN (DING)
KOON (DONG)
TIME FOR FIFTH PERIOD, AKIRA-SAN!

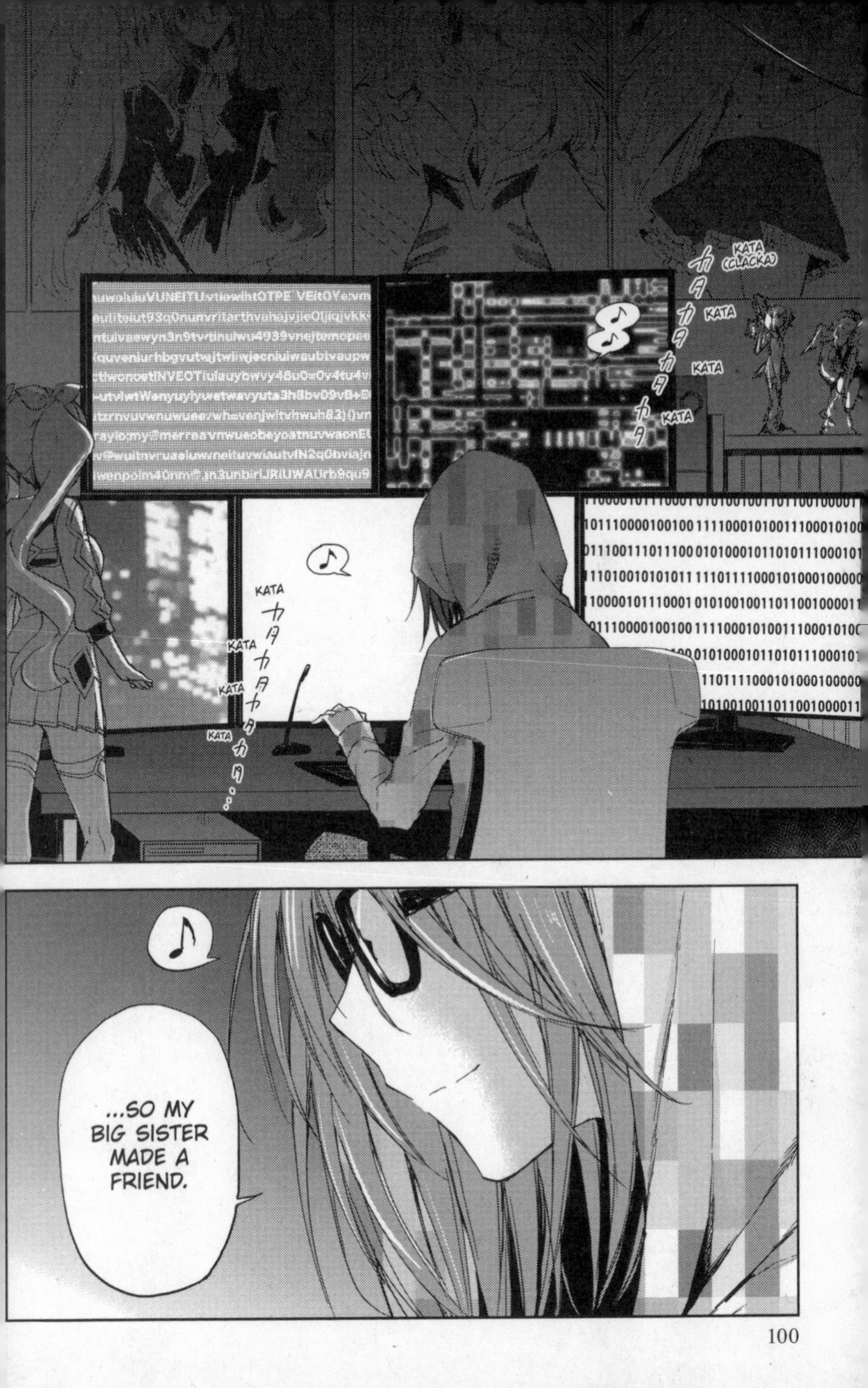
KATA (CLACKA)
KATA
KATA
KATA
♪
KATA
KATA
KATA
KATA
♪
...SO MY BIG SISTER MADE A FRIEND.

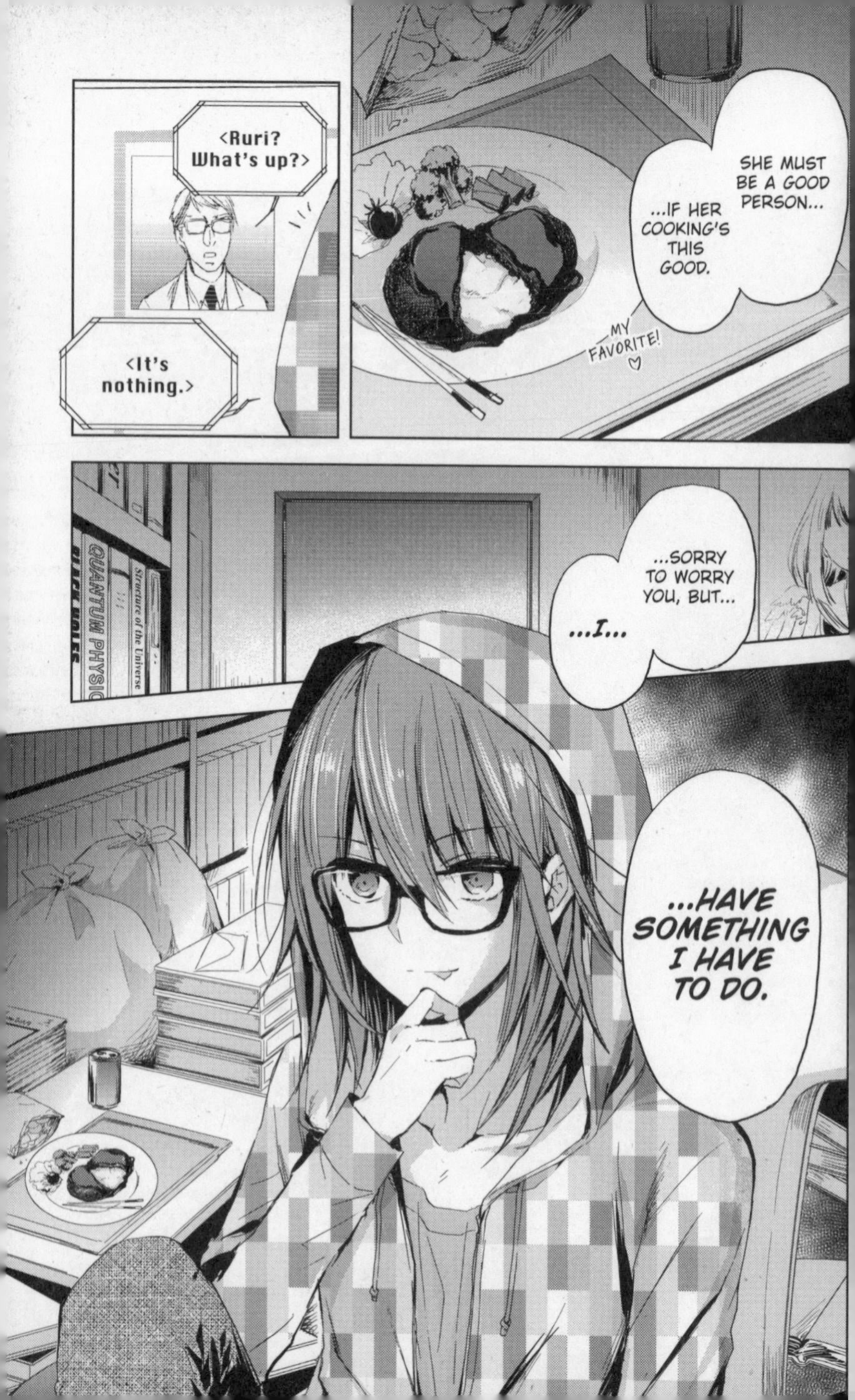
SHE MUST BE A GOOD PERSON...
...IF HER COOKING'S THIS GOOD.
MY FAVORITE! ♡
<Ruri? What's up?>
<It's nothing.>
QUANTUM PHYSIC
Structure of the Universe
...SORRY TO WORRY YOU, BUT...
...I...
...HAVE SOMETHING I HAVE TO DO.

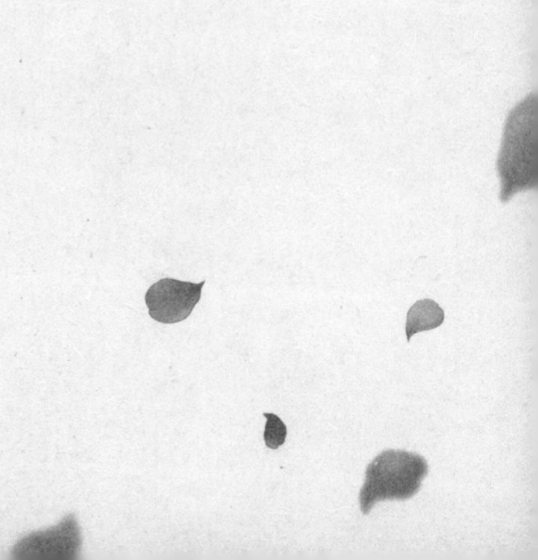

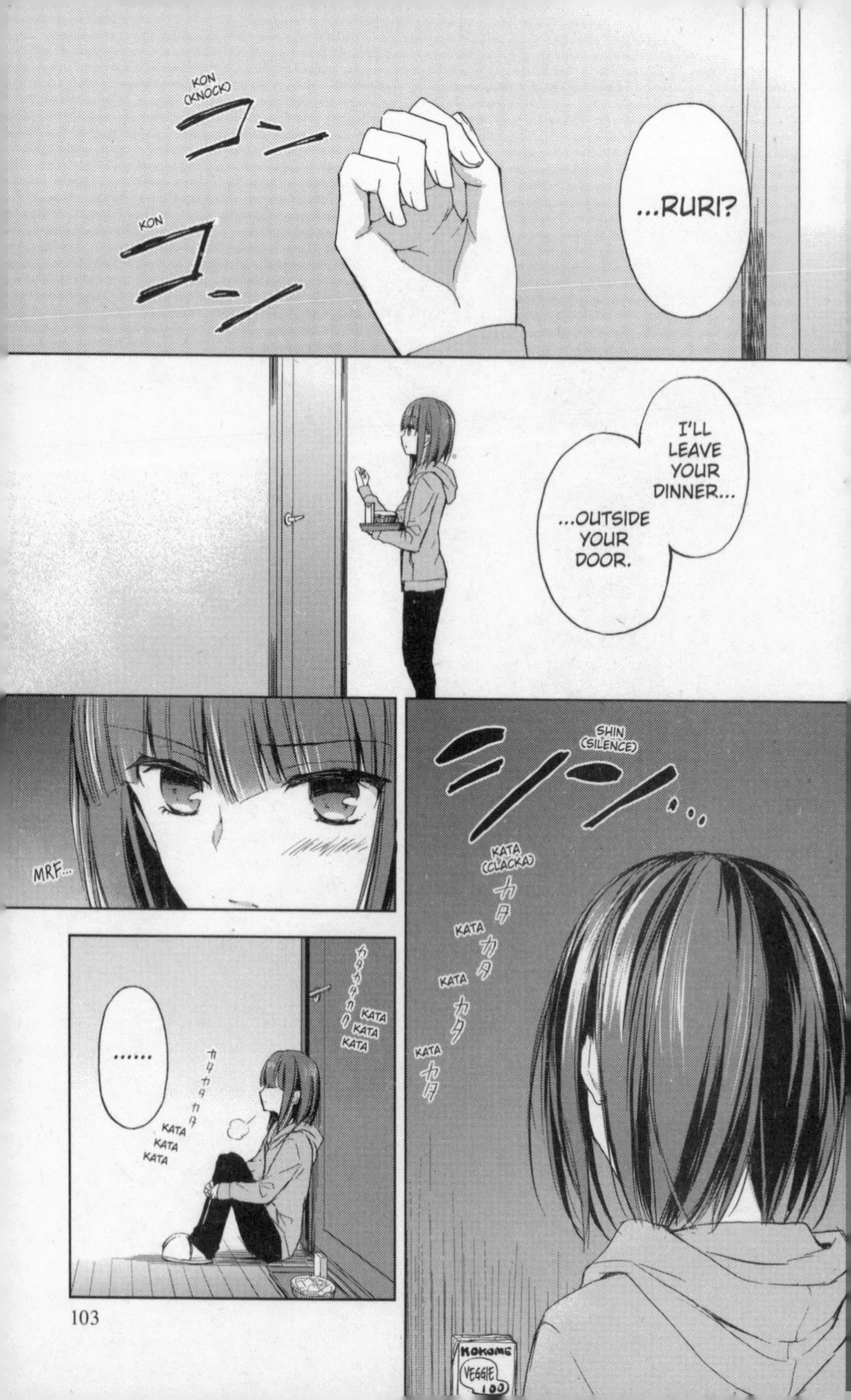
...RURI?
KON (KNOCK)
KON
I'LL LEAVE YOUR DINNER...
...OUTSIDE YOUR DOOR.
SHIN (SILENCE)
KATA (CLACKA)
KATA
KATA
KATA
KOKOME VEGGIE 100
MRF...
......
KATA KATA KATA
KATA KATA KATA

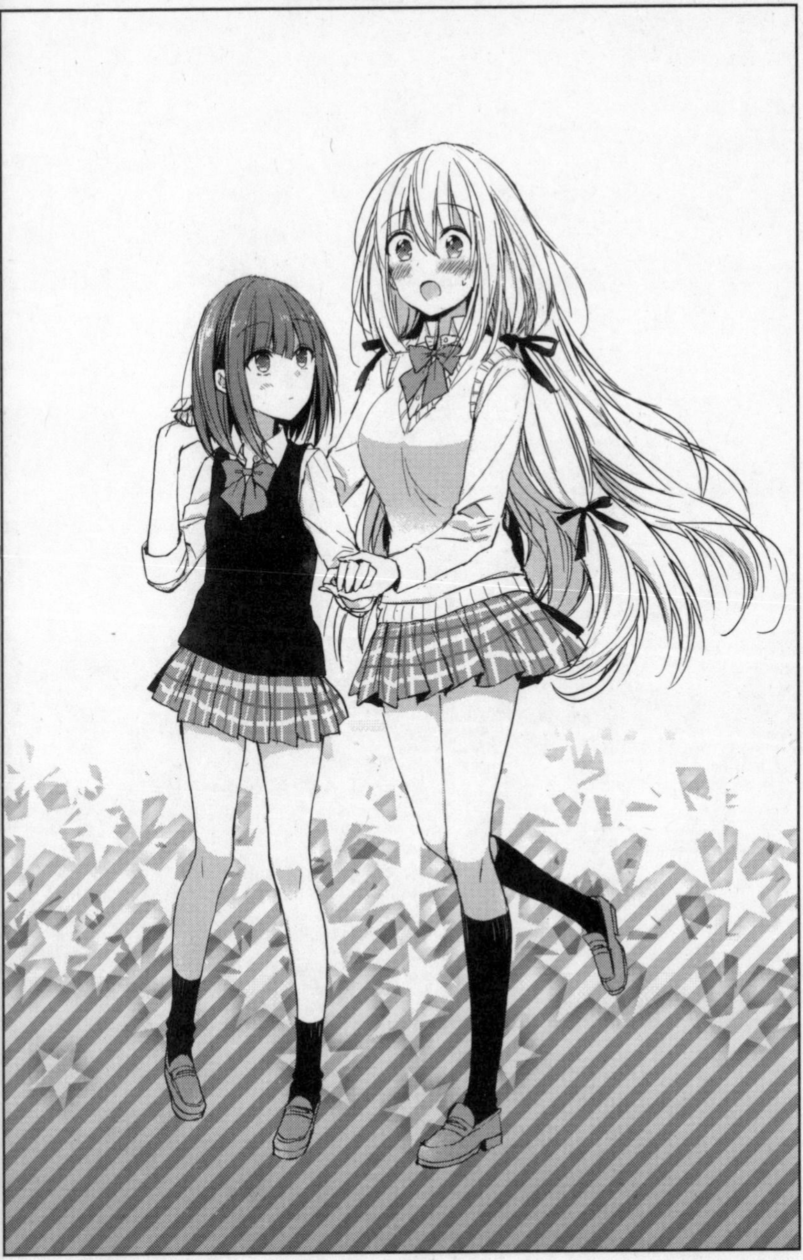

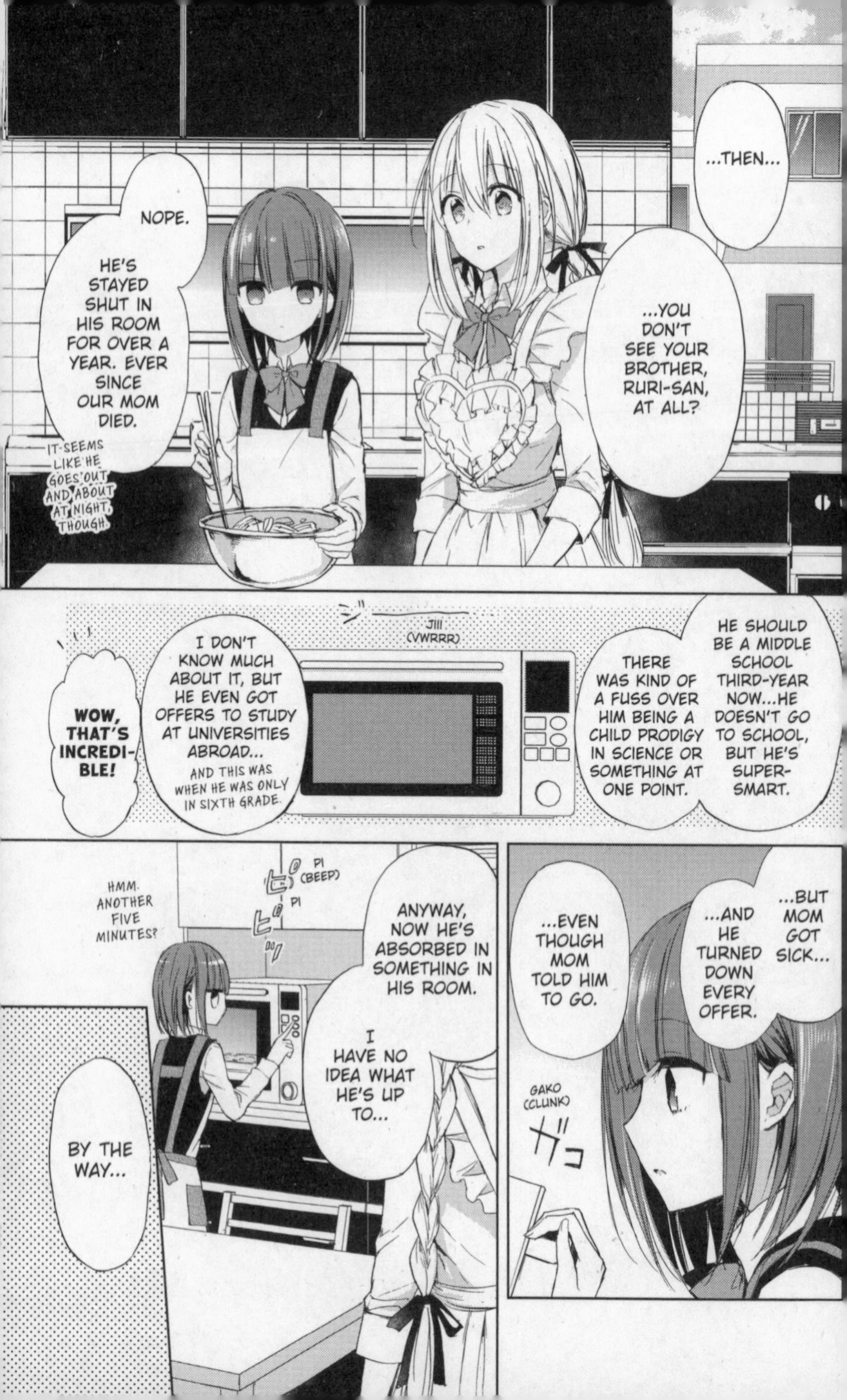
...THEN...
...YOU DON'T SEE YOUR BROTHER, RURI-SAN, AT ALL?
NOPE.
HE'S STAYED SHUT IN HIS ROOM FOR OVER A YEAR. EVER SINCE OUR MOM DIED.
IT SEEMS LIKE HE GOES OUT AND ABOUT AT NIGHT, THOUGH.
HE SHOULD BE A MIDDLE SCHOOL THIRD-YEAR NOW...HE DOESN'T GO TO SCHOOL, BUT HE'S SUPER-SMART.
THERE WAS KIND OF A FUSS OVER HIM BEING A CHILD PRODIGY IN SCIENCE OR SOMETHING AT ONE POINT.
JIII (VWRRR)
I DON'T KNOW MUCH ABOUT IT, BUT HE EVEN GOT OFFERS TO STUDY AT UNIVERSITIES ABROAD...
AND THIS WAS WHEN HE WAS ONLY IN SIXTH GRADE.
WOW, THAT'S INCREDI-BLE!
...BUT MOM GOT SICK...
...AND HE TURNED DOWN EVERY OFFER.
...EVEN THOUGH MOM TOLD HIM TO GO.
GAKO (CLUNK)
ANYWAY, NOW HE'S ABSORBED IN SOMETHING IN HIS ROOM.
PI (BEEP)
PI
HMM. ANOTHER FIVE MINUTES?
I HAVE NO IDEA WHAT HE'S UP TO...
BY THE WAY...

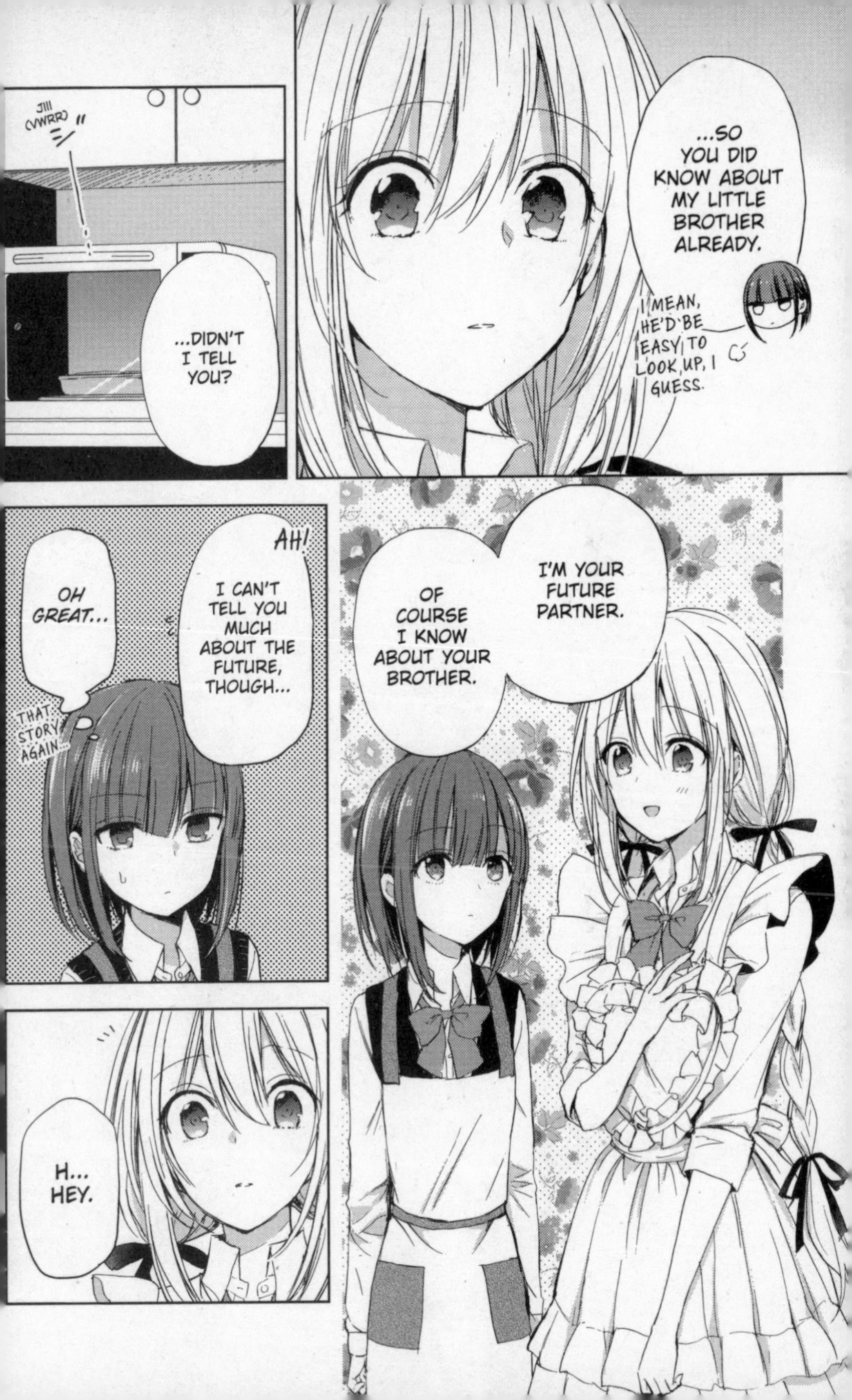
...SO YOU DID KNOW ABOUT MY LITTLE BROTHER ALREADY.
I MEAN, HE'D BE EASY TO LOOK UP, I GUESS.
JIII (VWRR)
...DIDN'T I TELL YOU?
I'M YOUR FUTURE PARTNER.
OF COURSE I KNOW ABOUT YOUR BROTHER.
AH!
I CAN'T TELL YOU MUCH ABOUT THE FUTURE, THOUGH...
OH GREAT...
THAT STORY AGAIN...
H... HEY.

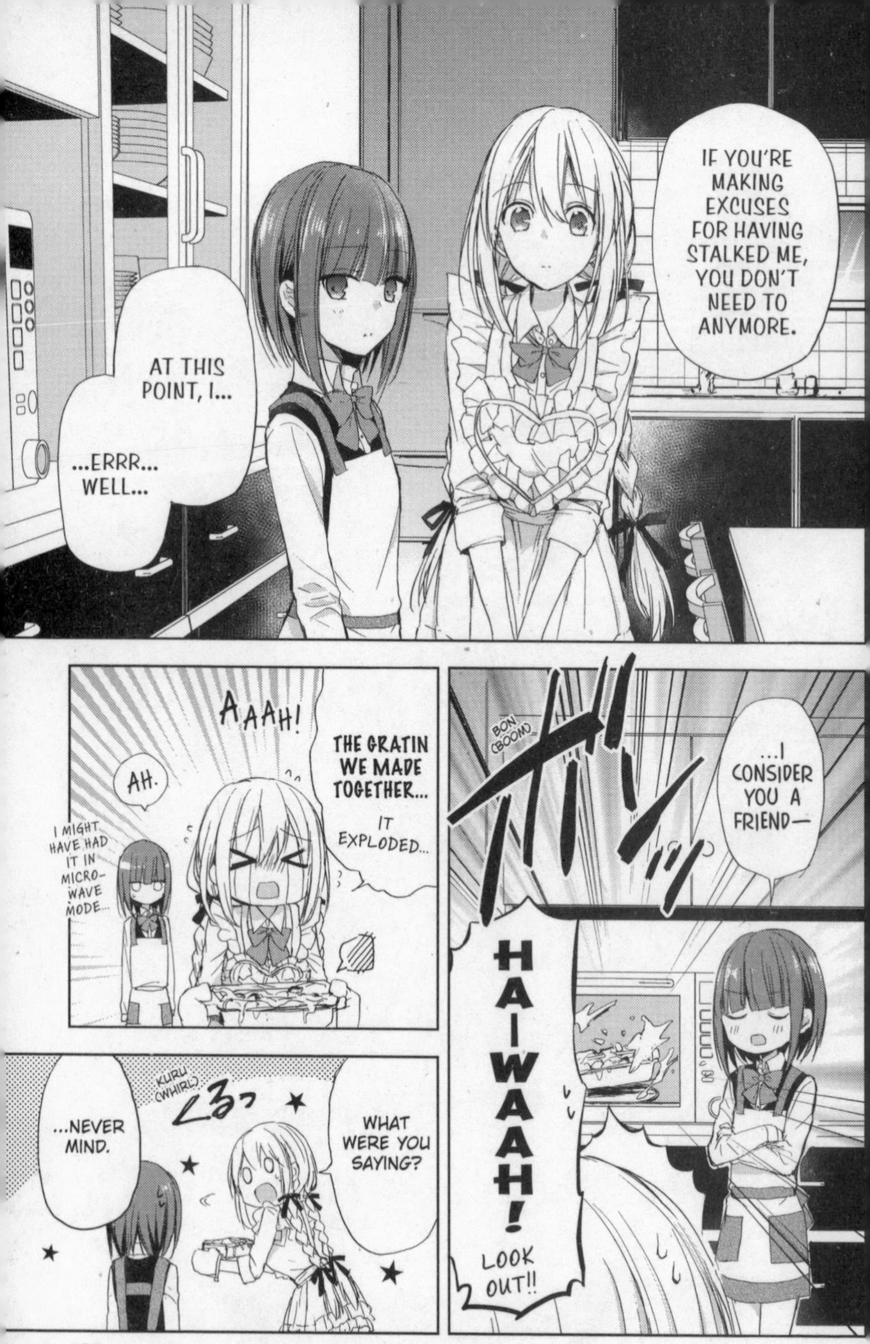
IF YOU'RE MAKING EXCUSES FOR HAVING STALKED ME, YOU DON'T NEED TO ANYMORE.
AT THIS POINT, I...
...ERRR... WELL...
BON (BOOM)
...I CONSIDER YOU A FRIEND—
HAIWAAAH! LOOK OUT!!
AAAH!
THE GRATIN WE MADE TOGETHER...
IT EXPLODED...
AH.
I MIGHT HAVE HAD IT IN MICRO-WAVE MODE...
KURU (WHIRL)
WHAT WERE YOU SAYING?
...NEVER MIND.

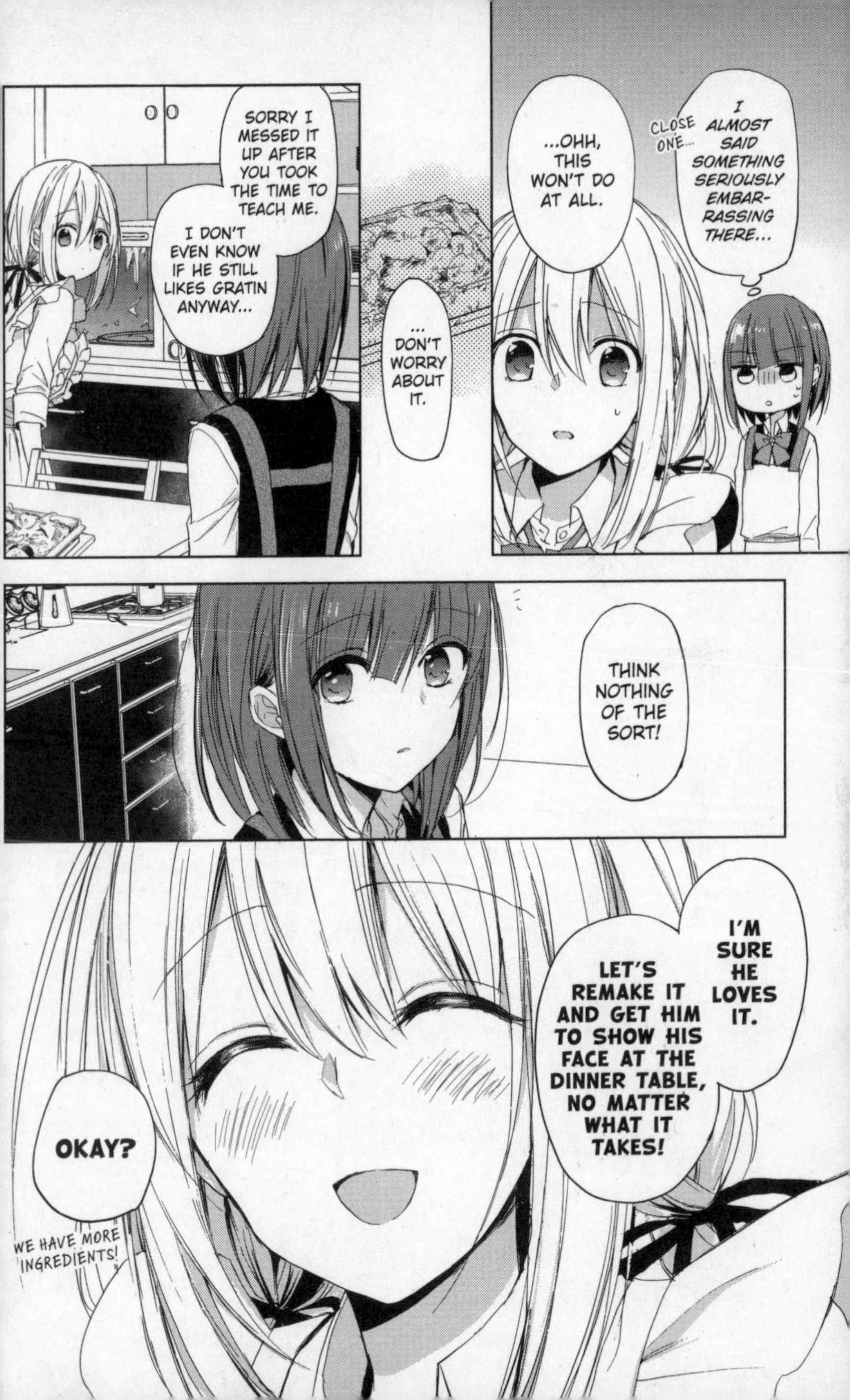
I ALMOST SAID SOMETHING SERIOUSLY EMBARRASSING THERE...
CLOSE ONE...
...OHH, THIS WON'T DO AT ALL.
... DON'T WORRY ABOUT IT.
SORRY I MESSED IT UP AFTER YOU TOOK THE TIME TO TEACH ME.
I DON'T EVEN KNOW IF HE STILL LIKES GRATIN ANYWAY...
THINK NOTHING OF THE SORT!
I'M SURE HE LOVES IT.
LET'S REMAKE IT AND GET HIM TO SHOW HIS FACE AT THE DINNER TABLE, NO MATTER WHAT IT TAKES!
OKAY?
WE HAVE MORE INGREDIENTS!

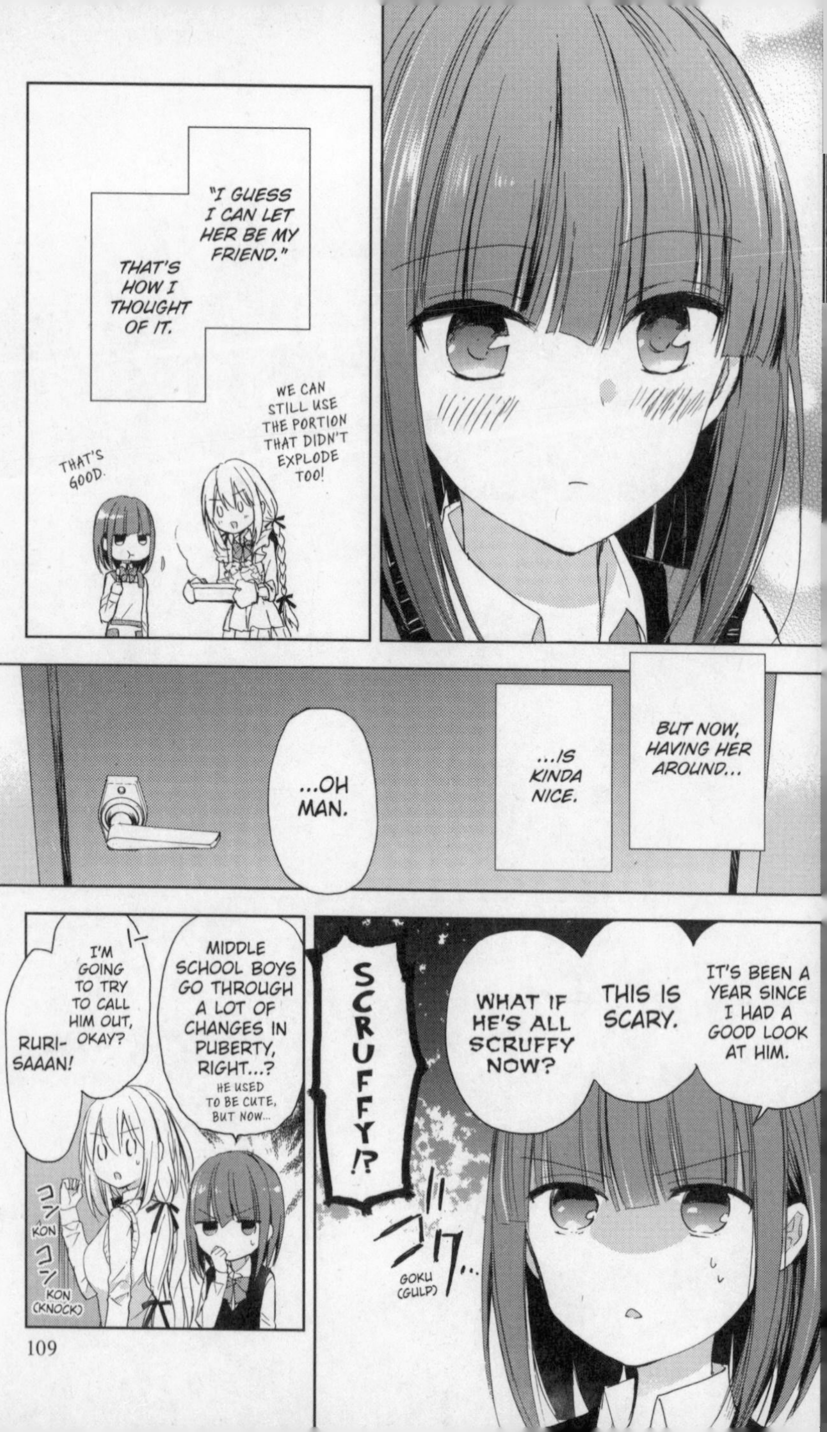
"I GUESS I CAN LET HER BE MY FRIEND."
THAT'S HOW I THOUGHT OF IT.
WE CAN STILL USE THE PORTION THAT DIDN'T EXPLODE TOO!
THAT'S GOOD.
BUT NOW, HAVING HER AROUND...
...IS KINDA NICE.
...OH MAN.
IT'S BEEN A YEAR SINCE I HAD A GOOD LOOK AT HIM.
THIS IS SCARY.
WHAT IF HE'S ALL SCRUFFY NOW?
GOKU (GULP)
SCRUFFY!?
MIDDLE SCHOOL BOYS GO THROUGH A LOT OF CHANGES IN PUBERTY, RIGHT...?
HE USED TO BE CUTE, BUT NOW...
I'M GOING TO TRY TO CALL HIM OUT, OKAY?
RURI-SAAAN!
KON
KON (KNOCK)

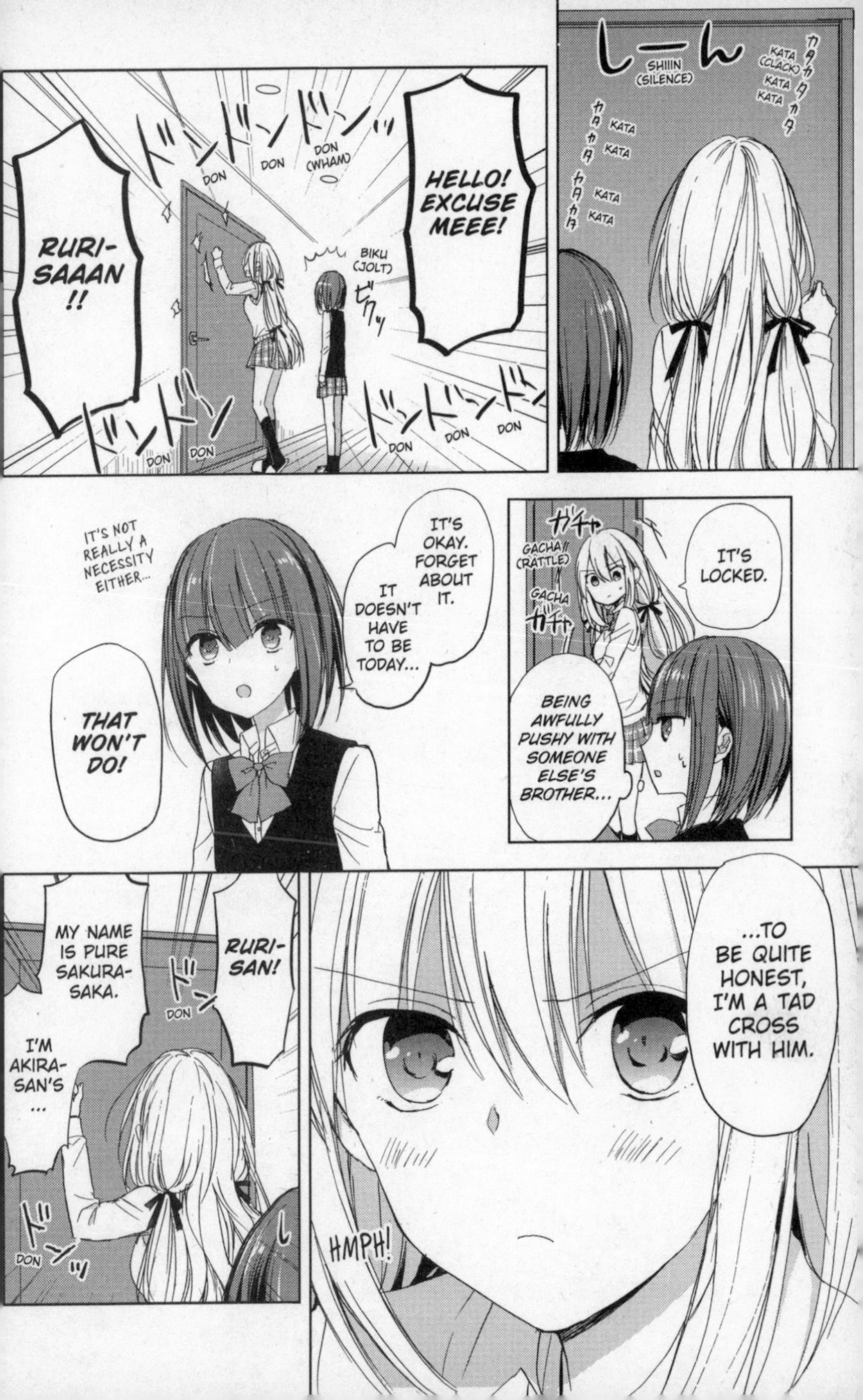
しーん
SHIIIN (SILENCE)
KATA (CLACK) KATA KATA
KATA KATA
KATA KATA
HELLO! EXCUSE MEEE!
DON (WHAM)
DON
DON
BIKU (JOLT)
RURI-SAAAN!!
DON DON DON
DON DON
IT'S LOCKED.
GACHA (RATTLE)
GACHA
BEING AWFULLY PUSHY WITH SOMEONE ELSE'S BROTHER...
IT'S OKAY. FORGET ABOUT IT.
IT DOESN'T HAVE TO BE TODAY...
IT'S NOT REALLY A NECESSITY EITHER...
THAT WON'T DO!
...TO BE QUITE HONEST, I'M A TAD CROSS WITH HIM.
HMPH!
RURI-SAN!
MY NAME IS PURE SAKURA-SAKA.
DON
I'M AKIRA-SAN'S ...
DON

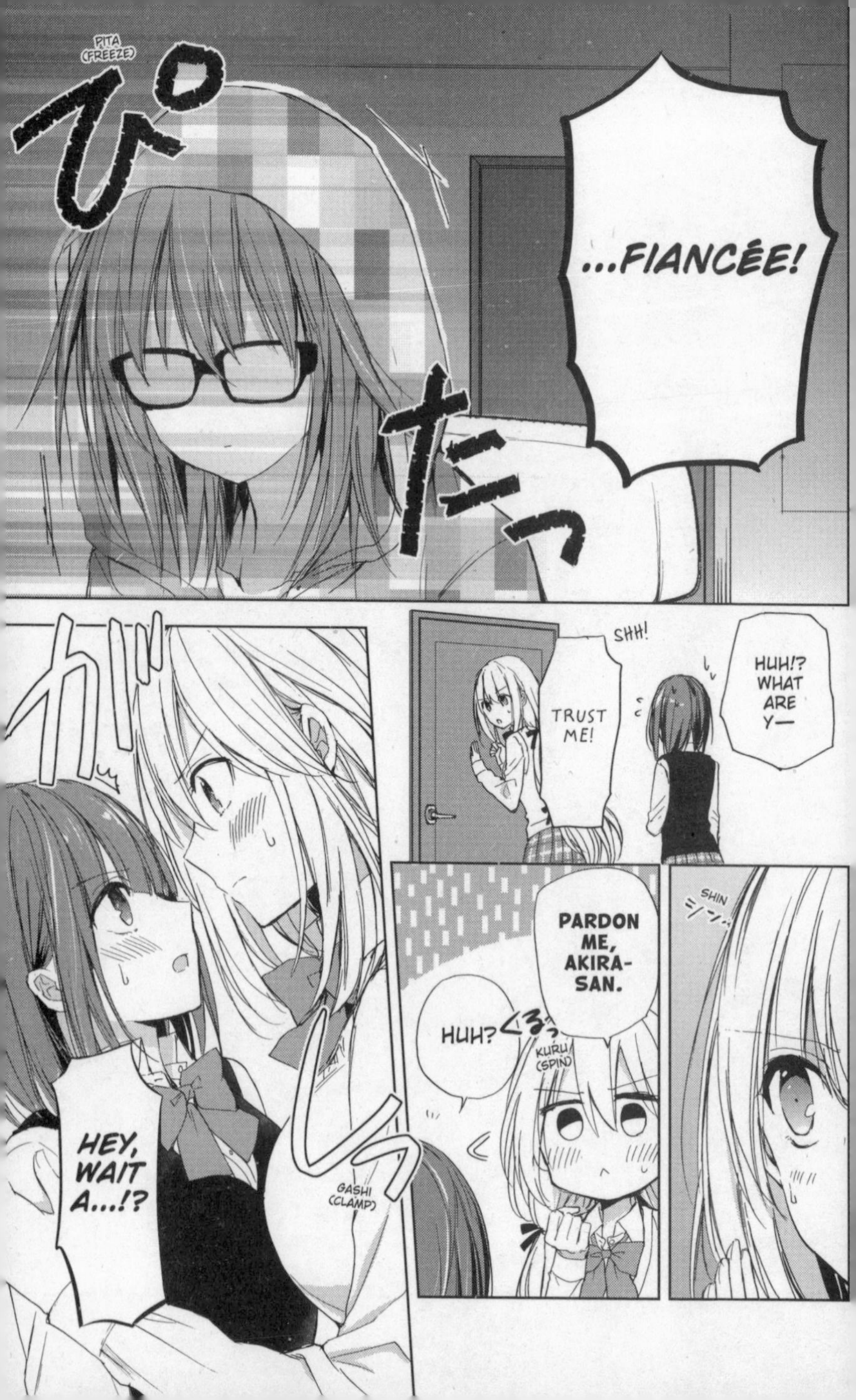
...FIANCÉE!
PITA (FREEZE)
HUH!? WHAT ARE Y—
SHH!
TRUST ME!
SHIN
PARDON ME, AKIRA-SAN.
KURU (SPIN)
HUH?
GASHI (CLAMP)
HEY, WAIT A...!?

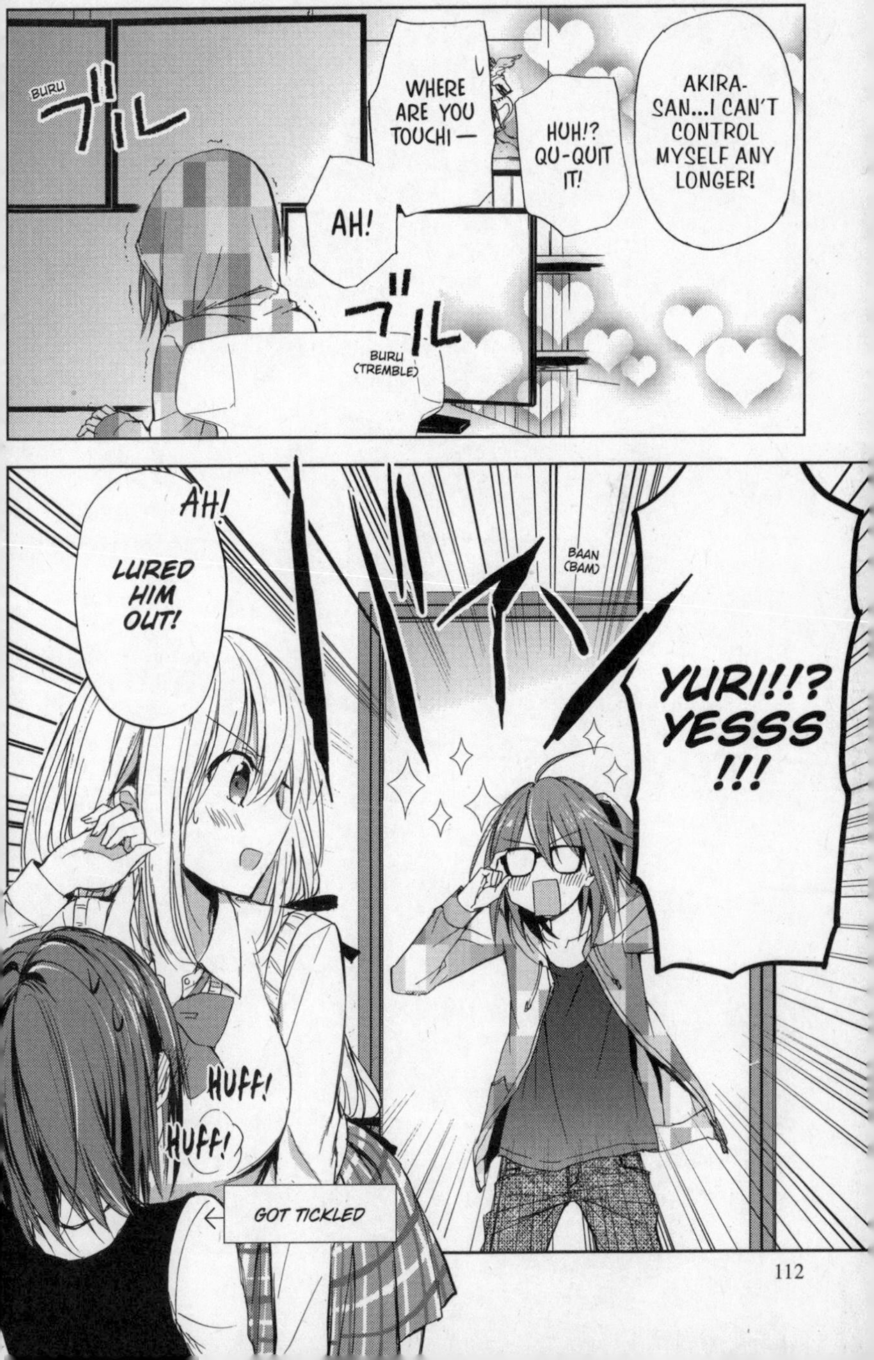
AKIRA-SAN...I CAN'T CONTROL MYSELF ANY LONGER!
HUH!? QU-QUIT IT!
WHERE ARE YOU TOUCHI—
AH!
BURU (TREMBLE)
BURU
YURI!!? YESSS!!!
BAAN (BAM)
AH! LURED HIM OUT!
HUFF! HUFF!
GOT TICKLED

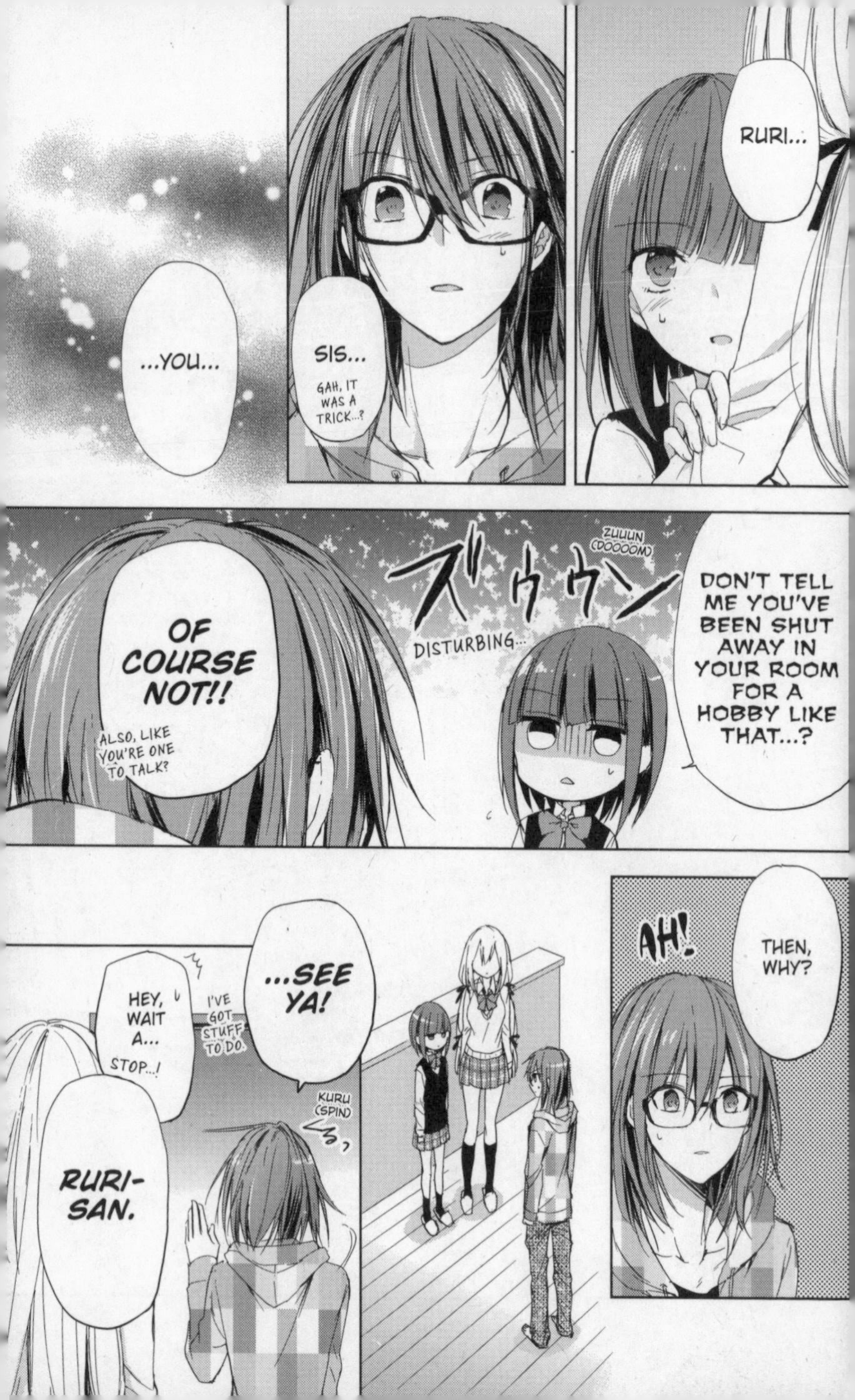
RURI...
SIS...
GAH, IT WAS A TRICK...?
...YOU...
DON'T TELL ME YOU'VE BEEN SHUT AWAY IN YOUR ROOM FOR A HOBBY LIKE THAT...?
ZUUUN (DOOOOM)
DISTURBING...
OF COURSE NOT!!
ALSO, LIKE YOU'RE ONE TO TALK?
THEN, WHY?
AH!
...SEE YA!
I'VE GOT STUFF TO DO.
KURU (SPIN)
HEY, WAIT A...
STOP...!
RURI-SAN.

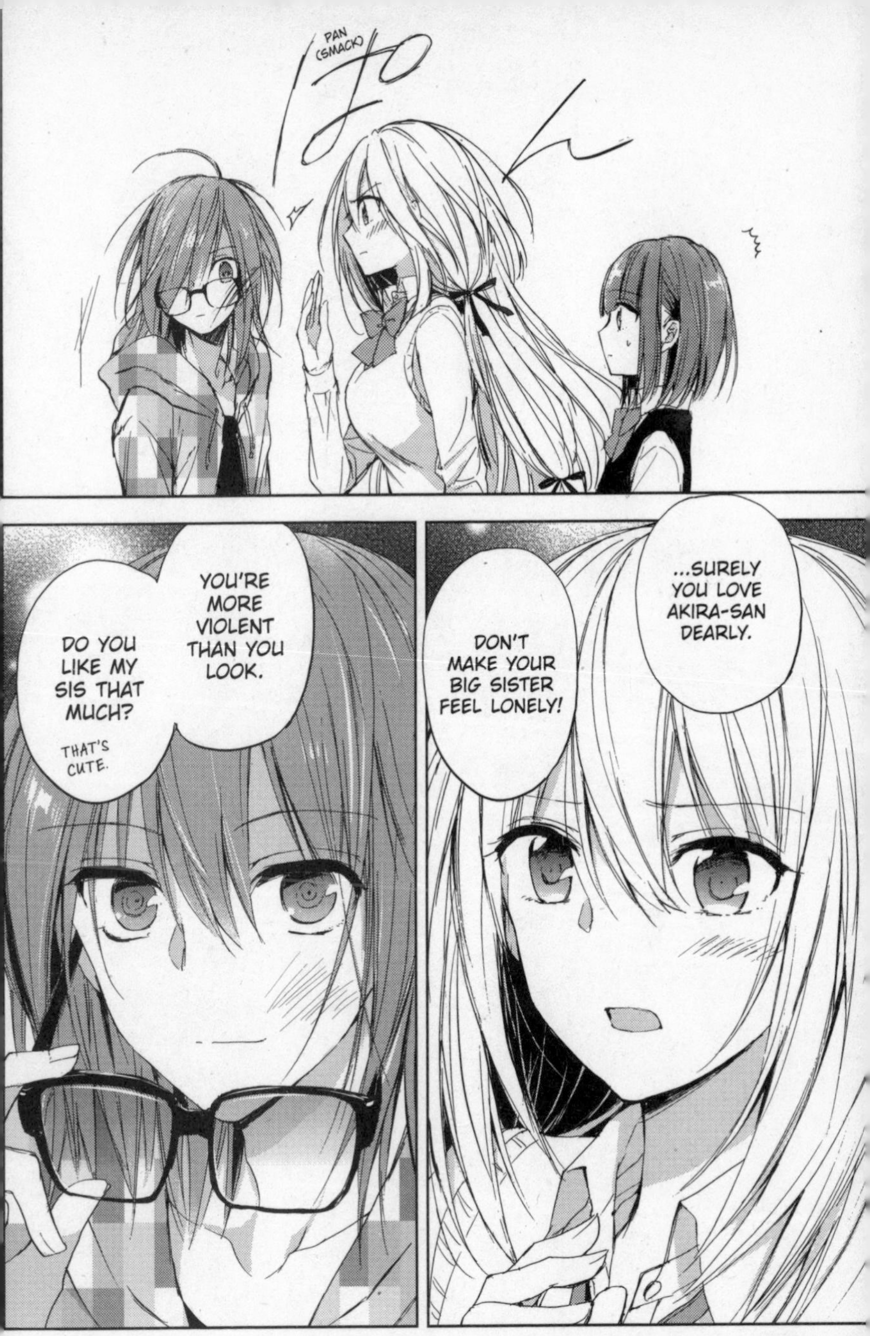
PAN (SMACK)
...SURELY YOU LOVE AKIRA-SAN DEARLY.
DON'T MAKE YOUR BIG SISTER FEEL LONELY!
YOU'RE MORE VIOLENT THAN YOU LOOK.
DO YOU LIKE MY SIS THAT MUCH?
THAT'S CUTE.

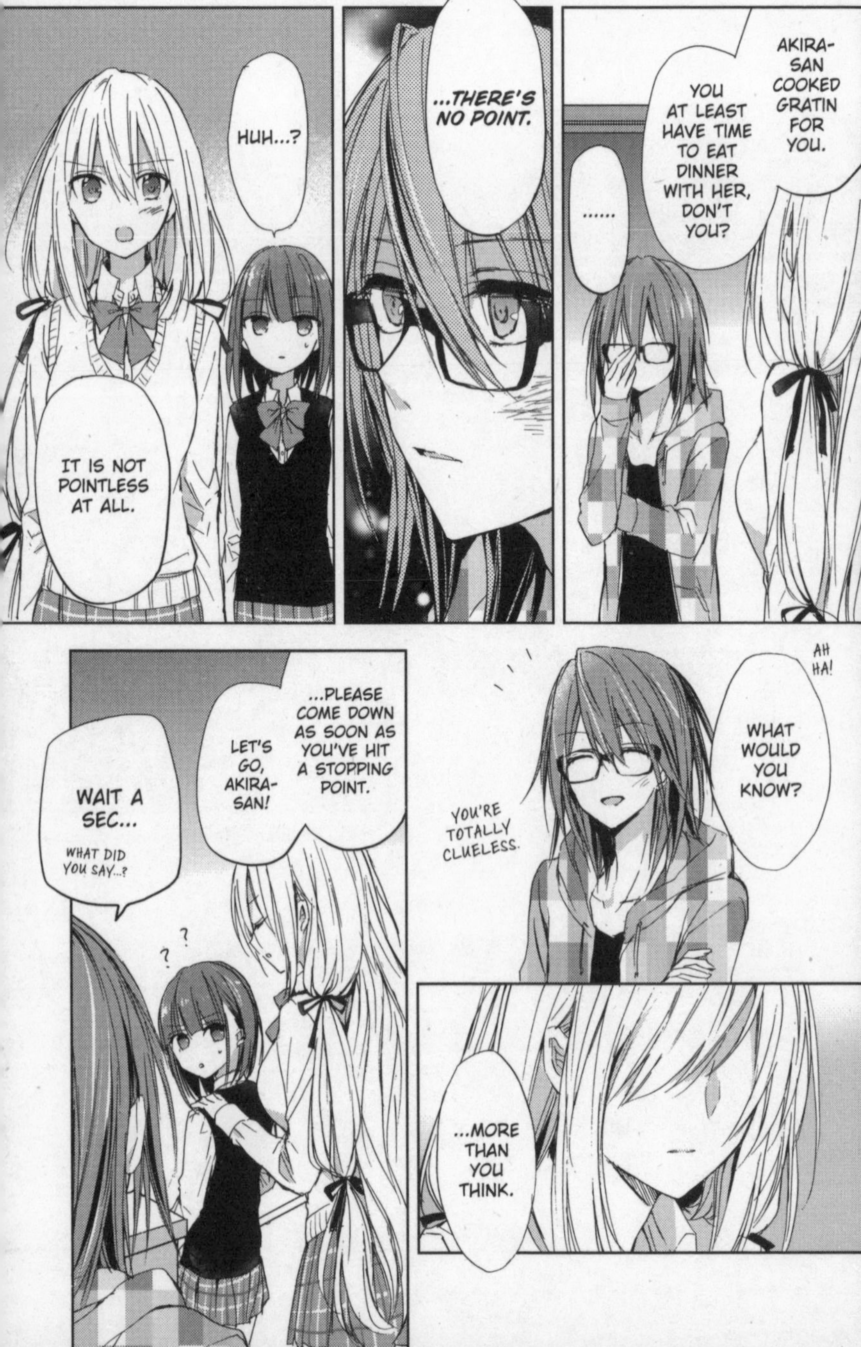
AKIRA-SAN COOKED GRATIN FOR YOU.
YOU AT LEAST HAVE TIME TO EAT DINNER WITH HER, DON'T YOU?
......
...THERE'S NO POINT.
HUH...?
IT IS NOT POINTLESS AT ALL.
AH HA!
WHAT WOULD YOU KNOW?
YOU'RE TOTALLY CLUELESS.
...MORE THAN YOU THINK.
...PLEASE COME DOWN AS SOON AS YOU'VE HIT A STOPPING POINT.
LET'S GO, AKIRA-SAN!
WAIT A SEC...
WHAT DID YOU SAY...?
?
?

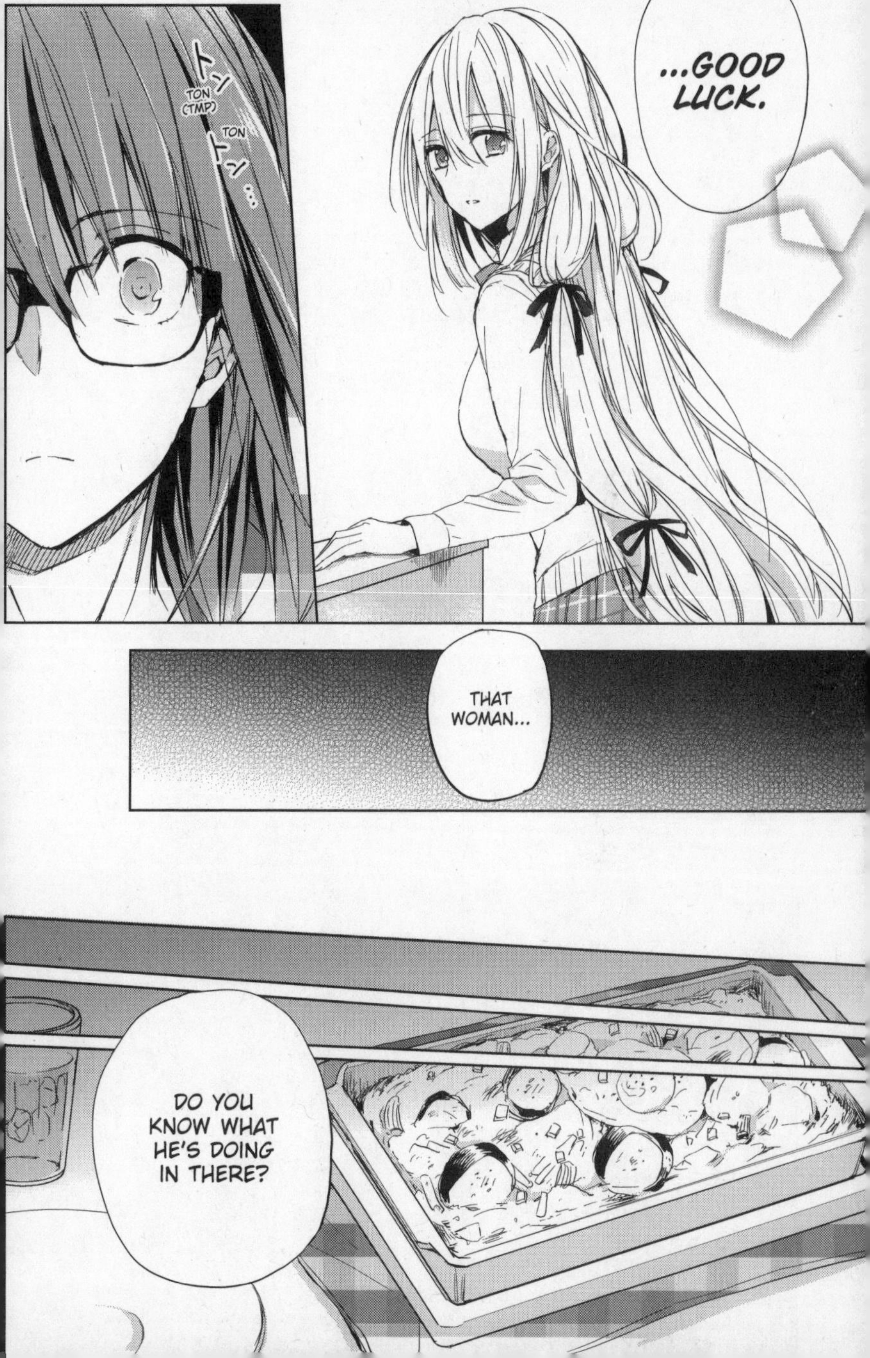
...GOOD LUCK.
トン TON (TMP)
トン… TON
THAT WOMAN...
DO YOU KNOW WHAT HE'S DOING IN THERE?

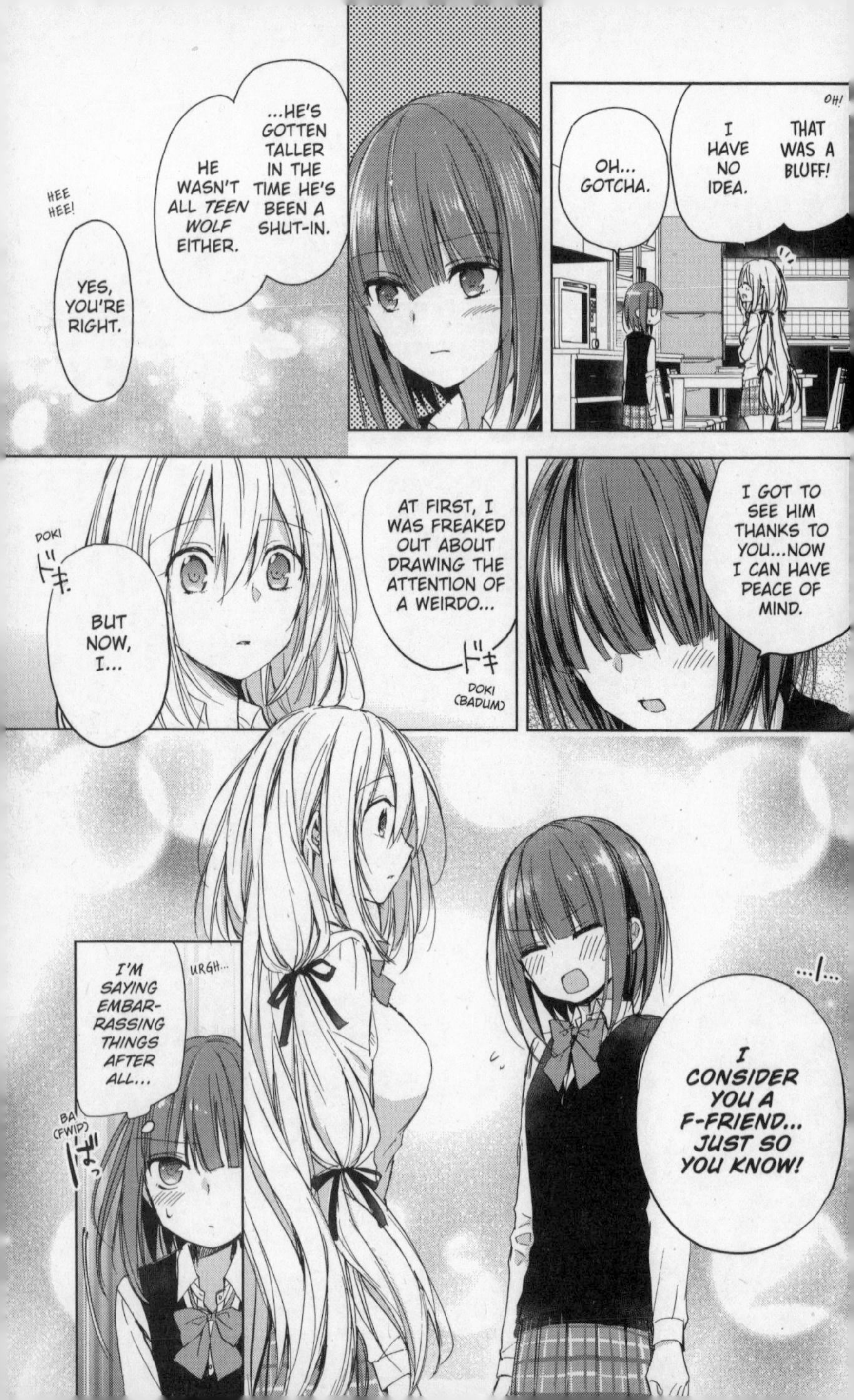
OH! THAT WAS A BLUFF!
I HAVE NO IDEA.
OH... GOTCHA.
...HE'S GOTTEN TALLER IN THE TIME HE'S BEEN A SHUT-IN.
HE WASN'T ALL *TEEN WOLF* EITHER.
HEE HEE!
YES, YOU'RE RIGHT.
I GOT TO SEE HIM THANKS TO YOU...NOW I CAN HAVE PEACE OF MIND.
AT FIRST, I WAS FREAKED OUT ABOUT DRAWING THE ATTENTION OF A WEIRDO...
DOKI (BADUM)
DOKI
BUT NOW, I...
...I...
I CONSIDER YOU A F-FRIEND... JUST SO YOU KNOW!
URGH...
I'M SAYING EMBARRASSING THINGS AFTER ALL...
BA (FWIP)

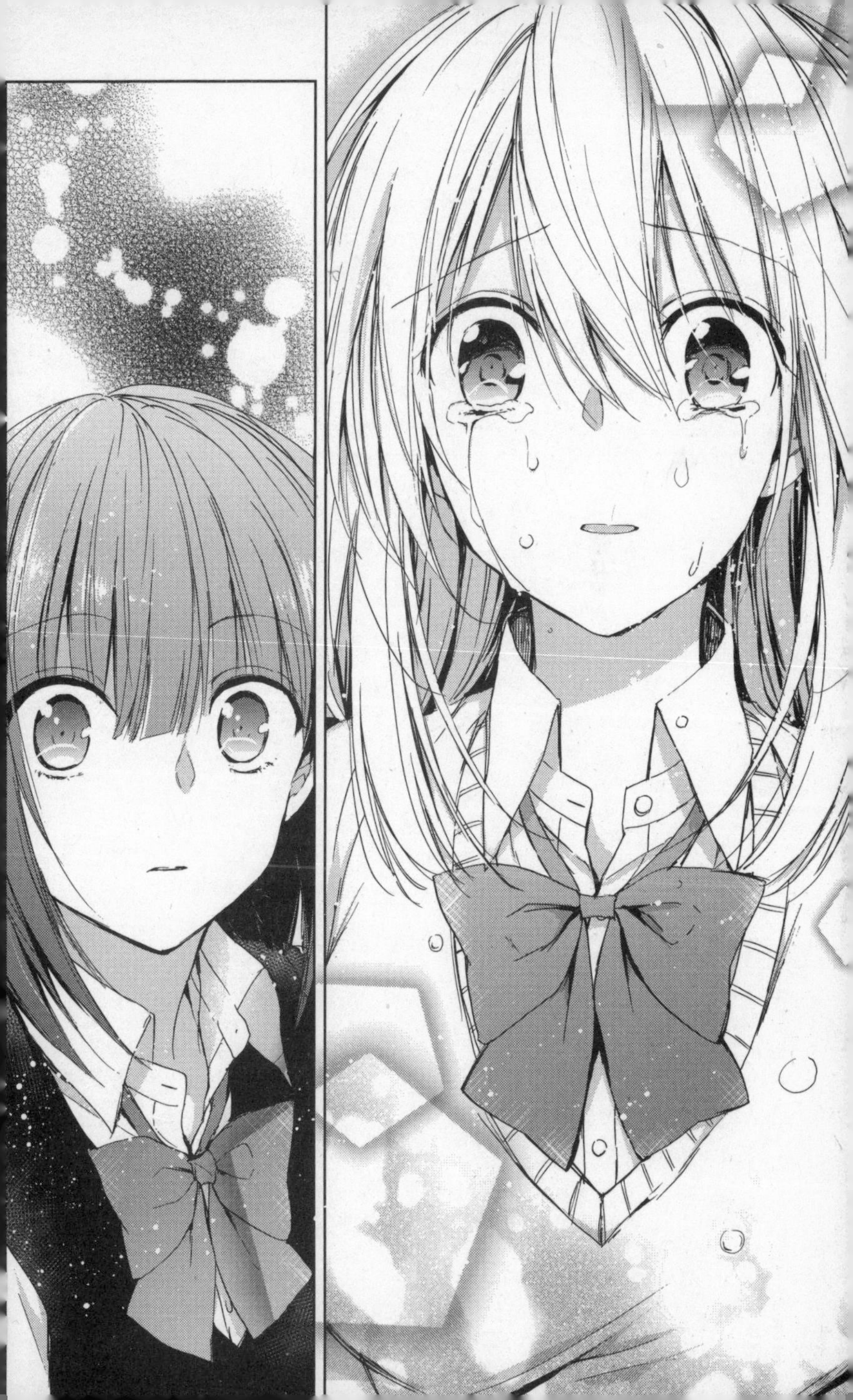

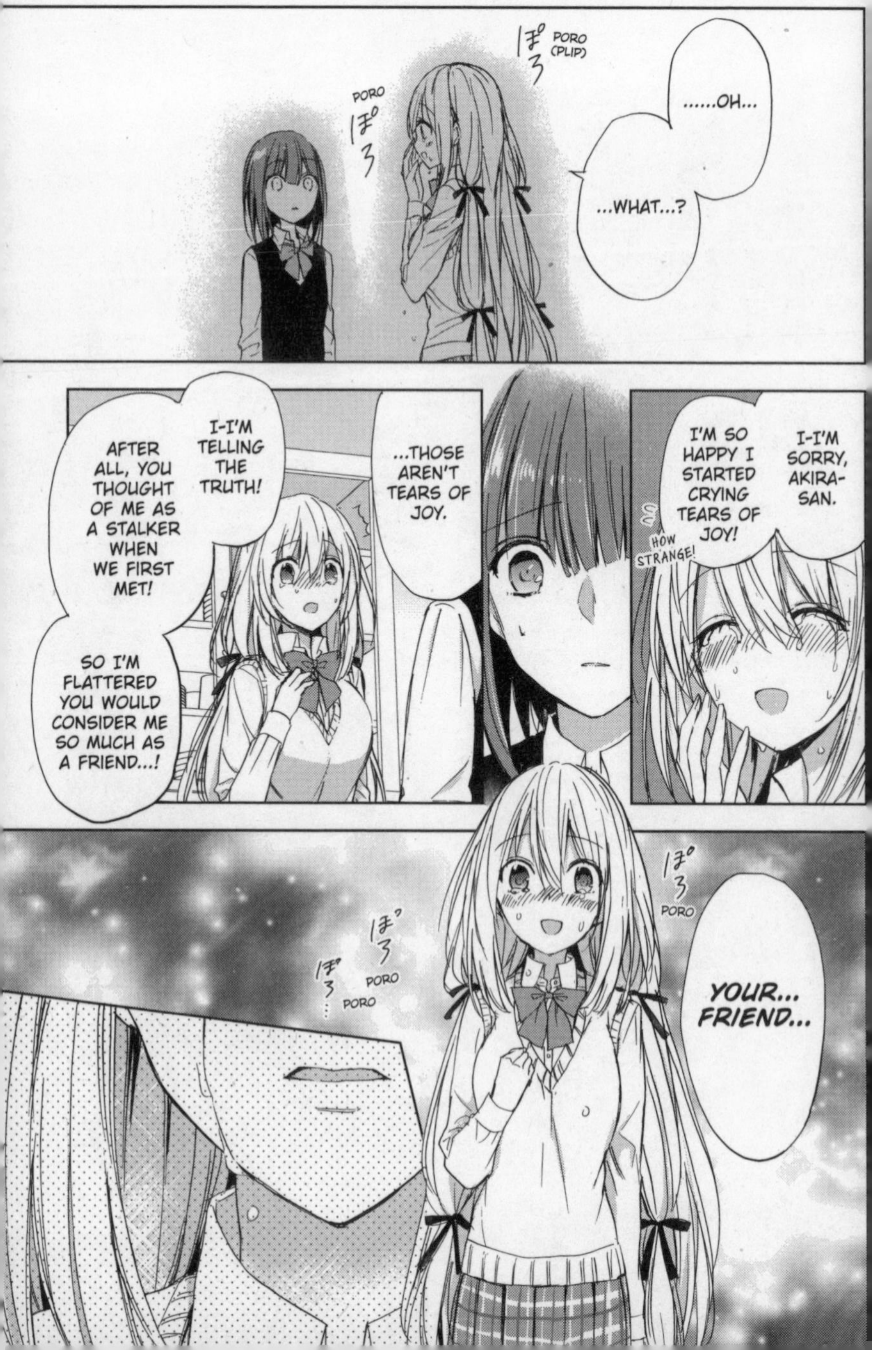
......OH...
...WHAT...?
PORO (PLIP)
PORO
I-I'M SORRY, AKIRA-SAN.
I'M SO HAPPY I STARTED CRYING TEARS OF JOY!
HOW STRANGE!
...THOSE AREN'T TEARS OF JOY.
I-I'M TELLING THE TRUTH!
AFTER ALL, YOU THOUGHT OF ME AS A STALKER WHEN WE FIRST MET!
SO I'M FLATTERED YOU WOULD CONSIDER ME SO MUCH AS A FRIEND...!
PORO
YOUR... FRIEND...
PORO
PORO

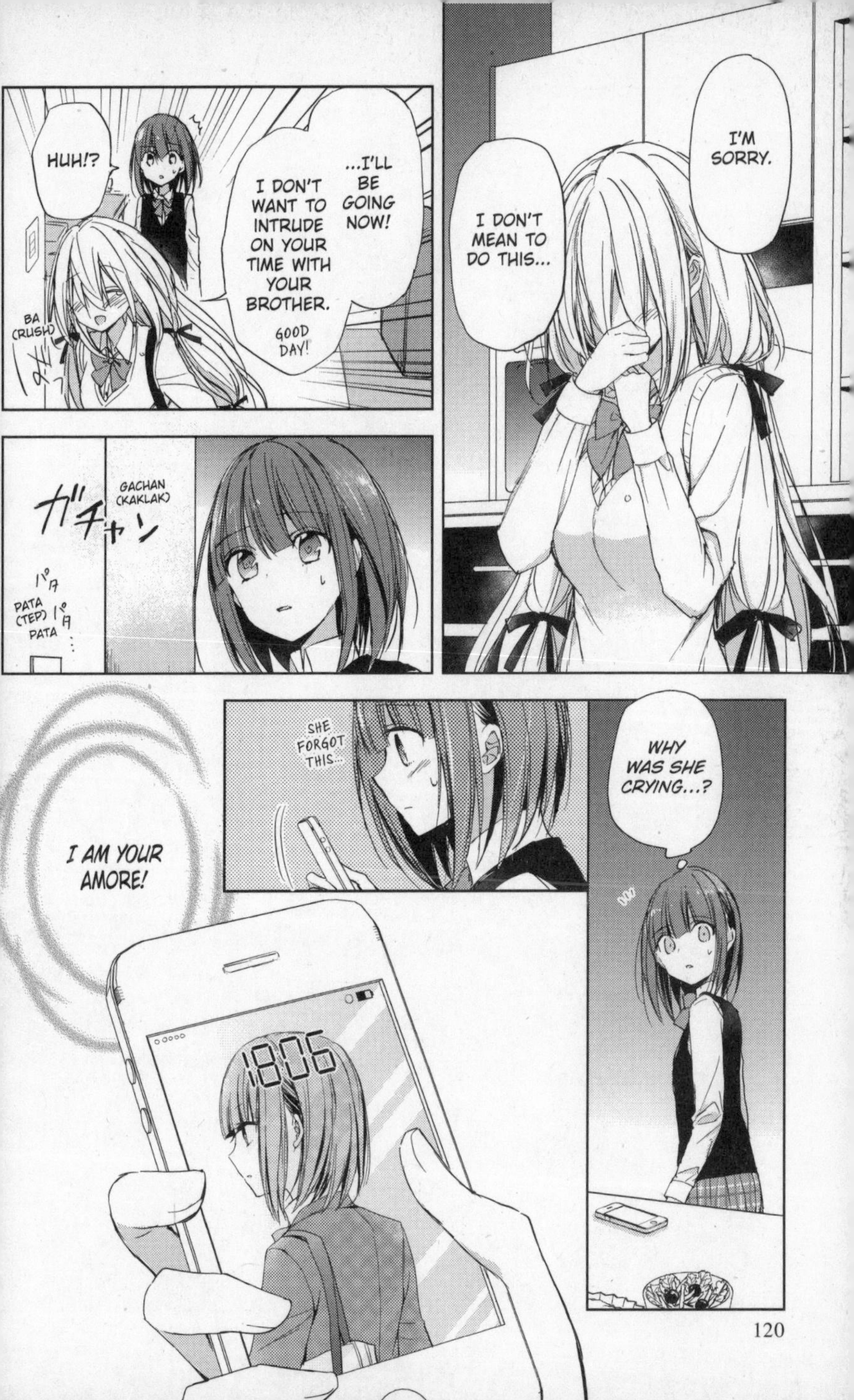
I'M SORRY.
I DON'T MEAN TO DO THIS...
...I'LL BE GOING NOW!
I DON'T WANT TO INTRUDE ON YOUR TIME WITH YOUR BROTHER.
GOOD DAY!
HUH!?
BA (RUSH)
GACHAN (KAKLAK)
PATA (TEP) PATA
WHY WAS SHE CRYING...?
SHE FORGOT THIS...
I AM YOUR AMORE!
1806

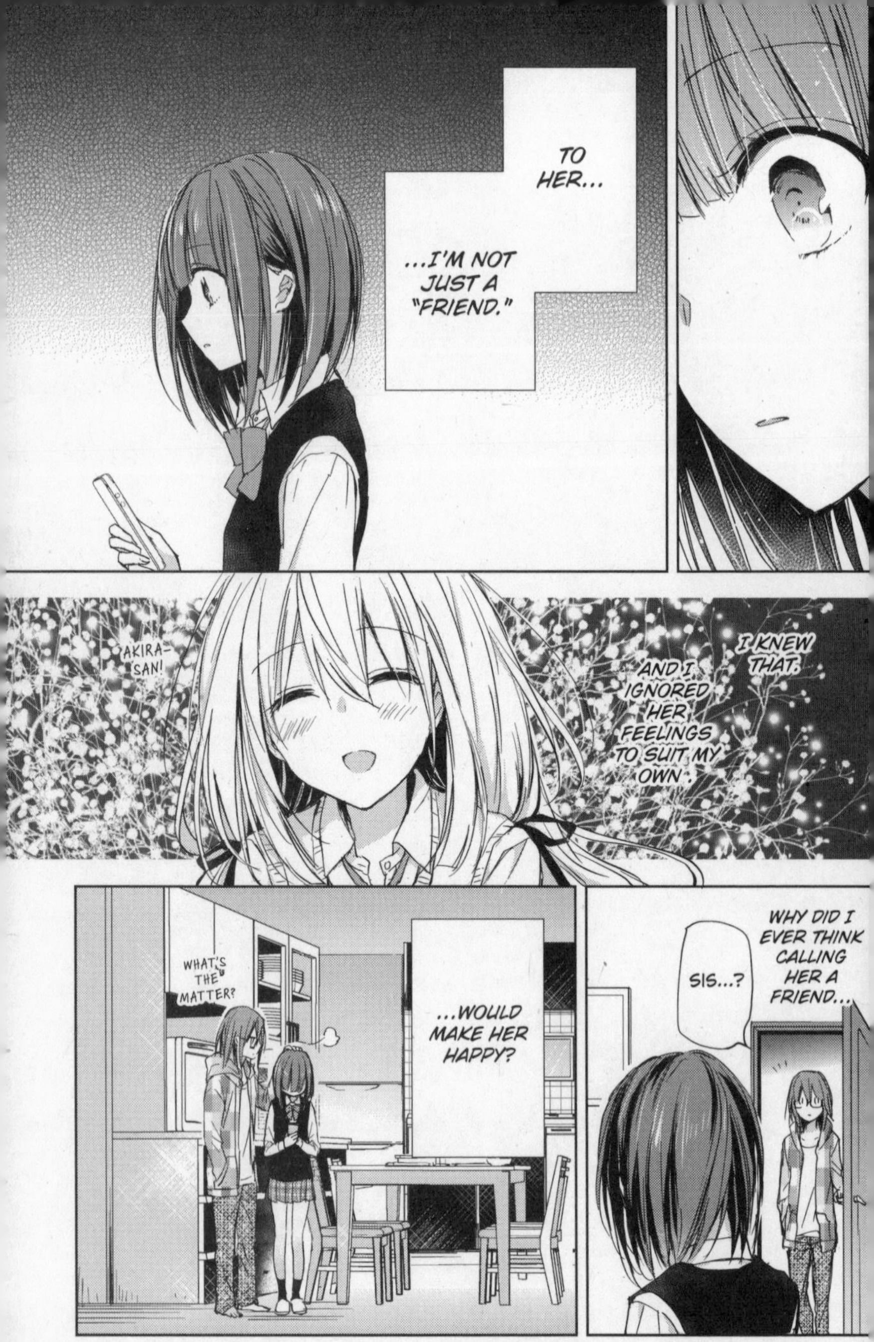
TO HER...
...I'M NOT JUST A "FRIEND."
I KNEW THAT.
AND I IGNORED HER FEELINGS TO SUIT MY OWN.
AKIRA-SAN!
WHY DID I EVER THINK CALLING HER A FRIEND...
SIS...?
...WOULD MAKE HER HAPPY?
WHAT'S THE MATTER?

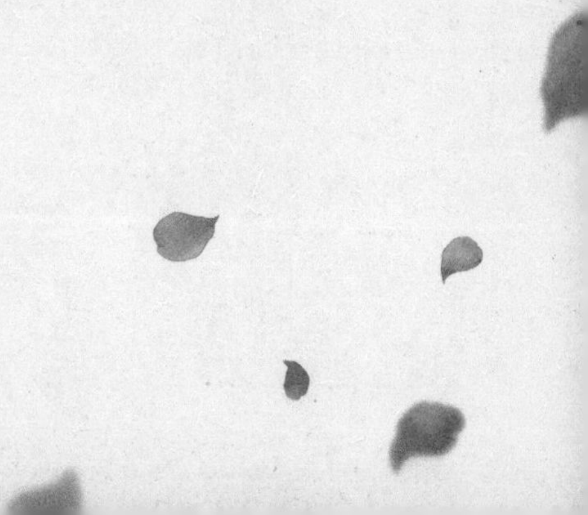

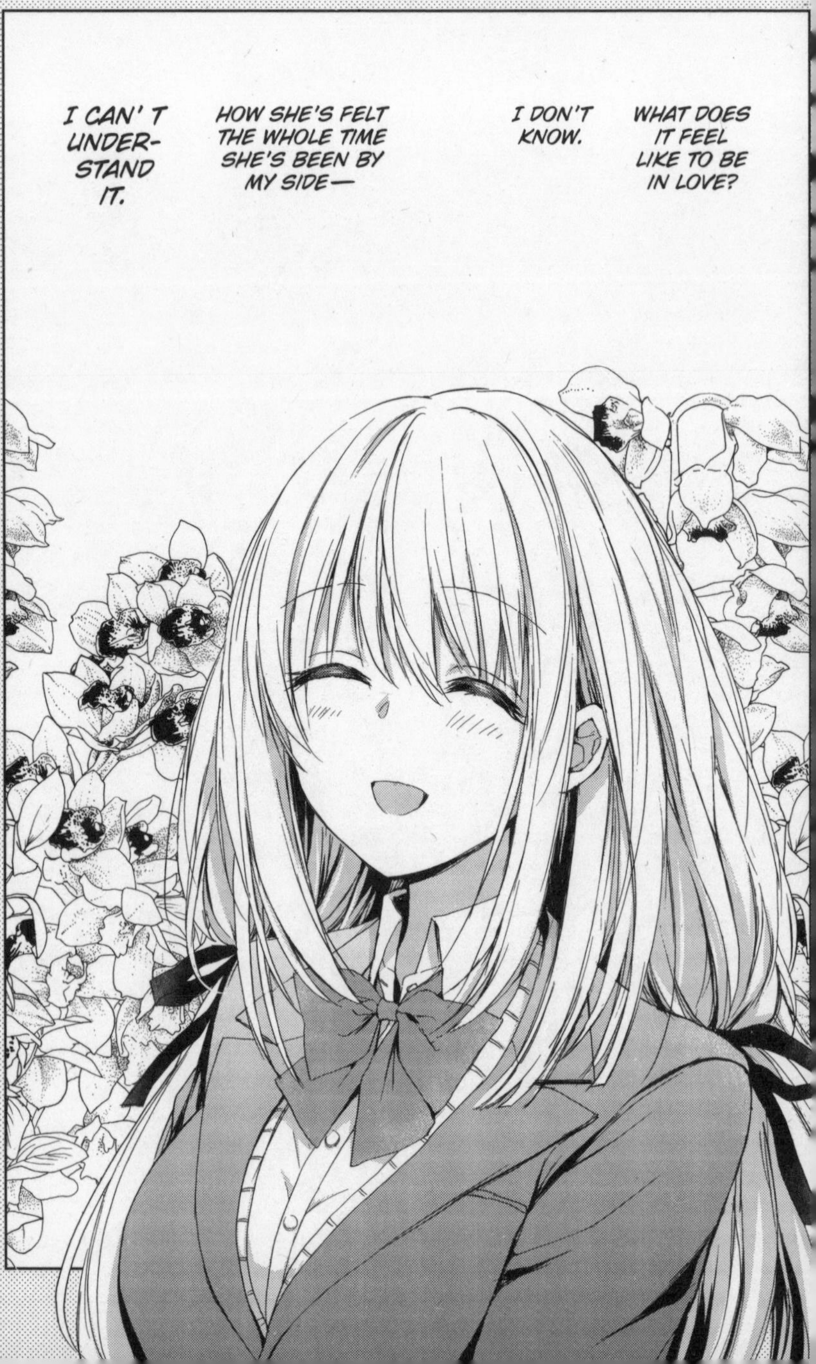
WHAT DOES IT FEEL LIKE TO BE IN LOVE?
I DON'T KNOW.
HOW SHE'S FELT THE WHOLE TIME SHE'S BEEN BY MY SIDE—
I CAN'T UNDERSTAND IT.

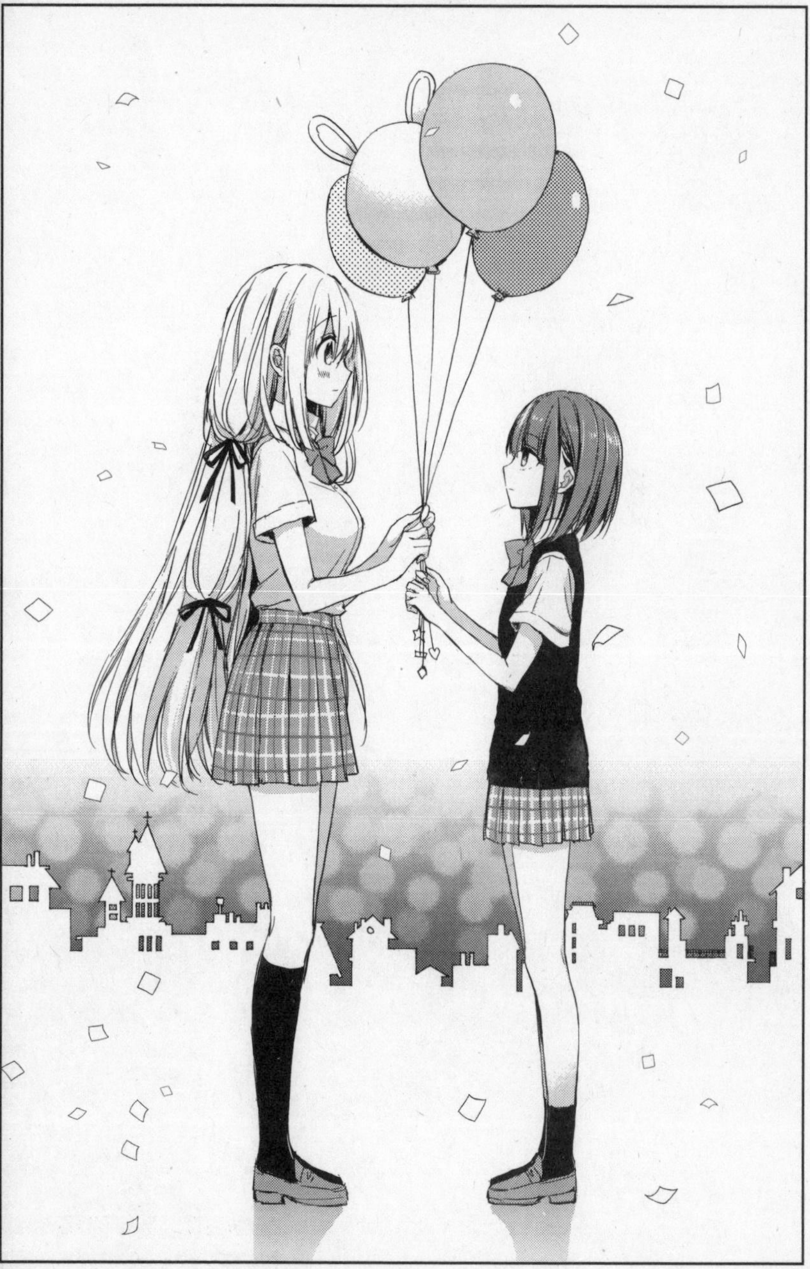

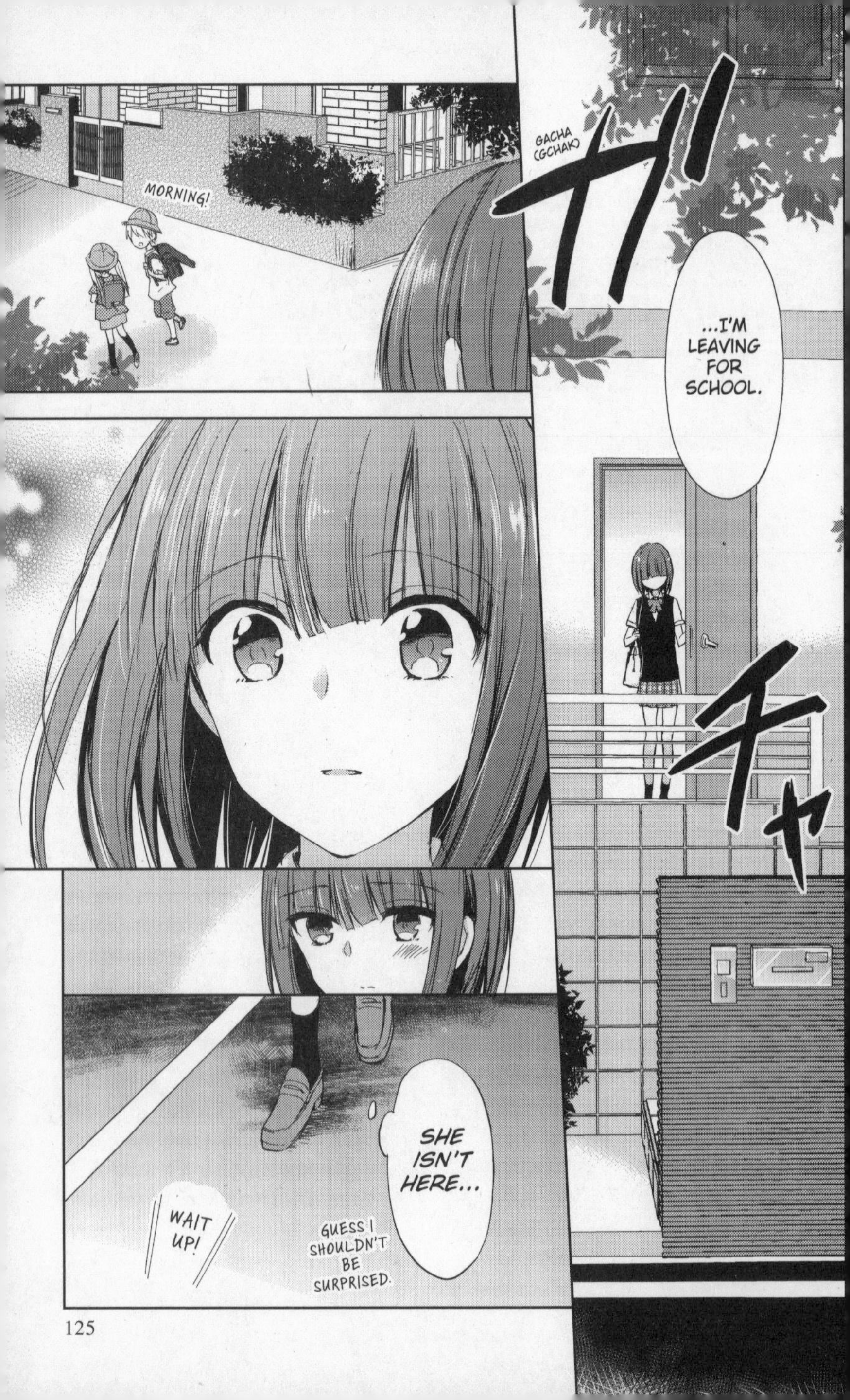
GACHA (GCHAK)
...I'M LEAVING FOR SCHOOL.
MORNING!
SHE ISN'T HERE...
GUESS I SHOULDN'T BE SURPRISED.
WAIT UP!

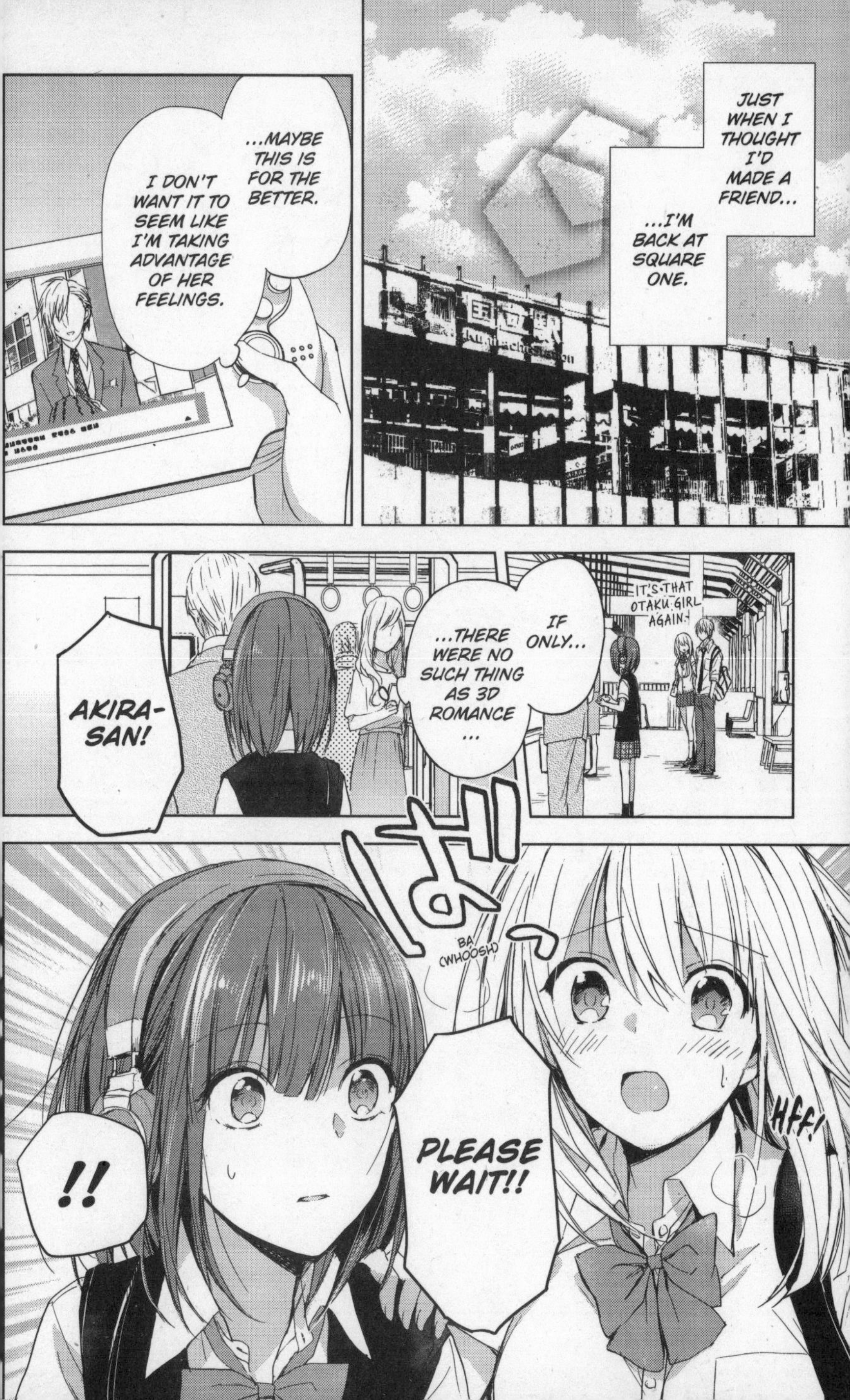
JUST WHEN I THOUGHT I'D MADE A FRIEND...
...I'M BACK AT SQUARE ONE.
...MAYBE THIS IS FOR THE BETTER.
I DON'T WANT IT TO SEEM LIKE I'M TAKING ADVANTAGE OF HER FEELINGS.
IT'S THAT OTAKU GIRL AGAIN.
IF ONLY...
...THERE WERE NO SUCH THING AS 3D ROMANCE...
AKIRA-SAN!
BA (WHOOSH)
HFF!
PLEASE WAIT!!
!!

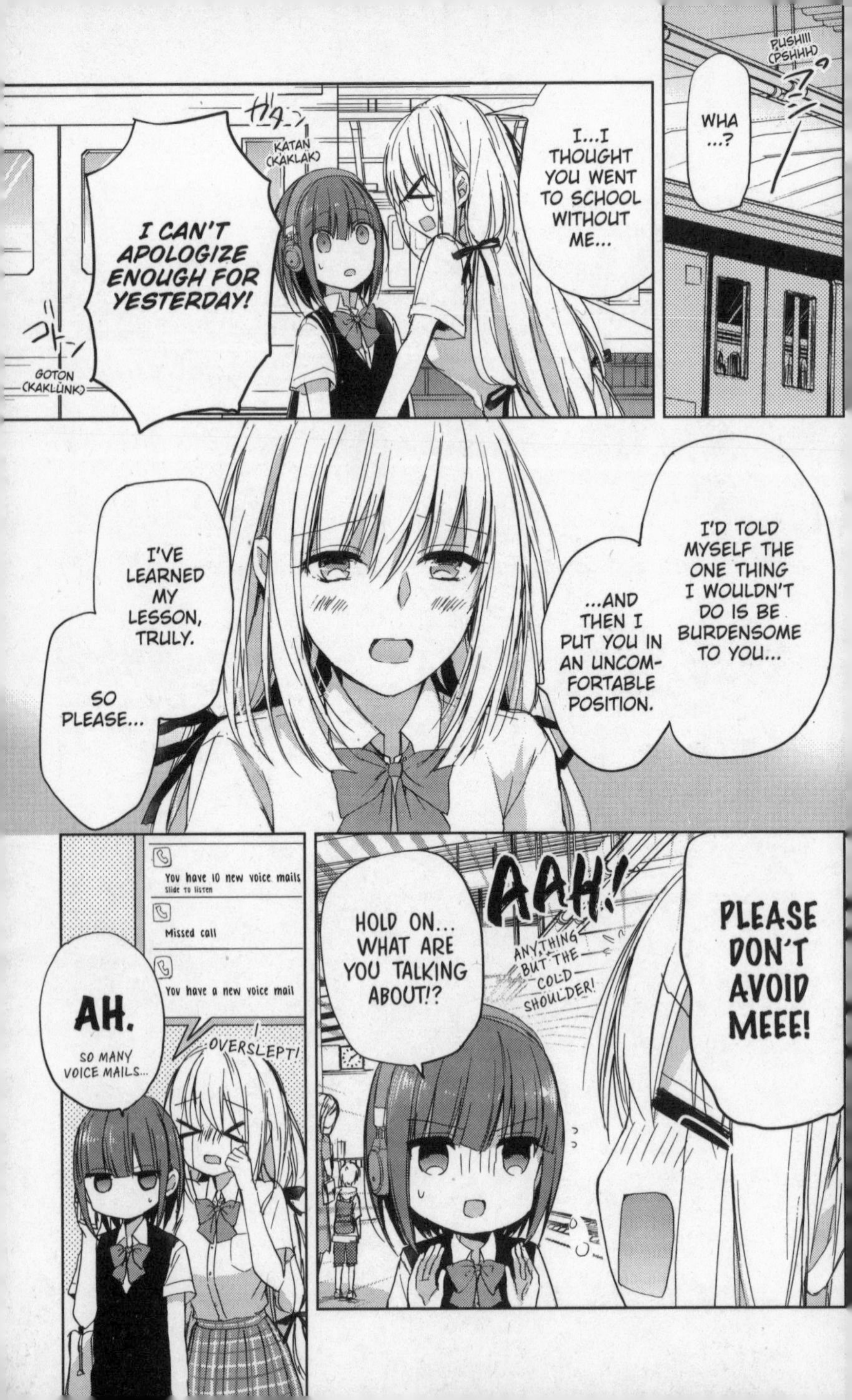
PUSHIII (PSHHH)
WHA ...?
I...I THOUGHT YOU WENT TO SCHOOL WITHOUT ME...
KATAN (KAKLAK)
I CAN'T APOLOGIZE ENOUGH FOR YESTERDAY!
GOTON (KAKLÜNK)
I'D TOLD MYSELF THE ONE THING I WOULDN'T DO IS BE BURDENSOME TO YOU...
...AND THEN I PUT YOU IN AN UNCOM-FORTABLE POSITION.
I'VE LEARNED MY LESSON, TRULY.
SO PLEASE...
PLEASE DON'T AVOID MEEE!
AAH!
ANYTHING BUT THE COLD SHOULDER!
HOLD ON... WHAT ARE YOU TALKING ABOUT!?
You have 10 new voice mails
Slide to listen
Missed call
You have a new voice mail
I OVERSLEPT!
AH.
SO MANY VOICE MAILS...

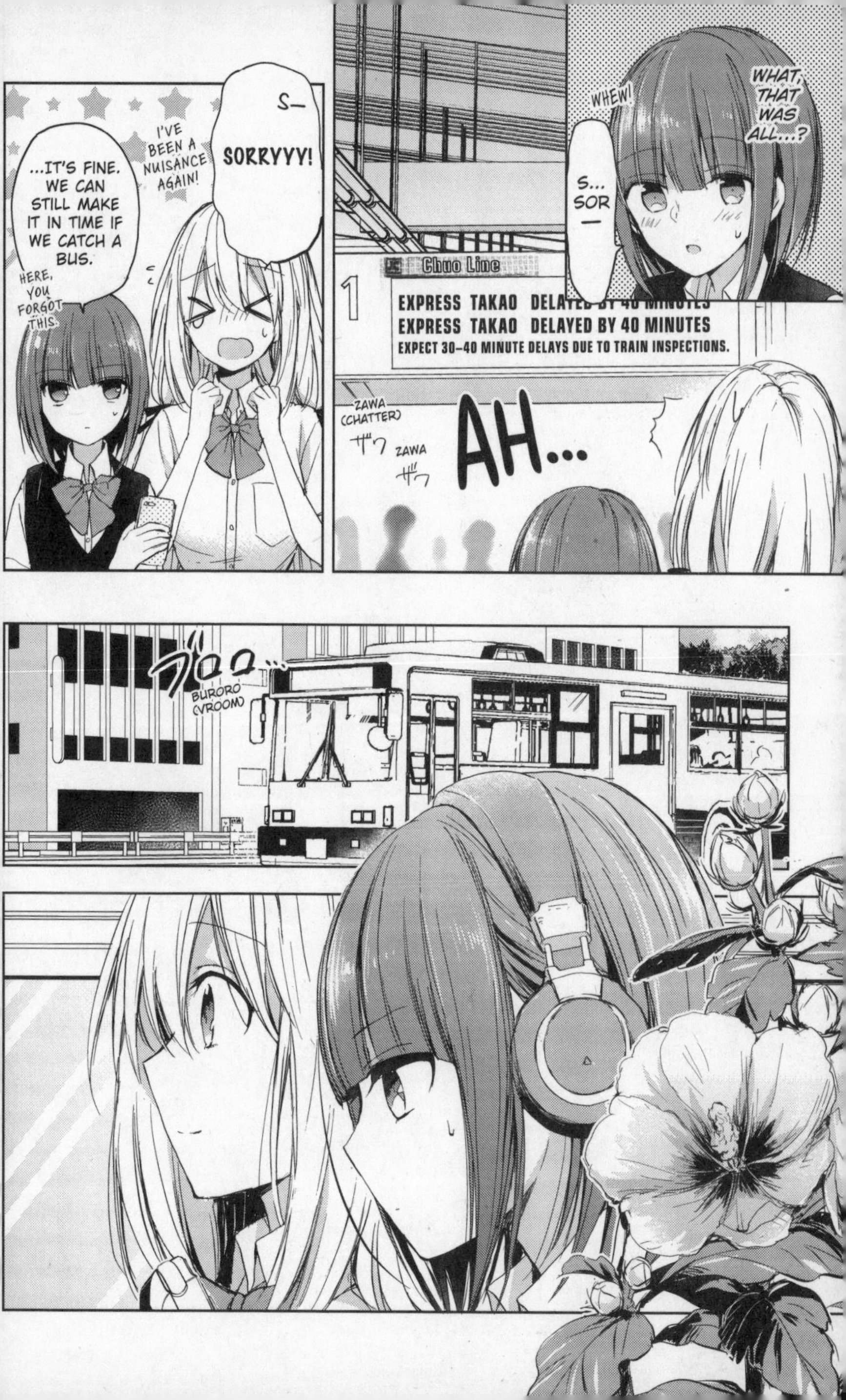
WHAT, THAT WAS ALL...?
WHEW!
S... SOR—
Chuo Line
1
EXPRESS TAKAO DELAYED BY 40 MINUTES
EXPRESS TAKAO DELAYED BY 40 MINUTES
EXPECT 30–40 MINUTE DELAYS DUE TO TRAIN INSPECTIONS.
AH...
ザワ ZAWA (CHATTER)
ザワ ZAWA
S—
SORRYYY!
I'VE BEEN A NUISANCE AGAIN!
...IT'S FINE. WE CAN STILL MAKE IT IN TIME IF WE CATCH A BUS.
HERE, YOU FORGOT THIS.
ブロロ…
BURORO (VROOM)

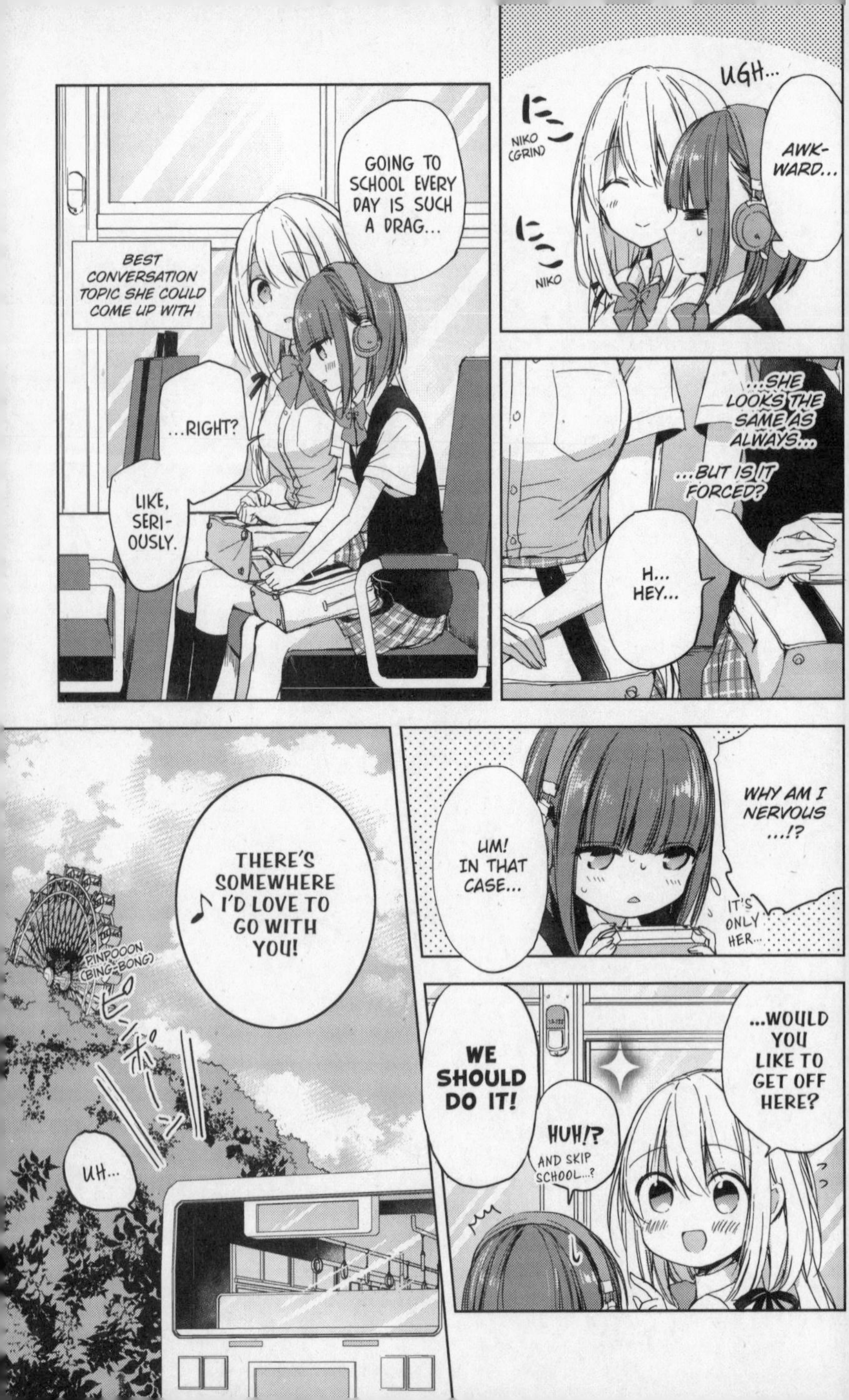

UGH...
AWK-WARD...
NIKO (GRIN)
NIKO
...SHE LOOKS THE SAME AS ALWAYS...
...BUT IS IT FORCED?
H... HEY...
GOING TO SCHOOL EVERY DAY IS SUCH A DRAG...
BEST CONVERSATION TOPIC SHE COULD COME UP WITH
...RIGHT?
LIKE, SERI-OUSLY.
WHY AM I NERVOUS ...!?
IT'S ONLY HER...
UM! IN THAT CASE...
...WOULD YOU LIKE TO GET OFF HERE?
HUH!?
AND SKIP SCHOOL...?
WE SHOULD DO IT!
THERE'S SOMEWHERE I'D LOVE TO GO WITH YOU!
PINPOOON (BING-BONG)
UH...

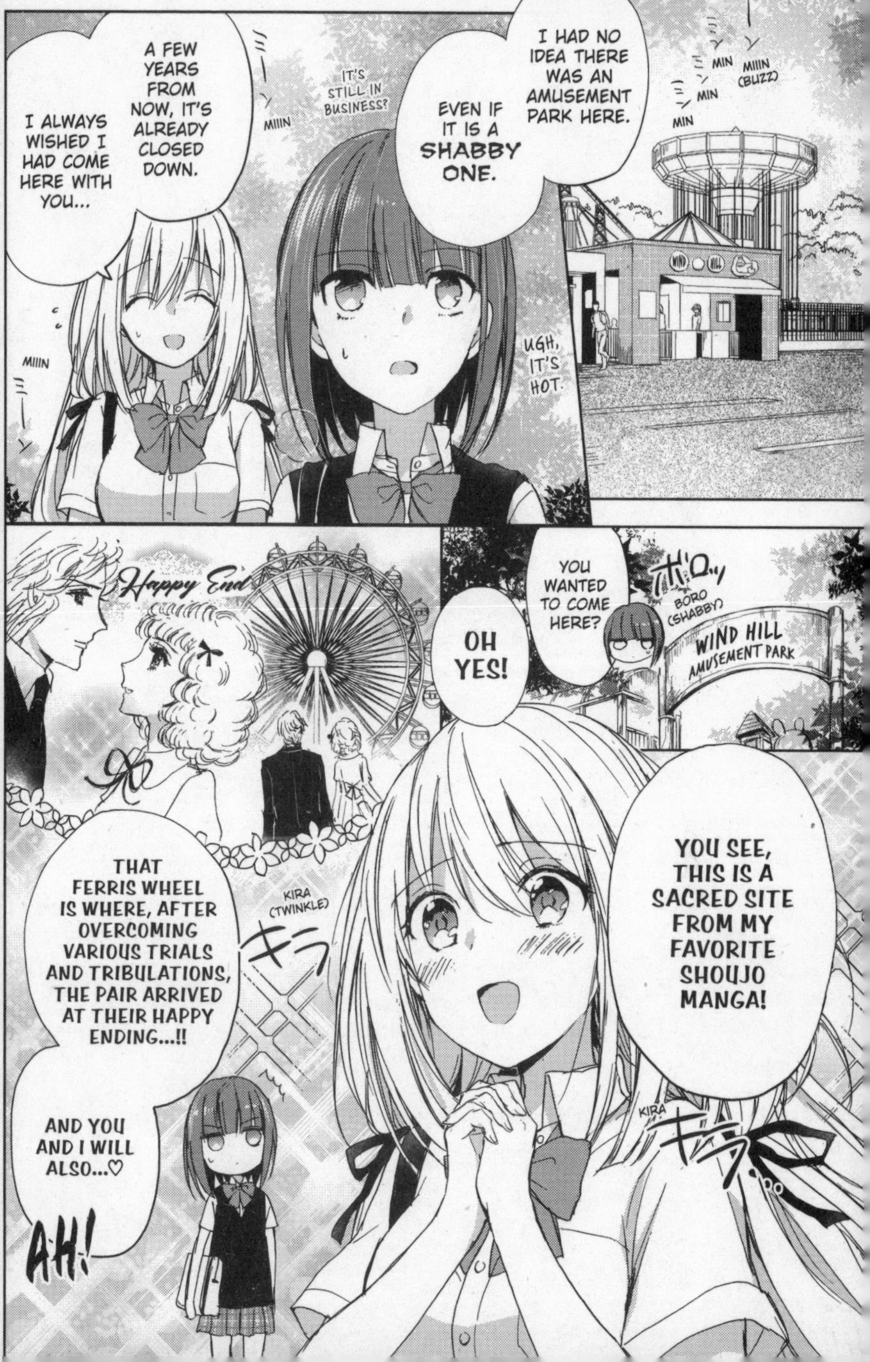
I HAD NO IDEA THERE WAS AN AMUSEMENT PARK HERE.
MIN
MIIIN (BUZZ)
MIN
MIN
WIND HILL
EVEN IF IT IS A SHABBY ONE.
IT'S STILL IN BUSINESS?
UGH, IT'S HOT.
MIIIN
A FEW YEARS FROM NOW, IT'S ALREADY CLOSED DOWN.
I ALWAYS WISHED I HAD COME HERE WITH YOU...
MIIIN
YOU WANTED TO COME HERE?
BORO (SHABBY)
WIND HILL AMUSEMENT PARK
OH YES!
Happy End
YOU SEE, THIS IS A SACRED SITE FROM MY FAVORITE SHOUJO MANGA!
KIRA
THAT FERRIS WHEEL IS WHERE, AFTER OVERCOMING VARIOUS TRIALS AND TRIBULATIONS, THE PAIR ARRIVED AT THEIR HAPPY ENDING...!!
KIRA (TWINKLE)
AND YOU AND I WILL ALSO...♡
AH!

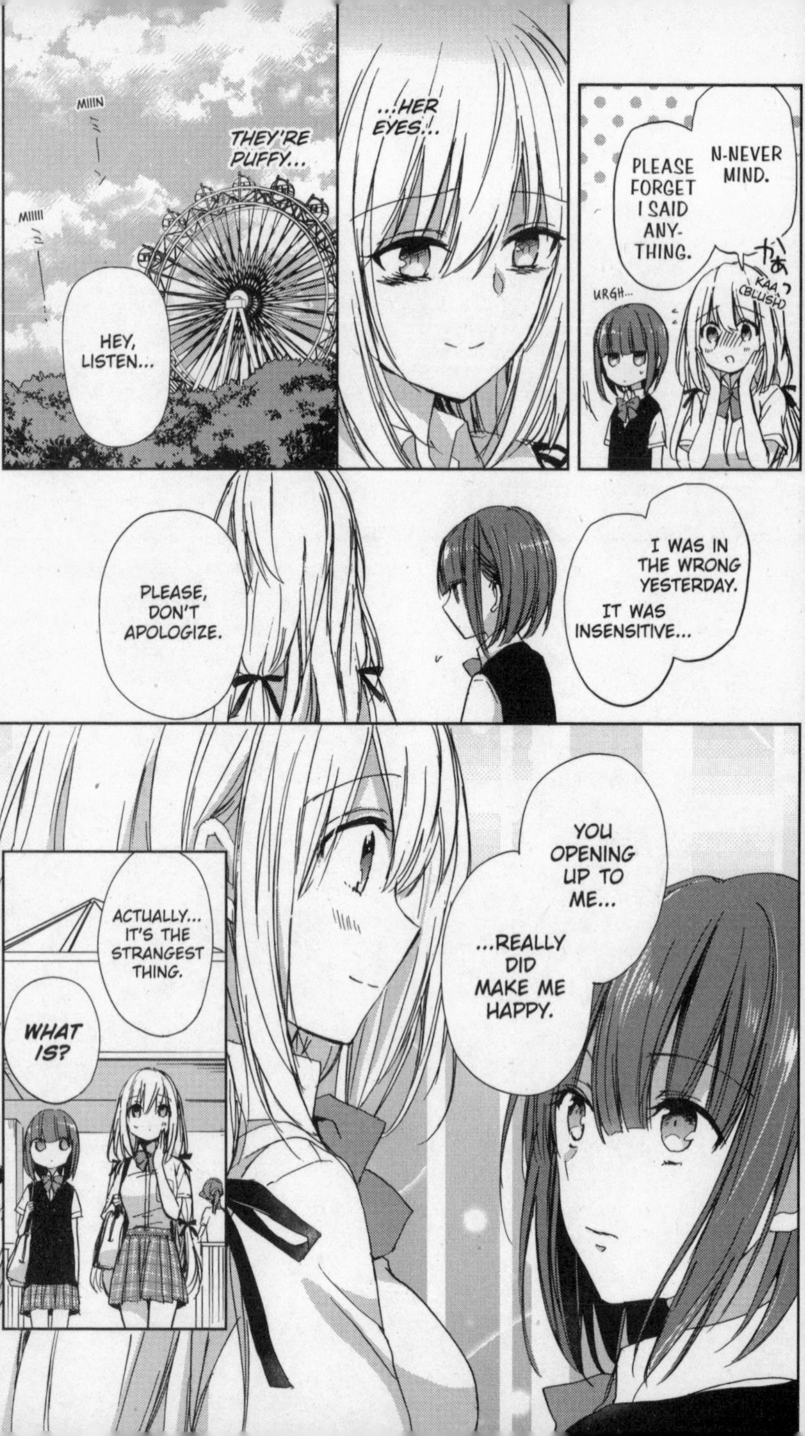
N-NEVER MIND.
PLEASE FORGET I SAID ANYTHING.
KAA (BLUSH)
URGH...
...HER EYES...
THEY'RE PUFFY...
MIIIN
MIIIII
HEY, LISTEN...
I WAS IN THE WRONG YESTERDAY.
IT WAS INSENSITIVE...
PLEASE, DON'T APOLOGIZE.
YOU OPENING UP TO ME...
...REALLY DID MAKE ME HAPPY.
ACTUALLY... IT'S THE STRANGEST THING.
WHAT IS?

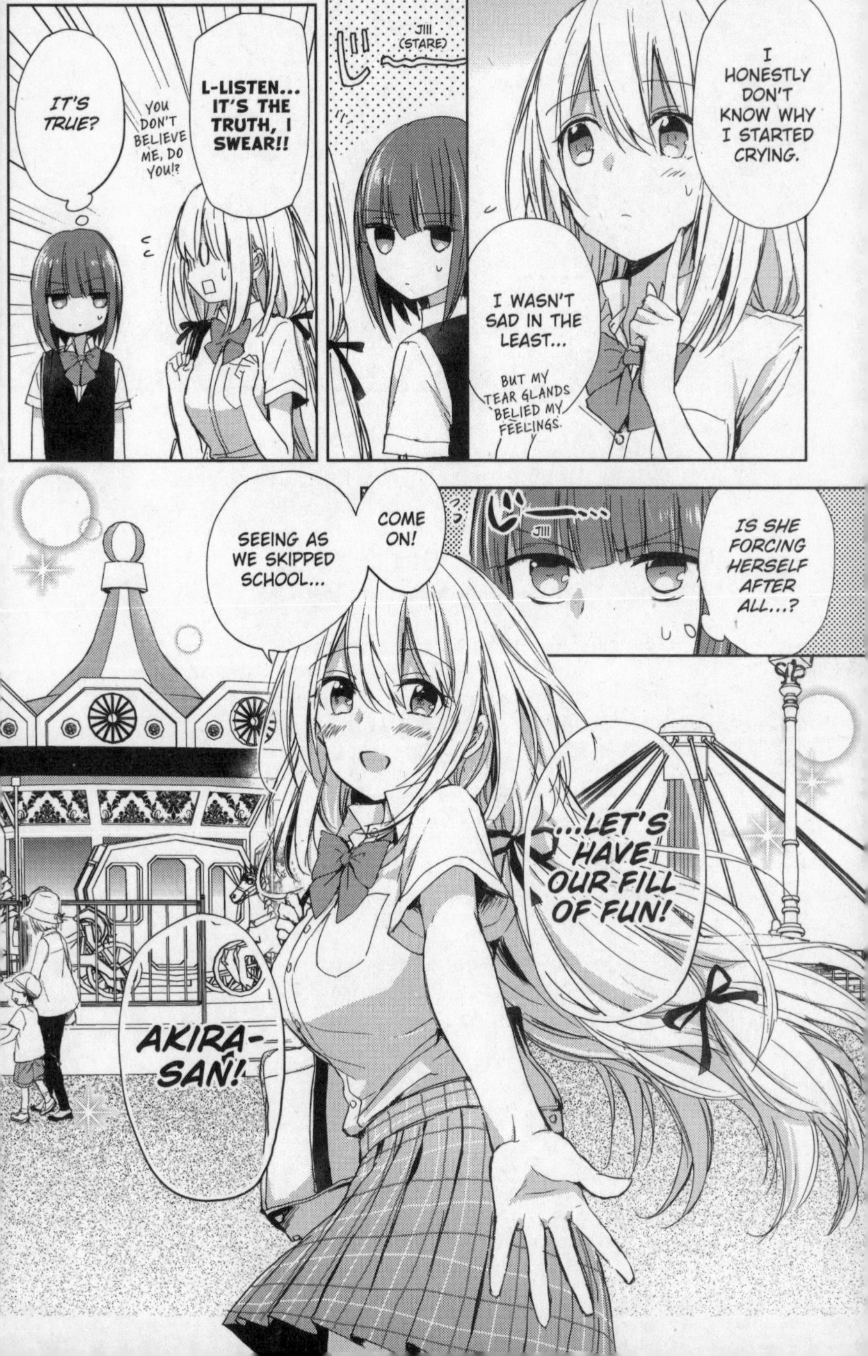
I HONESTLY DON'T KNOW WHY I STARTED CRYING.
I WASN'T SAD IN THE LEAST...
BUT MY TEAR GLANDS BELIED MY FEELINGS.
JIII (STARE)
L-LISTEN... IT'S THE TRUTH, I SWEAR!!
YOU DON'T BELIEVE ME, DO YOU!?
IT'S TRUE?
JIII
IS SHE FORCING HERSELF AFTER ALL...?
COME ON!
SEEING AS WE SKIPPED SCHOOL...
...LET'S HAVE OUR FILL OF FUN!
AKIRA-SAN!

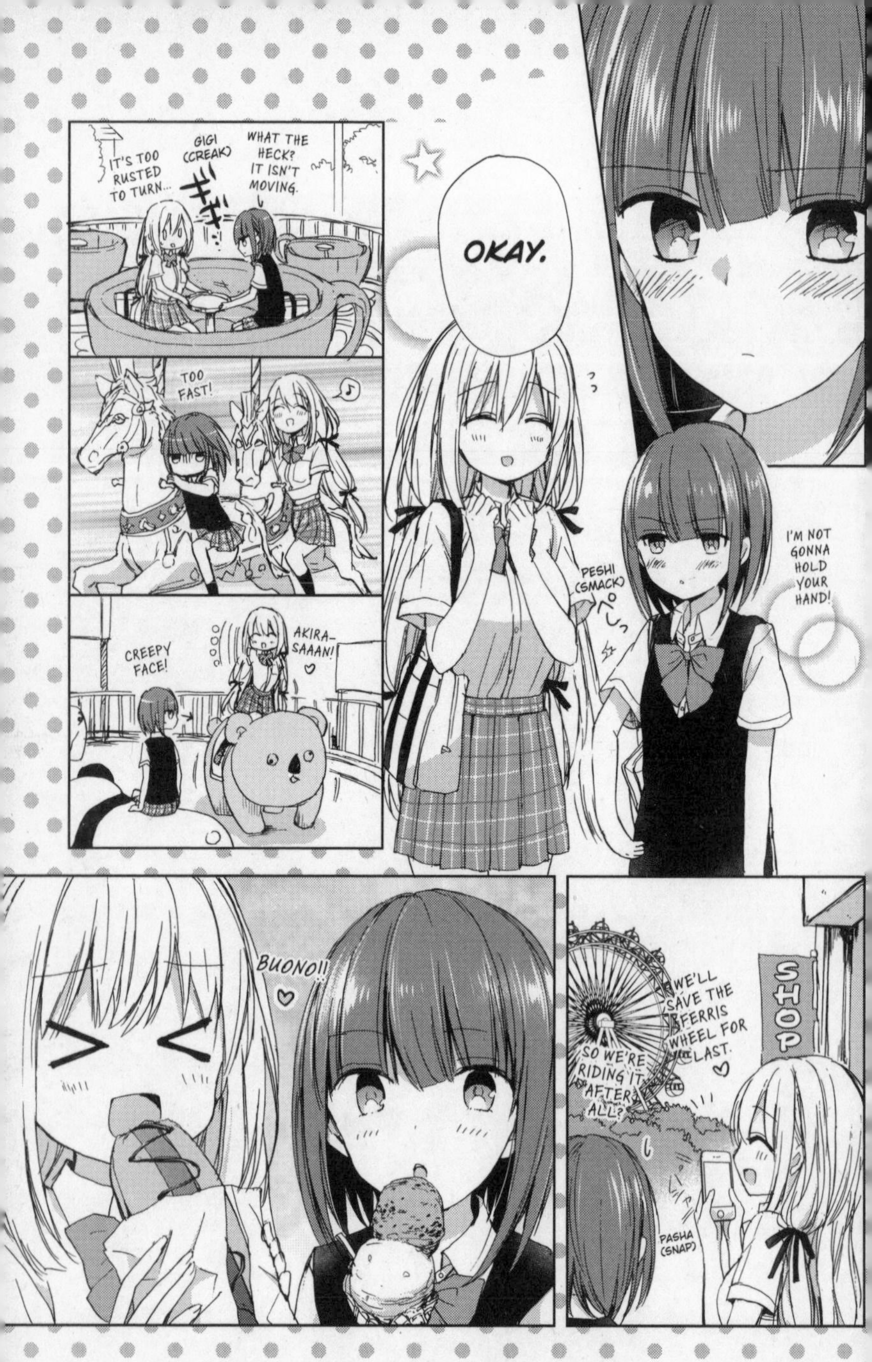
OKAY.
I'M NOT GONNA HOLD YOUR HAND!
PESHI (SMACK)
WHAT THE HECK? IT ISN'T MOVING.
GIGI (CREAK)
IT'S TOO RUSTED TO TURN...
TOO FAST!
AKIRA-SAAAN!
CREEPY FACE!
SHOP
WE'LL SAVE THE FERRIS WHEEL FOR LAST.
SO WE'RE RIDING IT AFTER ALL?
PASHA (SNAP)
BUONO!!

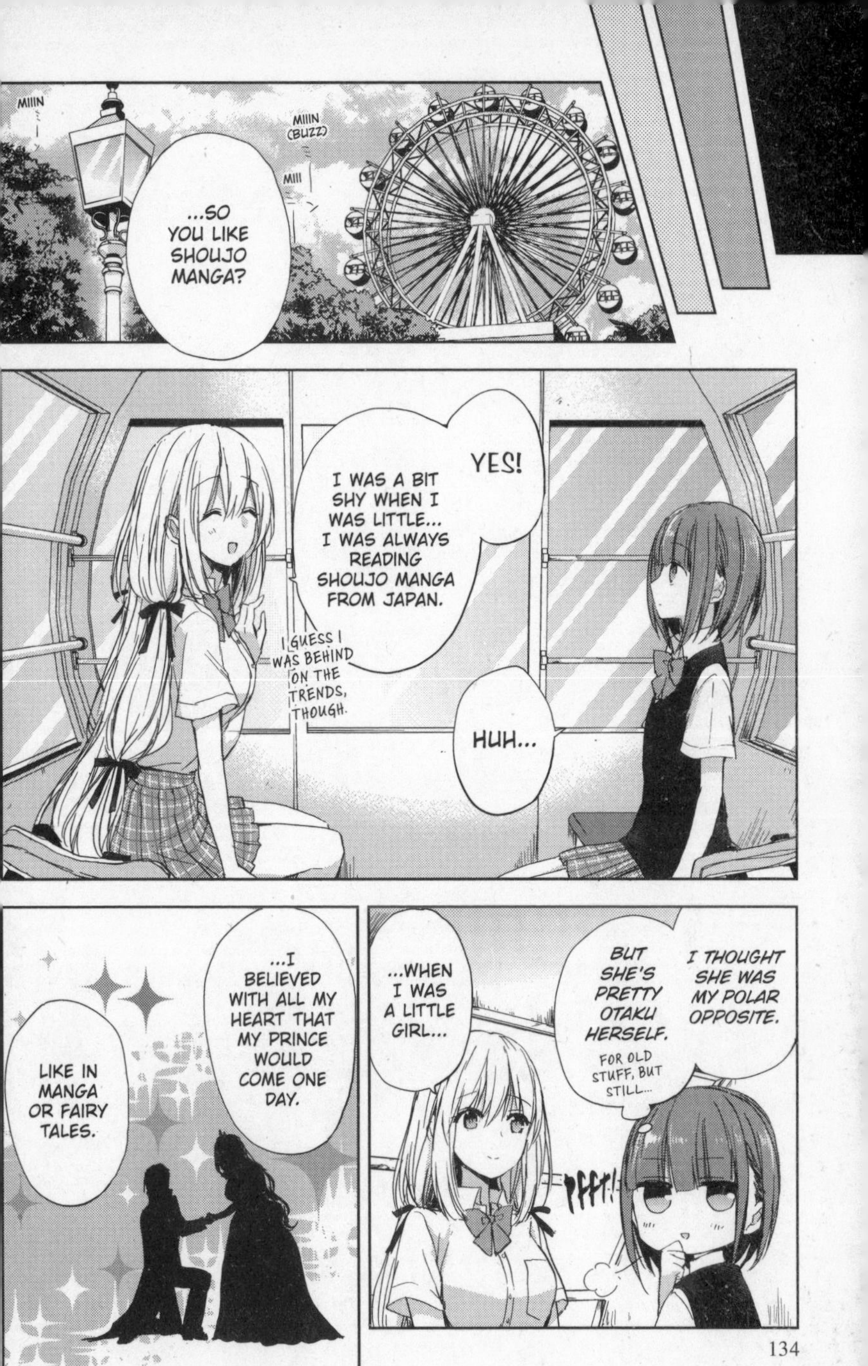
MIIIN (BUZZ)
MIII
MIIIN
...SO YOU LIKE SHOUJO MANGA?
YES!
I WAS A BIT SHY WHEN I WAS LITTLE... I WAS ALWAYS READING SHOUJO MANGA FROM JAPAN.
I GUESS I WAS BEHIND ON THE TRENDS, THOUGH.
HUH...
I THOUGHT SHE WAS MY POLAR OPPOSITE.
BUT SHE'S PRETTY OTAKU HERSELF.
FOR OLD STUFF, BUT STILL...
...WHEN I WAS A LITTLE GIRL...
PFFT!
...I BELIEVED WITH ALL MY HEART THAT MY PRINCE WOULD COME ONE DAY.
LIKE IN MANGA OR FAIRY TALES.

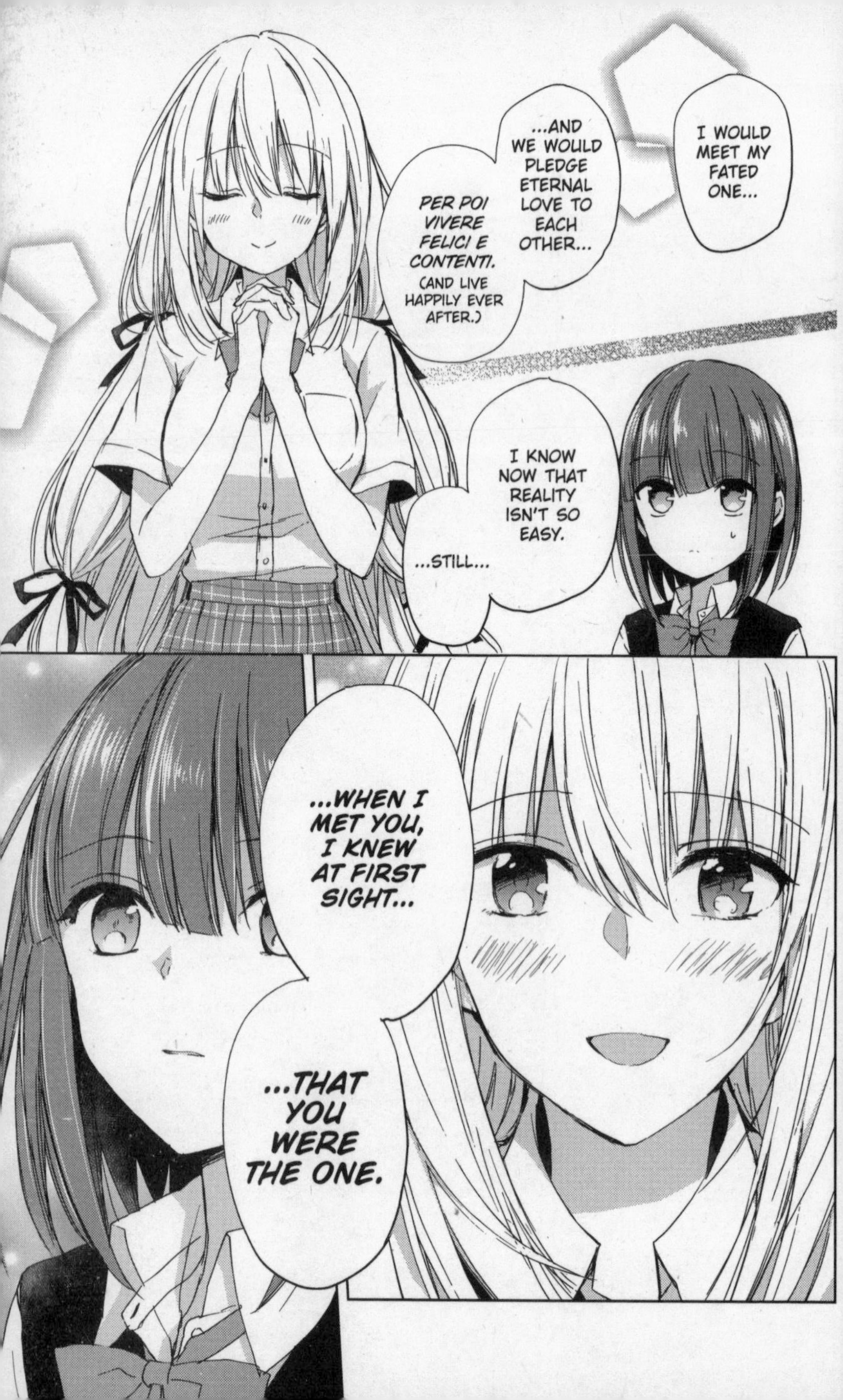
I WOULD MEET MY FATED ONE...
...AND WE WOULD PLEDGE ETERNAL LOVE TO EACH OTHER...
PER POI VIVERE FELICI E CONTENTI. (AND LIVE HAPPILY EVER AFTER.)
I KNOW NOW THAT REALITY ISN'T SO EASY.
...STILL...
...WHEN I MET YOU, I KNEW AT FIRST SIGHT...
...THAT YOU WERE THE ONE.

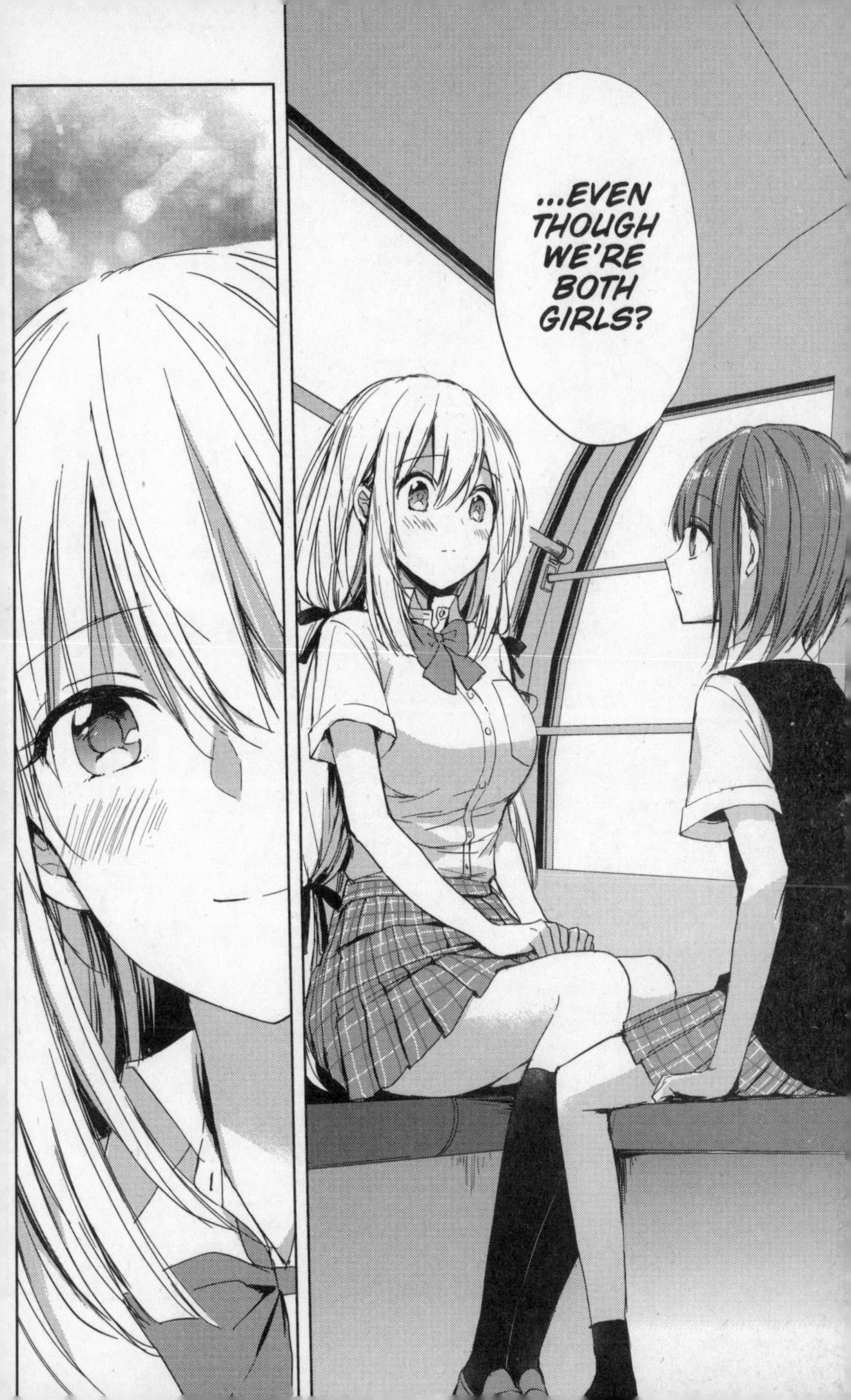
...EVEN THOUGH WE'RE BOTH GIRLS?

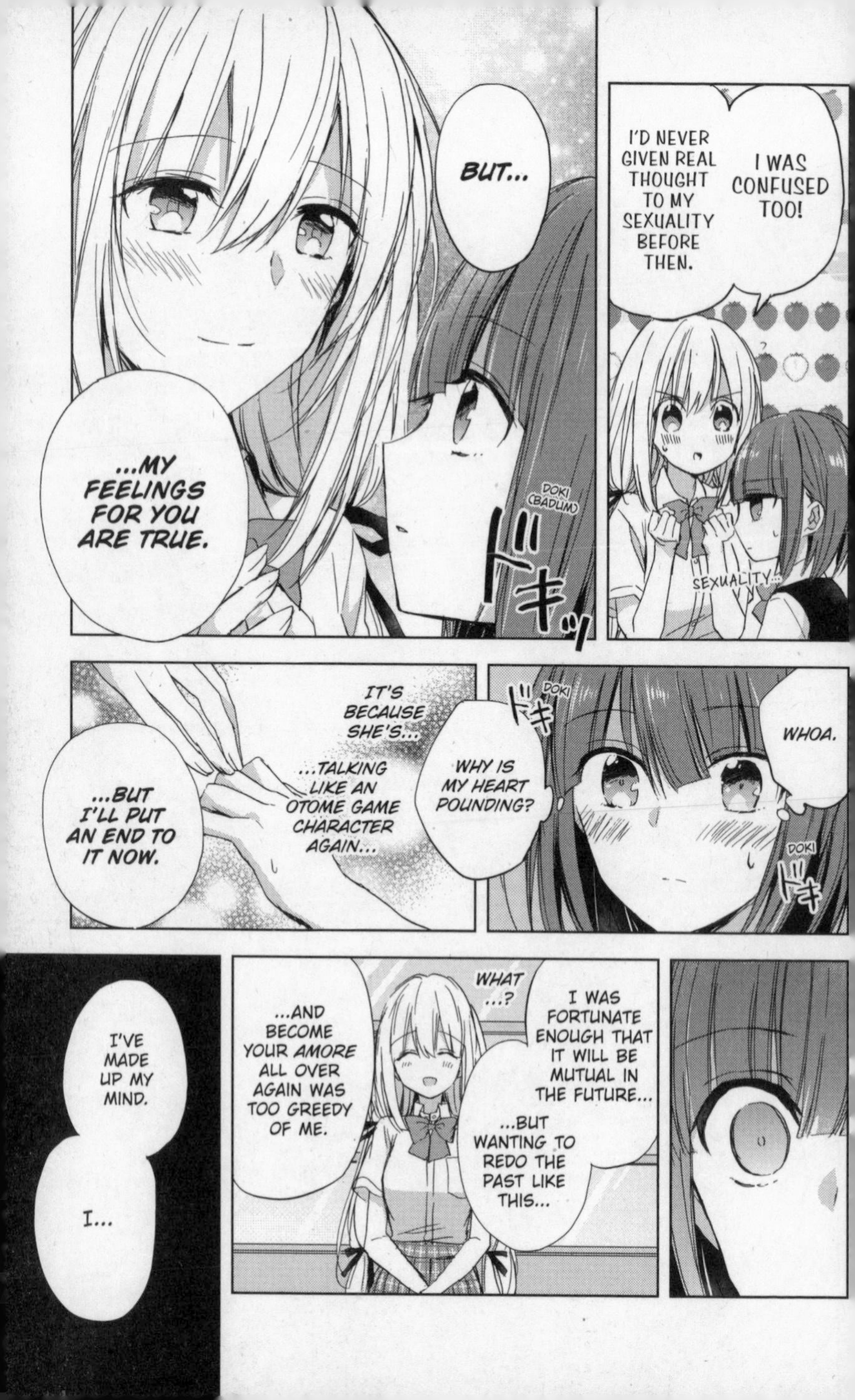
I WAS CONFUSED TOO!
I'D NEVER GIVEN REAL THOUGHT TO MY SEXUALITY BEFORE THEN.
SEXUALITY...
BUT...
DOKI (BADUM)
...MY FEELINGS FOR YOU ARE TRUE.
WHOA.
DOKI
WHY IS MY HEART POUNDING?
DOKI
IT'S BECAUSE SHE'S...
...TALKING LIKE AN OTOME GAME CHARACTER AGAIN...
...BUT I'LL PUT AN END TO IT NOW.
I WAS FORTUNATE ENOUGH THAT IT WILL BE MUTUAL IN THE FUTURE...
WHAT ...?
...BUT WANTING TO REDO THE PAST LIKE THIS...
...AND BECOME YOUR AMORE ALL OVER AGAIN WAS TOO GREEDY OF ME.
I'VE MADE UP MY MIND.
I...

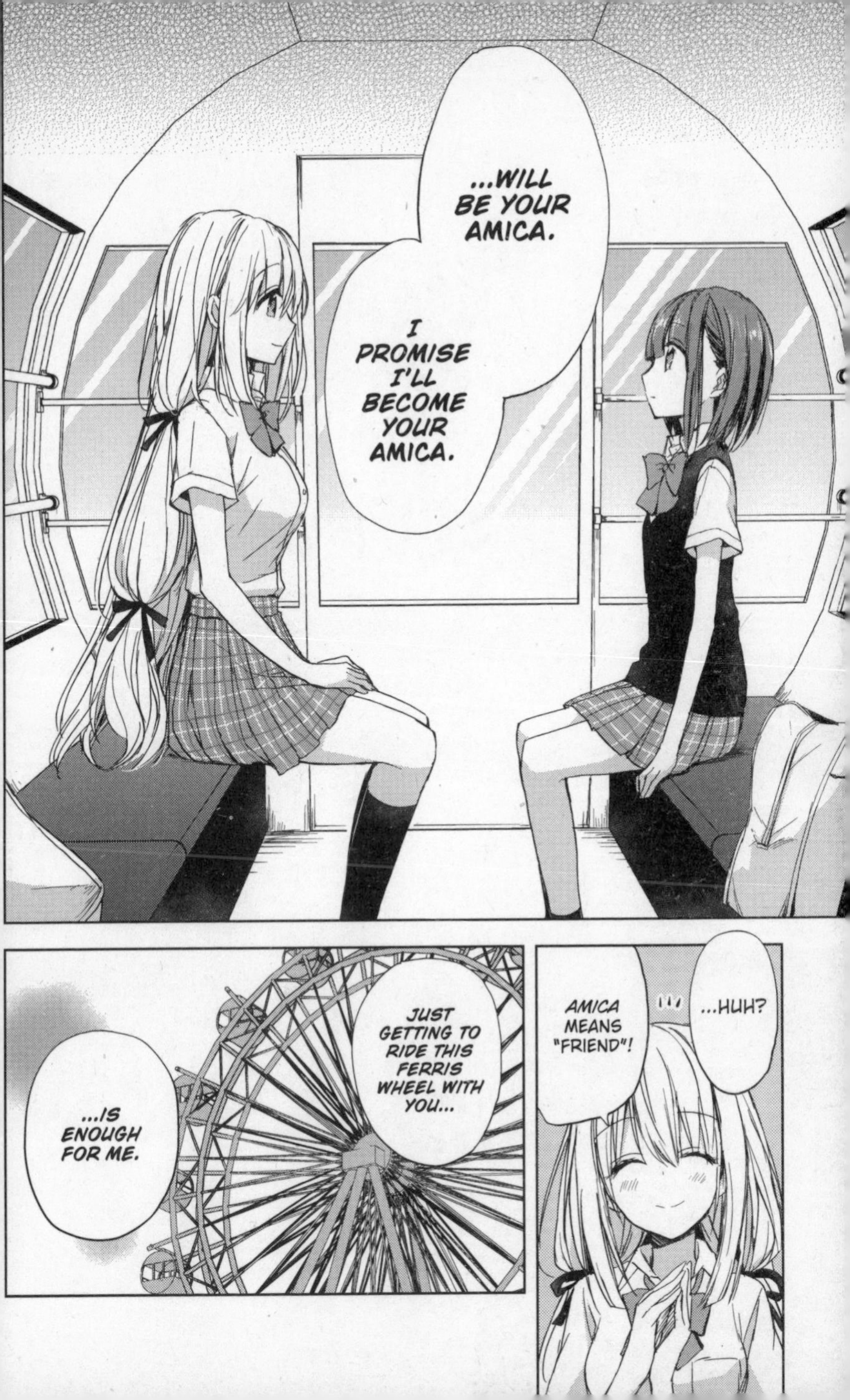
...WILL BE YOUR AMICA.
I PROMISE I'LL BECOME YOUR AMICA.
...HUH?
AMICA MEANS "FRIEND"!
JUST GETTING TO RIDE THIS FERRIS WHEEL WITH YOU...
...IS ENOUGH FOR ME.

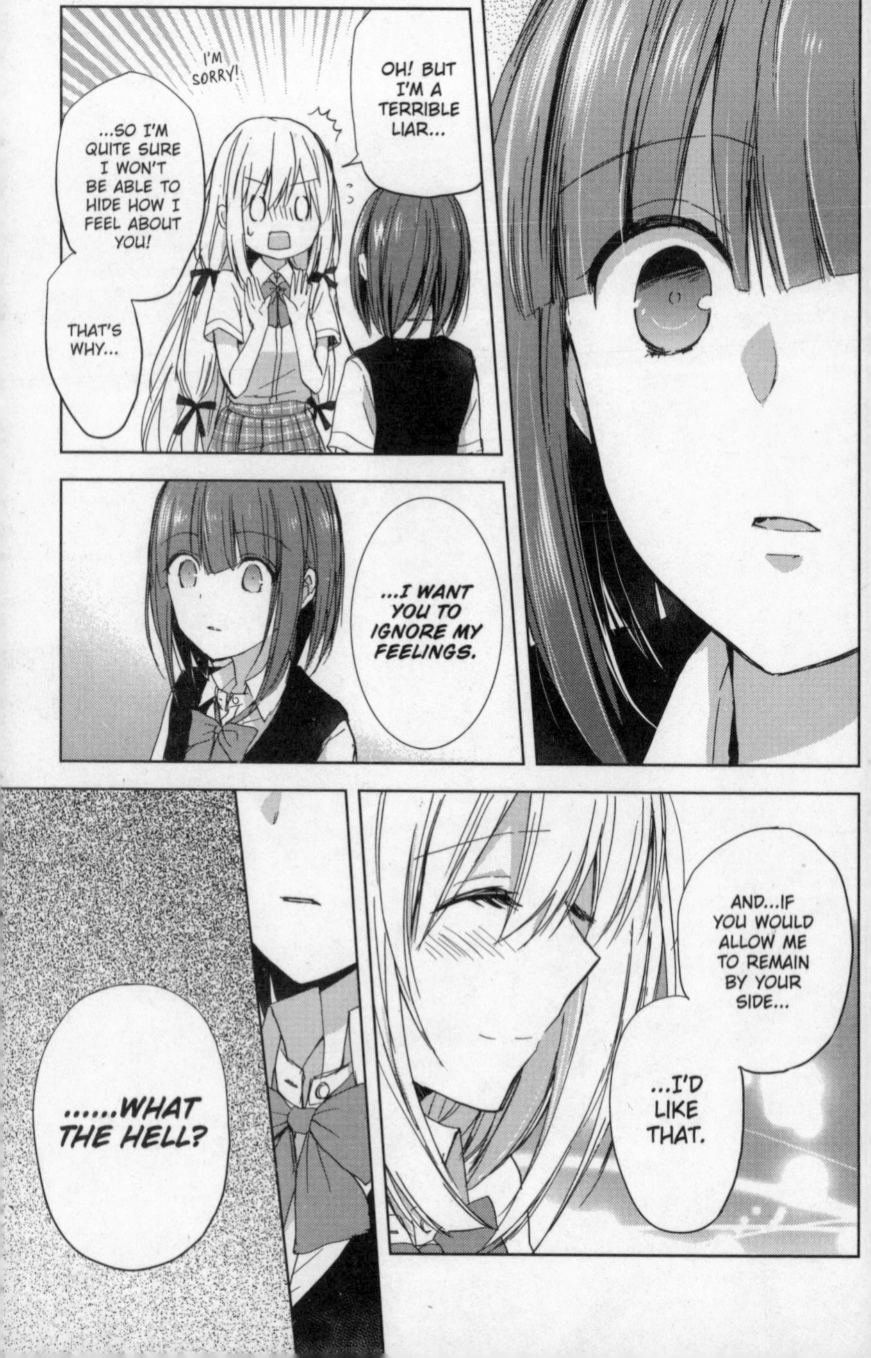
OH! BUT I'M A TERRIBLE LIAR...
I'M SORRY!
...SO I'M QUITE SURE I WON'T BE ABLE TO HIDE HOW I FEEL ABOUT YOU!
THAT'S WHY...
...I WANT YOU TO IGNORE MY FEELINGS.
AND...IF YOU WOULD ALLOW ME TO REMAIN BY YOUR SIDE...
...I'D LIKE THAT.
......WHAT THE HELL?

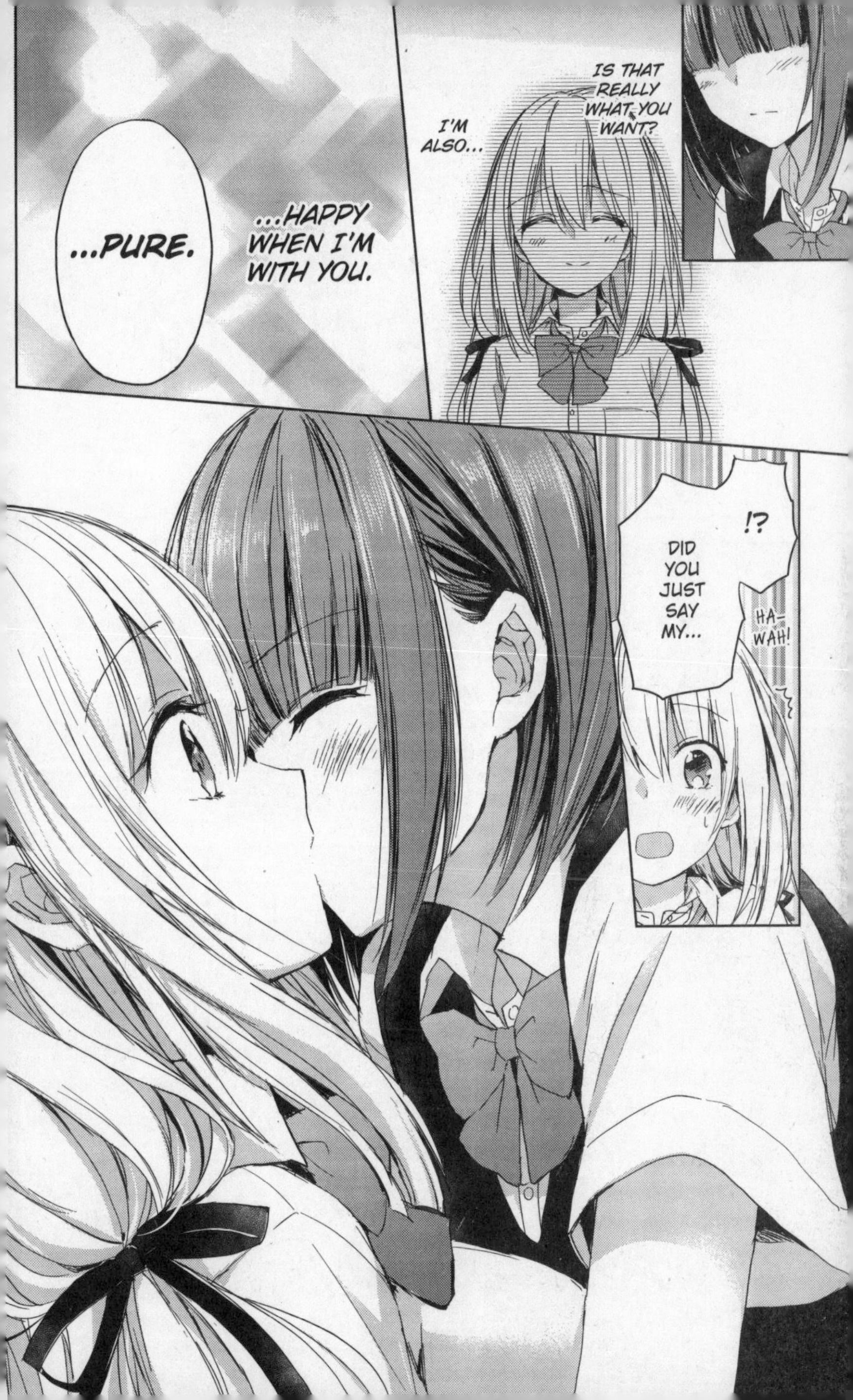
IS THAT REALLY WHAT YOU WANT?
I'M ALSO...
...HAPPY WHEN I'M WITH YOU.
...PURE.
!? DID YOU JUST SAY MY...
HA-WAH!

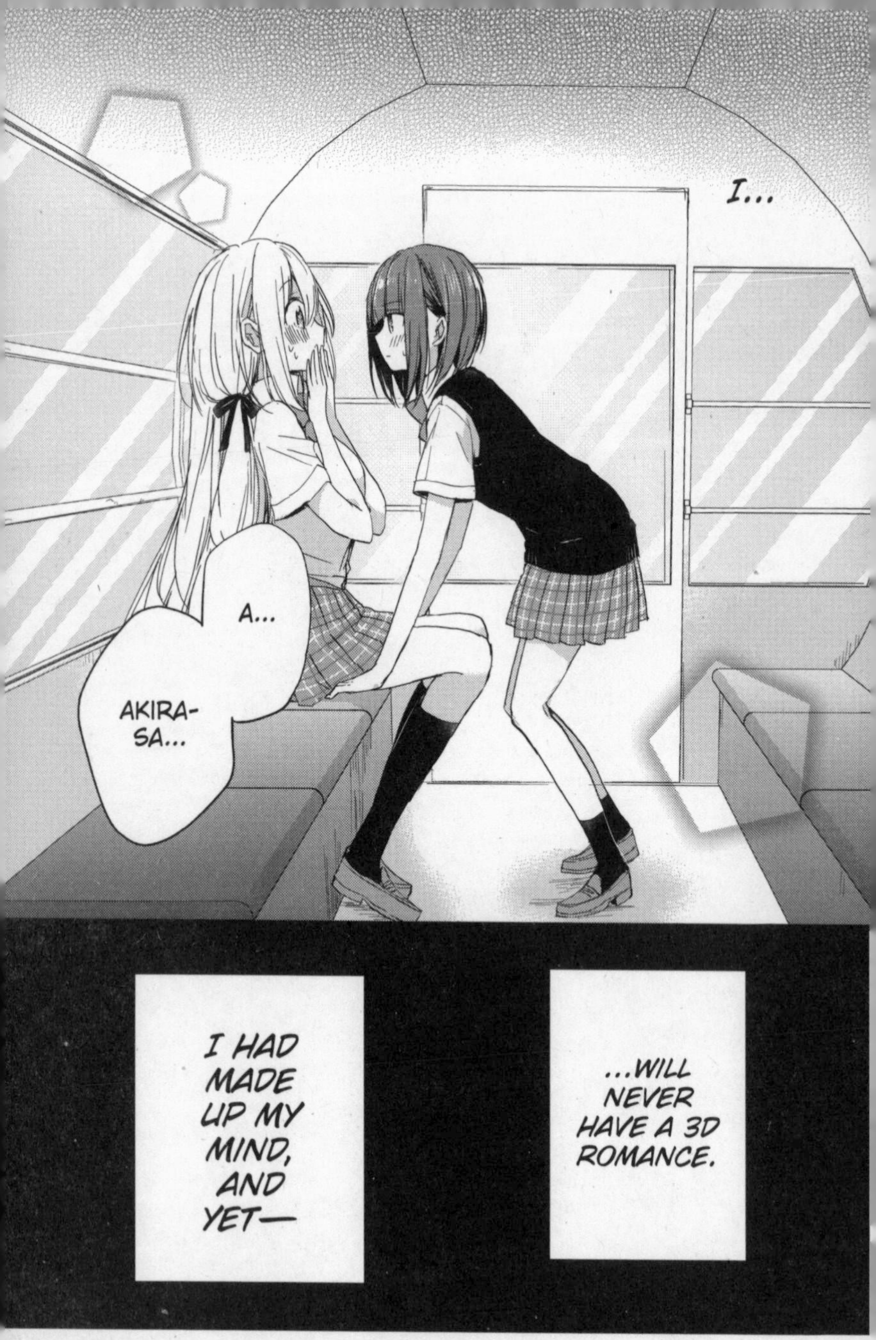
I...
A...
AKIRA-SA...
...WILL NEVER HAVE A 3D ROMANCE.
I HAD MADE UP MY MIND, AND YET—

CONTINUED IN VOLUME 2

🍓 TRANSLATION NOTES

Page 3
In visual novel games like the one Akira is playing, there may be multiple endings (bad and good) for different character routes, and there is often a so-called **"true ending,"** the ending considered final or canon.

An **otaku** is a person obsessed with a hobby, typically anime or manga (but it can apply to other hobbies as well)—a nerd or geek.

Page 6
Pure's given name is written with kanji characters **"pure"** and **"love."** It would be considered an unusual, unique name with a reading that isn't clear from its kanji characters.

Page 13
Otome **games** are visual novels or dating sims targeted toward women, generally with some degree of a romantic element, and love interests to choose from.

Page 39
LINE is a popular messenger service in Japan.

Page 71
Japanese families will typically have a **home altar** with photos of deceased family members, where they will pay respects by burning incense, leaving offerings, and praying. Although it hasn't been mentioned before this point, this is used as a visual cue that Akira's mother is deceased.

Page 73
Akira assumes that Pure left for the toilet because toilets and baths are typically in separate areas in Japanese homes. It's also common for there to be a separate changing room before the actual bath/shower area, with a door between them.

Page 96
Translated as **ax-crazy**, Akira compares Pure to a *yandere*, a character archetype or person who is romantically obsessed and possessive to the point of becoming violent.

Page 112
Yuri is a genre focusing on romantic relationships between women.

Page 130
Shoujo **manga** is a genre of manga targeted at young teen girls, often including romantic elements.

Page 143
The title of this bonus comic, **Yurimi-san is Watching** (*Yurimi-san ga Miteru*), is a reference to *Maria-sama ga Miteru* (*The Virgin Mary is Watching*), a novel series about a group of girls attending a girls-only Catholic school in Tokyo, that began in 1998 and later spawned anime and manga adaptations in the early 2000s. It's considered responsible for starting a wave of *yuri* stories.

Yurimi's name is written with the kanji characters for "*yuri*" (which can also mean "lily," a flower often used as symbolism for it) and "beautiful," but the *mi* also evokes the phonetic for "looking" (as in the title), which is fitting for her hobby of choice.

In Japanese, the name for a *yuri* **fangirl** is *yuri joshi* (literally, "*yuri* girl").

Page 155
The *tsundere* is a character archetype who acts cold or angry but eventually becomes affectionate (though they often deny or hide it).

Page 156
Doujinshi are self-published works, usually zines or manga.

Page 157
Luna is another unusual name—it uses the kanji character for "moon."

Page 158
Comiket (short for Comic Market) is Japan's most famous *doujinshi* convention.

OniShota is a subgenre in the boys' love fandom, a pairing of an older boy (from high school to young adulthood) and a *shota* (a much younger boy, either in grade school or middle school).

A **fujoshi** is a boys' love fangirl.

Page 159
The *yuri* **world's iconic couple** is a reference to Sailors Uranus and Neptune from *Sailor Moon*.

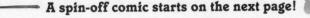

← **A spin-off comic starts on the next page!** 🍓

YURIMI-SAN IS WATCHING☆ ♥01

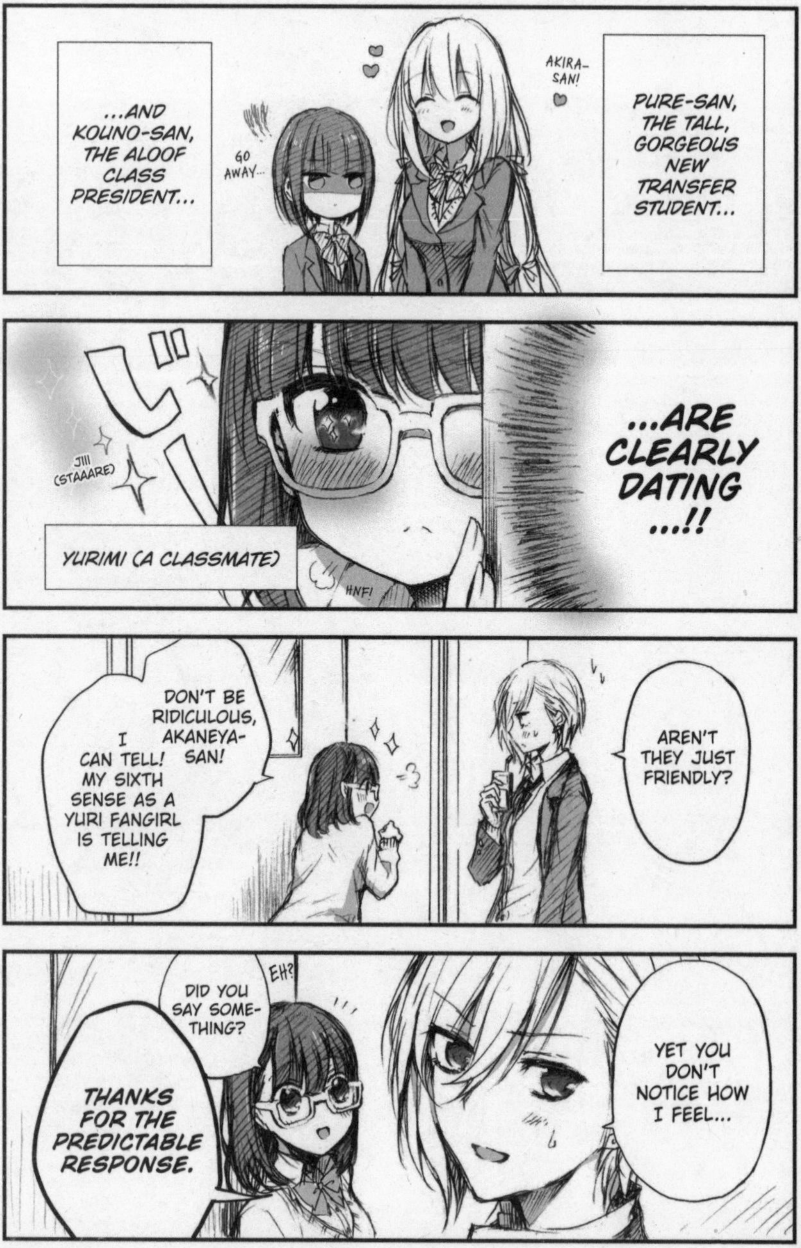
PURE-SAN, THE TALL, GORGEOUS NEW TRANSFER STUDENT...
AKIRA-SAN!
GO AWAY...
...AND KOUNO-SAN, THE ALOOF CLASS PRESIDENT...
...ARE CLEARLY DATING...!!
HNF!
YURIMI (A CLASSMATE)
JIII (STAAARE)
AREN'T THEY JUST FRIENDLY?
DON'T BE RIDICULOUS, AKANEYA-SAN! I CAN TELL! MY SIXTH SENSE AS A YURI FANGIRL IS TELLING ME!!
YET YOU DON'T NOTICE HOW I FEEL...
EH?
DID YOU SAY SOME-THING?
THANKS FOR THE PREDICTABLE RESPONSE.

YURIMI-SAN IS WATCHING☆ ♥02

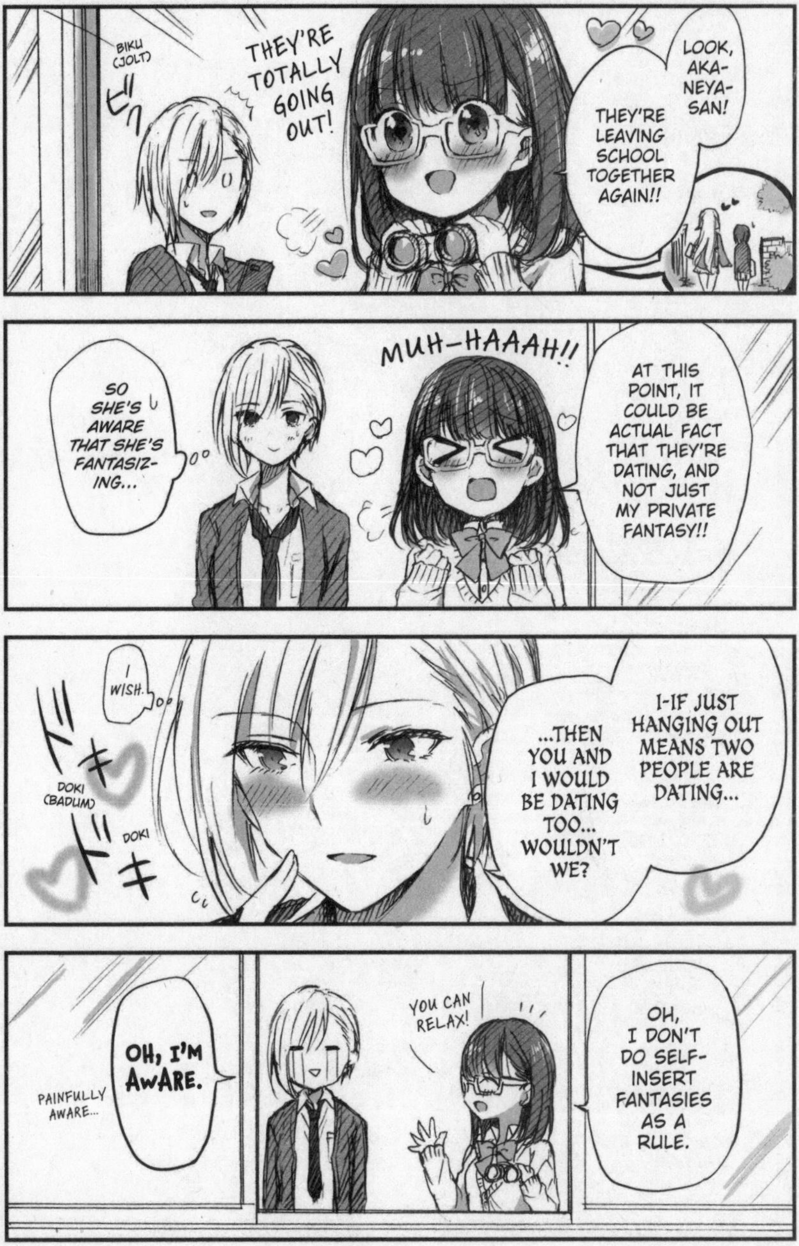
LOOK, AKANEYA-SAN!
THEY'RE LEAVING SCHOOL TOGETHER AGAIN!!
THEY'RE TOTALLY GOING OUT!
BIKU (JOLT)
MUH-HAAAH!!
AT THIS POINT, IT COULD BE ACTUAL FACT THAT THEY'RE DATING, AND NOT JUST MY PRIVATE FANTASY!!
SO SHE'S AWARE THAT SHE'S FANTASIZING...
I-IF JUST HANGING OUT MEANS TWO PEOPLE ARE DATING...
...THEN YOU AND I WOULD BE DATING TOO... WOULDN'T WE?
I WISH.
DOKI (BADUM)
DOKI
OH, I DON'T DO SELF-INSERT FANTASIES AS A RULE.
YOU CAN RELAX!
OH, I'M AWARE.
PAINFULLY AWARE...

YURIMI-SAN IS WATCHING☆ ♥03

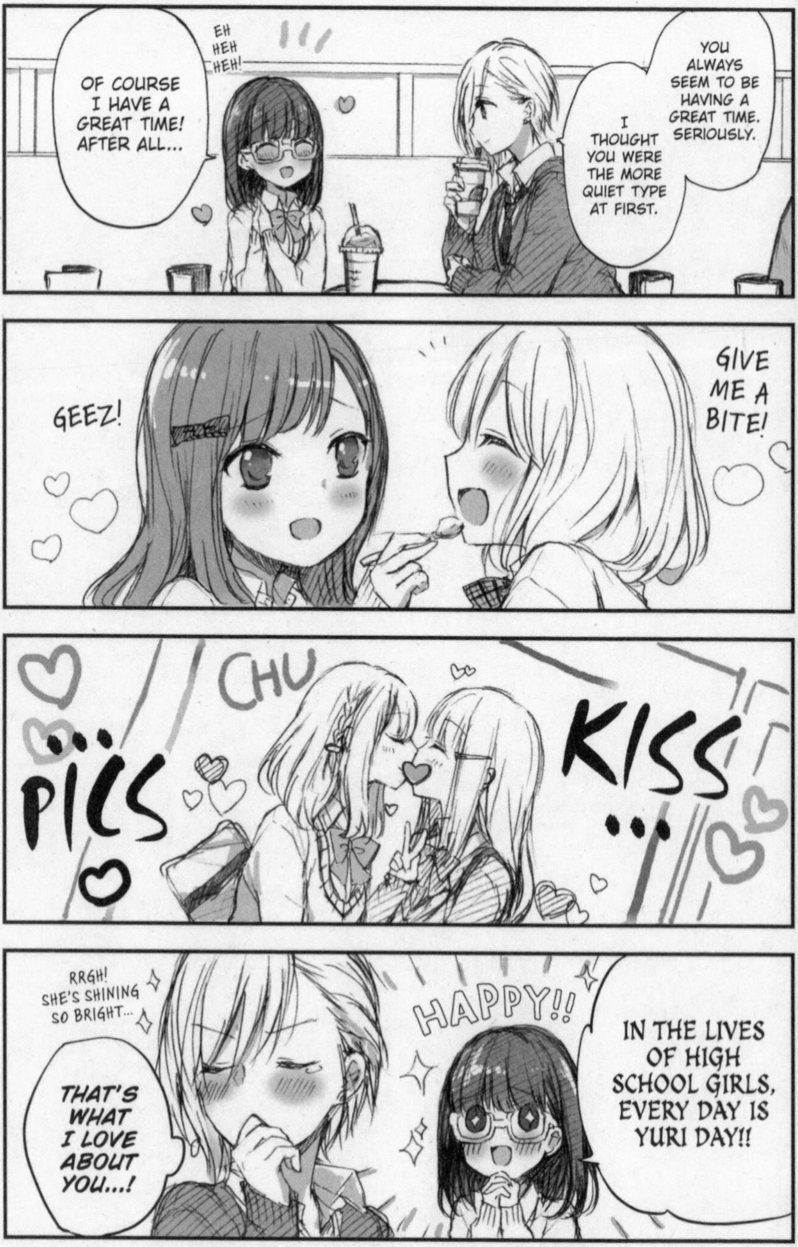
YOU ALWAYS SEEM TO BE HAVING A GREAT TIME. SERIOUSLY.
I THOUGHT YOU WERE THE MORE QUIET TYPE AT FIRST.
EH HEH HEH!
OF COURSE I HAVE A GREAT TIME! AFTER ALL...
GIVE ME A BITE!
GEEZ!
KISS...
CHU
...PICS
IN THE LIVES OF HIGH SCHOOL GIRLS, EVERY DAY IS YURI DAY!!
HAPPY!!
RRGH! SHE'S SHINING SO BRIGHT...
THAT'S WHAT I LOVE ABOUT YOU...!

YURIMI-SAN IS WATCHING☆ ♥04

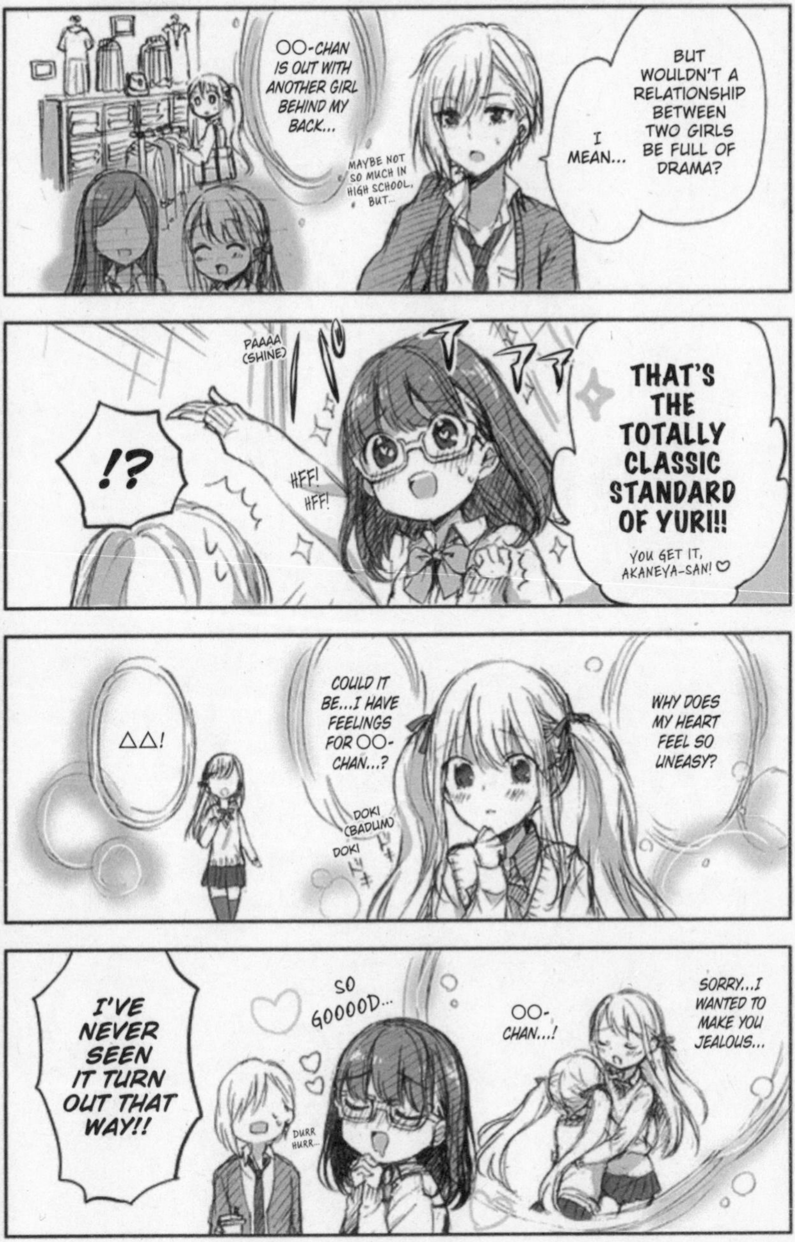
BUT WOULDN'T A RELATIONSHIP BETWEEN TWO GIRLS BE FULL OF DRAMA?
I MEAN...
MAYBE NOT SO MUCH IN HIGH SCHOOL, BUT...
○○-CHAN IS OUT WITH ANOTHER GIRL BEHIND MY BACK...
THAT'S THE TOTALLY CLASSIC STANDARD OF YURI!!!
YOU GET IT, AKANEYA-SAN! ♡
HFF! HFF!
PAAAA (SHINE)
!?
WHY DOES MY HEART FEEL SO UNEASY?
COULD IT BE...I HAVE FEELINGS FOR ○○-CHAN...?
DOKI (BADUM) DOKI
△△!
SORRY...I WANTED TO MAKE YOU JEALOUS...
○○-CHAN...!
SO GOOOOD...
DURR HURR...
I'VE NEVER SEEN IT TURN OUT THAT WAY!!

YURIMI-SAN IS WATCHING☆ ♥05

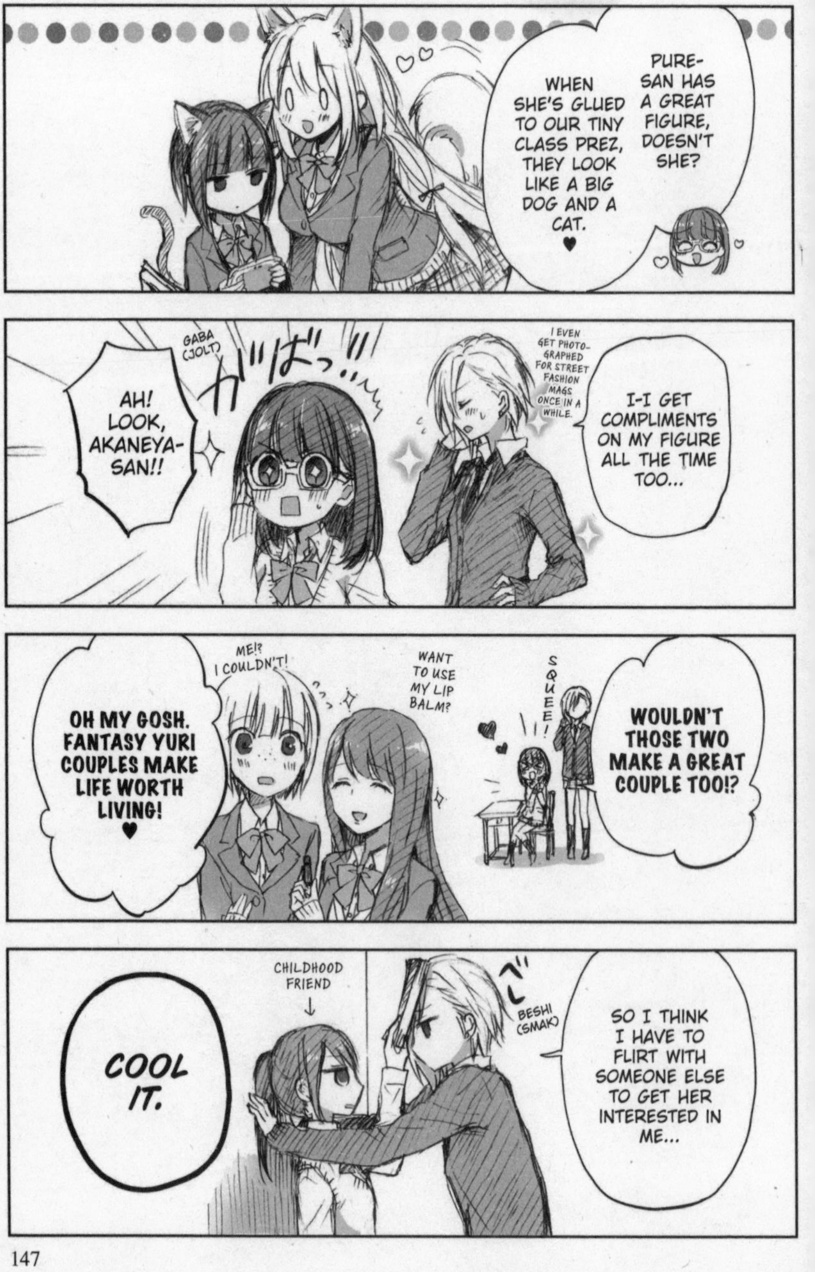
PURE-SAN HAS A GREAT FIGURE, DOESN'T SHE?
WHEN SHE'S GLUED TO OUR TINY CLASS PREZ, THEY LOOK LIKE A BIG DOG AND A CAT. ♥
I-I GET COMPLIMENTS ON MY FIGURE ALL THE TIME TOO...
I EVEN GET PHOTOGRAPHED FOR STREET FASHION MAGS ONCE IN A WHILE.
がばっ!!
GABA (JOLT)
AH! LOOK, AKANEYA-SAN!!
WOULDN'T THOSE TWO MAKE A GREAT COUPLE TOO!?
SQUEE!
WANT TO USE MY LIP BALM?
ME!? I COULDN'T!
OH MY GOSH. FANTASY YURI COUPLES MAKE LIFE WORTH LIVING! ♥
SO I THINK I HAVE TO FLIRT WITH SOMEONE ELSE TO GET HER INTERESTED IN ME...
べし
BESHI (SMAK)
CHILDHOOD FRIEND
COOL IT.

YURIMI-SAN IS WATCHING☆ ♥06

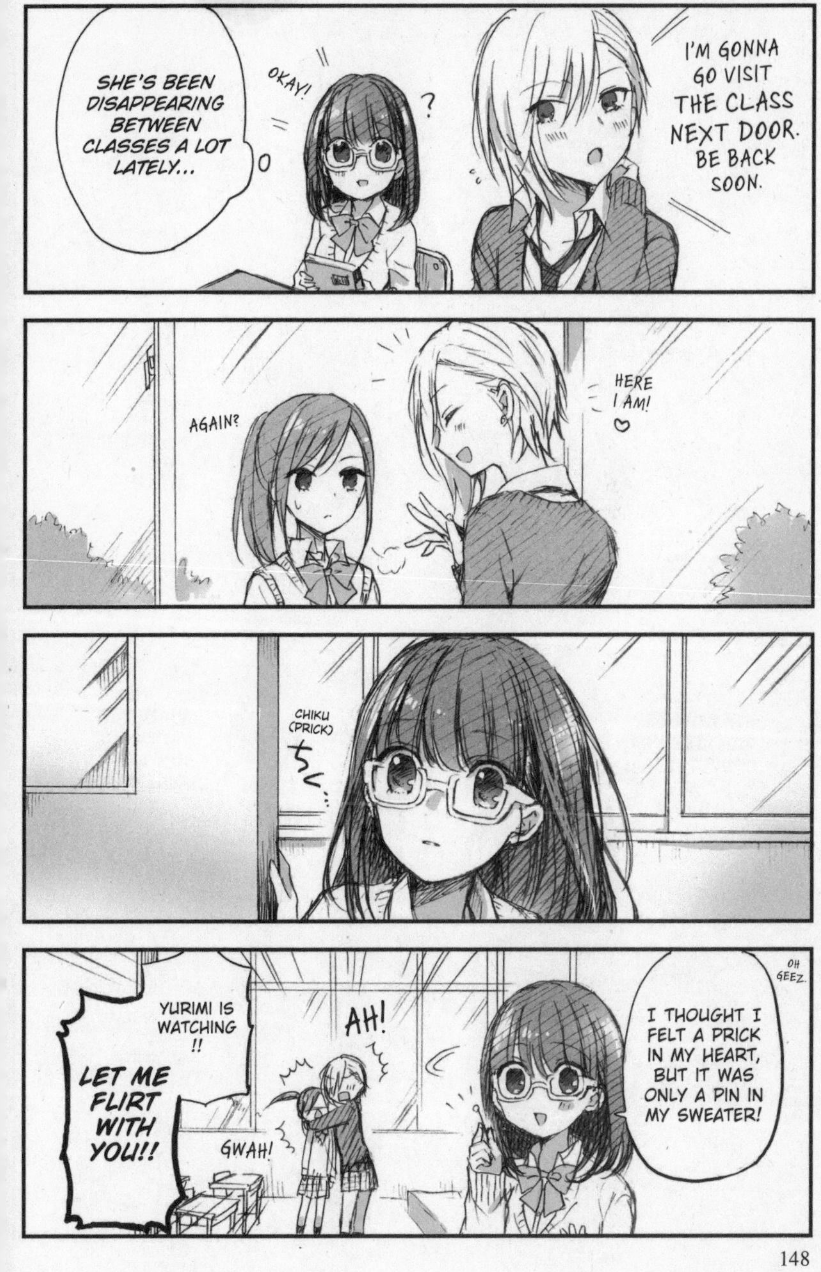

I'M GONNA GO VISIT THE CLASS NEXT DOOR. BE BACK SOON.
OKAY!
SHE'S BEEN DISAPPEARING BETWEEN CLASSES A LOT LATELY...
HERE I AM!
AGAIN?
CHIKU (PRICK)
ちく...
OH GEEZ.
I THOUGHT I FELT A PRICK IN MY HEART, BUT IT WAS ONLY A PIN IN MY SWEATER!
AH!
GWAH!
YURIMI IS WATCHING !!
LET ME FLIRT WITH YOU!!

YURIMI-SAN IS WATCHING☆ ♥07

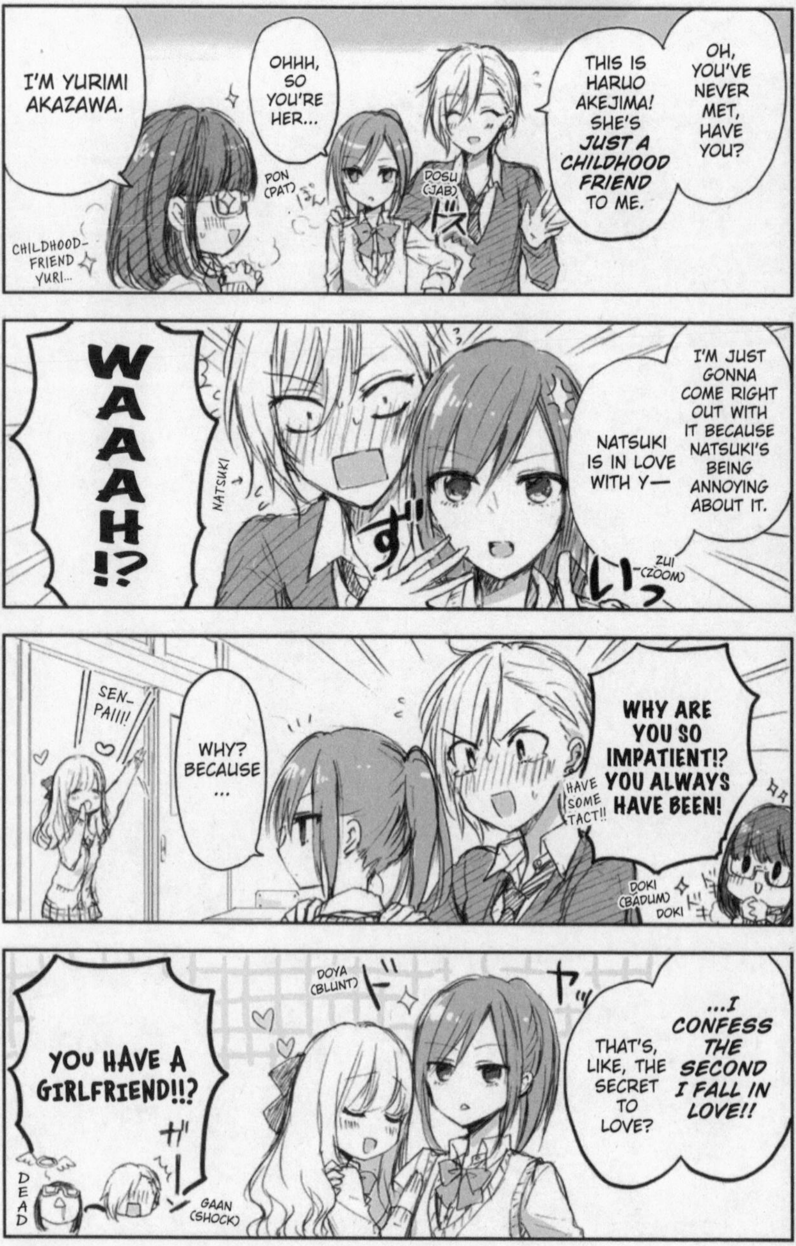
OH, YOU'VE NEVER MET, HAVE YOU?
THIS IS HARUO AKEJIMA! SHE'S JUST A CHILDHOOD FRIEND TO ME.
DOSU (JAB)
OHHH, SO YOU'RE HER...
PON (PAT)
I'M YURIMI AKAZAWA.
CHILDHOOD-FRIEND YURI...
I'M JUST GONNA COME RIGHT OUT WITH IT BECAUSE NATSUKI'S BEING ANNOYING ABOUT IT.
NATSUKI IS IN LOVE WITH Y—
ZUI (ZOOM)
NATSUKI
WAAAAH!?
WHY ARE YOU SO IMPATIENT!? YOU ALWAYS HAVE BEEN!
HAVE SOME TACT!!
DOKI (BADUM) DOKI
WHY? BECAUSE ...
SEN_PAI!!!
...I CONFESS THE SECOND I FALL IN LOVE!!
THAT'S, LIKE, THE SECRET TO LOVE?
DOYA (BLUNT)
YOU HAVE A GIRLFRIEND!!?
GAAN (SHOCK)
DEAD

YURIMI-SAN IS WATCHING☆ ♥08

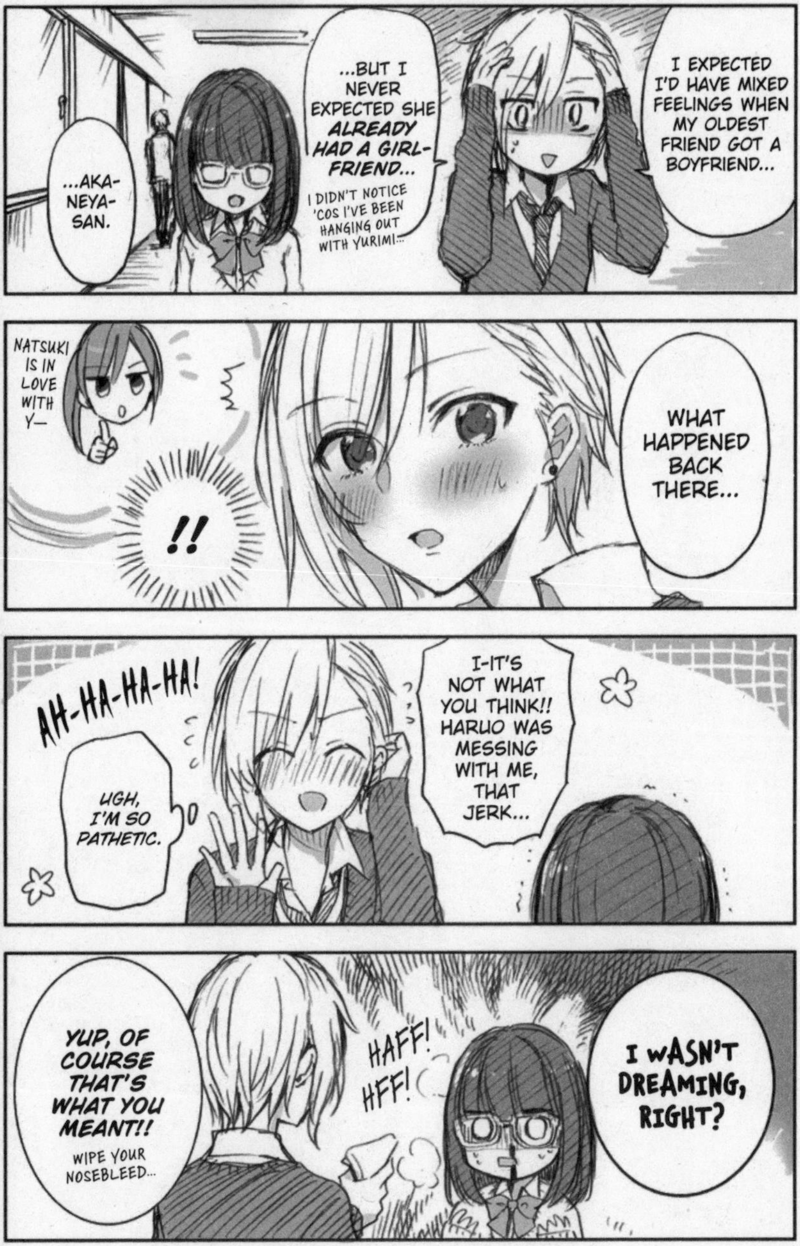
I EXPECTED I'D HAVE MIXED FEELINGS WHEN MY OLDEST FRIEND GOT A BOYFRIEND...
...BUT I NEVER EXPECTED SHE ALREADY HAD A GIRL-FRIEND...
I DIDN'T NOTICE 'COS I'VE BEEN HANGING OUT WITH YURIMI...
...AKA-NEYA-SAN.
WHAT HAPPENED BACK THERE...
!!
NATSUKI IS IN LOVE WITH Y—
I-IT'S NOT WHAT YOU THINK!! HARUO WAS MESSING WITH ME, THAT JERK...
AH-HA-HA-HA!
UGH, I'M SO PATHETIC.
I WASN'T DREAMING, RIGHT?
HAFF! HFF!
YUP, OF COURSE THAT'S WHAT YOU MEANT!!
WIPE YOUR NOSEBLEED...

YURIMI-SAN IS WATCHING☆ ♥09

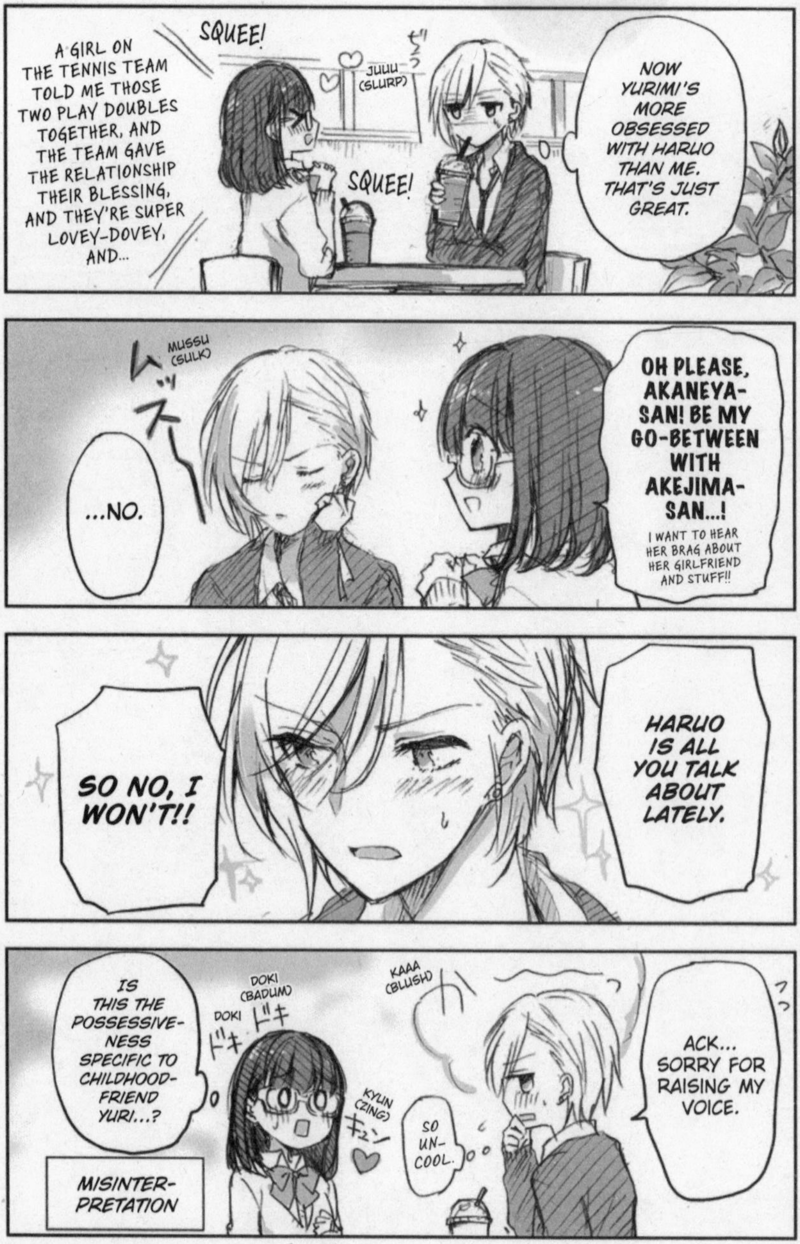
NOW YURIMI'S MORE OBSESSED WITH HARUO THAN ME. THAT'S JUST GREAT.
JUUU (SLURP)
SQUEE!
A GIRL ON THE TENNIS TEAM TOLD ME THOSE TWO PLAY DOUBLES TOGETHER, AND THE TEAM GAVE THE RELATIONSHIP THEIR BLESSING, AND THEY'RE SUPER LOVEY-DOVEY, AND...
SQUEE!
OH PLEASE, AKANEYA-SAN! BE MY GO-BETWEEN WITH AKEJIMA-SAN...!
I WANT TO HEAR HER BRAG ABOUT HER GIRLFRIEND AND STUFF!!
MUSSU (SULK)
...NO.
HARUO IS ALL YOU TALK ABOUT LATELY.
SO NO, I WON'T!!
ACK... SORRY FOR RAISING MY VOICE.
KAAA (BLUSH)
SO UN-COOL.
KYUN (ZING)
DOKI (BADUM)
DOKI
IS THIS THE POSSESSIVE-NESS SPECIFIC TO CHILDHOOD-FRIEND YURI...?
MISINTER-PRETATION

YURIMI-SAN IS WATCHING☆ ♥10

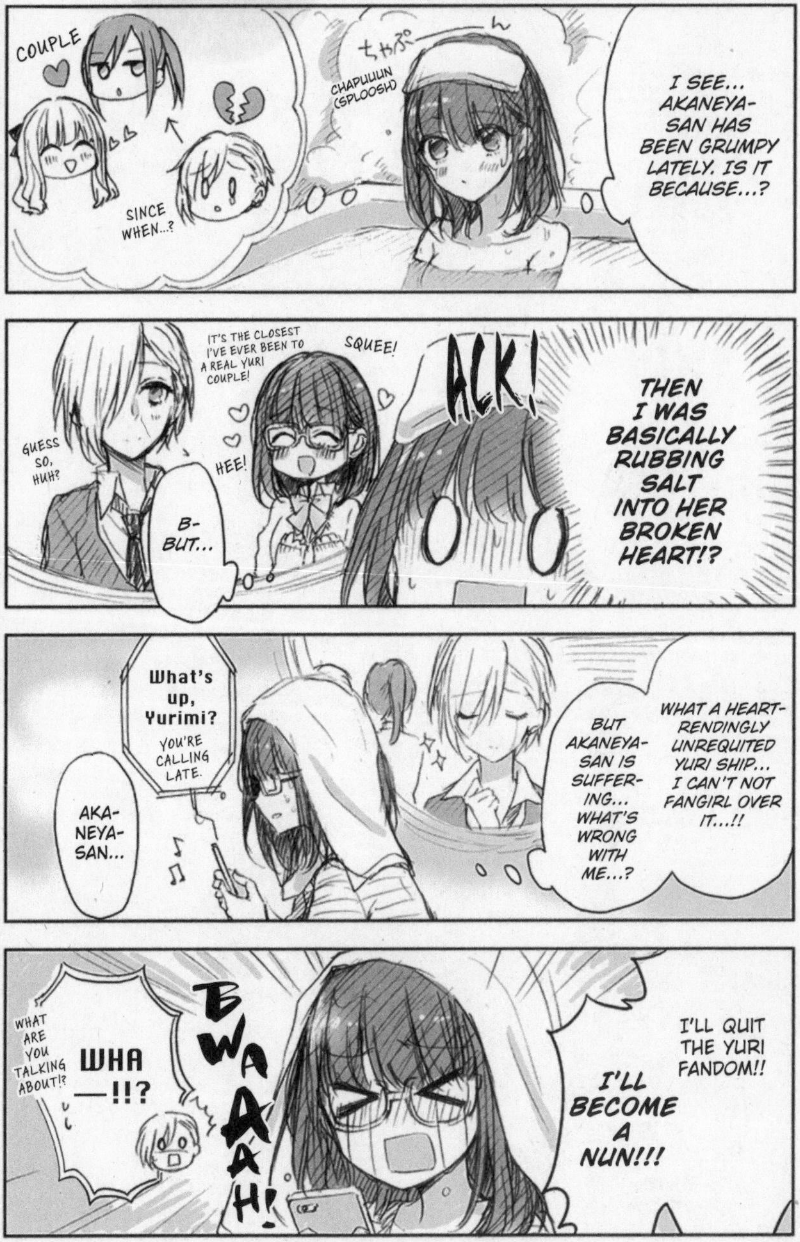
I SEE... AKANEYA-SAN HAS BEEN GRUMPY LATELY. IS IT BECAUSE...?
ちゃぷーーん
CHAPUUUN (SPLOOSH)
COUPLE
SINCE WHEN...?
THEN I WAS BASICALLY RUBBING SALT INTO HER BROKEN HEART!?
ACK!
SQUEE!
IT'S THE CLOSEST I'VE EVER BEEN TO A REAL YURI COUPLE!
HEE!
GUESS SO, HUH?
B-BUT...
WHAT A HEART-RENDINGLY UNREQUITED YURI SHIP... I CAN'T NOT FANGIRL OVER IT...!!
BUT AKANEYA-SAN IS SUFFERING... WHAT'S WRONG WITH ME...?
What's up, Yurimi? YOU'RE CALLING LATE.
AKA-NEYA-SAN...
I'LL QUIT THE YURI FANDOM!!
I'LL BECOME A NUN!!!
BWAAAAH!
WHA—!!?
WHAT ARE YOU TALKING ABOUT!?

YURIMI-SAN IS WATCHING☆ ♥11

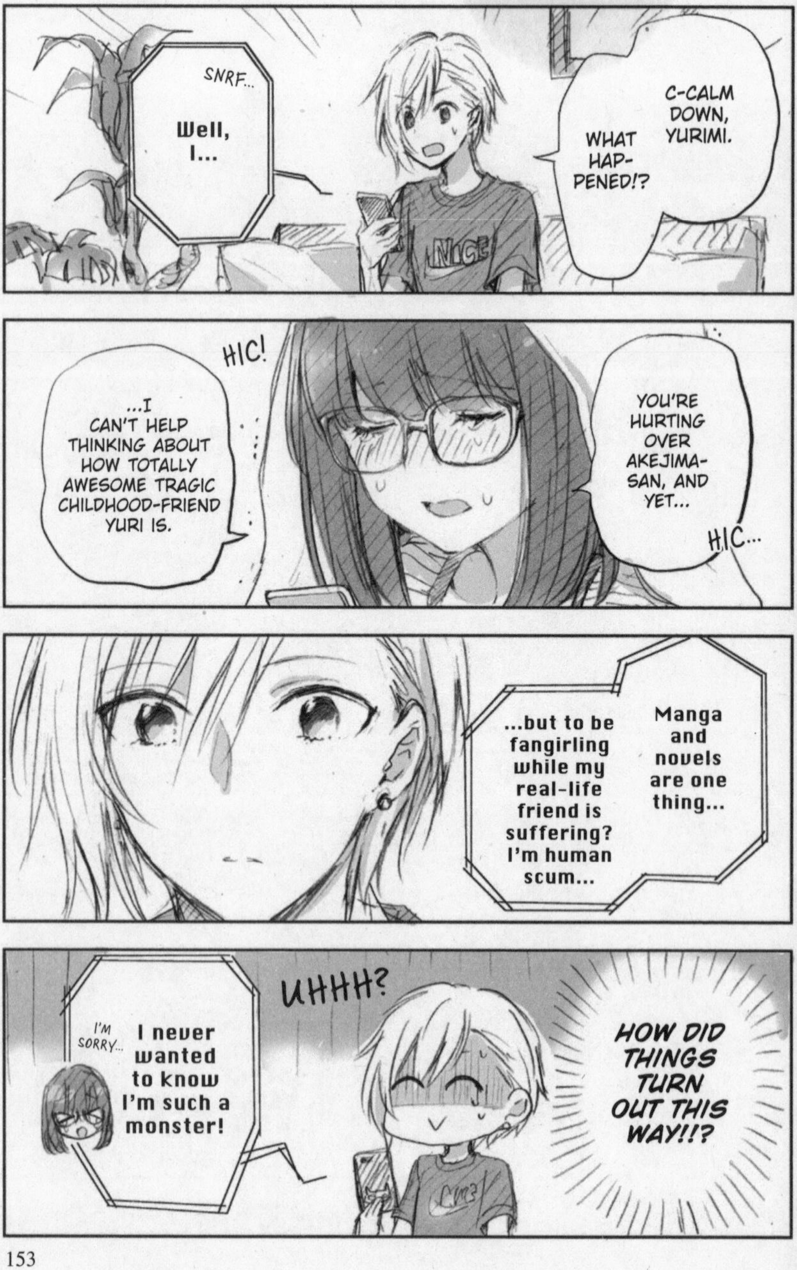
C-CALM DOWN, YURIMI.
WHAT HAP-PENED!?
SNRF...
Well, I...
YOU'RE HURTING OVER AKEJIMA-SAN, AND YET...
HIC...
HIC!
...I CAN'T HELP THINKING ABOUT HOW TOTALLY AWESOME TRAGIC CHILDHOOD-FRIEND YURI IS.
Manga and novels are one thing...
...but to be fangirling while my real-life friend is suffering? I'm human scum...
HOW DID THINGS TURN OUT THIS WAY!!?
UHHH?
I'M SORRY...
I never wanted to know I'm such a monster!

YURIMI-SAN IS WATCHING☆ ♥12

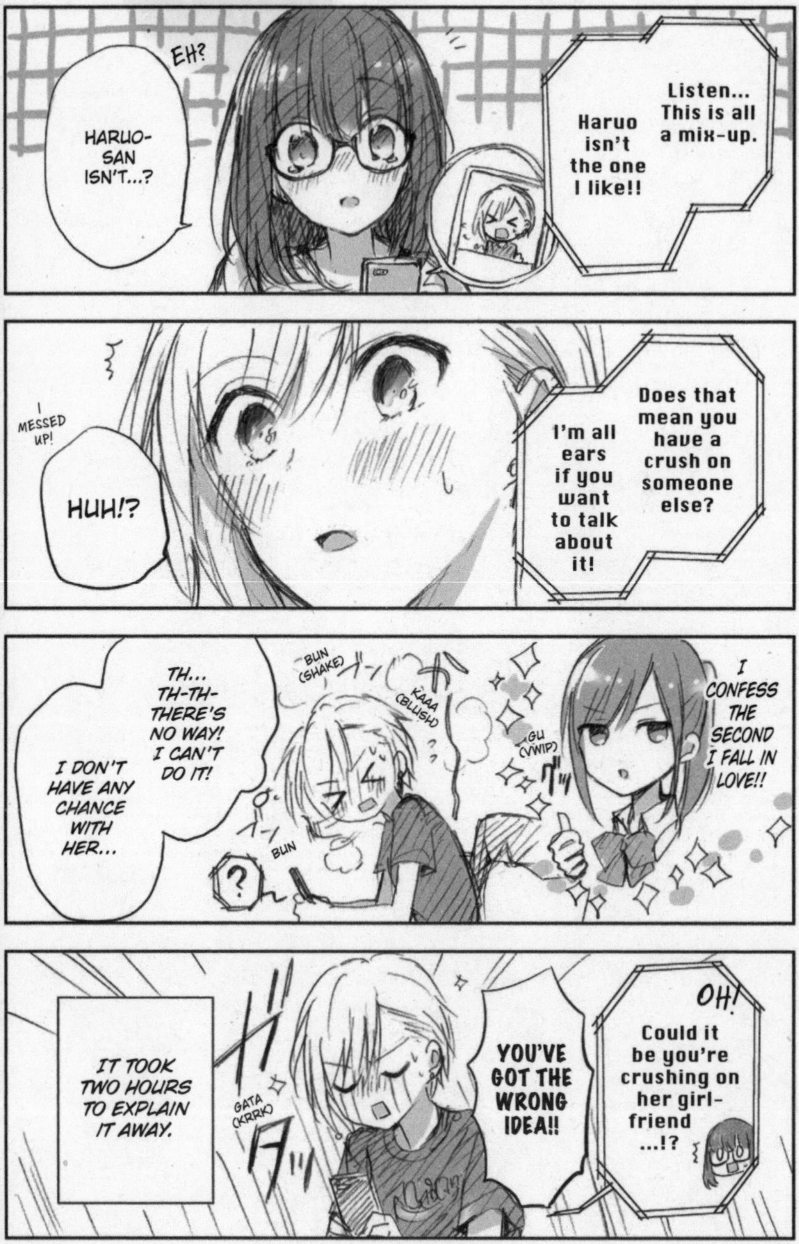
Listen... This is all a mix-up.
Haruo isn't the one I like!!
EH?
HARUO-SAN ISN'T...?
Does that mean you have a crush on someone else?
I'm all ears if you want to talk about it!
I MESSED UP!
HUH!?
I CONFESS THE SECOND I FALL IN LOVE!!
GU (VWIP)
KAAA (BLUSH)
BUN (SHAKE)
TH... TH-TH-THERE'S NO WAY! I CAN'T DO IT!
BUN
?
I DON'T HAVE ANY CHANCE WITH HER...
OH!
Could it be you're crushing on her girl-friend ...!?
YOU'VE GOT THE WRONG IDEA!!
GATA (KRRK)
IT TOOK TWO HOURS TO EXPLAIN IT AWAY.

YURIMI-SAN IS WATCHING☆ ♥13

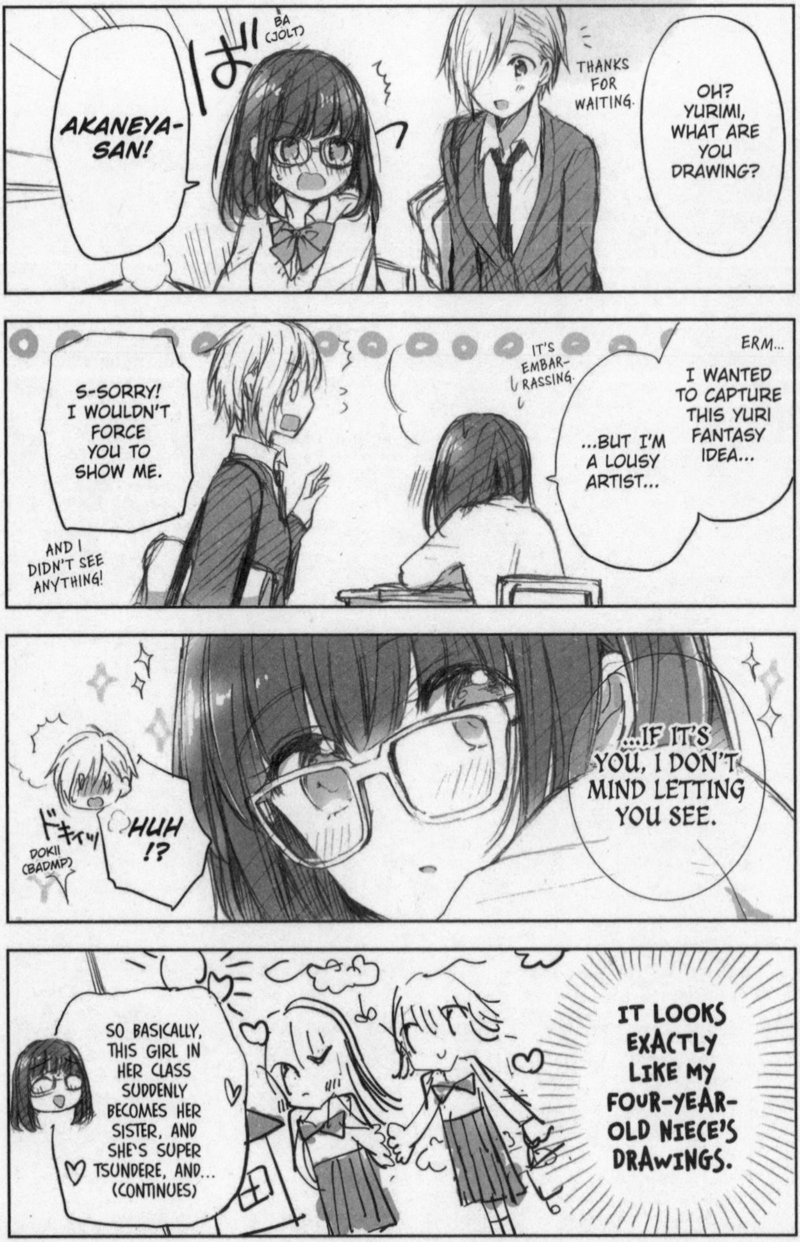

OH? YURIMI, WHAT ARE YOU DRAWING?
THANKS FOR WAITING.
BA (JOLT)
AKANEYA-SAN!
ERM...
I WANTED TO CAPTURE THIS YURI FANTASY IDEA...
...BUT I'M A LOUSY ARTIST...
IT'S EMBARRASSING.
S-SORRY! I WOULDN'T FORCE YOU TO SHOW ME.
AND I DIDN'T SEE ANYTHING!
...IF IT'S YOU, I DON'T MIND LETTING YOU SEE.
HUH!?
ドキィッ
DOKII (BADMP)
IT LOOKS EXACTLY LIKE MY FOUR-YEAR-OLD NIECE'S DRAWINGS.
SO BASICALLY, THIS GIRL IN HER CLASS SUDDENLY BECOMES HER SISTER, AND SHE'S SUPER TSUNDERE, AND... (CONTINUES)

YURIMI-SAN IS WATCHING☆ ♥14

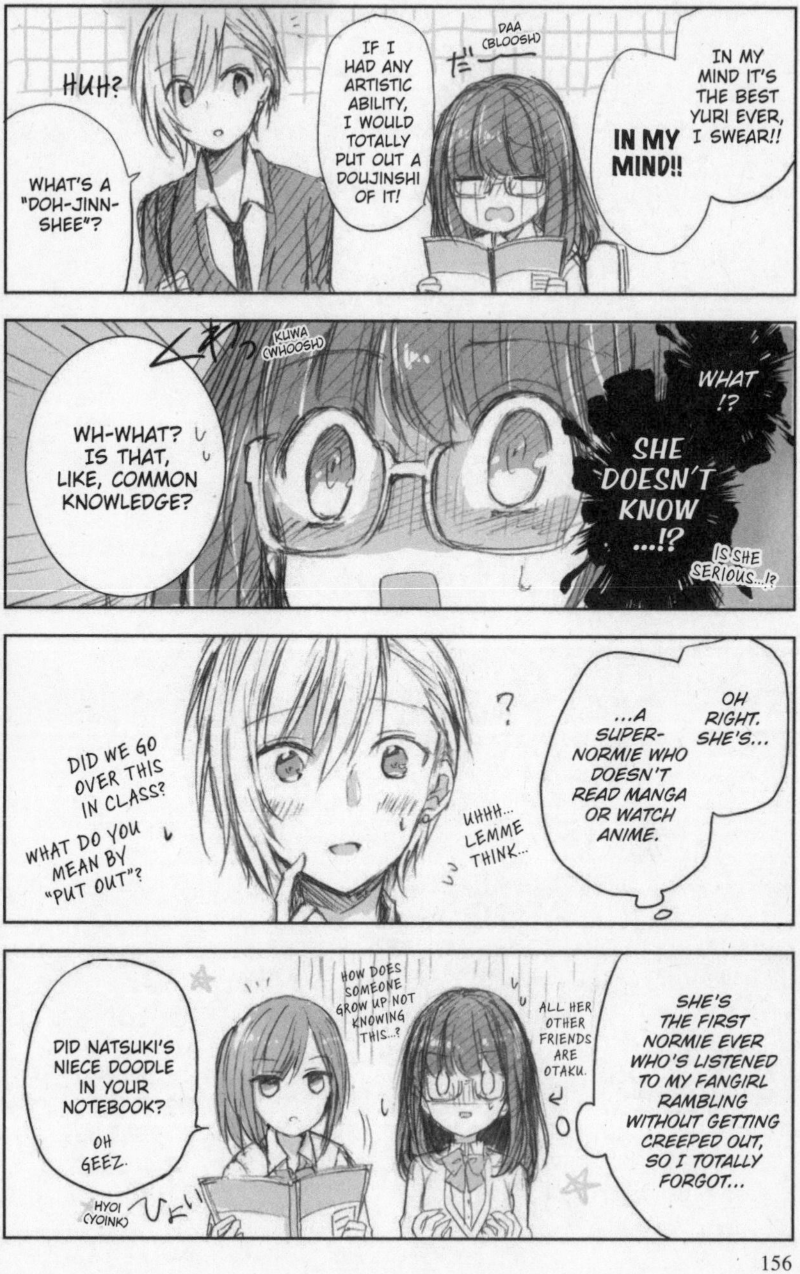
IN MY MIND IT'S THE BEST YURI EVER, I SWEAR!!
IN MY MIND!!
DAA (BLOOSH)
IF I HAD ANY ARTISTIC ABILITY, I WOULD TOTALLY PUT OUT A DOUJINSHI OF IT!
HUH?
WHAT'S A "DOH-JINN-SHEE"?
WHAT!?
SHE DOESN'T KNOW ...!?
IS SHE SERIOUS...!?
KUWA (WHOOSH)
WH-WHAT? IS THAT, LIKE, COMMON KNOWLEDGE?
OH RIGHT. SHE'S...
...A SUPER-NORMIE WHO DOESN'T READ MANGA OR WATCH ANIME.
UHHH... LEMME THINK...
DID WE GO OVER THIS IN CLASS?
WHAT DO YOU MEAN BY "PUT OUT"?
SHE'S THE FIRST NORMIE EVER WHO'S LISTENED TO MY FANGIRL RAMBLING WITHOUT GETTING CREEPED OUT, SO I TOTALLY FORGOT...
ALL HER OTHER FRIENDS ARE OTAKU.
HOW DOES SOMEONE GROW UP NOT KNOWING THIS...?
DID NATSUKI'S NIECE DOODLE IN YOUR NOTEBOOK?
OH GEEZ.
HYOI (YOINK)

YURIMI-SAN IS WATCHING☆ ♥15

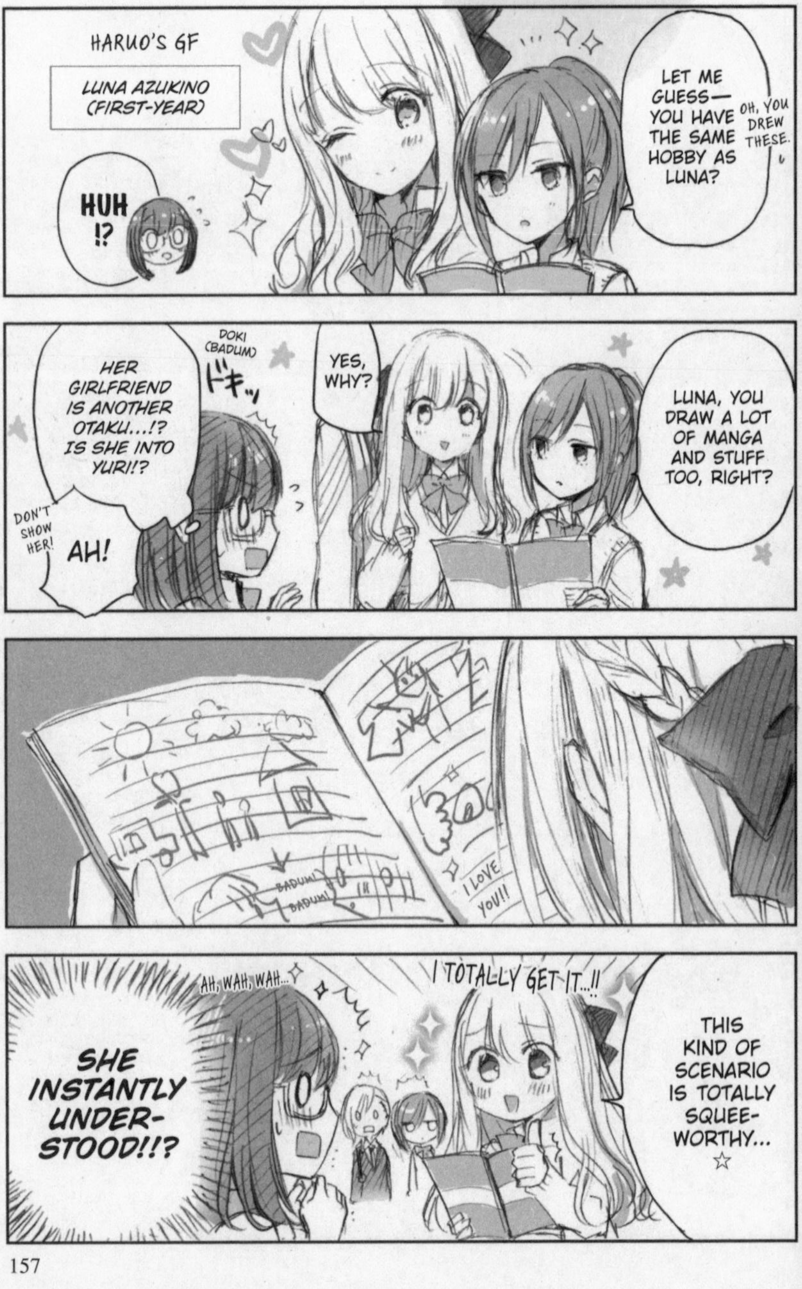
LET ME GUESS— YOU HAVE THE SAME HOBBY AS LUNA?
OH, YOU DREW THESE.
HARUO'S GF
LUNA AZUKINO (FIRST-YEAR)
HUH!?
LUNA, YOU DRAW A LOT OF MANGA AND STUFF TOO, RIGHT?
YES, WHY?
DOKI (BADUM)
ドキッ
HER GIRLFRIEND IS ANOTHER OTAKU...!? IS SHE INTO YURI!?
AH!
DON'T SHOW HER!
I LOVE YOU!!
BADUM! BADUM!
THIS KIND OF SCENARIO IS TOTALLY SQUEE-WORTHY... ☆
I TOTALLY GET IT...!!
AH, WAH, WAH...
SHE INSTANTLY UNDER-STOOD!!?

YURIMI-SAN IS WATCHING☆ ♥16

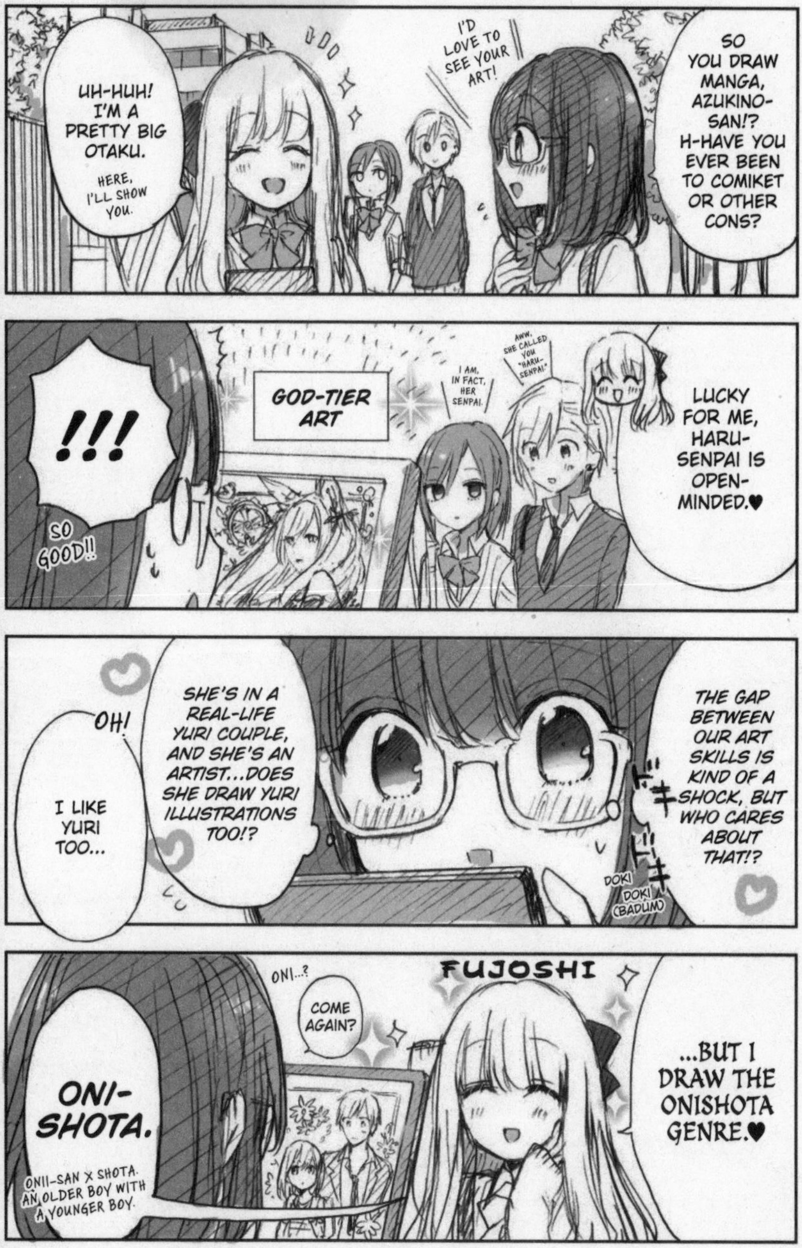

SO YOU DRAW MANGA, AZUKINO-SAN!? H-HAVE YOU EVER BEEN TO COMIKET OR OTHER CONS?
I'D LOVE TO SEE YOUR ART!
UH-HUH! I'M A PRETTY BIG OTAKU.
HERE, I'LL SHOW YOU.
LUCKY FOR ME, HARU-SENPAI IS OPEN-MINDED.♥
AWW, SHE CALLED YOU "HARU-SENPAI."
I AM, IN FACT, HER SENPAI.
GOD-TIER ART
!!!
SO GOOD!!
THE GAP BETWEEN OUR ART SKILLS IS KIND OF A SHOCK, BUT WHO CARES ABOUT THAT!?
DOKI DOKI (BADUM)
SHE'S IN A REAL-LIFE YURI COUPLE, AND SHE'S AN ARTIST...DOES SHE DRAW YURI ILLUSTRATIONS TOO!?
OH!
I LIKE YURI TOO...
FUJOSHI
...BUT I DRAW THE ONISHOTA GENRE.♥
ONI...?
COME AGAIN?
ONI-SHOTA.
ONII-SAN X SHOTA. AN OLDER BOY WITH A YOUNGER BOY.

YURIMI-SAN IS WATCHING☆ ♥17

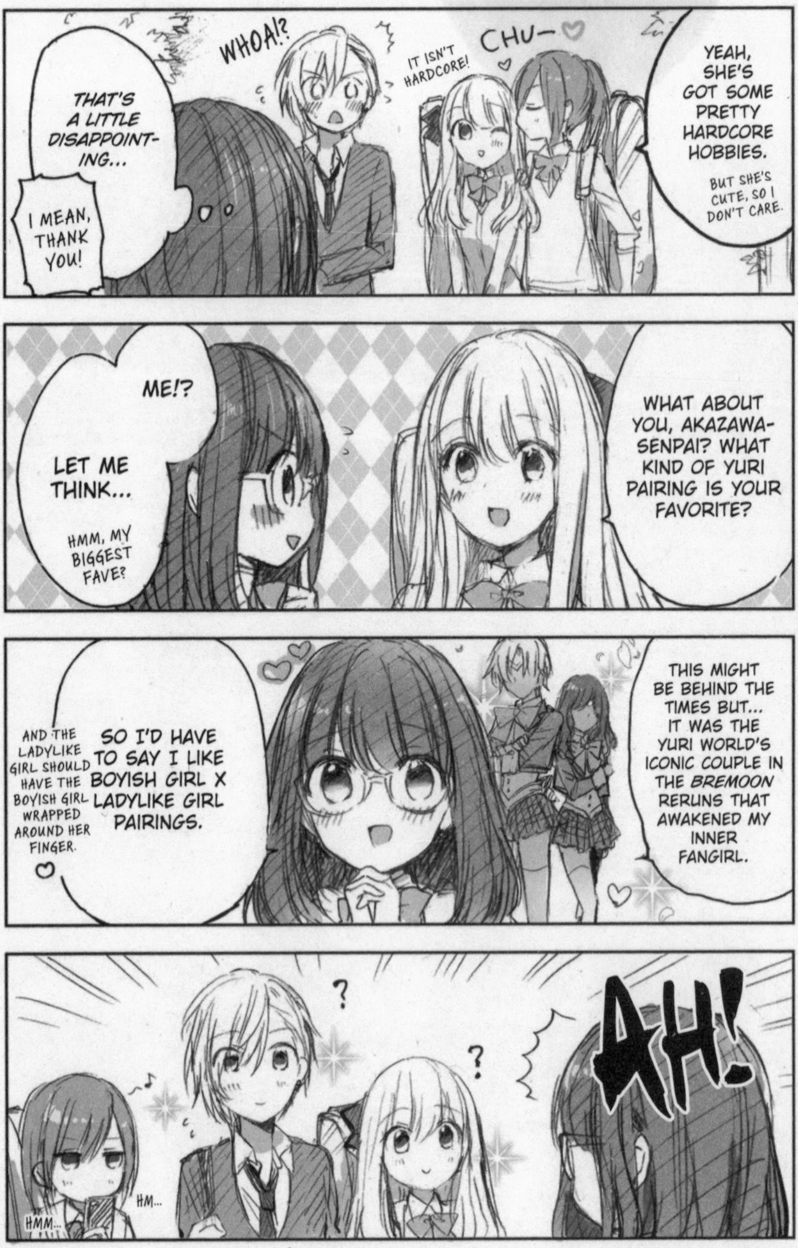
YEAH, SHE'S GOT SOME PRETTY HARDCORE HOBBIES.
BUT SHE'S CUTE, SO I DON'T CARE.
CHU–♡
IT ISN'T HARDCORE!
WHOA!?
THAT'S A LITTLE DISAPPOINTING...
I MEAN, THANK YOU!
WHAT ABOUT YOU, AKAZAWA-SENPAI? WHAT KIND OF YURI PAIRING IS YOUR FAVORITE?
ME!?
LET ME THINK...
HMM, MY BIGGEST FAVE?
THIS MIGHT BE BEHIND THE TIMES BUT... IT WAS THE YURI WORLD'S ICONIC COUPLE IN THE *BREMOON* RERUNS THAT AWAKENED MY INNER FANGIRL.
SO I'D HAVE TO SAY I LIKE BOYISH GIRL X LADYLIKE GIRL PAIRINGS.
AND THE LADYLIKE GIRL SHOULD HAVE THE BOYISH GIRL WRAPPED AROUND HER FINGER. ♡
AH!
?
?
HM...
HMM...

YURIMI-SAN IS WATCHING☆ ♥18

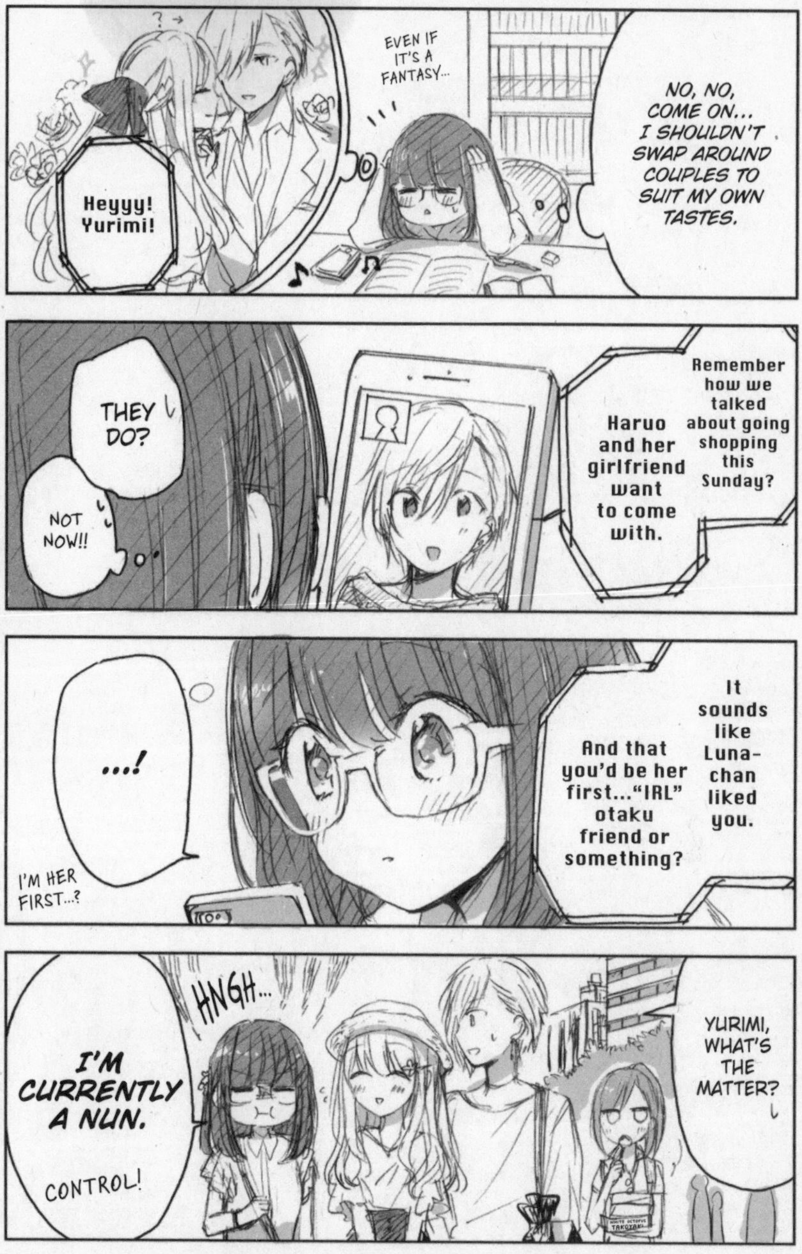
NO, NO, COME ON... I SHOULDN'T SWAP AROUND COUPLES TO SUIT MY OWN TASTES.
EVEN IF IT'S A FANTASY...
Heyyy! Yurimi!
Remember how we talked about going shopping this Sunday?
Haruo and her girlfriend want to come with.
THEY DO?
NOT NOW!!
It sounds like Luna-chan liked you.
And that you'd be her first..."IRL" otaku friend or something?
...!
I'M HER FIRST...?
YURIMI, WHAT'S THE MATTER?
HNGH...
I'M CURRENTLY A NUN.
CONTROL!

CONTINUED IN VOLUME 2☆

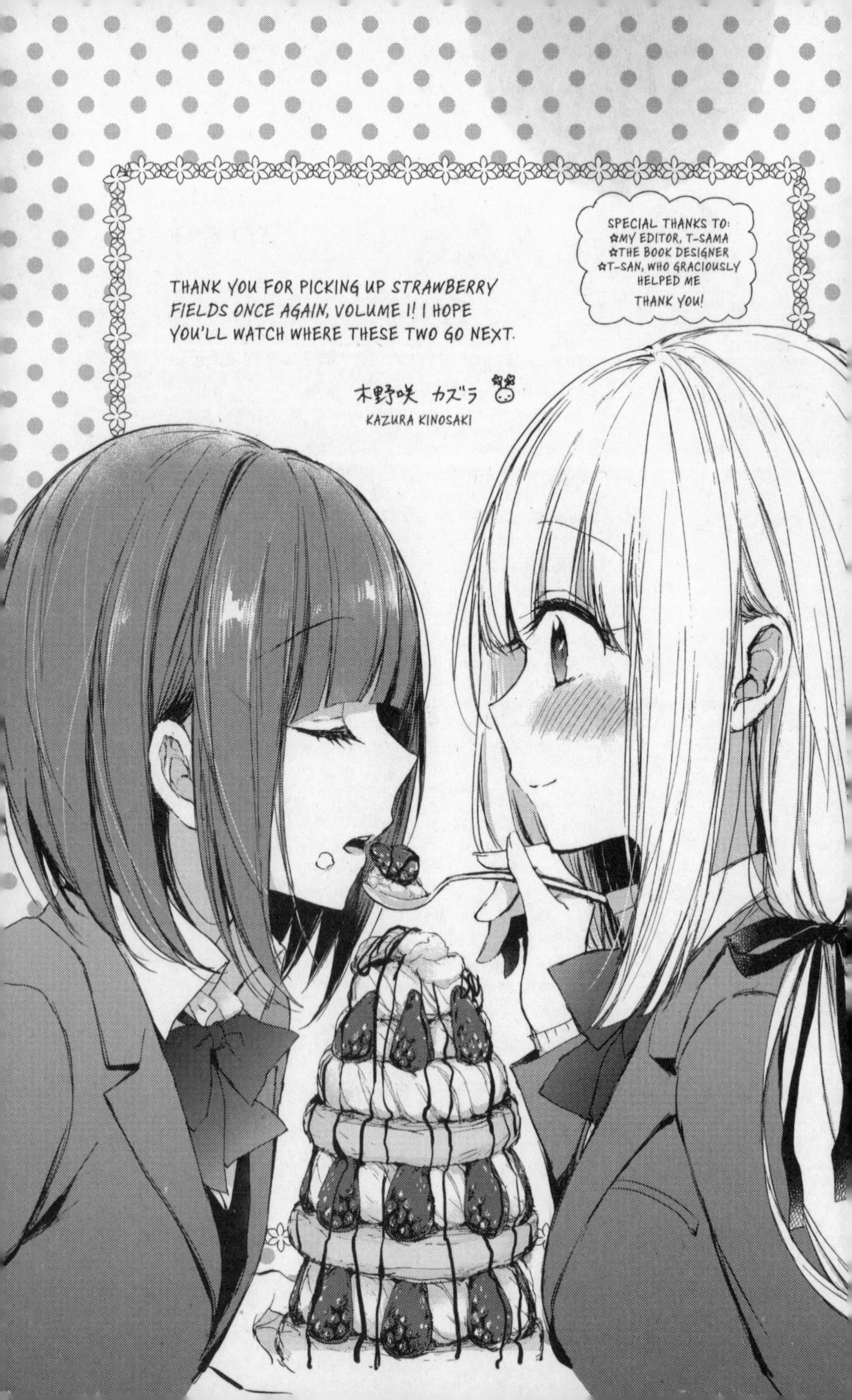
THANK YOU FOR PICKING UP *STRAWBERRY FIELDS ONCE AGAIN*, VOLUME 1! I HOPE YOU'LL WATCH WHERE THESE TWO GO NEXT.
SPECIAL THANKS TO:
☆MY EDITOR, T-SAMA
☆THE BOOK DESIGNER
☆T-SAN, WHO GRACIOUSLY HELPED ME
THANK YOU!
木野咲 カズラ
KAZURA KINOSAKI

Strawberry Fields Once Again

1

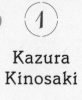

Kazura Kinosaki

Translation: **Amanda Haley** | Lettering: **Abigail Blackman**

This book is a work of fiction. Names, characters, places, and incidents are the product of the author's imagination or are used fictitiously. Any resemblance to actual events, locales, or persons, living or dead, is coincidental.

STRAWBERRY FIELDS WO MOU ICHIDO Volume 1

First published in Japan in 2017 by KADOKAWA CORPORATION, Tokyo
English translation rights arranged with KADOKAWA CORPORATION, Tokyo
through TUTTLE-MORI AGENCY, INC., Tokyo.

Yen Press
150 West 30th Street, 19th Floor
New York, NY 10001

Visit us at yenpress.com

facebook.com/yenpress
twitter.com/yenpress
yenpress.tumblr.com
instagram.com/yenpress

First Yen Press Edition: December 2020

Yen Press is an imprint of Yen Press, LLC.
The Yen Press name and logo are trademarks of Yen Press, LLC.

The publisher is not responsible for websites (or their content) that are not owned by the publisher.

Library of Congress Control Number: 2020946727
ISBNs: 978-1-9753-1922-9 (paperback)
978-1-9753-1921-2 (ebook)

10 9 8 7 6 5 4 3 2 1

WOR

Printed in the United States of America